Dear Marge:

Planet Earth and Humanity can use your help to make this a better place to live. Enjoy and be provoked!

Aloha

27 July 08

# Simple Solutions for Humanity

## Book 2

by PATRICK KENJI TAKAHASHI

authorHOUSE®

*AuthorHouse™*
*1663 Liberty Drive, Suite 200*
*Bloomington, IN 47403*
*www.authorhouse.com*
*Phone: 1-800-839-8640*

*This book is a work of non-fiction. Unless otherwise noted, the author and the publisher make no explicit guarantees as to the accuracy of the information contained in this book and in some cases, names of people and places have been altered to protect their privacy.*



*First published by AuthorHouse 2/27/2008*

*ISBN: 978-1-4343-6842-3 (sc)*

*Library of Congress Control Number: 2008901581*
*Printed in the United States of America*
*Bloomington, Indiana*
*This book is printed on acid-free paper.*

*There are a few controversial statements, particularly about nutrition and religion, representing opinions from specialists and the popular media. Should you have any issues with them, you are encouraged to directly contact the individuals or organizations listed in the REFERENCES. To provide some balance when necessary, I include various points of view not necessarily representing my personal beliefs.*

*There are items that appear in the literature or suddenly on the internet without any obvious attribution. Please notify me if you wish to be cited in the future for my second edition.*

*Finally, the superscript requirement led me to select Annals of Science as the reference style for* ***Book 1****. I did not particularly fancy the results, partially because the ENDNOTE program omitted information and entered strange punctuations. However, to maintain consistency, I again utilized this format, so, if you find information lacking on any particular reference, simply go to* ***Google*** *and use the provided notes as the beginning search point.*

# DEDICATION

I again thank all who appeared in ***Book 1, Simple Solutions for Planet Earth***. I would like to acknowledge the help of David Morrison, Jim Shon, Mildred and Richard Kosaki and my wife, Pearl, for reviewing portions of this ***Book 2***. Otherwise, while I renounce anything litigious for reasons cited in the Disclaimer page, yes, I am largely responsible for the many borderline ridiculous, and sometimes outrageous, solutions. I cite U.S. Senator Spark Matsunaga, who once told me, "shoot for the stars, and be gratified with landing on the Moon." You should, of course, use proper judgment and adhere to the Rainbow Solutions as you take steps to make a difference for Planet Earth and Humanity.

# SIMPLE SOLUTIONS
## For Humanity

## *Book 2*

# INTRODUCTION

## Background

***Book 1*** dealt with the present and future of Planet Earth. ***Book 2*** is about your life and death, and, perhaps, even beyond that. How and where did life originate? Will it be possible to eradicate crime and wars (*Chapter 1*) and find a cure for aging (*Chapter 2*)? The ultimate solutions will come from a better educational system (*Chapter 3*) and maybe even from above, extraterrestrials (*Chapter 4*) or God (*Chapter 5*). How truly possible is an afterlife? Just in case this is it, why not live in the best place on Earth (*Chapter 6*)?

Rather than complicate an already complex set of challenges, I have instead provided SIMPLE SOLUTIONS. How can we stop aging? Are there signals coming from space with clues on how to solve humanity's problems and attain our dreams? Can religion save itself and steer the way towards universal peace and a sustainable future for our society? What can you do to make the crucial difference?

Dan Boylan, Hawaii columnist for ***MidWeek***, headlined his August 22, 2007, comment with "There are No Simple Solutions." He said that things are always more complicated than they appear. He is, of course, absolutely right. My SIMPLE SOLUTIONS are part common sense, part sarcasm, and one reasonable, albeit extreme, point as any to begin the analysis.

***Book 1*** suggested SIMPLE SOLUTIONS to accelerate the development of green (*or clean*) technology and blue (*from the ocean*) resources. Certainly, simple solutions are not slam dunk answers, nor will they be easy to accomplish, and, in fact, might be downright impossible to achieve, for, depending on your point of view or belief, they could be inhumane or patently ridiculous. Even the more outrageous offerings, though, provide a platform for discussion so that society can more closely approach optimal solutions to seemingly despairing quandaries. These are the best of what others, mostly, have advocated.

Of course, I'm writing this primarily as an American for Americans. However, there are universal applications to virtually everything recommended. There was a saying some years ago something to the effect that what was good for General Motors was also good for the Nation. That logic failed the test of time, so I'm not saying that what is good for the USA would also be true for the World, but why not initiate the analysis with the most powerful country on the globe.

Why am I qualified to write this ***Book 2***? I had credibility in ***Book 1***, for the topics formed the basis of my professional life. ***Book Two*** is a bit more nebulous, but, nevertheless, is closely linked to my existence. I like to quote Arthur Schopenhauer, 19th Century German philosopher:

*All truth passes through three stages:*

- *First, it is ridiculed.*
- *Second, it is violently opposed.*
- *Third, it is accepted as being self-evident.*

Many of the technologies I advocated in ***Book 1*** passed through the first two stages. Most of the concepts I present here, though, could well still be in stage 1.

There is a book out, edited by John Brockman, entitled, ***Dangerous Ideas on the Loose*** (*HarperCollins, 2007*).[176] This anthology is a gathering of one hundred essays on the concept, and, while entertaining and provocative, could also be hazardous for the individual authors. As ***Book 1*** was written with a few dangerous ideas, I awaited with some trepidation for the repercussions…but half a year later, nothing. Well this ***Book 2*** is, perhaps, an order of magnitude more perilous, and a fellow author, George Carter, mentioned to me that Socrates was tried and executed just for such dangerous ideas, only one being an irreverence of religion, my Chapter 5. Well, this classical Greek philosopher was convicted by a 280 to 220 vote, and, frankly, I would be euphoric if as many read this publication, with 220 siding with me. Under any circumstances, I will find a way to forego the hemlock.

In the cosmic perspective of time, we only have a very short period left. Most of you no doubt have been too busy to do anything truly monumental for humanity, and, in fact, have generally been mostly in a survival mode, with a bit of pleasure tossed in now and then. If you are the average American, you are among the 61% who believe they are not living the American Dream. Only one in ten of you agree that it is easier today to attain that goal.[274] Maybe you can leapfrog over whatever that dream might be by making a crucial difference on something personally important or monumentally significant. You are encouraged, at any time, to leap to the very end, the Epilogue, to embark on your mission, guided by Rainbow Vision.

Occasionally you wonder if you're here for a purpose, and deep inside, would sincerely like to do something memorable for society…but, save for the occasional charity stuff, haven't done all that much yet. It is not too late! You still can make a difference, and throughout this book are stories of many who did just that…just normal people who took that fateful step. The EPILOGUE provides guidelines for you to consider. It is very similar to the guide from ***Book 1***. If this publication inspires only one tenth of one percent of the world, that means more than six million of you will be out there doing great things for humanity.

Finally, the cover shows my family crest or mon. I colorized this mon into the rainbow version shown on the cover of ***Book 1*** because most of the simple solutions represented a color. This time, the simple solutions are nearly all black or white, but nevertheless can still be represented by this same bridge (*Takahashi means high bridge*) connecting country to country, people to people, you to me, as is suggested in the Epilogue. However, as a testament to religion, or, perhaps, a marketing ploy to catch the buyer's attention, I have colorized the mon a metallic gold. That standard version, of course, is depicted on the inside cover page.

## Colors

My favorite class in college was "Color." It was taught out of the Art Department at Stanford, and I, actually, took or sat in on more art than chemical engineering courses. In my final undergraduate semester, it was a difficult decision whether to continue on some artistic track at Sophia University (*Tokyo*) or become a real chemical engineer. I took the latter pathway, and am glad I did, but these ***Simple Solutions*** books clearly show that I remain dedicated to colors.

While the cover of ***Book 1*** and chapters were an orgy of colors. ***Book 2*** is only **black** and **gold**, but, nevertheless filled with a **diamond**, which can be refracted to produce the full visible spectrum, and **rainbows**. ***Gold*** connotes power and royalty.

American designer Henry Dreyfus is widely quoted as saying that Japanese, compared to the Western world, associate colors with feelings. As a product of America and Japan, I have, thus, blended West and East, the emotion with reality. I am, though, now adding a third, and scientific, factor called chromatics to the mix, for the color you visualize depends on something called wavelength. The human eye can see between 380 (*violet*) and 740 (*red*) nanometers. But what does this mean?

This could get complicated, and will be the only time I attempt to get scientific (*and feel free to just skip the next few paragraphs*), but what you perceive is energy traveling at the speed of light (*186,000 miles per second, or 300 million meters per second*) in waves. Picture the beach and waves. The distance between the crest of two waves is the wavelength, and you can see this to be, say, 20 feet, traveling that distance in about 5 seconds. So the frequency would be 0.2 waves per second (*w/s*). That is, if you stand in the water, every five seconds you will feel a new wave *(the 20 foot distance never was incorporated into the calculation*) When it comes to a radio, the wave travels at the speed of light, so this results in a very large number, as for example, an AM station is in the range of 100,000 w/s, and when you listen to FM 92, it is 92,100,000 w/s, as you might note that you get a lot of static if you are exactly on the 92 line. The correct FM station is 92.1. Similarly, FM100 could well be 100,300,000, or, really at 100.3 on your dial.

The wavelength is the speed of light divided by this frequency, so the wavelength of the AM signal is 9835 feet, and the second FM signal is 9.84 feet. For color, the metric system is used, and the frequencies are so very high that, take the color blue, for example, the wavelength turns out to be 4750 angstroms = 475 nanometers = $475 \times 10^{-9}$ meters, a very short length. So the approximate wavelengths (*each has a broad range, except for the monochromatic colors*) of the following in meters are:

| | | |
|---|---|---|
| o | Radio/TV waves | $10^2$ (*range of from 2.5 to 4500 meters*) |
| o | Microwaves/Radar | $10^{-2}$ |
| o | Infrared | $10^{-5}$ |
| o | Red | $650x10^{-9}$ |
| o | Blue | $475x10^{-9}$ |
| o | Violet | $400x10^{-9}$ |
| o | Ultraviolet | $80x10^{-9}$ |
| o | X-Rays | $10^{-10}$ |
| o | Gamma Rays | $10^{-12}$ (*and down below* $10^{-15}$) |

Thus, we challenged humans can only view a very small part of this electromagnetic spectrum. In case you were wondering, brown is a low intensity orange-yellow. If a surface scatters all wavelengths, you see white; if there is total absorption...it's black. The shorter the wavelength, the higher the energy intensiveness, although, clearly, a microwave oven, which operates at around 2.5 GHz (*giga hertz, or billions of cycles or waves per second, in the microwave/radar band*), can cook food. Remember that the Gamma Ray Burst from ***Book 1*** was linked to the mass extinction on Planet Earth 443 million years ago. Infrared bursts could give you a sun tan, and is reported to be caused by a cyclotron maser instability operating at a few tens of neutron star radiuses above the poles of a magnetized neutron star in a binary system. This is a good time as any to return to more understandable language.

The human retina has 125 million rods that are colorblind, and 7 million cones, which can sense red, green and blue (*RGB*). Amazingly, these three colors, in specific combination, can produce all the hues. This was English doctor Thomas Young's experiment of 1801. Albert Munsell, an American painter, developed the color tree in the early 1900s, using hue, value and saturation values for the five primary and five secondary colors. Light colors are additive, while pigment (*paint, for example*) colors are subtractive. For the former, the absence of light is black, while a combination of all is sort of white, like sunlight. The RGB system prevails here, as determined by your cones.

Pigment theory is just the opposite, as a surface which absorbs all colors but green shows a green color. If all the colors are absorbed, you see black. The primary colors here are cyan (*greenish blue*), magenta (*a rich pinkish-purplish*) and yellow. This light signal goes to the brain, where cultural and other experiences become filters.

My wife and I do not agree on the color blue. She calls virtually any violet or purple flower blue. My blue is very specific. It has to be sky blue, or something similar. Spiders, marsupials, birds, reptiles and certain fish species have eyesight based on four primary colors. A lot more women are tetrachromatic. I think that explains it. Women are closer in the evolution chain to reptiles and spiders.

***Wikipedia*** has a topic called Blue Flower. However, the only blue flower they show is...purple. Roses are red, violets are blue, so maybe, something is wrong with my eyes. Blue flowers are rare. In 1840, the horticultural societies of Britain and Belgium offered a price of 500,000 francs for a blue rose. There was no blue rose, until Florigene of Australia and Suntory of Japan, using genetic engineering, finally succeeded. However, in the 2005 announcement by the Australian Scientific and Research Organization, the logo of CSIRO was a beautiful blue, but the flower itself was a violet lavender, the same color printed in the ***Japan Times***. Finally, the Hypography Science Forums released their blurb with a truly beautiful blue rose.[106] Plus, in 2006 I saw a blue rose in a flower shop in Tokyo. It was deep blue, but it could have been dried out. I'm waiting to buy one for Pearl, but I was told I might need to wait until this year (*2008*).

The notion of color has been with us from the beginning, of course, and the usual suspects wrote on this subject: Aristotle, Newton, Maxwell, Helmholtz etc. In 1810, Johann Wolfgang von Goethe published the ***Theory of Colors***. The science of colors is again covered in the rainbow portion of the education chapter.

I can go on and on, but, suffice to say that colors can add a special dimension to education and learning. So let me start with Black and White.

# CHAPTER 1: ENDING CRIME AND WAR FOREVER

## Black and White: Crime and Punishment / War and Peace

In my ***Book 1***, both black and white were used to represent subject areas, but never together. Black is the absence of color, and white, or transparent, could well include the full spectrum. They are opposites...ying and yang...good and bad...crime and punishment...war and peace.

I draw on the masterpieces of Russian writers Fyodor Dostoevsky and Leo Tolstoy because the former was an engineer and the latter a part time teacher. I am both. In the first novel, for two murders, the punishment was hardly worthy. In the second, while there was considerable agony from war, there was not much of a peace. There is a lot of character building and details about living in Russia in the 1800's, but in the end, what do you really get out of these notable works of fiction? Yes, something about life in Russia, then. Some might say, too, the satisfaction of having experienced greatness. **Simple Solutions** has only two characters—you and me. But we might accomplish a lot more than the two novels. Perhaps we will be able to provide the ultimate punishment to eliminate crime and the rational key to world peace. If we fail here, in this first chapter, there are a few others to which we can contribute.

My interest in crime and wars influenced me to look into studying law forty years ago when I applied to the New York University School of Law, was accepted, but till today feel a bit guilty for not informing them I was not coming. I do know that in parallel, I also took steps towards becoming a graduate student at Louisiana State University in chemical engineering, and went there because they offered a full fellowship, plus the sugar industry continued to pay me for a while if I did so. Later, after I got my PhD, during my early academic career at the University of Hawaii, the local School of Law began operations in 1973, the same year John Houseman in ***The Paper Chase***, convinced me that I should add a juris doctorate to my record. Again, there was something about the challenge. This is why, perhaps, people run marathons. However, sanity prevailed, I continued being an engineering educator and never ran the marathon, leading to my career in energy and extending to this book.

But on to the subject at hand, so let me start with the two most significant attacks on the United States, leading to World War II (*WW2*) and the World War against Terrorism (*WWT*), although a case has been made that terrorism is just a weapon, and the real world war is religious-based (*WWR*). In my mind, religion could well be the ultimate solution to wars, and is so pervasive, that I am spending a whole chapter on the Golden Evolution, the simple solution for religion, which itself, is in deep trouble.

On December 7, 1941, as a 15 month old child growing up in Honolulu, I witnessed the bombing of Pearl Harbor by the Japanese, or, at least was so told by my mother that she pointed to the smoke while I was in her arms. Two thousand four hundred and three Americans died, plus 59 Japanese airmen and sailors. A few more were killed almost 60 years later, on September 11, 2001, when Islamic terrorists hijacked four commercial jetliners; each loaded with nearly 25,000 gallons of jet fuel, and crashed them into the north and south towers of the World Trade Center (*WTC*) and the Pentagon, with the fourth falling in a Pennsylvania field. Nineteen terrorists died, plus 265 on board the planes, 125 in the Pentagon and 2,603 in the World Trade Center, with 24 still listed as missing and presumed dead. But this should not have been a particularly big surprise because al-Qaeda in 1993 detonated a 1,500 pound bomb in the basement of the WTC, hoping to wipe out up to 250,000 people, but ended up only killing six.

Pearl Harbor I don't really remember. Being an American of Japanese extraction, I have pondered on what would have happened if WWII did not occur. As terrible as any war is, I came to a conclusion that I, personally, actually benefited from this inferno, and to boot, the USA subsequently ascended to become the world economic leader and the champion for peace and prosperity. A close analysis shows that continued access to oil was an important reason why we won WWII, and the need to continue to protect this natural resource is mostly why WWT/R started. In fact, it turns out that we also won WWI because the Allies were able to convert from coal to oil more effectively.

Thus, one way to avoid future wars is to remove oil as a competitive resource. Solar, renewable, and all sustainable resources are de-centralized and universal. We will largely be able steer clear of these major conflagrations when Green Enertopia, the Free Hydrogen or Biomethanol Age and the Blue Revolution begin to flourish.

But, in a sense, war is not necessarily bad. The Falklands victory buoyed the spirits of Margaret Thatcher, Grenada gave Ronald Reagan and the American people our first military victory in a long time and the first Gulf War, plus eradication of the Taliban in Afghanistan, reinforced our international credibility. In each case, the Good Gal/Guys entered into a state of war through provocation. We did not start it. We wanted to be of assistance, and we benefited.

So, then, is war justified? War is bad, not good, though sometimes necessary. World War I was supposedly fought to end all wars. World War II stopped Hitler and the spread of fascism. Starting wars is immoral, but value systems are not the same. China will more and more become a concern because of its large size and a dissimilar culture. But there is a simple solution.

I was there via the omnipresence of television, lying in bed, on 9/11, and actually saw, live, that second crash into the south tower of the World Trade Center. It was 6:03AM in Hawaii. I, too, was stunned. How could this be happening to the United States?

Yet, the U.S. was not really threatened with extinction. Pearl Harbor could have been an imminent threat to my life and country, but terrorist acts today seem not unlike the television series, ***24***. Yes, terrible, but safe, for most of us. Subsequent to 9/11 I wondered about the passing of the Patriot Act and was troubled by those vexing airport rituals. Invading Iraq the second time was okay, for weapons of mass destruction (*WMD*) could have been there, and the Bush Administration did a great P.R. job on the public. Hey, world oil was protected and our globe was now a better place with Saddam disposed, and who knows, those other Arab Nations could have subsequently fallen in line. President Bush and Vice President Cheney would have then been considered beneficent heroes. The crucial factor in this Domino Theory was that Iraq would have served as the model for the rest of the Middle East to become democracies. But a few things went wrong.

We are all becoming increasingly frustrated at the inanity of how we are going about saving us from what, terrorists? Almost every day on the evening news, and certainly when I travel by air, I see increasing amounts of my tax dollars being spent protecting me from a rag-tag bunch of Islamic fundamentalists with a point to prove. Richard Reid, the shoe bomber, or his handler, is right up there with the person who invented those ads that fall out of magazines. From April 2005 to July 2006, 16 million cigarette lighters were confiscated at airports, representing 80% of all seized items.[256] It costs the Transportation Security Administration $6 million/year just to <u>dispose</u> of them, but the absurdity is that personnel could have spent the time looking for more dangerous articles. Or maybe fire everyone, stop being so paranoid, save a lot of my tax dollars and go on with our life, as those same terrorists, with what they carried, probably would pass through the TSA check routine today.

At this point, these amorphous terrorists are actually winning the war, maybe even smirking during prayer time. Yes, we won the Battle of Iraq, but we are losing the more important mission of securing the peace, and, like Vietnam, looking for any responsible way out.

I once worked for U.S. Senator Spark Matsunaga, who had, as his noblest goal, the establishment of the U.S. Peace Academy, for, if we are training warriors for war, he felt we should spend more to instruct peacemakers for peace. In the early 80's, the Matsunaga Commission listened to what amounted to 6,000 pages of testimony, and recommended a national peace academy. Matsunaga was the lead sponsor of a Senate bill that was adopted on June 22, 1984 to establish a U.S. Academy of Peace. The furthest this went, though, was the establishment in 1986 of the U.S. Institutes of Peace to conduct research on the subject. More recently, Representative Dennis Kucinich, in 2005, introduced a bill to establish a cabinet-level Department of Peace and Non-violence. He reintroduced HR 808 with 65 cosponsors in 2007.

I have on my office wall a press release from Spark M. Matsunaga entitled, "Matsunaga on Crime, Punishment and Energy." Dated April 1, 1981, it says Sen. Spike Matsunaga introduced a bold and historic measure called the National Crime Prevention, Research, Development and Demonstration Act, featuring mild to severe torture. This was apocryphal, of course, and only a reaction of fellow office-mate, Harvey Meyerson's, and my, playful response to a recommendation of Sparky's re-election campaign to feature crime as his major platform focus, something we thought was idiotic on strength of his past legislation. Certainly, this press release never was even shared with the staff, for we probably would have been fired if it ever got out.

Well, this is a fitting segue to start with combating crime. Why link crime to war? Well, both kill, or, otherwise inconvenience, our society. Can you imagine a world without crime and wars? Well, then, why not also eliminate natural death? Sure. But that's in the next chapter. What about needless infighting in a family or the injustices that go on in jungles? Where there are people, there will be differences of opinion. In the jungle, that's the law of nature…survival of the fittest…evolution. Let us focus on crime and major wars, something fundamentally human, yet potentially manageable.

## The End of Crimes

### History of Crime

Human nature being what it is, if there were no formalized social controls, the law of the jungle would take over. There are some, though, who believe that a civilized society is by nature honest and good, and Chapter 5 on religion will further discuss whether a Supreme Being is necessary for a crime-less future.

In any case, we are not mature as a civilization to enjoy utopia, so crime enforcement is necessary and defined by law, which somewhat differs and changes among cultures over time. Some form of government must be the operating element to impose order, carry out adjudication and punishment, and administer a penal system.

The Sumerians 4000 years ago had written criminal laws. A couple of centuries later, Hammurabi, ruler of Babylon, became known for his code of 282 entries, where "an eye for an eye" governed. Later, Roman and Teutonic laws formalized a court system and provided for compensation. Behind all this was the notion to maintain peace among clans and states. The position of the government came into prominence in England after the Romans left, thus the common law was born. Thomas Aquinas wrote about the natural law theory, to wit, it is morally appropriate to coerce citizens to conform to any morally acceptable law.[17]

Napoleon codified Roman law. Forty-nine states use English common law. Louisiana follows Napoleonic Law. At one point in my graduate career at Louisiana State University, I contemplated switching to law, but, after taking two courses, decided that this odd system might not be ideal for Hawaii. English law is based on court precedent, that is, the ruling of a judge can limit, if not control, a judge in a subsequent case. The Code of Napoleon takes the citizen law approach, that is, allow for the judge to interpret the legislated laws.

Our judicial system, to put it mildly, seems to be imperfect. How can we convict and jail a reasonably good citizen and model homemaker, Martha Stewart, and release so obvious a murderer as O. J. Simpson and child abuser, Michael Jackson? This is all the more ironic, because blacks are traditionally stereotyped by law enforcement agencies as guilty. Or, what frustrates the common citizen: how can a car thief be convicted a fifty times and still steal another vehicle? A solution will be offered, but, first, let us look at where it is safe, and not.

**Crime Statistics**

The island of Dominica was visited by Christopher Columbus in 1493. The French claimed it in 1635, but ceded it to the U.K. in 1763. Dominica, which should not be mistaken for the Dominican Republic, another Caribbean nation, became independent in 1978. Most of the 70,000 citizens are descendents of African slaves. If you scan through ***Wikipedia*** or the ***CIA World Factbook***, you might be tempted to plan a vacation there, although the latter reports that there is 23% unemployment and money laundering enforcement is weak. Actually, Dominica leads the world in crimes. A selected ranking from the latest, and seventh, United Nations Survey of Crime Trends and Operations of Criminal Justice Systems, covering the 1998-2000 period, can show the following (*all, per 1000 people*):[111]

- #1 Dominica 114
- #2 New Zealand 106
- #3 Finland 102
- #4 Denmark 93
- #5 Chile 88
- #6 United Kingdom 86
- #7 Montserrat 80
- #8 United States 80
- #10 South Africa 77
- #11 Germany 76
- #12 Canada 75
- #13 Norway 72
- #15 France 62
- #20 Switzerland 36
- #24 South Korea 32
- #30 Uruguay 21
- #34 Japan 19
- #40 Tunisia 12
- #47 Thailand 9
- #50 Malaysia 7
- #57 Papua New Guinea 2
- #59 India 2
- #60 Yemen 1

There are a lot of surprises here. Make that, incredible illogicalities. New Zealand at #2 and Finland at #3? Papua New Guinea at #57? I've been to all three places. The first two, I thought, were really safe and the third, truly dangerous. Is good, bad? Bad...good? What does all this mean?

Well, the 2006 Transparency International Corruption Perceptions Index lists Finland, New Zealand and Iceland at the top as the least corrupt countries in the world. [153] [244] For the record, the U.S. is #20, better than Spain *(#23*), but not as honest as France (*#18*) and Japan (*#17*). What this appears to mean is that honest countries report all their crimes. So, maybe, Dominica should not be tarnished by this crime ranking. Thus, **be careful of statistics**.

In the same 7th UN crime survey (*per 1000 people*):

| ASSAULTS | | MURDERS | | ROBBERIES | |
|---|---|---|---|---|---|
| o #1 South Africa | 12 | #1 Colombia | 0.6 | #1 Spain | 12 |
| o #2 Montserrat | 10 | #2 South Africa | 0.5 | #2 Chile | 7 |
| o #3 Mauritius | 8 | #3 Jamaica | 0.3 | #3 Costa Rica | 5 |
| o **#6 U.S.** | **8** | #5 Russia | 0.2 | **#11 U.S.** | **1.4** |
| o #12 Iceland | 5 | #12 Papua NG | 0.08 | #19 Russia | 0.9 |
| o #31 Dominica | 1 | **#24 U.S.** | **0.04** | #27 Papua NG | 0.6 |
| o #50 Costa Rica | 0.2 | #50 Tunisia | 0.01 | #50 Macedonia | 0.1 |
| o #57 Azerbaijan | 0.03 | #62 Quatar | 0.01 | #64 Quatar | 0.005 |

Overall, NationMaster.com reports that Columbia has 0.62 crimes/1000 people, South Africa (*0.50, #2*), U.S. (*0.043, #24*) and Qatar (*0.001, #62*).[213] Another way of looking at this is that Columbia has about 15 times more crimes than in the USA and more than 600 times that of Qatar.

Well, I've heard that South Africa and Colombia are bad places, and I personally almost was robbed in Spain, so, the worst countries, here, make sense. Yet, I was recently in Cartegena and did not feel in any way threatened, so there are micro-climates of good and bad within one country and any city. Yet, as you can see, if you want to avoid crime, live in Azerbaijan or Qatar. Also interesting that Costa Rica is about the safest place for assaults, but the third most prone to robberies. The United States is not a good place to be for crimes…but maybe that is because we report well. As for example, in police efficiency (*there were only 17 countries listed*):

- o **#1 United States 89%**
- o #2 Canada 87%
- o #3 New Zealand 79%
- o #16 Italy 52%
- o #17 Netherlands 52%

You can reasonably guess that most other countries, if they were included, would have fared worse.

In the United States, Statemaster.com reports:[300]

- o Lynchings (1882-1968): #1 Mississippi (581), #2 Georgia (531) (six states had zero)

- o Murder (per 10,000): #1 DC (3.6), #2 Louisiana (1.3) #51 Maine (0.1)

- o Burglary (per 10,000): #1 North Carolina (117), #2 Arkansas (108) #51 North Dakota (30)

Since 1993, property and violent crime rates have dropped by more than half, while rapes and robberies by two-thirds. Now, there is "only" one violent crime each year per 47 residents.[287] Why the drop? There are more criminals in prison and there are 100,000 additional police officers. It can be better, for in Honolulu alone, which is not far from the norm, there was in 2006 a backlog of 61,500 bench warrants (*mostly for traffic crimes*) because of a lack of personnel. The city of Chicago saw a 25% drop in killings to 445 for its 2.9 million citizens. Yet, Berlin, with 3.4 million, experienced only 71 murders in 2004.

There was a disturbing reversal beginning in 2007, though, as ***Google*** on July 24, 2007 showed that the crime rate was rising in New Orleans and San Bernardino, and murder rates in New York City and Philadelphia. Murders and robberies increased in 2006 for the second year in a row, said the FBI, and watch out if you are a transgender lady of color in Northern California, as murder rates are really skyrocketing.[215]

Part of the problem with crime is that perpetrators are not caught. Only 15.6% of all crimes were solved in the U.S. in 2002. In Hawaii, 90% of crimes remain on the books, but most of this is due to an 8% conviction for property *(burglary, larceny, motor vehicle theft)* crimes. Then when you hear of car thieves actually arrested and convicted innumerable times...only to steal another car...the conclusion is that a whole lot of cars are stolen. A paltry 3.6% of burglaries were cleared in 2004. These are generally carried out by those on drugs, so while this sorry type just has to be lacking in sense, it then must be that it is really safe to live this lifestyle.[40] Then, if, somehow, they are thrown in jail, you, the taxpayer, will be saddled with their food, air conditioning and whatever bills. There has got to be a better way.

**Drugs**

If there is one thing different about crime a half century ago *(when I was in high school)* and today, it is the current presence of drugs, and how family and society are now affected. Much of the following comes from the 2007 United Nations World Drug Report, which you can access through ***GOOGLE*** at UNODC-World Drug Report.[74] The English version is all of 7.27 MB long. According to this tome, 200 million people have used illicit drugs at least once in the past 12 months. That's about 3% of the world population.

Tobacco, a licit (*legal*) psychoactive substance, is used by more than one fourth of the world adults (*approaching 2 billion smokers*), versus 4% on marijuana and 1% for all other illegal drugs. This legal drug (*tobacco*) is, actually, a relative newcomer, compared to the illegal variety, and probably gained prominence in the Americas in the early AD period. Columbus was given a few leaves, but threw them away, coining the term after his visit to Tobago. Portuguese and Spanish sailors spread the habit to Europe. Virginia colonists in the later 16th century were responsible for the introduction into England, where it was then called, sotweed, about the time Sir Frances Drake passed on the practice to Sir Walter Raleigh.

The more expensive drugs induce crime because they are illegal, and this is the case because responsible authorities have declared them bad for you. There are 25 million true illegal drug addicts, or one-third of one percent of the world population. Thus, it is this relatively small portion of society that is tormenting the rest. As any amount of threat will not cure these souls, a simple solution might well be to terminate this small fraction of living beings.

## Opium and Heroin

Opium contains two alkaloids, phenanthrenes (*morphine, codeine,* $C_{17} H_{19} NO_3$) and benzylisoquinolines. First exploited as a narcotic in Sumerian and European cultures 6,000 years ago, Muslims spread the use to India, then on to China. Clearly, throughout time, ancient priests and warriors found ways to utilize this powder. Homer described such a combatant, and so did the founder of medicine, Hippocrates. Laudanum, opium in ethanol, was widely prescribed into the 19th century.

For centuries in China, even a small village without a rice shop could have an opium distributor. British merchants in the early 1800's smuggled this drug as trade for tea, leading to the Opium Wars, through which the U.K. gained control of Hong Kong.

Chinese emigrants employed for the transcontinental railroad brought this habit to the U.S. Opium was smoked, but derivatives were used in various tonics. President Theodore Roosevelt convened an international conference in 1902, spearheading the control of this opiate at a time when 27% of the adult male population of China was addicted. Yet, if it is true that 6,630 metric tons were produced in 2006,[171] and the price on the streets is $16,000 per kilogram, then the value that year was in excess of $100 billion, with 150 times more going to drug traffickers than growers.[62] And that's only opium, which the general populace thought only was smoked by old Chinese men in dark dens. Further, this opium, losing 90% the weight, can be processed into heroin, which has a value of about $300,000/kg. We are now up to $200 billion/year if the entire crop were converted to heroin.

With apologies to Teddy, the media reports that international drug control as a multilateral program is older than the United Nations, even older than the League of Nations, beginning in 1912 to deal with opium. This has been a success story, for then, the production of opium was 30,000 metric tons. Today, it has dropped below 10,000 metric tons, so with four times more people today, the reduction of use per capita is down more than 90%. But was it this international organization, or just, plain, China, and how it governs? A century ago, with one third the present population, there were 25 million opium users. Today, there are 8.5 million drug addicts with a much larger population. The incidence is still high, but certainly better.

Regarding supply, in 2006, Afghanistan produced 92% of all the opium (*obtained by drying the milky juice of the unripe seed pods of poppy*), with Columbia, Mexico, Peru and the Golden Triangle (*Myanmar, Laos, Thailand, Viet Nam*) supplying the rest. Heroin (*which is diacetylmorphine, $C_{12}H_{23}NO_5$, is converted by your liver to morphine*) is synthesized from opium. In 2007, the Afghanistan supply went up 34%, but their world share only increased by 1%, meaning the rest of these countries also had in total a similar increase.

To make heroin, the raw opium is first boiled in water. Slaked lime (*calcium hydroxide—which is made by mixing lime, or calcium oxide, in water*) is then added to form a solution, which is filtered to remove any impurities. Ammonia is used to precipitate the morphine, which is filtered out as white chunks of morphine base, known as Heroin Number 1. But this is not yet real heroin. Heroin #1 is dissolved in acetic acid and heated at 85 degrees Celsius for two hours, chemically producing Heroin #2 in solution, to which sodium carbonate is added to produce heroin base. This is still not real heroin. To produce Heroin #3, or smoking heroin, #2 is mixed with hydrochloric acid, dried and crushed into what generally looks like brown sugar, and is thusly so called. At this point, the heroin is 20-30% pure. To make Heroin #4, or injectable heroin, both ether and hydrochloric acid are added to #2, filtered and dried. This 80-90% heroin can then be injected.

Thus, if one had that early vision of only smoking opium in hazy oblivion, well, the true danger is injecting the refined product into the blood stream. Where total cultivation dropped from 275,000 hectares in 1991 to 150,000 today, production is bullish and growing. Looks like we did not decimate the Taliban, for they are largely responsible for this recovery.

## Cocaine, Marijuana and Ice

Cocaine, a crystalline tropane alkaloid, was first isolated by German chemist Albert Niemann in 1860, and has a chemical formula too long to include here, but is simply, $C_{17}H_{21}NO_4$. The powder is commonly snorted, that is, inhaled through the nose. It can be dissolved in water and injected, and smoked as crack. The drug has been used by South American Indians for 5000 years. Mama Coca was considered to be a benevolent goddess, and chewing the coca leaf provided contact with the spiritual world, while maintaining endurance. In pre-Columbian times, coca was reserved for Inca royalty. The Spanish conquistadors initially banned it, so, it is said, the Catholic Church took on the cultivation. In recent times, during the 1980's, the American CIA teamed with drug dealers to fight communism.

South America (*Columbia, Peru and Bolivia*) produces most of the world cocaine, but cultivation has dropped from 221,200 hectares in 2000 to 159,600 in 2005. Cocaine production has remained relatively constant, as efficiency has improved. Columbia is the largest producer of cocaine, but it is reported that Bolivia has almost doubled its production since current president Evo Morales took office and is already the second largest producer to Columbia. Almost all the cocaine produced in South America finds its way to the U.S. Cocaine is valued at $1,762/kg.

I'm writing this, but not quite believing it. You surely have seen those tiny black poppy seeds on cakes and rolls. Well, eating two rolls or a slice of poppy seed cake will, for 24 hours, produce a positive drug test from your urine sample. There is some exaggeration here, for the official test was raised in 1998 to a higher level, but, yes, that innocuous bakery additive comes from that same poppy flower from which heroin is produced.

Cannabis (*marijuana and hashish*) is grown in 176 countries, and even in Hawaii, where Maui Wowee and Kona Gold are noteworthy. There is paleontological evidence that this plant was smoked as far back as the Neolithic Age. Three thousand year old mummies from China showed such evidence, too, and are mentioned in Greek and Roman bacchanalias. Certainly, cannabis was used by Hindus in India and Nepal, and as a religious sacrament by ancient Jews and early Christians.

It is tetrahydrocannabinol, normally 10-15% of hashish, that creates intoxication. Hashish is the dried resin from the flowering tops only of female hemp, *Cannabis sativa.* Marijuana is a concoction of various parts of the plant, and has one-eighth the potency.

While the prevailing sociological and medical politics are that cannabis is addictive, causes psychosis, augments cancer and heart ailments, and can affect perception, memory and coordination, there is countervailing evidence to the contrary, or, at best, only little evidence of medical support. An important point is that anything to excess can be dangerous. All in all, marijuana and hashish appear to be less harmful to the individual and society than any illicit drug, or, even, tobacco and alcohol. But there is bio-development progress, as breeders have created a strengthened indoor-produced sinsemilla, a highly potent form, obtained from unpollinated female plants.

How significant is marijuana? Well, it has been reported that, at $35 billion/year, pot boasts the largest farmed crop, bigger than corn or wheat.[21]

There are amphetamines, or a-methylphenthylamine, a synthetic drug that is used as pep pills and called Bennies. Then came methamphetamine, a slight chemical variation, with a stronger effect and more addictive properties, known as speed. A particularly dangerous variant is crystal methamphetamine, a colorless and odorless form of d-methamphetamine or methamphetamine hydrochloride, which is inhaled or smoked, although it can also be injected. It resembles shiny blue-white rocks and is, therefore, called ice. The cheapest form is a smelly yellow ice called crank. Up to 5% of high school seniors have used ice at least once.

These non-biological, amphetamine-type stimulants were once mostly produced in Europe, but the danger is that with a few accessible chemicals, they can be churned out in any home, and are. Use causes violent behavior, paranoia, anxiety, confusion and insomnia. Psychotic symptoms can last for years.

There was a period when crystal methamphetamine (*ice*) began to replace cocaine, until 2006, when enforcement success hiked the price of ice from $2,000/ounce to $3,500/ounce. Cocaine held below $2,000/ounce. In any case, both drugs are truly bad.

## Status of Drug Control

The enforcement is relatively simple: prevent growth, seize product, exterminate (*make that, legally, arrest and convict*) suppliers, educate the youth, treat users the first time and revert to more odious punishment subsequently. The White House in 2006 reported that violent crime, homicides and property crime dropped from 2003 to 2004, except for drug abuse violations, which increased.[301] The FBI reported in 2007 that murder and robberies were up for the second year in row, as mentioned in the previous section, so illegal drug use must be increasing.

The U.N. Office on Drugs and Crime, though, reported in mid 2007 that the world drug situation has been stabilized and brought under control.[124] U.S. Drug Czar, John Walters, agreed. Sure, but the United Nations indicated in September of 2006 that the Afghan opium crop jumped 59% that year, for opium is 35% of the local economy, and American Ambassador William Wood said in July of 2007 that the Karzai government destroyed nearly 50,000 acres (*about 10% of the cultivated acreage*) of poppies this year, yet the opium crop set another record.[238] The key is understanding what is being said. Simply, "under control" means not wildly out of control.

We do have a problem. The U.S. Department of Justice reports that 80% of the increase in the federal prison population from 1985 to 1995 was due to drug convictions. Is there a better way to control this problem other than sending them to jail?

### Prisons

The world prison population in 2003 was 8.75 million, which is a little more than a tenth of one percent of the world population. The number of inmates in the United States' now exceeds 2 million.[335] This is particularly interesting, for with 5 percent the world population, the U.S. has almost one quarter the number of citizens in prison, which is curiously close to the disproportionate rate at which we use energy. We have the highest incarceration rate in the world at 686 per 100,000. Worse, 7 million of us—one in every 32 Americans—were either in jail or on parole at the end of 2005.[149]

In 2005, America added about 1,000 new inmates each week, increasing the prison population to 2.2 million (*726 prisoners per 100,000 people*), or almost 1% of this society. However, 62% are not yet convicted, as they are awaiting trail. Actually, the situation is worse, for 4.8 million adults were on probation or parole in 2003, and 40% of them will again be jailed someday. Men are ten times more likely to be in prison.[348] Expectedly, but still shocking, 11.9% of black males in the 25-29 age group are in jail, with, in comparison, 3.9% Hispanic and 1.7% white.

While China has 1.43 million (*119 per 100,000*) incarcerated, they have four times more people than the U.S. The U.K. has the highest rate in the European Union, at 139/100,000. In south central Asia (*including India*), the figure is 54/100,000, or less than a tenth that of the U.S. However, prison populations are growing worldwide. [336] Is there a better way?

In terms of jails (*per 1000 population*):

| | | | |
|---|---|---|---|
| o | #1 | Maldives | 2.2 |
| o | #2 | Czech Republic | 2.1 |
| o | #3 | Papua NG | 1.7 |
| o | #4 | Hong Kong | 1.5 |
| o | #9 | Dominica | 0.014 |
| o | **#22** | **United States** | **0.005** |
| o | #50 | Thailand | 0.002 |
| o | #62 | Kazakhstan | 0.0001 |

Nearly 10% of all prisoners are there for life.[184] In 2005, that was 127,677 inmates, an increase of 83% since 1992.

In 2001 (*most recent U.S. Department Justice analysis*), the average cost of an inmate was $62, which should be about $75/prisoner in 2007.[303] This sum means a tax to each citizen of about $125/year, or in the range of $500 for each family of four. Your taxes, of course, pay for prisoners suffering in this largely air-conditioned comfort. When you add the total correctional expenditures, each family contributes about $1200/year. Most actually welcome this tolerable safety tax. But there must be a better way.

Any poll will show that the general population applauds more policemen and placing more criminals in jails. Here I go again, but I disagree. There is a better way...immoral, yes... depraved, maybe, but as Al Jolson might have said, "you ain't seen nothing yet." The ideas are not mine. Some came through sardonic or facetious columnists, such as Rick Hamada of ***Midweek***: remove eyes of car thieves so they cannot steal another car, commit a rape and provide the victim's family five minutes in a room with baseball bats, cut hands off burglars, etc.[131] Okay, he was not serious, but there are extremes, and I will advocate a particularly ghastly one, later.

**About the American Civil Liberties Union**

In 1920 the American Civil Liberties Union [11] was founded by Crystal Eastman, a lawyer who helped write the Equal Rights Amendment (*women suffrage*), and Roger Nash Baldwin, who served as the executive director until 1950. It is reported to have more than half a million members.

Very simply, the ACLU provides assistance when civil liberties are at risk, including religious freedom. It tends to attack Republicans more, but, of course, because of their beliefs. It has defended the Ku Klux Klan, neo-Nazi organizations, the North American Man/Boy Love Association and Lt. Colonel Oliver North. The ACLU lost the Scopes Trial and was fined $100; filed an amicus curiae (*legal opinion*) brief in the Brown v. Board of Education trial, which led to the ban on racial segregation; and was the first major national organization to call for the impeachment of President Richard Nixon.

This organization receives nearly $100 million each year in donations, almost 90% from the general public. It actually rejected $1.5 million from the Ford and Rockefeller Foundations in 2004 because there was a stipulation prohibiting the underwriting of terrorism, which the ACLU viewed as a threat to civil liberties, a remarkable point of view.

In the State of Hawaii, and much of the nation, the labor unions were essential to bring equality to the masses. They still have an important role to play, but are they being smart about their current mission? Times have changed. The ACLU, I fear, is suffering the same obsolescence when it comes to crime. They are continuously on the back of Sheriff Joe Arpaio (*who is later suggested as a simple solution to minimize crime*), always happen to be on the side of the criminal, and exact considerable cost to government, which means taxpayers money. I would like to plead for the ACLU to mature into a more responsible organization, and, now and then, consider the innocent public as your primary constituency.

Convicted criminals have certain restrictions in society. They have legally nullified their contract with society and are, therefore, at risk. Here, ACLU steps in, for the convict is still human. If some understanding can be reached that government has the right to treat the offender in a manner that maintains reasonable health, at minimal expense to the community, this will provide the ACLU with more resources to scrutinize the Patriot Act and sundry other more important issues.

**On the Morality and Efficacy of Death Sentences**

The ACLU has eight objections to the death penalty:[11]

- unfair,
- irreversible;
- barbarous,
- unjustified retribution,
- **costs more than incarceration,**
- **not a deterrent to capital crimes,**
- less popular than the alternatives, and
- inhuman and anachronistic.

Others say, the death penalty:[95, 123]

- violates America's founding principles;
- is the hallmark of authoritarian regimes;
- creates more victims;
- is arbitrary and capricious;
- is racist, classist and financially contingent;
- deprives us of our own human dignity;
- denies our ability to change;
- is cruel and denigrating;
- **is unanimously excluded in international jurisdictions**; and
- as no one is beyond redemption, it detracts from the transformative power of God.

Much of the above is moralistic, but let us look at some of them.

## Life in Prison is Cheaper than a Penalty of Death

While at first glance it seems that it should be cheaper to swiftly inject a lethal dose than to keep a lifer in air conditioned comfort, there are sound arguments that the added cost of capital trials is greater than a simple one maintaining the prisoner in jail. Duke University estimated that death penalty trials take 3-5 times longer than typical murders, plus, they are invariably followed by appeals. It costs North Carolina $2.16 million more per execution trial than one for a life sentence. At $100/day, this would keep a prisoner for nearly 60 years.

Thus, the matter of deterrence, perhaps, becomes more important. That, and the diminishing need for trials, if economics were of consequence.

## The Death Penalty Does Not Work

With the exception of assassins, most people who kill are not in a rational frame of mind. These murders occur on impulse.

The reality is that:[263]

- While executions in the U.S. from 1976-1996 increased from 0 to 60, the homicide rate per 100,000 remained constant at just under 10.
- About 80% of criminologists believe that executions do not have a deterrent effect.
- Two-thirds of U.S. police chiefs do not believe that the death penalty reduces murders.
- A 1998 United Nations study concluded that executions do not deter.

What do work are reduction in drug use, a better economy with more jobs, simplification of court rules and longer prison sentences. In fact, in 1996, those states with the death penalty had an average murder rate of 7.1 per 100,000, and those which did not had a rate of 3.6. In Canada, the homicide rate dropped 27% after the death penalty was abolished.

In September 2000, a ***New York Times*** survey showed that during the last 20 years, the homicide rate in states **with** the death penalty was 48 to 110 percent **higher** than in states without the death penalty. This was reported in a press release by Amnesty International USA, where "action for human rights" and hope for humanity" are their themes. It went on further to state that the threat of execution at some future date is unlikely to enter the minds of those acting under the influence of drugs and/or alcohol, or in a grip of fear or rage, or is mentally retarded.

## The Death Penalty Works

In 2005, there were 16,692 cases of murder in the U.S. There were 60 executions.

On June 11, 2007, Robert Tanner of the ***Chicago Sun-Times*** reported that the death penalty acts as a deterrent to murder.[317] Further, each execution saves from three to 18 lives. Naci Mocan, an economics professor at the University of Colorado at Denver, who opposes the death penalty, was one of the authors of one of those studies. He said that each execution saved five innocent lives.

Since 2001, there have been a dozen such papers, and they ALL say the death penalty deters crime, as for example:

- 2003 Emory University conclusion that each execution deters an average of 18 murders and
- 2006 University of Houston study that the Illinois moratorium on executions in 2000 led to 150 additional homicides over four years.

The acceptance of this notion—that executions deter crime—has significant ramifications, as in 1975, Isaac Ehrlich's analysis that each execution saved eight lives influenced the Supreme Court to end the death penalty moratorium, even though a National Academy of Sciences panel decided that Ehrlich's conclusions were flawed.

Predictably, critics responded:

- there were profound mistakes in the methodology so the results are untrustworthy;
- we don't have enough data to say anything; and
- this is an open question.

The latter two opinions, actually, came from a very scholarly 2006 paper by John Donahue and Justin Wolfers, published in the **Stanford Law Review.**[363]

Well, does the death penalty work or not? **It works, crime is deterred.**

## Capital Punishment and the World

One of the bullets above implied that the U.S. is the only country that executes. This reference was to international tribunals, which have tended not to carry out the death penalty on even the most heinous of crimes. Japanese war criminals? They were judged by the International Military Tribunal for the Far East or Khabarovsk War Crime Trials, and 1000 were sentenced to death. Nuremberg was a military tribunal. Military trials can be terminal. Adolph Eichmann? He was tried in an Israeli court and hanged.

While there were only 18 nations prohibiting the death penalty in 1977, today, 89 countries have totally abolished this practice, 10 use it only under very special circumstances, and 30 others have not used it during the past decade. In comparison, 38 U.S. states do not allow death. China carried out from 1,010 to 8,000 executions in 2006, depending on the source, as compared to 53 in the USA. Ten years ago, 40 countries had executions, compared to 26 in 2006. Thus, while the trend is towards more clemency, the U.S. is not the only country that terminates the life of a wanton convict.

## How Does the Public Feel about the Death Penalty

Over the past two decades, the percent of Americans who thought that death should be the penalty for murder has vacillated between 49% and 61%. Life imprisonment has ranged between 29 and 47%.[206] However, to the question, "favor or oppose death penalty for those convicted of murder," the favor opinion from 1936 to 2004 had a low of 45% in 1965, rose to 80% in the 90's and seems to be around 70% today. Opposition ranged between 13% and 43%, settling at 25% of recent. Thus, most Americans FAVOR the death penalty.

A curious shift has occurred to the question, "is the death penalty a deterrent to the commitment of murder," sitting at 61% for yes in 1985, and dropping to 35% in 2004. The no response rose from 31% to 62%. So the average citizen does not think that the death penalty deters crime. They are wrong but don't know it.

Thus, on June 15, 2007, the Death Penalty Information Center reported that 58% of Americans now want a national moratorium on executions.[87, 294] Executions rose in the 1990s, but has tailed off since then. The reason? John Grisham books, movies and TV shows. While 39% of the general population believe they should be disqualified from capital juries (*because of their views on the subject*), the figure for African Americans is 68%.

Around the world:

- 55% of Brazilians support the death penalty, a 14 year high.
- 29% of Finns;
- 42 % of French favor reinstating the death penalty;
- 81% of Japanese; and
- 28% of New Zealanders want to reinstate the death penalty.

In general, support for the death penalty is dropping globally.

## How are the Condemned Executed?

Early on, suffocation was the means, but the more humane dropping of the body a longer distance to dislocate the neck or sever the spinal cord was then instituted. There was a time when stones, swords and axes were used. Then firing squads and hanging became the termination actions of choice. There were also the Scottish Maiden and the Halifax Gibbet, instruments that crushed the neck by blunt force to take off the head.

In France, there was sentiment for ending life with minimal pain, so a committee was set up, with professor of anatomy, Joseph-Ignace Guillotin, credited with developing the concept of a falling triangular blade with a beveled edge. The device in 1792 became known as the guillotine in France and fallbeil (*falling axe*) in Germany, was universally used in Europe, and finally retired in 1977. Gas chambers were also used, but that is another story of the holocaust.

In the U.S., the gas chamber was also utilized, but the electric chair (*EC*) had a dreadful history and showed some bitter rivalry between Thomas Edison, an advocate of DC electricity, and George Westinghouse, who was responsible for AC currents, the eventual winner. In 1887, Edison held a public demonstration, setting up a 1,000 volt Westinghouse AC generator to execute a dozen animals on an electrified plate. The term "electrocution" was invented that day. It was gruesome, but the point was made that AC electricity was dangerous. Edison's smear campaign did not work, but it did get the Westinghouse chair adopted for executions. In 1889, Westinghouse's chair became law, but he refused to sell any AC generators for this purpose, and, even funded the appeals for the first so sentenced prisoners. Edison, through subterfuge, then provided the AC generators. The media referred to the process as being "Westinghoused."

William Kemmler was the first to be executed in New York in 1890, and it wasn't pretty. The first 17-second jolt did not kill him, so the voltage was increased, and on the second attempt, blood vessels ruptured and the body caught fire. It took eight minutes. He died. Westinghouse commented that they should have used an axe. Notable victims were Sacco and Vanzetti, Bruno Hauptman, Julius and Ethel Rosenberg and Ted Bundy. Nebraska is today the only state to solely use the electric chair, but the May 8, 2007 execution was stayed while the courts looked closer at the EC as cruel and unusual punishment.

## The Seven Minute Solution: Lethal Injection

Every American execution since 2005 was conducted by lethal injection. The basic idea was proposed in 1888 by Julius Mount Bleyer, a New York doctor, because it was more humane and cheaper. Nothing much happened, though, until 1977, when Jay Chapman, the state medical examiner for Oklahoma, introduced the Chapman Protocol, a two-stage intravenous drip. Thirty-seven states have adopted this treatment, and so has China.

The technique has now been refined into a three-step sequence, with parallel drips, in case the first one does not work:

- sodium thiopental: induces unconsciousness;
- pancuronium bromide: stops all muscle movement, except the heart; and
- potassium chloride: causing cardiac arrest.

It usually takes 7 minutes for death to occur.

The Supreme Court has indicated that death-row inmates can challenge lethal injection as cruel and unusual, but has not themselves decided if this protocol is illegal or not. The American Medical Association believes that it is a personal decision. The debate is in two parts: first, is the death penalty too terminal, and, second, if acceptable, is there a more humane method.

The Florida Catholic Conference and Amnesty International USA reported on the Bennie Demps execution, a Muslim, who in 1971 murdered two people, was convicted to death, but was saved in 1972 when the Supreme Court declared capital punishment unconstitutional. However, in 1976, the Florida death law was upheld, soon after when Demps participated in a jail stabbing murder, and was sentenced to death for the second time. After all this time in jail, on June 7, 2000, D-Day came, technicians couldn't find that second vein, and Demps was quoted by witnesses to have remarked, "They butchered me back there...This is not an execution, it is murder."

In 1981, Michael Angelo Morales, a heavy drug user, was recruited by his gay cousin, Ricky Ortega, to kill Terri Winchell, 17, who was dating Ortega's boyfriend. According to testimony, Morales strangled, hit her head 23 times with a claw hammer, raped, and then stabbed her four times. A quarter century later, in February of 2006, he ate his "last meal" of pork chops, bacon, a lettuce/tomato sandwich, milkshake and strawberry shortcake. Two hours before the second attempt at execution, it was postponed because a judge determined that there was a risk that the death might be painful, having something to do with not having a licensed professional do the job. Barbara Christian, Terri's mother, remarked, "Here our beautiful daughter lies murdered, and there they worry about the way this monster feels and if he'll feel any pain."[296] In mid-2007, U.S. District Judge Jeremy Fogel said that he would visit California's new death chamber later this year to issue a follow-up ruling. Morales still lives.

## Nitrogen: The Next Generation

Ah, but on the horizon is nitrogen asphyxiation, known as killing with kindness.[73] Nitrogen is 78% of the atmosphere we breathe. But if the content is less than 10% oxygen, death can result. Nearly 100 industrial deaths have been caused by too rich a nitrogen atmosphere over the past couple of decades.

In 1981, during final countdown for the Columbia Space Shuttle at the Kennedy Space Center, two NASA technicians entered the aft engine compartment, which was purged with nitrogen to reduce any hydrogen-oxygen build-up, and died in minutes from anoxia (*lack of oxygen*). Nitrogen has no distinct smell or taste. The same happened to the European Space Agency in 1995 when two more lost their lives from a nitrogen leak into the launchpad.

The body feels suffocation only when the carbon dioxide concentration in your lungs exceeds a certain threshold, as when you hold your breath. The beauty of using nitrogen, if you can call it that, is that in a nitrogen atmosphere, you exhale the carbon dioxide normally, but without the 20% oxygen on inhalation. Thus, death is painless without the feeling of suffocation.

### Draco the Lawgiver

Draco wrote the first constitution of Athens. His laws were severe, as a debtor became a slave and there was death for even minor offenses. In time, this form of punishment became known as Draconian.

Draco means dragon in Latin. I'm a dragon. Maybe there is more to all this than I can imagine. The solution to crime might well be Draconian.

**The Three Strikes Law**

There is almost total agreement that the solution to crime is in the prevention. Upbringing and education mean everything, and every care and reasonable expense should be expended to mold a solid citizen. I highly advocate early education as the means to remediate potential criminals in Chapter 4. Unfortunately, there will still be crimes.

Civilization has exacted a range of punishments over time. In Exodus 21:23-27, an "eye for an eye" provided the principle of proportionate punishment. Equitable retaliation was the belief. This same concept is presented in the Code of Hammurabi. Of benefit to the criminal, this type of law prevents excessive punishment. The Quran actually urges the victim to accept a lower compensation, if not totally forgive, with an unwritten belief of a later reward, such as, perhaps, paradise. Martin Luther King has been quoted to say, "the old law of an eye for an eye leaves everyone blind."

Fair enough, as everyone makes a mistake now and then. If the crime can be forgiven, fine, now do everything possible to remediate that person. Be protective, be reformative. Rehabilitate. A second crime is committed and there is a conviction. Now what? Is there a way to prevent habitual offending? Do longer and longer prison sentences make sense? Alas there could be a third strike. Chaperoned, air-conditioned comfort, for life?

In baseball, if you get three strikes, you are out. In the U.S., with three strikes, or convictions, you go to jail, maybe even for a long time, perhaps life. This is a relatively new concept, which started in the state of Washington in 1993 and California the following year, with three felonies and you're in prison for life. Kevin Weber was sentenced to 26 years to life for stealing four chocolate chip cookies (*his two previous convictions were for burglary and assault*). There are 344 shoplifters in prison for 25 years or more, one who stole a $3 magazine. Les Miserables? Their prisons now hold double the designed capacity. And, you're paying for all this.

More than half of the states now have some form of this law. In March 5, 2003, the U.S. Supreme Court ruled that the three strikes law was **not** "cruel and unusual punishment."

Here is my problem with this law. As immoral as keeping someone in jail for the rest of his life might be, I think it is not worth my tax dollars. Does this mean I am against such a concept? No, I like the fact that seasoned criminals are kept away, only, let us be truly sensible, maybe, even **draconian**. First, do we want a better educational system or should we build more prisons? Second, isn't it cruel to keep someone locked up for a lifetime? Third, how, really, can we actually best prevent that fourth crime. This simple solution will soon be announced.

## The Singapore Solution to Crime

In March 2004, Michael Peter Fay, 18, from Missouri and Ohio, pleaded guilty in a Singapore court to vandalism (*spray painting cars*), mischief and receiving stolen property (*No Smoking and No Exit signs*). He was sentenced by Judge F. G. Remedios to four months in prison, six strokes of the rattan and a fine of $2230. Fay's partner, Shiu Chi Ho, 16, of Hong Kong, was given 8 months in jail and twelve strokes of the cane. This is not a slap on the knuckles by a nun wielding a ruler. An official trained in the martial arts, with firm strength, swings a half inch cane, many times causing shock and usually permanent scars. It is reported that around 1000 canings occur every year. There is no graffiti problem here and, furthermore, chewing gum was once banned (*lifted in 2004*). I think it's still illegal not to flush a public toilet. You don't want to be caught for this neglect.

While Americans seemed aghast about Michael, more than half of us in a poll of 23,000 favored whipping and other harsh sentences as an acceptable deterrent to crime in the U.S. That year, Mike Royko, the Voice of the Working Class for the ***New York Daily News*** (*both have since passed away*), said that 99% of the letters he received said, yes, Fay should be flogged. Yet, President Clinton did send an official protest, and so did six U.S. Senators. Officials in Singapore were unapologetic, wondered how the leader of the most powerful country could worry about a spoiled brat and remarked that they did not have situations where vandals spray-painted police cars, such as in New York City.

Well, Singapore President Ong Teng Cheong, ever so kind, reduced the penalty to four strokes and they were applied on May 5, 1994, in private. Americans again griped that the penalty was excessive and inhumane. Not long thereafter, after Michael Fay returned to the U.S., he was admitted to the Hazelden rehabilitation program for butane abuse (*he sniffed this fossil fuel gas*), was cited for reckless driving in Florida and then arrested for possession of marijuana and drug paraphernalia. I guess he is one person who never learns his lesson.

In 2002, Van Tuong Nguyen of Melbourne was arrested at Changi Airport with nearly 400 grams (*almost a pound*) of heroin. He was convicted and sentenced to death. The Australian and New Zealand Prime Ministers, the Pope and many others, called for clemency. Singapore has a mandatory death penalty for the importation of more than 15 grams of heroin, 30 grams of cocaine and 500 grams of cannabis. Singapore executes more people per capita that any other country, about 35/year, mostly for drug trafficking. Van Tuong Nguyen was hanged in Changi Prison on December 2, 2005.

In the 1800's, before Singapore became a nation, opium was supplied to laborers and addiction became increasingly widespread. After World War II, opium smoking was made illegal. By the 1970's heroin took over. Well, is there a drug problem in Singapore today? Yes, but mostly synthetic drugs such as nimetazepam, because it was new and not yet subject to control (*it now is*). Today, heroin is #7. Zero tolerance seems to be somewhat working.

**The Simple Solution to Crime**

According to a 2005 report of the National Crime Victims' Rights Week, crime costs Americans somewhere in the range of $500 billion annually.[341] However, in 1999, David Anderson published in the ***Journal of Law and Economics*** a paper outlining that the net burden of crime in the U.S. was $1.7 trillion per year, or $5667 for each person in the country.[233] This did not include the physical pain, long-term mental anguish and general fear anyone has about stepping out at night and such. Wouldn't it be wonderful if we could just eliminate this compromise in our daily life forever? The savings of $1.7 trillion/year would be wonderful, but just the lifestyle enhancement alone would be huge.

Let me be candid by saying that this not my idea, but, if society is willing to stomach some morality issues to prevent crime, what about a real three strikes law. This one is called Three Strikes and You're Dead (*TSAYD*)! To repeat, THREE STRIKES AND YOU'RE DEAD.

**First conviction**: Someone commits a crime. Do everything possible to reform the culprit. Of course, even before the first crime, it is in the upbringing and educational process where people begin to go bad. It would make eminent good sense to spend tax dollars at this early stage. But, regarding the lawbreaker, there are shelves of books with ideas on how to remediate an individual.

One option is restorative justice, promoting repair, reconciliation and the rebuilding of relationships. The process attempts to build partnerships, seeking balanced approaches for victim, wrongdoer and community. There will be a lot of counseling and, as necessary and possible, some restitution. New Zealand legislated in 1989 restorative justice for juvenile crime. Then, there were 64 violations per 1,000 in the population. Today, this figure has dropped to 16.

The concept is hardly new, as the Pentateuch, the so-called books of Moses, advocated compensation for property crimes, as did the Code of Hammurabi (*1700 BC*). The Code of Ur-Nammu (*2000 BC*) required amends for violence.

Spend the bigger bucks on shoring up the early life, but be generous, too, on reclaiming this individual after a tolerable first offense. The primary objective will be to prevent those potential second and third crimes. Half of all inmates are back in jail only two years later. A simple way to reduce this rate is to strike fear into the offender so that he abandons all thought of committing another crime. Thus, the penalty for entering stage two should be terrible, if not horrendous.

**Crime #2** is committed and the defendant is judged guilty. Standard prison? Nope. Save that money to build better schools. Find some hellacious environment where the prisoner will need to support himself, and where the cost to society will be minimal. A mild form—I was thinking more in terms of dungeons or caves—of this concept is represented by Joe Arpaio, sheriff of Maricopa Arizona County:

- jail meals, such as bologna sandwich, cost 40 cents/serving, and he charges inmates for them;
- no smoking, no coffee and no porno magazines;
- chain gangs to do free work on county projects;
- took away cable TV, but was forced to put them back because a federal court required that for jails, so he played only the Disney and weather channels, and added Newt Gingrich lectures;

When inmates complained, he told them don't come back. Two thousand prisoners in tents with no air conditioning, even when the temperature is more than 116 degrees F. Sheriff Joe says that our soldiers in Iraq are in tents where the temperature exceeds 120, in full battle gear.

News flash! Hawaii announced in 2008 that seven prison tents will be built with federal funds. No, they are not following the Arpaio strategy. These will be for minimum custody inmates. But get ready to relocate them to more secure cites if TSAYD is instituted.

The question is, will those who survive be more apt not to return? The answer is, heck, yes, but mostly because of the consequences of a third conviction! Anyway, why waste good money on the hopeless, which is defined as anyone who is stupid enough to commit a second crime knowing that the punishment will be hell. The prison of Sheriff Joe is a reasonable simple solution for **strike two**.

**Third conviction: termination!** Yes, death. The U.S. has now had more than 1000 executions since the Supreme Court ended a moratorium three decades ago. Under the TSAYD formula, this number could seriously increase in the first few years, but should decline with time. The odds are astronomically high that crime rates will significantly drop within the decade.

Oh yes, there are millions of questions and issues. First, some particularly odious crimes will immediately go to step three, as is the case today. But what about a white collar criminal or traffic violator? Can you execute someone for stealing a chocolate chip cookie or a magazine? You've no doubt read of a car thief, who is convicted, convicted mind you, a hundred times (*well, I'm not sure what the record is, and I can't imagine our court system being so efficient as to actually convict the same person this many times*), and still somehow runs loose and is arrested for stealing yet another car. Maybe enough should be three convictions for anything. The odds are high that this will all stop after the first arrest. But what about those on drugs who cannot control themselves or the few so idiotic as to absent mindedly commit that third crime? Answering this question will only irritate churches, social workers and mothers.

What about those with mental illnesses? A Bureau of Justice Statistics study reported in 2006 that half of those in jail suffered from mental health problems:[337]

- o 73% of females and 55% of males in State prisons,
- o 61% female / 44% male in Federal prisons and
- o 75% female / 63% male were certifiably sub-normal.

Sounds menacingly Hitleresque, but perhaps an argument can be made that the elimination of this drag on society can only improve the quality of life for the innocent. Former Education Secretary William Bennett, on his radio show, is quoted to have said:[239]

*To reduce crime, you could—if that were your sole purpose—you could abort every black baby in this country, and your crime rate would go down...That would be an impossible, ridiculous and morally reprehensible thing to do, but your crime rate would go down.*

He said his statement was taken out of context, and many of my simple solutions definitely fall in this framework of being "taken out of context." Could a "Three Strikes and You're Dead" law ever be enacted anywhere in the world today? Of course not! But it should be debated and considered, for, perhaps, a compromising intermediary first step might well be universal application of the Sheriff Joe penal system.

Thus, the nature of a human society could well be the primary impediment to ending crime forever. Well, let us now go on to something simpler, mega-crimes, or wars. How to prevent them? The solution is surprisingly simple, and not as draconian as **TSAYD**.

## The End of World Wars

### World War Trends

Evolution is a process of survival, and war is just a more organized development to prevail. There no doubt were wars in one million B.C. But something happened to the mind of man, and the greatest strategist of all, Sun-tzu, author of ***The Art of War***, written as far back as the fourth century B.C., hypothesized that the ideal winning strategy was one without bloodshed.[122] But men will be men, and our civilization has been laced with just the opposite. Ah, but there has been progress. It has been reported that 30% of males died in violence during our cavemen-hunter-gatherer days. Since that perilous period, this number dropped to 1% in the 1900's, and in this 21st Century, perhaps a tenth of that.

In World War I, everyone exploited chemical warfare. The French began the practice, using xylyl bromide tear-gas grenades in 1914. In 1915, chlorine gas was employed by Germany, killing at least 5,000. The British responded in kind. Phosgene came into use by all. In 1917, to slow the Allied advance, mustard (*yperite, a carbon, hydrogen, chlorine and sulfur compound*) gas was used by Germany, which actually was a liquid, not a gas. The French employed a nerve gas, hydrocyanic acid, spiked with a little arsenic, but not too effectively because, by then, gas masks actually worked. The Americans entered the war quite late, but General John Pershing had available a range of chemical agents.

In this supposed war to end wars, it is estimated that there were **15 million killed**, although there are indications that up to 66 million actually died, maybe more from the Spanish Flu than anything else. Many don't realize that the Russian Civil War, which ran from 1917 to 1922, experienced 9 million deaths, and the Stalin regime eliminated 20 million from 1924 to 1953. Armistice outlawed poison gas in 1925 and the ban worked, as World War II saw no use of chemical warfare. [90]

However, in 2007, it was reported that the British tested mustard gas on Indian soldiers during the 1930s and during the second world war, the U.S. Naval Research Laboratory experimented with Lewisite and mustard gas on 2,000 American personnel, who got special weekend passes if they participated.[323]

**World War II had 55 million deaths**, or up to 72 million by other accounts. With regard to high technology, the Atomic Bombs dropped on Hiroshima and Nagasaki killed somewhere between 100,000 and 200,000 people. The world will forever debate whether this was morally right or not, but the devastation ingrained a MAD (*mutually assured destruction*) mentality that probably served to prevent total nuclear warfare during the Cold War.

Post WWII saw 2.5 million killed in the Chinese Civil War from 1945 to 1949, and Mao Zedong's reign was responsible for 40 million deaths from 1949 to 1975. For the record, the Korean War (*1950-53*) lost 3.5 million (*33,000 to 54,000 Americans, depending on whom you ask*), Vietnam War (*1960-75*) 5 million (*67,000 Americans, including almost 10,000 who committed suicide*) and the more recent Kinshasa Congo Civil War has seen 5 million deaths (*although 8 million perished from 1886 to 1908*) thus far.[350] Total fatalities in the ongoing Afghanistan-Iraq skirmish are reported to be less than 1 million (*less than 5,000 American deaths*).[193]

In summary, then (*highest estimate of deaths*):

| **WAR** | **LOCATION** | **PERIOD** | **DEATHS** | **RATIO** |
|---|---|---|---|---|
| Three Kingdom Wars | China | 184-280 | 40 million | 0.27 |
| An Shi Rebellion | China | 756-63 | 36 million | 0.17 |
| Mongol Conquests | Asia/Europe | 1207-79 | 60 million | 0.15 |
| Conquests (Timor the Lame) | Asia Major | 1369-1405 | 20 million | 0.056 |
| Napoleonic Wars | Europe | 1804-15 | 16 million | 0.016 |
| Taiping Rebellion | China | 1851-64 | 50 million | 0.04 |
| American Civil War | U.S. | 1861-65 | 1 million | 0.0007 |
| World War I | Europe | 1914-18 | 66 million | 0.04 |
| World War II | World | 1939-45 | 72 million | 0.03 |
| Korean War | Korea | 1950-53 | 3.5 million | 0.0014 |
| Vietnam War | Vietnam | 1945-75 | 5 million | 0.0017 |
| Iraq War | Iraq | 2003-08 | 700,000 | 0.0001 |

The RATIO represents maximum deaths divided by the approximate world population of that period, and you will note the rapid decline compared to those early wars.

Americans tend to get wrapped up in their own conflicts. No one outside of China remembers the Taiping Rebellion, a so-called Rebellion of Great Peace, a religious revolt against the Qing government, which occurred at the same time period as the American Civil War. The Chinese civil war lost 50 times more, and the American 1 million is somewhat exaggerated, as the correct estimate is around 970,000. But even that Asian war is puny compared to the Mongol Conquests and the Three Kingdom Wars. Ominous, though, that all these truly great wars occurred in, or otherwise were caused by, China.

World War I is anomalous because most of those deaths were due to the Spanish Flu. However, you can see how relatively insignificant were the Korean, Vietnam and Iraq wars. The trend, as surmised in the opening paragraph, indeed, seems promising. Our major wars are killing fewer and fewer people, per capita.

Adjusted for 2000 dollars, our wars have cost:[196]

| | |
|---|---|
| o Civil War | $62 billion |
| o Spanish American War | $5 billion |
| o World War I | $290 billion |
| o World War II | $2,300 billion (*or $2.3 trillion*) |
| o Korean Conflict | $111 billion |
| o Vietnam War | $165 billion |
| o Iraq War | $2,400 billion (*estimated, $2.4 trillion*)* |

These wars are certainly not cheap, and it is startling that this second Iraq War will cost more than the entire World War II. Further, we LOST that Vietnam War to communists, and they still went away, while we rose to become #1. If those Iraq War funds were instead used to sidestep Peak Oil or prevent Global Warming, where would we be today?

Well, perhaps we still can democratize the Middle East. But, things are not going well, so one wonders what better priorities for those trillions of dollars. There is a report by Nobel Laureate Joseph Stiglitz that projects more than $2 trillion for the Iraq War[28] and a Congressional Budget Office estimate that the Afghanistan/Iraq War if continued over the next decade will cost $2.4 trillion* *(that is $8,000/person in the U.S.)*.[229] There are, of course, hidden costs to all wars, and a Joint Economic Committee of Congress reported that the Iraq and Afghanistan wars have already cost $1.5 trillion, that is 1,500 billion dollars.[349] Remember the entire annual renewable energy budget for the U.S. Department of Energy for the past decade averaged under $1 billion/year, or one-thousandth of a trillion dollars.

Jumping to today, the latest Grimmett Report says that the world spends about $1 trillion/year on the military.[282] More than a third of all arms sales in the 1998-2005 period, close to $100 billion, can be attributed to the U.S:

- o We specialize in providing arms and training to countries harboring terrorists, good because our soldiers are not killed, but one wonders where these rifles go, and whether they might someday be pointed right back at us.
- o Twenty of the top twenty-five U.S. arms clients in the developing world were either undemocratic regimes or governments with records of major human rights abuses. But, then, again, maybe this is the way to wean them towards democracy.

Russia is #2 with about $41 billion. Numbers alone, however, do not portray the reality. The U.S. government provides subsidies to allow countries to purchase these military arms, a kind of foreign aid. There is, of course, widespread corruption and bribes, for this international industry has no oversight, generally because the matter of national security provides for confidentiality. President Jimmy Carter in 1976 said that "we can't be both the world's leading champion of peace and the world's leading supplier of arms." But we are!

While Iran and North Korea at one time were feared to be capable of utilizing nuclear arms, the greater danger today has to do with terrorism and dirty bombs, that is, standard explosives spiced with nuclear wastes. In time, an actual Atomic Bomb could well be within the capability of a well-financed group, and it is logical to predict that biological weapons could well become an even more dangerous alternative. While the 1972 Biological Weapons Convention signed by most countries outlaws the creation and stockpiling of germ warfare weapons, amazingly, it does not prohibit their usage. Not that this would make much of a difference for renegade organizations. Russia kept building bio-weapon stockpiles until 1992, and it is suspected that the number of countries capable of producing biological weapons has increased since then.

While biological warfare sounds futuristic, in the 6th Century B.C., the Assyrians poisoned enemy wells with a delusional fungus (*whatever that means*) and in 184 B.C., Hannibal's soldiers threw clay pots filled with venomous snakes unto the decks of Pergamene ships. Diseased bodies were used to infect enemy water supplies in Medieval Europe, Black Death casualties were catapulted into besieged cities during the Middle Ages and as recently as 1710 by Russian forces attacking Sweden. The British Army is said to have used smallpox as a weapon during the Indian Wars in North America. In World War II, Japan reportedly infected foodstuffs with the plague and cholera, killing 58,000. China and North Korea protested in the Korean War that American troops used biological weapons against them. There is considerable evidence today of continuing R&D (*which is permitted by the ban*) at the Dugway Proving Grounds in Utah and Fort Detrick, Maryland.[351]

Conventional biological weapons have animal origins, and, as would be expected, these tend to be the test subjects. Not necessarily for warfare experiments, but a relatively peaceful nation today such as the United Kingdom in 2001 used more than 2.5 million animals, including 20,000 hoofed mammals, 125,605 birds and 170,459 fish. [26] Where are the People for the Ethical Treatment of Animals (*PETA*), the Animal Liberation Front [173] or Brigitte Bardot? At the other end of the killing spectrum, Norway fishermen must now humanely terminate the life of any caught seafood variety.

In 1979 at a test site in Sverdlovsk in the Soviet Union, sheep became ill with anthrax 125 miles (200 kilometers) away from the lab. Washington, D.C. is only 30 miles from Fort Detrick. On a targeted basis, only 220 pounds of anthrax can virtually eliminate the 3 million in the District.[146] Reportedly, Saddam Hussein at one time had at his disposal 25 missiles able to carry 11,000 pounds of biological agents, including botulism and anthrax.

The fear, of course, is that, with the advent of the Genome Table, a whole new stratum of super-biological microorganisms can be created, especially for warfare. The ultimate virus could well eliminate human life forever. How do we prevent all this? Easy, prevent wars.

But you would hope, actually, that the world someday promotes wars for beneficent causes. The 9/11 death toll was around 3,000. Each year 470,000 die in traffic accidents, a little less than 10% (*43,000*) of that in the U.S. Now that would be a worthwhile crusade, a "War on Highway deaths." Or, the UN reported that there were 13 million deaths in 2006 due to environmental causes.[378] What about the "World War to Prevent Environmental Deaths?" We will soon need a World War to Combat Peak Oil and Global Warming, and while already maybe be too late to avoid the economic crunch, perhaps this potential calamity can serve to catalyze world peace. Huh? Read on.

## Civilizational Trends

Babylon, the ancient city of Mesopotamia, famous for its Hanging Gardens, one of the Seven Wonders of the World, located where what today is Iraq, had a population of maybe 100,000. But this was way back in 3000 B.C. Today, Iraq has a population of 26 million, and has lost its charm.

Athens was all of 50,000 in its heyday 2,500 years ago. It grew to 300,000 by 432 B.C. (*only half citizens, as 50,000 were aliens, with 100,000 slaves*). Today, while it has lost its dominance, the population is approaching 4 million.

Early in the 17th Century, London became the first city to reach 1 million. Today, nineteen cities have populations ranging from 10 to 25 million.

Conversely, Europe in the 16th Century had 500 autonomous governments. By 1975, this had been reduced to 35, and with the European Union, 27 countries will be reduced to one. But, then, the Soviet Union did increase from one to 15, and there are projections that China could someday suffer the same fate. Irrespective, those Soviet entities will someday all join the EU and those potential Chinese states will link with the budding OU, or, Orient Union. The trend is towards one unifying world government.

The world today can be represented by what came to me through the internet. If the world population could be reduced to 100 people, there would be:

- 60 Asians
- 14 Africans
- 12 Europeans
- 8 Latin Americans
- 5 U.S. Americans and Canadians

Or looking at population another way:

- 82 non-white
- 80 live in sub-standard housing
- 67 non-Christian
- 67 unable to read
- 50 malnourished

The United Nations has 191 members, and, according to the chapter on the Blue Revolution in ***Book 1***, this could increase to thousands with each floating city becoming independent. So much for one global government. However, strength in number of members could well someday mature into one governing body. Either this model or a dominant global corporation, for one of the simple solutions to ending wars will be one ascendant and benevolent government. Then there will someday be colonization of outer space and the whole cycle begins again. But that's a millennium away.

**What about the United States of America?**

Let me skip the history of the USA, and start with a comparative table:

| | **World** | **United States** |
|---|---|---|
| Age | Dawn of Humanity (150,000 BC or so) | About 200 years |
| Size (land) | 510 million sq km | 10 million sq km |
| Population | 6,700 million | 302 million |
| Gross Domestic Product | $66,000 billion | $13,000 billion |
| GDP/Capita | $10,200 | $44,000 |
| Military Expenditures | $1,320 billion | $528 billion |
| Military Expenditures as %GDP | 2% | 4.1% |

From ***Time*** magazine:

- 80% White, 15% Hispanic, 13% Black and 4.4% Asian. By 2050 it will be 50% White and 24% Hispanic.
- Until 1960 less than 5% of births were to unmarried women. Today, this figure is approaching 40%.
- Per 1000 Americans, 370 believe in ghosts, 250 deem flying saucers as being real, 126 live in poverty, 122 are 65 or older, 50-100 doubt the existence of a God (*which means 900 to 950 believe*), 27 are cashiers (*$16,260*), 23 are in prison, 4 are lawyers (*$98,930*) and 1 is in kindergarten

Our national budget for 2008 is $2.387 trillion, of which slightly more than half goes to current and past military expenses, at least according to the War Resisters League, an anti-war organization that first formed in 1923.[183] The official government pie chart shows a military and domestic security figure of 19%. The Bush EY 2009 budget exceeds $3 billion because of war.

During World War II, the military budget as a percentage of the Gross Domestic Product was around 38%. It dropped to 5% by 1950, but jumped to 14% in 1953 because of the Korean War. At the peak of the Vietnam War it was just over 9% in 1968. Today, with the war in Iraq, this figure is 4.1%. A final way of looking at this is, in 2002 dollars:

| **Year** | **Outlay for National Defense in Billions** |
|---|---|
| 1945 | $830 (*World War II*) |
| 1953 | $357 (*Korean War*) |
| 1968 | $424 (*Vietnam War*) |
| 1986 | $449 (*Reagan defense spending increase*) |
| 2008 | $550 (*Iraq War*) |

It is reported that President Bush will seek $200 billion only for the Iraq War in 2008. In any case, there is considerable expenditure for war, as we shall see.

## The Most Powerful Nation on Earth, Ever?

Without a doubt, the United States is the most powerful nation because of current technology. The Mongol Empire with all of 250,000 warriors, some on horses, would not stand a chance. The Roman Empire had less than half a million soldiers, with which they controlled most of Europe, including England and Turkey. A war would not last a day. The British Empire lorded over 25% of the world population (*458 million in 1921*), covering about 25% of the world land area. It's true that the Sun never set over its possessions. But submarines and nuclear carriers, plus planes, against ships?

Yet, the Vietnam War and the war against terrorists taught us a bitter lesson. Advanced technology cannot win all wars. Is the current and future of wars linked to sabotage and terror? Thus, the most powerful nation, ever, can be beaten, or neutralized. We did find Saddam Hussein, but that was almost by accident through a snitch. With all our intelligence and advanced weapons, we can't get to Osama bin Laden. On the other hand, maybe he did die from typhoid or some liver ailment. It might well be impossible to locate someone who is already dead and secretly buried.

But, in any case, the question, really, should, perhaps, be broader, in terms of relative economic/ trade or cultural power. The $500 billion each year in excess profits going to the OPEC nations are fueling the enemy. This economic windfall is neutralizing our obvious superiority. To win all wars, we also need to prevail at the sociological and cultural level. Democracy is not catching on in many parts of the world because we have not gotten to the hearts and minds of the people. But the full analysis of this phase of power would need to be another book.

In a 2007 WorldPublicOpinion.org poll, 70% of Americans felt that China's influence would increase over the next decade, while 60% of Russians chose their country over China at 50%. Both Russia and the U.S. gave the U.S. future influence rating of around 32%. Is the U.S. slipping?

## Why are Americans so Despised?

Just for fun, to be perverse, I typed into ***Google***, "why America is tops." This yielded ten sites on everything from tops *(that toy that spins)* to restaurants to models to music to American Idol. So I tried, "the United States is the best country." Well, first, nothing appeared in the top ten that even resembled anything close to being best. But, #4 was, "United States of America (*the **Best** Violator of International Law*)." This is then a perfect lead-in for this section.

In a BBC World Service Poll published in March of 2007, thirteen countries were rated:[58]

| | COUNTRY | MAINLY POSITIVE | MAINLY NEGATIVE |
|---|---|---|---|
| o | Canada | 54% | 14% |
| o | Japan | 54% | 20% |
| o | EU | 53% | 19% |
| o | France | 50% | 21% |
| o | GB | 45% | 28% |
| o | China | 42% | 32% |
| o | India | 37% | 26% |
| o | **USA** | **30%** | **51%** |
| o | Russia | 28% | 40% |
| o | Venezuela | 27% | 27% |
| o | North Korea | 19% | 48% |
| o | Iran | 18% | 54% |
| o | Israel | 17% | 56% |

China has a higher positive rating than the USA and Russia has a lower negative reputation than the USA. Israel, apparently, is really unpopular. Only Nigeria, Kenya and the Philippines gave us positive scores exceeding 70%.

What doesn't the world like about the U.S.?[241]

| | ISSUE | APPROVE | DISAPPROVE |
|---|---|---|---|
| o | North Korea's nuclear program | 30% | 54% |
| o | Iran's nuclear program | 28% | 60% |
| o | Global warming | 27% | 56% |
| o | The Israeli-Hezbollah war | 21% | 65% |
| o | The war in Iraq | 20% | 73% |

A good place to start is by introspection. We find every excuse for deriding China on virtually everything it does. So why did the United States in 2006 choose not to seek a seat on the new U.N. Human Rights Council? Why didn't the conscious of the world, us, continue our attempts to improve the world? Very simple, the potential embarrassment that we would not win one of the seats, for we now rest at the top of the list for the exploitation and manipulation of human rights, that's why.[191] Add to these the Patriot Act, which provides an excuse for eavesdropping and circumventing civil rights at home, and one gets an uneasy sense of really Big Brother.

Internationally, America the Protector! A little loyalty, perhaps, might be nice. Our only wish is for you to become democratic. Why, then, in a poll taken early in 2006, half of South Korean youths who will be old enough to vote in the next elections, say that Seoul should side with their neighbors to the North if the United States invades North Korea? Also, 40% chose China as their most important partner, with the U.S. tying North Korea with 18%.[295]

What kind of thanks is that? U.S. attack North Korea? Preposterous! But, in a ***CBS/New York Times*** Poll taken in February of 2003, 52% of Americans responded that if diplomacy fails, military action should be taken if North Korea begins to develop nuclear weapons. [242] Well, Great Leader Kim Jong Il finally did shut down his nuclear reactor in mid-2007.

Further, we saved France in World War II. How many there feel good about the ole US of A? Well, as a matter of fact, there is a book called ***The Arrogance of the French: Why They Can't Stand Us—and Why the Feeling is Mutual.*** [57] Written by a ***U.S. News and World Report*** correspondent in Paris, the bottom line being that France sucks. Remember our Freedom Fries and boycotts of French wine after their complicity with Saddam Hussein? The why has to do with a combination of arrogance and envy. I went to an energy conference in La Reunion Island in the Indian Ocean in 2005. I was the only American. There were some initial chidings and jokes. Then, I made a remark that I can't understand why my President scuttled the Kyoto Protocol and how I can't agree with him on virtually everything. All true. I became a virtual celebrity and relationships began to gel. So, maybe the problem is our Great Leader, George W. Bush.

I travel the world. Japan kind of likes us, especially their Ministry of Foreign Affairs, particularly when a Republican is president. Singapore seems okay, especially if you talk business. Ah....I don't remember, though, encountering too many friends anywhere else. In Edinburgh, Scotland, at their annual Arts Festival, there were more down with Bush signs than any other protest. Anytime President Bush visits any site, from Pakistan to the U.K. to Timbuktu, you can count on significant to massive demonstrations.

## President George Bush, #43

I can't help but insert here another one of those internet jokes that comes across everyday as almost spam:

> ***Subject:*** *Presidential Alert*
>
> *Donald Rumsfeld briefed the President this morning. He told Bush that three Brazilian soldiers were killed in Iraq.*
>
> *To everyone's amazement, all of the color ran from Bush's face, then he collapsed onto his desk, head in hands, visibly shaken, almost whimpering.*
>
> *Finally, he composed himself and asked "Just exactly how many is a Brazillion?"*

No, this did not, in fact, occur, and the entire above aside, President George W. Bush, actually, just might have the clue to insuring for world peace forever. I have tended to disagree with him on just about everything else, but I support my President on maintaining the effort in Iraq. Why? As Ronald Reagan played a key role in ending the Cold War, **George Bush the Younger could well have the solution to world peace**, forever. We will discuss this later in the simple solution to wars.

But President George W. Bush is certainly unpopular. In 2004, historians rated Bush a disaster, as 81% of 415 classified this presidency a failure. This was in his first term.

I count more than 300 polls taken of his overall job rating since then, from August 2005 to 2007.[242] During 2005, approve averaged around 40% and disapprove 55%, with unsure at 5%. "Approve" began dropping to a low of 28% level in 2007, and almost always above 60% for disapproval. The end of presidency job approval ratings were: Bill Clinton (*65%*), Ronald Reagan (*64%*), Dwight Eisenhower (*59%*), John F. Kennedy (*63%*), George Bush the Elder (*56%*), Gerald Ford (*53%*), Lyndon Johnson (*49%*), Jimmy Carter (*34%*) and Richard Nixon (*24%*).[9] The only question now is whether GWB will sink below Nixon's 24% by the end of 2008.

Let's look at the pluses. The economy is going well. A few dips in the stock market now and then, but with those high oil prices, it is remarkable that interest rates are reasonable and the financial base sound, although notion of a recession keeps popping up as a fear. Bush has "incredible passion and resolve." His religious feelings I place as a non-negative. He was quoted to say to Prince Bandar of Saudi Arabia in 2004, courtesy of Bob Woodward in his ***State of Denial***, "I get guidance from God in prayer," and has thusly received guidance.[365] God is great in the Middle East countries.

We recovered from 9/11. He routed the Taliban and took out Saddam Hussein. On August 9, 2007, he put Iran on notice for supporting terrorism. Oh…oh. They overreacted and professed that they gave up on nuclear weapons to undercut any insanity on part of the Americans.

Oh yes, he did win re-election, although the ***Daily Mirror of London*** headlined: "How can 59,054,087 people be so dumb." The U.K. is our closest ally. Further, people are still wondering how John Kerry was tainted by his heroics in the Vietnam war when Bush himself, Dick Cheney, Dennis Hastert, Paul Wolfowitz, Karl Rowe, John Ashcroft, Richard Perle, Andrew Card and Tom Delay somehow managed to avoid that conflict. Speaking of Delay, there was also that Jack Abramoff scandal that the White House deftly sidestepped.

A destructive influence on President Bush was Vice President Richard Cheney. During the transition period before entering the White House, I noticed his arrogance shown in secretly meeting with oil and nuclear executives to carve a national energy policy. During my U.S. Senate days, I recall Cheney as an authoritative figure with commanding presence working for Senator Scoop Jackson (*who was a Democrat from Washington*). Cheney's one percent doctrine, from the book by Ron Suskind, might have been particularly damaging. In essence, if there was a 1% chance that certain terrorist acts were possible, he treated it as a certainty, or a 100% probability.[309]

This is but a short list of President Bush's crises and travails:

- Started a cowboy war in Iraq without finding any weapons of mass destruction, while being unable to win the peace.
- Responded late and disastrously to the Hurricane Katrina destruction of New Orleans.

- Appointed a friend to the Supreme Court, which was rejected.
- Recommended a "no child left behind" education policy that failed.
- Promoted an anti-environmental program that included defying the Kyoto Protocol, dismantling federal control over protected areas, diluting federal rules governing air pollution, approving the drilling for oil and gas in pristine wilderness areas, easing rules for coal-fired power plants, permitting the continued use of 31 popular but controversial pesticides and allowing the sale of PCB-tainted lands.
- Formed an unholy alliance with the moral majority and religion in general, dismantling the wall between church and state.
- Developed a ruinous foreign policy program engendering considerable international distrust.
- Reversed the $5 trillion surplus earlier predicted for the first decade of this century to a deficit of $5 trillion.
- Disregarded personal rights through advocacy and conduct of the Patriot Act.
- Promoted fossil fuels and nuclear energy, with only token support for sustainable resources.
- Sponsored a health program biased towards rich people.
- Disregarded scientific integrity in policy making and disdained inconvenient research, with notable examples being for global climate change, lead poisoning, air pollution and stem cell study. Leading researchers (*62, including 20 Nobel laureates and 19 recipients of the National Medal of Science, including a few advisors to Nixon and Eisenhower*) gave Bush failing marks, and were joined by 12,000 other scientists.[277]

The above no doubt caused the Democratic takeover of the U.S. Congress in the 2006 elections and his 28% approval rating.

But the President of the United States is the most powerful person on the face of the Earth. His declarations carry a lot of influence. Plus, he is right about democracy and the Middle East.

## Bush's Axis of Evil

George W. Bush's State of the Union Address on January 29, 2002, identified the Axis of Evil that sponsored terror: Iraq, Iran and North Korea. But while he devoted only 17 words to North Korea and 19 to Iran, he spent all of 84 words on Iraq, showing, no doubt, his priorities. In World War II there were the Axis Powers: Nazi Germany, Fascist Italy and Imperial Japan. These three are now close allies, maybe our most important ones, next to the U.K. So is it a matter of time before these terror regimes, too, become buddies?

Iraq and North Korea are worrisome because of their nuclear interests. North Korea's exhibitionist tendencies with rockets are troublesome, although they have now shut down their nuclear program. Israel just might serve as the armed angel of mercy for a safer Middle East, and Japan, might just step up its activity level because of those rockets, although the U.S. policy seems to be to just wait for the collapse, which more times than not in the past has worked, as both countries have now abandoned their original nuclear ambitions.

One of the problems with terrorism and the Middle East is that the U.S. is just not wanted there. On the same day, July 9, 2006, ***The Honolulu Advertiser*** had two articles on the very same page [12]:

- "7 suspected terrorists escape from Saudi prison"
- "19 al-Qaida suspects acquitted in Yemen"

One would have thought that both Saudi Arabia and Yemen were close allies with us against terrorism, but actions speak louder than words. Word of the escape in Saudi Arabia was not reported until several days after the jailbreak and the Yemen judge said that these terrorists did not violate Yemeni law because Islamic Sharia law permits jihad against occupiers.

The primary terrorist organizations in the Middle East are (*mostly from* ***Wikipedia***):

- **Al Qaeda (AQ)**, also spelled Al-Quaeda or Al-Qa'ida or Al Qaida or Al-Qaidah, among many variations is a Sunni paramilitary organization which was named, of all things, by the U.S. Justice Department. The literary translation is "the foundation or base." While it's really more than this, the popular story is that Osama bin Laden, a Saudi Arabian, met in 1979 with Ayman Al-Zawahiri, an Egyptian medical doctor, to form the group. Interestingly enough, the U.S. provided funds to this outfit in the 1980's. After they "beat" the Soviets out of Afghanistan in 1989, the first Gulf War of 1990 provided another opportunity to rid the region of infidels, especially the U.S. By some accounts, this is when AQ really organized. The 1998 U.S. Embassy bombings in Nairobi, Kenya and Dar es Salaam, killing more than 200 and wounding 5,000, and the 2000 attack on the U.S.S. Cole, killing 17 sailors, were by AQ. Their September 11, 2001 strike of the World Trade Center and Pentagon, slaughtering nearly 3,000, set the table for the second Gulf War in 2002. The 2005 London, Jordan and Egypt bombings resulting in more than 200 deaths were reportedly AQ operated. Supposedly, 100,000 have received AQ training, but "only" 20,000 seem active world-wide.
- The **Taliban** is an Afghanistanian, indigenous, Sunni movement that formed in the midst of the Soviet-backed Democratic Republic government being overthrown in 1992, leading to a civil war among American bankrolled warlords. There, however, also is an important connection to the Inter-Services Intelligence of Pakistan, which received some funding from the American CIA. Yes, the U.S., thus, had a hand in establishing both AQ and the Taliban, and to boot, the Taliban were initially the good guys, bringing some military and economic stability to the country, including eliminating the payments businesses had to make to the warlords, and banning the growing of opium. In 1996, the Taliban established the Islamic Emirate of Afghanistan, winning recognition from Pakistan and Saudi Arabia in 1997. In what have become almost standard reverse operations, the U.S. succeeded in an international effort called Operation Enduring Freedom to depose the Taliban in 2001. While in 2001 opium had been reduced by 98%, after their fall, by 2004, Afghanistan was supplying 87% of the world opium supply. One practice objected to by the liberated world is that the movement believed women should stay at home and take care of the children. Hmmm, that's not all, bad, actually. The Taliban is aligned with bin Laden through family

marriage, and is an enemy of Shiite Iran, and also, now, the U.S. There supposedly are more Taliban fighters than AQ terrorists.

- **Hamas** is an acronym corresponding to an Arabic word for zeal or fanaticism, has a meaning of courage, and is a Sunni organization that was democratically elected to govern Palestine in the 2006 elections. This legislative takeover was an embarrassment to the Bush Administration. Created in 1987, it is known for suicide bombings and acts against Israel. Their charter calls for destruction of the State of Israel. They have thousand of supporters, but only a small number of active soldiers.
- The Sunni Palestinian **Islamic Jihad** Movement (*PIJM*), also called Al-Jihad, has dual goals to liberate Palestine and destroy Israel. It was founded in the 1970's as a branch of the Egyptian Islamic Jihad, which today, is led by Ayman al-Zawahri, the second in command of AQ. While far smaller than Hamas, the PIJM specializes in suicide bombers, using even women and teens. It is most famous for assassinating Egyptian President Anwar Sadat, is headquartered in Damascus, the capital of Syria, and receives financial aid from that country and Iran. It has several hundred hard core members.
- The **Palestine Liberation Organization** (*PLO*) was created in 1964 by the Arab League to form an independent Palestinian state. It is recognized for their 1972 Black September splinter group's attack on the Israeli Olympic squad in Munich. Known to be extremely wealthy, the PLO has $50 billion in secret investments in Zimbabwe and Somalia. Mohammed Abdel-Raouf "Yasir" Arafat, a Sunni, the man with the checkered kaffiyeh, became chairman in 1969. In 1988 Arafat renounced terrorism and gained metastable peace through the Oslo Accords of 1993. He, along with Yitzhak Rabin and Shimon Peres, were awarded the Nobel Peace Prize in 1994. While President Bill Clinton got personally involved in the peace process, President George Bush the Younger refused to meet with Arafat. After surviving numerous assassination attempts and illnesses, he finally succumbed to a blood ailment in 2004. But the PLO lives on as a quasi-terrorist organization still dedicated to the dissolution of Israel.
- **Hezbollah** or Hizbullah or Hizballah or—this is a bit more complicated, as the spelling varies with grammatical usage—but let us use the most common, Hezbollah, a Shiite political party and military organization. Ayatollah Khomeini was the founder in the early 1980's. Most Iranians are Muslim and 90% of them belong to the Shia community, which also is Lebanon's largest religious group, about 40% of 3 million citizens. Financial aid unofficially comes from Iran and Syria. Hezbollah is credited with the 1983 suicide bombings of the U.S. Embassy, killing 63, and the U.S. Marine barracks in Beirut, with 299 slain, plus the 1994 bombing of the Israeli Embassy in London. Hezbollah is to Lebanon as Hamas is to Palestine, and Hezbollah supports the Hamas' death to Israel policy, noting that the former is Shiite and latter Sunni. Israel overrides religious differences here. However, the Sunni-Shiite split is why Al-Queda and Hezbollah had strained relations...until the war between Israel and Hezbollah in Lebanon erupted in 2006. Then, Ayman al-Zawahri weighed in with a call for all Muslims to rise up in a holy war against Israel. There are several thousand supporters, but only a few hundred Hezbollah warriors.

You could just as well also add Iranian President Mahmoud Ahmadinejad to the above list.

When you read books and articles about this topic, it is helpful to understand the terms:

- o Jihad: Islamic holy war.
- o Mujahidin: person who wages a jihad.
- o Intifada: rebellion.
- o Diaspora: migration away from ancestral homeland.
- o Shiite: a Muslim of the Shia branch of Islam, which believes in Ali and the Imams as the only rightful successors of Muhammad.
- o Sunni: a Muslim of the branch of Islam that adheres to the orthodox tradition (yes, they don't seem to be too different).
- o Fatwa: a decree handed down by an Islamic leader, as for example, Ayatollah Khomeini, calling for the execution of Salman Rushdie in 1989, and bin Laden and Zawahiri and others in 1997 issuing the ruling to kill Americans and their allies, including civilians.

There are variations and sectarian differences, such as that represented by Wahhabism and Takfiri concepts, as for example, Al Queda may be considered the generic name for all those movements that have in common what is called the Takfiri ideology, but the above should suffice for this discussion.

Thus, the terror scorecard in the Middle East:

| **Terrorist Organization** | **Headquarters** | **Sect** | **Living Notables** |
|---|---|---|---|
| Al Queda | Afghanistan and Pakistan | Sunni | Osama bin Laden<br>Ayman Al-Zawahiri |
| Taliban | Afghanistan | Sunni | Mohammad Omar |
| Hamas | Palestine | Sunni | Khaled Mashal<br>Ismail Haniyeh |
| Palestinian Islamic Jihad | Syria | Sunni | Ramadan Shallah<br>(Ayman Al-Zawahiri) |
| Palestine Liberation Org. | Palestine | Sunni | Mahmoud Abbas |
| Hezbollah | Lebanon | Shiite | Hassan Nasrallah |

But how many active terrorists are out there? The State Department supposedly had a list of 65,000 names, but that was before 9/11. Certainly, there are more now, but not anything close to a million, and, actively, probably, around 100,000. The world population is approaching 7 billion. Don't place all one billion or so Muslim's in the terrorist pot. Only a very few extremists are the problem. It is a bit disconcerting, though, that our government is not really sure if there are 1 million or 7 million Muslims in the U.S. Then again, we shouldn't categorize people by religion, so, so much for that. The U.S. Census has it right in the middle, or 4 million. What is truly troublesome is that former Department of Defense Secretary Donald Rumsfeld was asked, how is the U.S. faring against terrorists' extremist ideology in the global "battle of ideas," and he gave our country a D or D+ grade.

To recap about Middle East religion:

| | |
|---|---|
| o Egypt | Sunni Muslim |
| o Turkey | Sunni Muslim |
| o Saudi Arabia | Sunni Muslim |
| o Syria | Sunni Muslim |
| o Jordan | Sunni Muslim |
| o Pakistan | Sunni (77%) Muslim |
| o Iraq | Shi'a (63%) Muslim – Sunni (35%) |
| o Iran | Shi'a (89%) Muslim |
| o Israel | Jewish (77%) – Muslim (16%) |
| o Lebanon | Christian (41%)–Sunni (27%) –Shi'a (26%) |
| o India | Hindu (81%) – Muslim (13%) |

For completeness, the following terrorist organizations can also be mentioned:

- Japanese Red Army: formed in 1970, they were known to operate in Israel and the U.S., and are dedicated to fomenting world revolution. There are only six hard-core members. Their leader, Fusako Shigenobu, co-founder, was captured in 2000.
- Earth Liberation Front: is the collective name for individuals and small groups in the U.S. and U.K. dedicated to ecotage: damaging property to save the environment. Originally founded in 1992 in the U.K., by 2001, the FBI classified ELF as the top domestic terror threat in the U.S. An earlier ELF, the Environmental Life Force, had similar strategies. However, today, the current ELF web site merely states that this underground movement has no leadership, membership nor official spokesperson. Participation is anonymous. There is no known leader, because, if known, would be arrested, convicted and placed in jail.
- United States and Australia: labeled by some, if not many, as eco-terrorists for not signing the Kyoto Protocol (*global climate warming*). Kevin Rudd replaced John Howard as Prime Minister of Australia, and was reported to be more supportive of the agreement, but the day following the Bali talks at the end of 2007, appeared to be unhappy with such deep cuts in greenhouse gas emissions.

### About Iraq

Where was the Garden of Eden? The Tower of Babel? Mesopotamia? The Cradle of Civilization? Daniel's lion den? Babylon? Where did Noah build his Ark? From where did come the Three Wise Men? Why, of course, Iraq, home to the first civilizations!

However, it was not until 1919 that Iraq became an official Middle East country. After the first world war, the League of Nations made Iraq a British mandate, but independence was granted in 1932. After WW II, there was a monarchy, then a coup d'etat, a couple of overthrows and, finally, the ascendance of Saddam Hussein in 1979. The Iran-Iraq war of the 1980's had, officially, half a million deaths, but other estimates at least double that total. The first Gulf War (*Iraq-Kuwait*)of 1990 had a reported kill total of close to 150,000, including civilians, with only 148 American battle casualties. The America-Iraq war of the 21st century will have up to 1.5 million violent deaths, around 4,000 being American casualties.

Comparing the two countries (*all these tables come from the CIA World Factbook*):

| | **Iraq** | **United States** |
|---|---|---|
| Age | 7000 years | About 200 years |
| Size | 0.437 million sq km | 9.826 million sq km |
| Population | 27.5 million | 302 million |
| GDP | $88 billion | $13,000 billion |
| GDP/Capita | $2,900 | $44,000 |
| Military Expenditures | $7.6 billion | $528 billion |
| Military Expenditures as %GDP | 8.6% | 4.1% |

Is Iraq to become our next Vietnam? Yes and no. 2007 turned out to be the year with our highest deaths in Iraq. Amazingly enough, 2007 was also the year we also experienced our highest casualties in Afghanistan after that 2001 invasion year. Yet, by the time we leave Iraq in what could be in ignominy, our military deaths will only be around 5% that of the Southeast Asian conflict known as Vietnam, which resulted in around 80,000 American deaths. Mind you, an estimated 5 million died in that war, including enemy and civilians. The guerillas of VN attacked at their advantage, not unlike the terrorist bombers of Iraq.

The enemy in the 70's had open access to China and, even, Russia. Today, it is Iran and every other Arabic country. Not quite as intimidating this time. But oil, I guess, suffices.

The purpose of VN was to check the spread of communism, while in Iraq we are there to spread democracy. You might say, this is almost the same thing. We lost the VN war because of television. We just didn't have the heart to continue the embarrassment and tragedy unfolding while we had dinner. The exact same thing is happening this time, although the American public seems satisfied with Republican-Democratic politics taking the place of anguished public protests. So, yes, it's the same, but no because this new one is an almost trivial affair with no world power points at stake.

But you've heard too much already about weapons of mass destruction, or the lack of them; the high cost of this war; and the quagmire it has become. Read about this war in another book.

In any case, at least we have a stooge in place to represent sane democratic policy and righteousness in the Middle East. Well, maybe no. On May 27, 2006, not very long after establishing their government, Iraq Foreign Minister Hoshyar Zebari, and his Iranian counterpart, Manouchehr Mottaki, all smiles, faced the public in Baghdad, and reiterated friendship with each other. Zebari went on to say that Iraq supports Iran's right to develop nuclear energy, a position at complete odds with the U.S. view. [328] Now, surely, there were the appropriate diplomatic checks and there was some sort of blessing ceremony in White House ranks for Iraq to appear to be one of the Muslim gang. If nothing else, this reverse negative psychology should serve a useful purpose of confusing the enemy. On the other hand, one has to wonder.

In 2007, Baghdad awarded more than a billion dollars in contracts to Iranian and Chinese companies to build electrical powerplants. Part of the deal was that Iran would also provide cheaper electricity to the grid. There was no backlash from the U.S., for, the thinking might have been that we need to have a greater part of the world participate in the restoration of Iraq. Maybe we have learned a lesson. Then again, maybe we are losing influence already.

One final issue about these minor wars. Yes, there is the matter of cost and casualties. The 4,000 deaths and 30,000 injuries is one thing. However, there is more. It is reported that in the 12 month period from 2006 to 2007, 70% of Iraq and Afghanistan war veterans sought treatment for post-traumatic stress.[381] Scarily, there is even more, as this percentage does not include those treated at storefront Vet Centers operated by department stores nor, of course, those who value their future career (*either in the military or later in life*) and choose not seek aid. Compound this matter with the affect on families and communities and you get a closer appreciation about the wickedness of even a minor war.

Then we attempted a last gasp surge, which was somewhat puny, but, apparently, seems to be turning the tide. In August of 2007, the UN Security Council voted unanimously to expand presence in Iraq, that is, serve as the transition government after the U.S. and U.K. move out. Call it peace keeping if you wish, at least there is an international organization capable of providing a solution.

### Then there is Iran

The Islamic Republic of Iran, meaning "Land of the Aryans (*Indo-European*)," known as Persia until 1935, has a population of 69 million, and is a bit smaller than Alaska. Iran is a puzzlement. Various scenarios have cast this country as being THE Middle East by 2050, first, because it has that intention, and two, because of its central location. Its neighbors are Armenia, Azerbaijan, Turkmenistan, Pakistan, Afghanistan, Turkey and Iraq. Across the Persian Gulf you will find Kuwait, Saudi Arabia, Bahrain, Oman, Qatar and the United Arab Emirates. From the 9th to 11th century, Persia was the heart and mind of the Islamic Golden Age.

In 1921, Reza Shah Pahlavi gained control of the country, but was forced to abdicate by the British and USSR in 1941 in favor of his son, Mohammad Reza Pahlavi, who was more malleable. After WW II, in 1953, Mohammed Mossadegh won a democratic election and forced Pahlavi to leave the country. However, Operation Ajax, a British Intelligence Service led, CIA cooperated, venture overthrew Mossadegh, and the Shah returned later that year. Twenty-six years henceforth, in 1979, Ayatollah Khomeini led the Iranian Revolution, and the Shah again fled the country. This is when the American hostage incident took place, and lingered for 444 days. In 1980, with favorable signals from Uncle Sam, Iraq invaded Iran, initiating a war which lasted eight years and killed up to a million Iranians. It is reported that the Americans provided chemicals for weapons of mass destruction, providing a historical footnote on why there was so much certainty about Saddam still having them. Is there any wonder about why the U.S. is mistrusted in the Middle East? Overthrowing a democracy and supplying materials for weapons of mass destruction? Us, the freedom fighters? I guess so.

The Supreme Religious Leader is Ali Khamenei and the President, the secular leader, is Mahmoud Ahmadinejad. Who is in charge? Well, there are a lot more portraits of Khamenei throughout the nation, plus, he has definite seniority.

In comparison with the U.S.:

| | **Iran** | **United States** |
|---|---|---|
| Age | 9000 years | About 200 years |
| Size | 1.648 million sq km | 9.826 million sq km |
| Population | 69 million | 302 million |
| GDP | $562 billion | $13,000 billion |
| GDP/Capita | $8,300 | $44,000 |
| Military Expenditures | $4.3 billion | $528 billion |
| Military Expenditures as %GDP | 3.3% | 4.1% |

We spend 100 times more than Iran on our military, so why is that country a concern? From all reports, there is now a new developing axis of evil: Iran, Pakistan, and Russia. Russia is in it for oil and has the technology to share. There are some disturbing rumors about Cuba and Venezuela being courted. Hizbollah in Lebanon and Hamas in Palestine are being funded by Iran. Then there is that nuclear issue that comes, goes and continues to irritate the free world, even if we have ours and they don't. Iran is, thus, today, the most prominent catalyst for evil.

What nurtures the influence of Iran are oil (*second largest OPEC producer*) and natural gas (*second to Russia in terms of reserves*). But there is a limit of how long these fossil fuels will produce, making a nuclear future understandable. One would hope, of course, that solar energy could, instead, dominate. This never comes up for discussion.

The notion of the entire Middle East becoming the Iranian Empire is not far-fetched. The lightening rod for unity is Israel. Everyone else in the region is an enemy of this "American satellite." Ironically, the U.S. eliminated the Iranians two worst enemies, the Taliban and Saddam Hussein. President Ahmadinejad has unwisely and royally ticked off Israel with statements like calling the Nazi Holocaust a myth and boasting of the need to wipe Israel off the map. One more provocation and a surgically precise bombing of potential nuclear or rocket launching sites by the Israeli Air Force could serve as a useful warning shot, except the latest intelligence is that they don't really exist, yet.

On the peace front, though, on May 8, 2006, President Ahmadinejad sent an 18-page letter to President George W. Bush, the first such communication between Iranian and American heads since 1980. While the letter was generally courteous, it criticizes Bush for attacking

Afghanistan and Iraq, supporting Israel and other nit-picking subjects, and wondered how Jesus and his prophets would have judged these acts. Ahmadinejad simply asked Bush to justify his Middle East policies and those of his predecessors.

This would have been a golden opportunity to first question Iran's sense of equity and freedom, but, then, state the obvious validations and propose a sincere dialogue on various important issues. As far as I know, Bush's only response was at a press conference with Tony Blair later that month indicating that he had read the letter but expressed distaste that the nuclear matter was not addressed. Unfortunately, but not unsurprisingly, there came no official response, further reinforcing the common belief that the U.S. blatantly ignores the concerns of the Middle East. A telling comment came from think tank Chatham House: "While the U.S. has been playing poker in the region, Iran has been playing chess."[285]

Finally, further embarrassing our intelligence experts, late in 2007 it was determined that Iran had stopped its nuclear weapons program four years earlier. I guess the pressure is now off, for now.

## What about North Korea

By legend, Korea was founded in 2333 BC by Dangun, and is referred to as Choson, loosely interpreted to be "Land of the Morning Calm." Through invasions and religions, Three Kingdoms formed, and were unified by Silla in 676 AD. The Mongols invaded in the 13$^{th}$ century, King Sejong ruled and the Korean alphabet han-geul was created in the 15$^{th}$ century. Japan first invaded in the 16$^{th}$ century.

The modern history of Korea begins in 1910 with the annexation by Japan. After WW II, the peninsula was split, with the northern half coming under communist sponsorship and the south going democratic. Almost 7 million Americans served in the Korean War of 1950-53, with 54,000 deaths, but the total killed approached 3.5 million, all that to maintain the 38$^{th}$ parallel as the line separating North and South. Founder Kim Il-song passed away in 1994, and the leadership passed on to his son, Kim Jong Il.

North Korea serves a useful purpose for American policy. Their hilarious leader is more an embarrassment than foe. Their toothless pronouncements, now and then reinforced by a pointless lob in the Pacific, cause sufficient panic in Japan and allow our military-industrial complex to justify ridiculous expenditures for billion dollar radar stations. Even U.S. Senator Daniel Inouye (*D-Hawaii*) has expressed concern about Hawaii someday becoming a target of a nuclear missile from North Korea. But the fact of the matter is that North Korea is more bizarre than dangerous, and there is no evidence whatever of their forming an evil axis with any country. Maybe not surprisingly, the Bush White House policy of ignoring them finally worked when Great Leader Kim caved in by dropping his nuclear program in 2007. However, this relationship in the past has been a flim-flam game where Kim has been the consummate confidence man.

There, too, remains a dark side to this untrustworthy country, as reported in various publications, but well summarized in the July 23, 2007 issue of ***TIME***.[376] Legitimate exports totaled $1.7 billion. Illegitimate ones approached $1 billion:

| | | |
|---|---|---|
| o | 41 billion contraband cigarettes | $160 million |
| o | Counterfeit currency | $48 million |
| o | Illegal drugs | ?? |
| o | Weapons | ?? |

Diplomatic immunity has helped their own consulate people bring in and distribute these items. Finally, $25 million was seized in a Macau bank, representing revenues from Mafia-like operations, but were released as part of the package for Kim to give up their nuclear weapons program.

Although there are overtures from the South Korean media for a quick transition into normal relations with the North, the fact of the matter is that the South is not falling all over itself to accelerate anything. They saw what happened between East and West Germany, and have decided that prudent discretion is the smart economic plan. To summarize:

| | **North Korea** | **South Korea** | **United States** |
|---|---|---|---|
| Age | 4000 years | 4000 years | About 200 yrs |
| Size | 120,540 $km^2$ | 98,480 sq km | 9,826,000sq km |
| Population | 23 million | 49 million | 302 million |
| GDP | $40 billion | $1,196 billion | $13,000 billion |
| GDP/Capita | $1,800 | $24,500 | $44,000 |
| Military Exp. | Not Available | $32 billion | $528 billion |
| Military Exp. %GDP | Not Available | 2.7% | 4.1% |

Clearly, South Korea, since the Korean War, has flourished, but the North has putrefied.

### Then the Rest of the Terrorist World

Twenty-four bombs exploded at the same time on August 31, 2006. [298] They were homemade and triggered by mobile phone signals. Baghdad? Nope! Southern Thailand, where, more and more, Muslim insurgency seeks to create a separate country from the Buddhist dominated nation at large. Women were among those planting these bombs, and this time only one person was killed, indicating a sense of humanity. However, since 2004, 1,500 people have been killed in this civil war.

There, too, are terroristic acts in India, Indonesia, Philippines, Russia and China. Most of these deeds are Muslim inspired, even in those Chechnya incidents, for while separatism is the goal, they are Islamic militants.

### Let Me Add Israel

Judaism is older than ***The Bible***. The Patriarchs, Abraham, his son Isaac and grandson Jacob, settled in the Land of Canaan (*present day Israel*) around 1800 BC, but famine, say some historians, forced the Israelites to migrate to Egypt. The First Exodus, led by Moses out of Egypt, say essentially these same historians, occurred in the 13th century, and around 1020 BC, King David made Jerusalem the national and spiritual center. In 586, most Jews were exiled to Babylonia, but they returned a half century later. They were then ruled by the Greeks, Romans, Byzantines, Arabs and, finally, Ottomans, for 400 years, until 1917, when the British pledged support for establishment of a Jewish national home in Jerusalem. The League of Nations granted Britain the Mandate for Palestine. In 1947, the United Nations proposed the establishment of Arab and Jewish States, leading to proclamation of the State of Israel in 1948 after the War of Independence. Israel joined the UN in 1949, prevailing in the 1967 6-day war against Egypt and neutralizing aggressors Syria and Egypt in the Yom Kippur War of 1973.

Israel became an associate member of the European Common Market in 1975. Since then, with sporadic peace periods, Israel has been besieged by its neighbors. Israel has subsequently depended mostly on the U.S. for security and diplomatic support. The October 1973 war saw massive American airlifts of military equipment and from 1948 to 1985 the U.S. provided $31 billion, mostly grants. There have been innumerable agreements, accords and attempts at peace, including a latest last gasp attempt in 2008 by President George W. Bush.

A comparative look at the primary Middle East challengers would be useful:

| | **Israel** | **Iraq** | **Iran** |
|---|---|---|---|
| Age | 9,000 years | 7000 years | 9000 years |
| (*Current Government*) | (*59 years*) | (*just forming*) | (*28 years*) |
| Size | 20,770 km$^2$ | 437,000 km$^2$ | 1,648,000 km$^2$ |
| Population | 6.4 million | 27.5 million | 69 million |
| GDP | $170 billion | $88 billion | $562 billion |
| GDP/Capita | $26,800 | $2,900 | $8,300 |
| Military Expenditures | $12 billion | $7.6 billion | $4.3 billion |
| Military Exp. %GDP | 7.3% | 8.6% | 3.3% |

Israel, about the size of New Jersey, is much smaller in population and territory than Iraq and Iran. But Egypt has twelve times more people and lands nearly 50 times larger, but got embarrassed in the 6-day War.

The countries of the Middle East believe that Israel is for all intents and purposes a puppet of the United States, and history has shown this to be largely correct. For example, Israel served as the secret channel for the U.S. to provide arms to Iran in the middle '80's. Now, Israel is strategically positioned to take out possible nuclear facilities in Iran, if they ever came to be, something the U.S. would have difficulty perpetrating in view of our Iraq quagmire and need to shore up international respect. That Israeli air strike in October of 2007 on a suspected

North Korea nuclear site in Syria could well just have been an appetizer. Thus, Israel will continue to serve as the catalyst for future conflicts for a long time to come, as today, that has become a necessary problem.

## But, Darn It, America is the Best Country

So I typed into ***Google***, again, but this time, "in what way is the United States the best country," and saw only one obvious site that looked promising:[127]

10. Even lowly interns can meet the President.
9. Them other countries got nothing but foreigners!
8. The Pamela and Tommy Lee tape.
7. Three glorious words: "World Wrestling Federation."
6. In the U.S. it is acceptable for a grown man to wear skimpy shorts and a lot of oil.
5. Mexico invented the burrito. But we made it microwaveable!
4. Jeopardy's host: Canadian. Nine out of 10 winners on Jeopardy: American.
3. If you're really good at sports, you get to kill people.
2. Europe may be architecture, but we've got Hooters!
1. No fruity accents.

Okay, what's happening? Is ***Google*** breaking down? So I tried ***Ask.com***. Nothing! Bernard Goldberg wrote, ***100 People Who Are Screwing up America***. Try typing that in and see what you get…nearly 2 million entries close this subject. "Why America is good" yielded more items about we not being so.

There clearly are areas where the U.S. is lacking:

- National medical coverage is one. South Africa is the only other developed country with a similar absence, but their silver bullet is a consumer driven health savings account. The American Medical Association is just too strong, as Michael Moore's ***Sicko*** disclosed. As a symptom, we rank anywhere from #38 to #45 in various rankings of life expectancy. Andorra is (#1).[139]
- We are the only country to drop the Atomic Bomb on civilians, and we did this twice.
- We are #36 in infant mortality, soundly beaten by Cuba, with Singapore at #1.
- With 5% of the world population, we emit 25% of all the greenhouse gases and maybe as much as 50% of all civilian-owned guns (*270 million firearms for our 300 million people*).[44]

There is a definite problem: congressional lobbyists. The farm lobby is legendary, so is the fossil fuel industry and, of course, the National Rifle Association. Campaign reform occurs every year, but only for show. This is a definite challenge that has withstood the test of time.

We seem to be shrinking in height, at least Caucasians, on a relative basis. In 1860 the average height of white males in the U.S. was about 5' 8 ½". Today, it is 5'10 1/2"'. But, the 5'5" Dutch male of 1830 is now over 6', and similar growth was shown by Danish men.[72] Worse, according to the Organization for Economic Cooperation and Development, the U.S. is #1 on the world obesity scale. However, we will later see that there are countries in the Middle East, particularly, fatter than us.

We are stingy. There is a "Commitment to Development Index," which ranks rich nations by how well they help poor ones. The U.S. is #13, with Japan at #21 and Netherlands #1. There is a Global Peace Index comparing 121 countries. Iraq is last, Iran is #97 and the USA sits at #96.[148] Norway is #1. The Scandinavian countries all seem to fare well in these two categories.

Life is not equal in our country. Those running the company can get 500 times more than the average worker and Howard Stern in half a minute makes more than most of us in a week. If you are of a minority race, of the female gender or handicapped, you will generally not be uniformly treated. However, there are innumerable laws that provide an intent to be fair. But this is a free enterprise system, with merit and effort usually producing rewards.

But, certainly, freedom of the press, this we have. We can say almost anything in the USA. Well, maybe not. Reporters Without Borders announced its third annual worldwide index and placed Denmark, Finland, Iceland, Ireland, Netherlands, Norway, Slovakia and Switzerland, tied as #1.[37] The U.S., with Belgium is in...22nd place. We were also beaten by Lithuania (#16) and Bosnia and Herzegovina (#21). Well, we were better than Turkmenistan, Myanmar, Cuba (#76) and North Korea (#77).

What about happiness? According to Ruut Veenhoven, who is responsible for the World DataBase of Happiness, citizens of Denmark rank #1, with Switzerland #2 and Austria #3.[305] The U.S. sits at #15. In the survey of Global Projection of Subjective Well-Being by Adrian White, again, Denmark, Switzerland and Austria ranked one, two and three.[60] The U.S. took 23rd place. Interestingly, Bhutan, which focuses on Gross National Happiness, ranked #8.

Okay, then, what about our national stability? ***Foreign Policy*** magazine announced its Failed State Index for 2007, and had Sudan at #1 and Iraq at #2. The U.S. came in at #160, but Norway took the top spot at #177.[236]

In addition to all the energy we use and carbon dioxide we produce, there is also the matter of lifestyle and what we eat. I got this from the internet, without any reference attribution, so this might not be entirely accurate, but the order of magnitude seems reasonable:

| | | | | | |
|---|---|---|---|---|---|
| o | Cost of food for 1 week for a family of | 6 | in | Chad | $1.23 |
| o | | 12 | in | Bhutan | $5.00 |
| o | | 4 | in | USA | $300 |
| o | | 4 | in | Germany | $500 |

So if the above table is anywhere close to being real, we do set aside a lot of money for food, but there are other countries that spend more.

There are other defects, of course, but let us look at the positives. The United Nations Human Development Index rates Norway as #1 and the U.S. as #8. Not so good, but better than

170 other countries. Plus, if you don't like cold, you can move south and still remain the country.

The International Labor Organization of the United Nations reports that the U.S. is the #1 rated nation in productivity.[231] Each employed person in 2006 produced $63,885 of value. Ireland, at #2, was nearly $8,000 behind, and Japan, at #16, only produced $44,877/person. How did we accomplish this? Part of the success is that we work longer during the year—1804 hours, versus 1401 for Norway and 1564 for the French—and have a system with no paid holidays and vacations, and no guaranteed health care. Use of information and communications technology also contributed. We are #2 in wealth created per hour at $35.63, but Norway, at #1 with $37.99, is temporarily in the lead only because of its oil exports. Adjusted for inflation, though, since 1973, average wages grew by a total of only one half of one percent. Labor unions, which in the 50's represented more than a third of all workers, have seen this percentage drop to 7.4% today. Part of this is the result of shipping labor intensive work offshore and the use of migrant labor for menial tasks. All this makes for good business sense, but comes with the discomfort that Big Brother could well be industry, with too much of an influence over the legislative and administrative branches of government.

Yet, a lot more people want to come here than leave. From 2002 to 2006, 1,342,570 immigrants, annually, were legally admitted. The Pew Hispanic Center estimates that an additional unauthorized half a million sneak into the country each year. It is estimated that there are between 11 million and 21 million illegal immigrants now residing in the U.S. This has created some difficulties, to the point where Congress has regularly considered building the Great Chain-Linked Wall of Texas, New Mexico, Arizona and California to stem southern migration. I can agree with President George Bush, who has his heart in the right place on this issue, for he is not as ruthless as some Congressional Republicans on this issue, as this party generally believes that our borders should be protected and rights must be earned.

Of course, there would be no all-powerful United States were it not for immigration, and as a grandson of one, I particularly appreciate this good fortune. Partly due to this influx, the USA is the only developed country that is growing at a healthy rate, if you subscribe to the theory that a little population growth is good for the economy. Finally, 123 of the 300 2006 Intel (*formerly Westinghouse*) Science Talent Search semifinalists had foreign sounding names, mostly from the Orient.

So, it's no wonder that ***The Economist*** reported America boasts 17 of the world's top 20 universities and 70% of all the Nobel laureates. The best three universities are Harvard, Stanford and Cambridge.[20]

So how great is the USA? Greatest ever! Are we declining, after only a little more than two centuries? Probably not, but let's look at a really bad case scenario. Over the next hundred years, we continue to embarrass ourselves in minor wars. China rises, but they will have their hands full just maintaining order within. Plus, what good is it, these days, with a global economy, to conquer nations militarily. So, the U.S. does, in fact, begin to decline. By mid-millennium we become like Rome and Italy, which still has fine wines, great food, and culture. Not a bad way to go, actually.

I could cite other studies and get scholarly. However, preparing the reader for Chapter 6, let me just say: preeminent in higher education (*which will extend our position as the world's most powerful*), outstanding scientific minds, Gross National Product, first to the Moon, film-making, baseball, Grand Canyon, freedom and opportunity. Plus, we did save the world from imperialism, fascism and communism, are doing our best on terrorism...and still only a little more than 200 years old. Warts and all, America is the best today, and, perhaps, ever. We should learn from past failures, and generally listen to what the world is saying, but, nevertheless, for now, consider much of global rhetoric to be, at least in part, sour grapes and jealousy.

### Japan, the European Union and India

Further analysis only includes Russia and China because the European Union, India and Japan don't appear to be particularly dangerous future military foes. But for comparative purposes, here are some statistics, mostly from the ***CIA World Factbook***:

| | **Japan** | **European Union** | **India** |
|---|---|---|---|
| Age | 30,000 years | 2 million years | 500,000 years |
| *Central Government* | (*1300 years*) | (*50 years*) | (*60 years*) |
| Size | 377,835 km$^2$ | 4,323,782 km$^2$ | 3,287,590 km$^2$ |
| Population | 128 million | 490 million | 1,130 million |
| GDP | $4,218 trillion | $13,000 trillion | $4,156 trillion |
| GDP/Capita | $33,100 | $29,900 | $3,800 |
| Military Expenditures | $33 billion | $293 billion | 103.9 billion |
| Military Exp., %GDP | 0.8% | 2.3% | 2.5% |

In the spirit of the previous sections, though, one point worth mentioning is that, India, a Hindu nation, with a minority of 150 million Muslims, still has more Muslims than Pakistan or the entire Middle East. The unemployment rate for Indian Muslims is 52%, and, while making up 11% of the total population, they are 40% of the prison population. Yes, India is incredible and making a major economic move. However, there is a loudly ticking time bomb here that has to be defused.[222]

### What About Russia?

Founded in the 12th century, it was conquered by the Mongols in the 13th century and did not really emerge until after the 15th century. By the 17th century, the Romanov Dynasty expanded the country to Siberia and the Pacific, then, under Peter I, to the Baltic Sea, for the first time naming the country the Russian Empire.

The communists led by Vladimir Lenin gained control in 1917, calling it the Union of Soviet Socialist Republic. Under a quarter century of rule by Josef Stalin until 1953, the USSR became a serious challenger to the United States. General Secretary Mikhail Gorbachev, who led from 1985 to 1991, introduced glasnost (*openness*) and perestroika (*restructuring*) to modernize the country, leading to the fall of the Berlin Wall and ending the Cold War, breaking apart the union into 15 countries. On his 75$^{th}$ birthday, Gorbachev was quoted to say that "despite the great opportunity that the end of the cold war presented to the U.S. to build a safer and more stable world, it only strengthened America's arrogance and unilateralism." Current Russian President Vladimir Putin also blames the U.S. for militarism and global instability, while he clamps down on internal dissent and takes over fossil fuel operations. Putin wants his country to become the next Saudi Arabia, at least for natural gas.

A comparative U.S.-Russian tally shows the following:

| | **Russia** | **United States** |
|---|---|---|
| Age | Almost 1000 years | About 200 years |
| Size | 17 million sq km | 9.826 million sq km |
| Population | 141 million | 302 million |
| GDP | $1,746 billion | $13,000 billion |
| GDP/Capita | $12,200 | $44,000 |
| Military Expenditures | Not Available | $528 billion |
| Military Expenditures as %GDP | Not Available | 4.1% |

Thus, Russia has less than half the population of the U.S., but is almost twice as large in area. Our Gross Domestic Product is seven and a half times larger than that of Russia.

The clue to world peace forever could well be influenced by one crucial series of understandings between the Soviet Union and the U.S. When Gorbachev and Reagan agreed to disarmament and all its repercussions, humanity overcame our greatest threshold of madness: mutually assured destruction.

Russia today plays the field, and, you might say, is enterprising. An Israeli satellite launched by Russia in 2006 now allows the gathering of data, with 27.5 inch resolution, on Iran's military assemblage. Russia happens to be building Iran's Bushehr nuclear power plant at a cost of $800 million. Also, too, Russia is more and more keeping bad company, Iran and North Korea being prime examples. With China, the growling Bear has more and more again tended to confront the U.S. on international politics.

Perhaps most worrisome, Putin's recent moves have reasserted dominance of the Kremlin, while limiting media and judiciary independence. In September of 2007, Putin flew close to NATO airspace his antique Tu-95 strategic bombers, which where escorted back by British and Norwegian fighter planes. He also announced a $200 billion rearmament plan to modernize his military. The U.K. has called to task Russia's violations of human and democratic rights. Yet, it's gratifying to note that on being awarded the 2014 Winter Olympics, Dmitry Chernyshenko called the victory a "key moment in Russian history...The games will help Russia's transition as a young **democracy**."[360]

The next war for resources could well be Russia versus Canada and Denmark, with the U.S. serving as an associate to the new enemy coalition. On August 3, 2007, a Russian scientific crew planted a flag (*actually, dropped a titanium capsule containing the flag*) on the ocean floor under the North Pole, leading President Putin to claim the rights to the half million square mile seabed for oil and gas. Canada, in an earlier response ordered several billion dollars worth of military equipment and facilities to assert their claim on the same territory, and Denmark, teaming with Canada, contends that the North Pole is merely an extension of Greenland, which they own. The United Nations, actually, in 2001, had already rejected Moscow's claim to that seabed. For the record, the U.S., Canada and Norway already have claims on that space, too.

Why the ruckus? There is speculation that the bottom of the ocean over the North Pole has as much untapped oil and gas as Saudi Arabia. For the record, too, Vladimir Gruzdev and Artur Chilingarov saw yellowish gravel, but no creatures of the deep, at the bottom. The Antarctic is a continent. The Arctic just floats over water.

**Peace with the People's Republic of China?**

Dated stone tools indicate that China was inhabited by Homo erectus 1.36 million years ago. The use of fire might have been discovered here 1.27 million years ago.[261] The discovery of Peking Man is an adventure that started in 1921 when Swedish archeologist Johann Gunnar Andersson and Austrian paleontologist Otto Zdansky found two teeth of an early man. American geologist William Grabau gave the teeth a name, Peking Man, although the scientific term was Homo erectus pekinensis, certainly not Homo sapiens. Later, in 1927, with funding from the Rockefeller Foundation, a systematic excavation was initiated at Zhoukoudian (*now a World Heritage Site*), located about 50 km southwest of Peking, now Beijing. In 1929 an almost complete skull was found. French paleontologist Father Teilhard de Chardin participated in the analysis.

This unearthing went on into 1966 when Peking Man consisted of portions of at least 6 different skulls, and assorted other parts, although there is some intrigue dealing with the Japanese invasion of China and the possibility of the fossils being smuggled to the U.S. The early fossils remain missing today. Peking Man (*more accurately, men and women*) lived from about 500,000 years to 240,000 years ago. Thus, they lived in the same cave for more than a quarter million years.

The history of China has been recorded over five millennia:

- It was only a couple of centuries before Jesus, though, that the country became unified, when Qin Shi Huang formed the first dynasty. While this reign only lasted for 12 years, the most famous of the Great Walls of China gained more prominence (*actually, the building, in fits, began in the 5th century BC*).
- The following Han Dynasty governed for 400 years, from two centuries before to two centuries after Jesus. The Silk Road to the West was established.
- Four centuries of disorder followed when in 589 the Sui Dynasty united the country, but was superseded by the Tang Dynasty in 618, ruling for almost three centuries until chaos took over for half a century.

- Then, the Song Dynasty, maintained control for three centuries, a time when science flourished and gunpowder was invented, about 1040.
- The Mongol Empire began to form around Genghis Khan from 1206, and his grandson, Kublai Khan established the Yuan Dynasty later in that century. The capital moved from Xian to Beijing, but in this interval the Chinese population dropped from 100 million to 60 million.
- These barbarians were then replaced by the Ming Dynasty in 1368 under Zhu Yuanzhang, a peasant. China during this period ruled the oceans with Zhang He, Forbidden City reached its grandeur and the Great Wall of China, a project that took 1000 years, was completed.
- Finally, after nearly three centuries of control, the Manchus invaded from the North, and the Quin Dynasty endured from 1644 to 1912 various internal wars and external influences. The Last Emperor, Henry Puyi was born in 1906, was not quite 3 when he was named emperor by Dowager Empress Cixi, but just at the age of 6 abdicated, officially ending the rule of the Dynasties. Puyi was restored as Emperor in 1917, but was almost instantly deposed, finally becoming Emperor of Manchukuo as a Japanese puppet, then at the end, a Chinese pawn of Chairman Mao.

There, in less than a page, is the entire history of China.

A following comparative table compares China with the U.S.:

| | **China** | **United States** |
|---|---|---|
| Age | A million years?? | About 200 years |
| Size | 9.598 million sq km | 9.826 million sq km |
| Population | 1,322 million | 302 million |
| GDP | $8, 182 billion | $13,000 billion |
| GDP/Capita | $6,300 | $44,000 |
| Military Expenditures | $81 billion | $528 billion |
| Military Expenditures as %GDP | 4.3%* | 4.1% |

China and the U.S., thus, are about the same in land area, with China having one billion more people than the U.S. *(* The 4.3% for Military Expenditures as % of GDP comes straight from the CIA report, but my calculations show a figure of ONLY 1%.)*

Additionally:

| | **China** | **United States** |
|---|---|---|
| Energy Consumption Ratio | 1 | 9 |
| Tobacco Use | 36% | 24% |
| Meat Consumption/Capita/Year | 104 pounds | 269 pounds |
| Paper Consumption/Capita/Year | 73 pounds | 730 pounds |
| Water Use/Capita/Year | 116,000 gallons | 484,500 galloons |
| Vehicles/Capita | 0.0016 | 0.774 |

The U.S. uses a lot more energy than China, but, because of the population disparity and the type of energy, ***Guardian Unlimited*** reported on June 19, 2007 that China had overtaken the U.S. as the world's biggest carbon dioxide emitter.[376] Also because of the population difference, China eats more meat (*67 million tons versus 38 million tons*), consumes more grain (*380 million tons to 260 million tons*) and uses more steel (*258 million tons versus 104 million tons*) than the U.S.[43] The Chinese internet population grew by 53% from 2007 to 2008 to 210 million, and will surge past the U.S. this year.[156] As the economy further improves and censorship is relaxed, the growth should be even more spectacular. Oh yes, China already has more cell phones (*461 million to 219 million*), television sets and refrigerators. With only 12 million cars, versus 140 million for the U.S., China has 90,000 traffic deaths each year, while we kill less than 50,000 on our roads.[223] I've been there. I believe it. Ah, my day in Hangzhou could just as well have been my last on Planet Earth. See Chapter 6.

Where China is truly trouncing the U.S. is in trade. First, a possible surprise...Germany is the #1 exporter. By mid-2006, China had supplanted the U.S. for #2, with exports surging by 27% from the previous year.[170] Germany should be overtaken by 2009. The trade deficit between China and the U.S. in 2006 was $232 billion. China did increase overall imports by 20% in 2006 to $792 billion. So what did the U.S. do? We went to the World Trade Organization and complained. Okay, there are some valid copyright and patent issues worthy of resolution, but, the overall attitude should be to take stock of our deficiencies and rectify them.

To no one's shock, here is the reason why China is so successful: low cost. But, higher quality is also a key. China exported $14 billion worth of furniture in 2006, surpassing Italy for #1. A beautiful executive chair from Italy wholesales for $348 in America. The Chinese price is $56, for essentially the same chair. A 23 year old farmer, Zhu Kanglin of Anjin, in 1993, begged, borrowed and persevered a sum of $3000 to start a chair factory. Today, he has 1000 different office chair models...not chairs, models. His workers toil up to 10 hours per day through six days a week to make $185/month. The equivalent Italian worker makes $1000/month.[155]

Three particularly amazing examples of growth can be mentioned:

- Shenzhen, on the China side, was a fishing village of 25,000 in 1979, a short metro train to Hong Kong. As an experiment in capitalism, but using Chinese socialism, this location that year was designated as an industrial and business center, growing by 2008 to 9 million people living in town, with an additional 9 million in the immediate urban area.
- In 2002, China decided to convert the seedy gambling town (*the only site with Hong Kong horse racing where gambling is allowed in China, although various mainland cites are now beginning to be approved*) of Macau to compete with Las Vegas. In 2006, revenues of close to $7 billion surpassed Las Vegas, leapt passed $10 billion in 2007, and will surge beyond the State of Nevada in 2008, with Wynn Macau, MGM Mirage, the second Sands (*the Venetian, with the world's biggest casino*), second Mirage and two Shangri-La/Traders leading the way. The 1400 gambling tables of 2006 will increase to 4,000 by 2009. The ten year plan is such that by 2012, the gambling revenues of Macau could well double that of Las Vegas. Sheldon Adelson of the Sands is the new Stanley Ho, although his daughter, Pansy Ho Chiu-king, is in

partnership with Mirage. All of which galvanized Las Vegas to commit $40 billion by 2012 to build more magnificent palaces for their losers to spend more, as Macau only attracted 27 million victims last year, while Sin City drew 39 million. The Chinese lose more elaborately and quickly in craps, roulette and baccarat, while Americans contribute more slowly with slot machines, poker and black jack.

- In 1985, the U.S. and China both conferred 70,000 bachelor degrees in engineering. In 2000, the U.S. number dropped to 53,000 and China's increased to 220,000. Worse yet, if you toss in Japan and South Korea, the bachelors degrees in engineering go up to 380,000.[255] Then in 2008...not that engineering is crucial to the future of a nation, but this growing discrepancy most definitely is a warning signal.

The economy should be the fear, but the singular apprehension about China seems to be as a dangerous military threat. So let's look at defense expenditures. The Center for Arms Control and Non-Proliferation showed that the 2005 military budget for the United States was $419 billion, with Russia second at $65 billion and China third at $56 billion. The U.S. accounts for almost half the world military outlays, and alone exceeds the combined total of the next 42 highest spending countries. So the U.S. pays out seven and a half times more for the military than China, according to those figures, or 33 times more per capita.

It is said, though, that much of the China armed forces budget is hidden. In 2003, the published amount was $25 billion. The CIA said it could have been $65 billion, and, considering relative purchasing strength, perhaps as much as $114 billion. The U.S. Department of Defense, when reporting on their $419 billion budget for 2005, speculated that the Chinese actual amount was $90 billion. Even at that escalated level, the U.S. commits 4.6 times more than China on military expenditures. Thus, the U.S. spends 4.1% of our GDP on the military, while China's percentage is 1.1%. Further, on a per capita basis, the U.S. sets aside $1638/person for defense, while China provides only $68/person.

Worse yet, that U.S. budget above does **not** account for wars, nuclear weapons research and sundry other military-related items. For FY2008, President Bush has asked for $861 billion to cover the DOD, plus veterans' affairs, homeland security and war costs. China announced its military budget for 2007 at $45 billion. Thus, on this basis, using official statistics, the U.S. spends nearly twenty times more than China for warfare. There must be a more effective way to wage peace than to ridiculously outspend your rivals.

So U.S. Defense Secretary Robert Gates' questioning of Chinese officials on November 5, 2007, about why they are spending so much money on arms build-up could have had monumental impact if he had instead said, look, friends, the U.S. will reduce defense expenditures by $100 billion next year. You think you can cut yours by $10 billion? Now, that would be a Gorbachev-like one-upmanship that could have set the table for total disarmament in a decade.

China and the U.S. are both Republics. So is Iran. However, there are republics and there are republics. At least China appears to be on the road from dictatorship towards democracy.

**Weapons of Mass Destruction**

The term, weapons of mass destruction (*WMD*), was first used either in 1937 in reference to an aerial bombardment of Spain or in 1945 from the Hiroshima/Nagasaki A-bombs. President George W. Bush again made WMD popular in the 2003 Iraq invasion.

Although WMD can be chemical, radiological, biological and nuclear, the latter two today are of concern, biological because of unseen dangers from genetic engineering, and nuclear, because the Soviets had at one time built a 100 megaton (*MT*) H-bomb and exploded a 57 MT monster in 1961. The Oklahoma City fertilizer bomb was said to be 0.000002 MT, and the largest A-bomb possible (*Little Boy as much as 0.000015 MT and Fat Boy 0.000022MT*) is less than 1 MT. The greater menace, though, now, are the potential dirty radioactive bombs of terrorists. For the sake of peace, at least nuclear WMD devices have shrunk from 100 MT to 0.00000001, plus or minus a couple of decimal points.

## How to Make a Dirty Bomb

Jon Ronson of ***Guardian*** was commissioned in July 2002 by his newspaper company to purchase materials to make a nuclear weapon, but be careful with the expenses.[265] He couldn't have gone to "How to Build a Nuclear Bomb and Other Weapons,"[24] because Frank Barnaby did not publish that book until 2004. Ronson very quickly found that The Bulletin of the Atomic Scientists indicating it could take billions of dollars was probably true. So Ronson set out just to make a dirty bomb—typical terrorist weapon laced with radioactive material. No, he couldn't have accessed the Al Qaeda website on the subject, containing 80 pages of detail, because that manual was not made available until 2005. Russia seemed to be the best place to secure a supply, but some simple intelligence showed this was just too scary, so he ended up calling the Nuclear Security Administration in Las Vegas, where Darwin Morgan told him that U.S. businesses have misplaced some 1,500 pieces of radioactive equipment, especially density gauges, because they are commonly used by road building crews. But securing one would be a problem.

At this point he had come to the conclusion that actually killing a victim through radiation was not necessary, for the mere detection of any sort of radiation would discombobulate the citizenry. So, perhaps the internet? Ronson asks Jeeves, which sends him to eBay, which had an ongoing uranium auction: 22 grams of U-238 now going for $18.41, but useless as an A-bomb material. His expert contact said that was not frightening enough, so on to Cobalt-60 from food processing plants, which are mostly poorly guarded. Al Qaeda, incidentally, recommends radium. At this point, his expert stops giving him information, so he came to the conclusion that a terrorist posing as a ***Guardian*** reporter might someday be able do better than he. Ronson's article is worth a read.

There is a second type of dirty bomb, a biological one. Al Qaeda actually has a website on how to build such a bomb.[102] Posted on October 6, 2005, the forum, titled Al Firdaws, or Paradise, provides lessons, and more.

To be operationally correct, the biological weapon of mass destruction (*WOMD*) will probably not be a bomb. Other than actually gaining access to anthrax, botulinum toxin, ricin, smallpox, tularemia, plague and viral hemorrhagic fevers (*these are the Category A BWOMD, a B is Q fever and C is hantavirus*) a second important step will be the delivery system. The U.S. Post Office has been used with devastating results, but, some means of aerosolization and dissemination in the field to maximize breathing the biological agent is also known as germ warfare.

So making a dirty bomb is not a particularly difficult challenge. Why such a device has not been exploded in America defies all logic.

## How to Make an Atomic Bomb

It's true, you can go to the internet and find out how to make an atomic bomb, at least, all disclaimers aside, with the principles to guide you. The wild card is the billion dollar price tag, which is conservative.

The literature says that all you need to do is to shape 110 pounds of Uranium 235 into a sphere with a small piece missing, and use a conventional explosive bullet detonator to shove the absent portion of the material into the ball to attain critical mass.[332] Other guides suggest that 10 pounds of U235 might be sufficient. The explosion itself occurs in one millionth of a second. Little Boy on Hiroshima was of this type. If you need to start with the uranium ore, you also must separate the good stuff, U235 (*about 0.6%*), from the waste, U238, which is over 99% the batch. Thus, begin with 18 million pounds of crude uranium ore to obtain the required amount of U235 through a simple three step process of gaseous diffusion, magnetic separation and gaseous centrifugation. Harold Urey, who had in 1931 won a Nobel Prize for demonstrating the existence of heavy water, was instrumental in devising the gaseous diffuser to separate U235 from U238, and later again gained fame when his graduate student, Stanley Miller formed amino acids in a flask with water, methane, ammonia, hydrogen and lab lightning.

Clearly, then, terrorists will not be setting up a mining operation. All they need to do is steal or purchase enriched uranium or plutonium. While the 1974 days of Karen Silkwood at the Kerr-McGee plant in Oklahoma, are over, where 40 pounds of plutonium were supposedly lost, either Israel, the CIA or terrorists did steal some plutonium from the Nuclear Materials and Equipment Corporation in Pennsylvania. Nonweapons grade U-235 can be purified with centrifuges, certainly within the capability of a lab in the desert. Weapons grade U-235, reportedly, can be purchased on the black market. The accessible spots are the former Soviet nations, but North Korea, apparently, is now out of the business. Syria? Well, Israel kiboshed that attempt, but Iran? Someday, maybe.

Only 22 pounds of Plutonium 239 can also be used, but that's another process requiring a nuclear reactor, implosion and a U238 casing. Detonation occurs in one ten-millionths of a second. The process is difficult and uncertain. The first version of this bomb was The Gadget at Trinity on July 16, 1945 in New Mexico and second was Fat Man three weeks later on Nagasaki. An audition was necessary because scientists did not know for sure if this concept was going to work. Little Boy was a sure thing because of the type of technology.

With tongue firmly in cheek, an unacknowledged how to do it guide also pondered the psychological state of a possible American terrorist:

- o Subscribes to one or more of the following: ***Soldier of Fortune*, *Hustler*, *Popular Mechanics*, *Self*.**
- o I am my own best friend.
- o I have seen the movie, ***Deer Hunter***, more than once.
- o I have read evidence that solar energy is a Communist conspiracy.

There were several more, but you get the point, of course. Don't you?

The best brains on Earth in the Forties spent the 2007 equivalent of $23 billion (*$2 billion then*) to hit the nuclear jackpot three straight times. Can a terrorist group today repeat this act?

## How to Build a Hydrogen Bomb…Not

If it's very expensive and, further, not all that easy, to build an A-Bomb, the notion of a terroristic H-Bomb must border on the nonsense. However, the Father of this ultimate of weapons, Edward Teller, weaves through ***Books 1*** and ***2***, and his involvement in the Einstein to FDR letters to build the A-Bomb inspired the Hydrogen Romantics to affect the G8 Nation gathering in Germany in 2007, where we at least received a couple of nice gestures, and is continuing to inspire our attempts for the 2008 Hokkaido Summit, so this subject serves as another node linking elements of my life, including one of my stops at the Lawrence Livermore National Laboratory on laser fusion. Teller also presented a paper in 1997 on some geoengineering options for remediating global climate change. So on to how to build the ultimate bomb on a relative shoestring budget.

The initial step is to first build an atomic bomb. Hint: you might need four of these. Then have this simultaneous blast ignite the hydrogen bomb. Very simple. The first test in 1952 of a 10.4 MT—700 times more destructive than Little Boy—bomb was all of two-stories tall and destroyed the Pacific island of Elugelab. Then there were a few more, capped by the USSR 57 MT, the Tsar Bomba, in 1961.

If the Al Qaeda terrorists on 9/11/01 were so successful in carrying out their mission, as difficult as it is to build a hydrogen bomb, it remains possible, remotely, of course, that a well-financed team might be able to detonate such a device to again capture the imagination of the world. Maybe they're waiting for such a spectacle. That said, as an ultimate disclaimer, I have decided not to provide any details on exactly what to do with the atomic bombs, except that you need to attain about 100 million degrees Celsius and have access (*can easily be purchased from any chemical supply house*) to lithium deuteride, or, if this has any potential of setting off warning alarms, just a hundred pounds of lithium hydride. Theoretically, this H-Bomb could be a thousand times more powerful than Little Boy over Hiroshima.

What about the morality and ethics of all this? Well, our Federal Government and military-industrial complex do it all the time and even sell it to former enemies, or friends who could in a few short years become a foe. Certainly, there must be a better way, as I will soon suggest.

**Global Terrorism, Redux**

World War II was "easy." Against all initial intentions, we vanquished Japan and Germany, saving the world for freedom. Well, it did cost an equivalent of $12 trillion and 400,000 American lives, with another 100,000 still missing. But the world suffered a lot more, with 24 million dying just in the Battle of Stalingrad, and, perhaps a 100 million in total, so it could have been a lot worse for the U.S. Were it not for the USA, the world today could well be dominated by fascists. There are varied books on this subject matter.

The Cold War against communism was tense, but we also prevailed. We have yet to lose a major war. Western democracy is undefeated. We might lose minor struggles, such as Vietnam and Iraq, and still harbor internal imperfections, but observing the larger picture, we find a way to continue the effort towards the global good, save for climate warming.

In 1992, Frances Fukuyama released the ***End of History***,[110] suggesting that liberal democracy had conquered monarchy, fascism and communism, ending the evolution of human society. Thus, the end of history.

We have reached perfection, so there will be no further adjustments necessary. Samuel Huntington, in his 1996 ***Clash of Civilizations***,[150] disagreed, and proposed that cultural and religious differences would provoke future conflicts. In my mind, both are right. Yes, terrorism continues on the rise, but, in the end, democracy will triumph. Terrorism, though, is a matter of strategy, the correct reference should be, War on Islamic Fundamentalists, or some variation which will change over time.

September 11, 2001 was not when this war began. Certainly, you can go back to:

- 1968 Bobby Kennedy assassination,
- 1972 Munich Olympics massacre,
- 1979 Iran Embassy hostage crisis,
- 1980's kidnapping of Americans in Lebanon,
- 1983 Beirut bombing of U.S. Marine barracks,
- 1985 hijacking of cruise ship Achille Lauro and TWA flight 847,
- 1988 bombing of Pan Am Flight 103,
- 1993 first World Trade Center attack (*which killed six, injured 1000 and caused $300 million in damages*),
- 1998 bombing of U.S. embassies in Kenya and Tanzania, and
- 2000 assault on the USS Cole in Yemen.

Plus, the Daniel Pearl murder and London bombings, of course. The constancy in all these attacks was that they were all committed by male Muslim extremists, generally in the 17-40 age category.

There was never a full confirmation on what the 9/11 terrorists used as weapons. The official release indicated plastic knives and box cutters, but that might have been for legal reasons. There was a stabbing, a chemical weapon was used, a terrorist probably had a bomb and one shot was fired, killing a passenger. Fifteen of the 19 terrorists came from Saudi Arabia, and were all in large part well, educated, skilled, middle-class professionals.

Thusly triggered, the Iraq war was launched on March 19, 2003, and was essentially over in less than a month. American casualties will be about 4,000, but it is reported that 700,000 civilians have died. Yes, it is troublesome and unfortunate that the 100% school attendance during the days of Dictator Saddam is now down to 30%, nearly half the professionals and 2 million citizens have left Iraq, with 2000 doctors murdered, and worldwide terrorism has increased seven-fold.[158]

I once lived in D.C., and the firearm death rate of that city was about 80 per 100,000. In the Iraq theatre, this same death rate is 60 per 100,000 soldiers. But I wouldn't want to live in either location. Of some surprise, the number of American soldiers was not at a maximum during the initial days of the war, the peak was reached in August of 2007, 52 months after that. Attaining a satisfactory peace will take a long, long, time, way after we leave.

The United Kingdom has more recently experienced various successful terroristic events and uncovered a number of plots. It approaches miracle status that nothing has happened in the U.S. since 9/11. The sense is that the next target has to result in a more spectacular message.

The problem with fighting terrorists is that the enemy is scattered. Further, there is no worldwide conspiracy. Yes, the Jihadis, the militant Muslims, seek to control the Middle East, Europe next (*and France is already 20% Muslim, and a likely target*), then the world. But, as the relatively defined Iraq War showed, it is not a simple matter of blanket bombing the terrorists. Al Queda seeks to unify the Islamic community around the world. Even if they should they succeed in their holy war, ultimately, the more conventional, and less irrational, beliefs of the Koran will dominate.

This conflict between largely Christian nations and Wahhabi Islam believers will last several generations. Europe fought Germany from 1870 to 1945, or 75 years. The Cold War lasted 42 years. The U.S. pullout of Vietnam, a war that was our longest military conflict, was more than thirty years ago. For some, that was the beginning of the conflict with China. When we leave Iraq, this will occur in the infancy of the War on Terror.

Simple solution for Iraq? Use the India-Pakistan formula, creating at least three sections by religion: Sunni, Shiite and other. Provide equitable land and value relative to population and strength. Have the UN manage the country as three competing democracies, with a referendum every ten years to review the possibility of unification. The availability of petroleum revenues will go a long way to insure for cooperation and peace. Over the next century, as oil runs out, it is possible that the entire Middle East could end up being three countries: Sunni, Shiite and "other." Religious differences—not the dogma, but the deep hatreds—will require several generations to overcome.

Thus, some means must be found to have the people police themselves. In the 1930's, only a very few in Germany were Nazis. While many enjoyed the return of German pride, most were too busy with their lives to bother about the rise. In fact, there are statements of fact that most felt that these Nazis were a bunch of fools. The people of Japan were not warmongering sadists. While only a few at the top were responsible for 20 million being killed in Russia and 70 million in China, the vast majority, exhibiting their irrelevance, did nothing.

Today, yes, there is some jealousy about the American lifestyle, our arrogance, the fact that we are not Muslim and the loathsome reality that we are camped in their backyard. But most are, like in Germany and Japan in the period leading to World War II, just citizens trying to get on with their life. This 99.9% of the population needs to overcome the fanatical 0.1%.

One final treacherous and precarious fact is that nine nations belong to the nuclear club, and who knows how many more, including terrorists, harbor nuclear weapons or potent radioactive materials. A Russian "accident" could still trigger a worst case scenario for a nuclear winter. For these reasons, the Doomsday Clock was advanced to 5 minutes on January 17, 2007.

Alas, there seems to always be Black and White…fascism vs democracy…imperialism vs democracy…communism vs democracy…terrorism vs democracy. Wouldn't it be a lot better to end all wars, forever? Let us explore how this might be accomplished. If only an active catalytic few can, having experienced the past, be influenced by this simple solution.

## The United Nations

But before getting to the punch line, as the world will need a coordinating entity to organize the peace, let us start with some interesting facts:

- The World population took twelve years to increase from 5 billion in 1988 to 6 billion in 2000, and will take another dozen years to reach 7 billion, in 2012.
- There are 194 countries, 192 with membership in the United Nations, plus the Vatican and Taiwan, which in July 2007 again was rejected.
- China and Russia each border 14 other countries.
- The Gross World Product is $66 trillion (*2006*), with that of the United States being $11 trillion, so GWP/person is $10,000/year, compared to GNP/person of $37,000 for the U.S.
- Globally, the median age is 28, and the current life expectancy at birth is 66 years.
- One-third are Christians and one-fifth are Muslims.

The only global organization with any kind of influence today was founded in 1945, replacing the League of Nations. Franklin D. Roosevelt is credited with first suggesting the name, United Nations. The headquarters are located in New York City on land purchased from funds donated by John D. Rockefeller, Jr., and the Secretary General is Ban Ki-moon of South Korea.

Much of the global climate change leadership came from the 1992 UN Earth Summit in Rio de Janeiro. The UN also has convened conferences on population, trade efficiency, disarmament and social development. Peacekeeping (*with a staffing of 70,000*), human rights development, international law adjudication and humanitarian assistance are leading missions of this organization.

The UN budget is intricate. While in 2006 the U.S. was assessed 22% (*the maximum*) of the nearly $2 billion, or $424 million *($1.42 per American citizen*), it is estimated that we actually are contributing about $3 billion *($10/person*) / year because of special assessments, primarily for peacekeeping. The International Criminal Tribunal for Rwanda, as an example, was an added cost to the UN of $260 million. Japan paid $374 million *($3.94/citizen*) to the regular budget, the second most by far, and Liberia provided $19,000. Yes, the U.S. is arrears on some payments as a protest in principle, and also is regularly tardy, but late payments are standard international practice.

Many families don't manage their affairs too well. So too can be said for villages, companies, universities and governments. The UN is the worst of all, but understandably so. Reforming the UN has become a mantra: membership on the Security Council, bureaucracy, transparency, accountability, efficiency, etc. Thus, in 2005, the UN convened a World Summit involving the heads of state of member countries to make a once-in-generation attempt to craft bold decisions on areas of development, security, human rights and reform. The conferees agreed to:

- create a Peace building Commission and a Human Rights Council;
- step-in when any national government does not fulfill their responsibility to protect their own citizens from atrocity crimes;
- increase internal oversight ;
- commit significant funds toward achieving Millennium Development Goals;
- condemn terrorism; and
- found a Democracy Fund.

In 2004, President George W. Bush, at the UN General Assembly, said:

> *Because I believe the advance of liberty is the path to both a safer and better world, today, I propose establishing a Democracy Fund within the United Nations. This is a great calling for this great organization...To show our commitment to the new Democracy Fund, the United States will make an initial contribution.*

One hundred forty-one ministers meeting at the Community of Democracies in Santiago, Chile the following year embraced the concept, and on July 4, yes, Independence Day for the USA, UN Secretary-General Kofi Annan announced the establishment of a UN Democracy Fund. The program will promote and consolidate new and restored democracies.

Well, that's terrific, but, alas, unless Mars Attacks, nothing much will happen and things will continue to proceed as poorly as they have, forever. That said, the UN remains our best hope to lead the way to eternal peace.

## Is it Possible to Survive Without a Military?

In a word, yes. There are 24 countries with no military. Costa Rica, Iceland, Mauritius and Panama have no defense expenditures. However, they form alliances and maintain a police force of some sorts. Grenada actually gave theirs up after the U.S. invasion in 1983.

None of these countries seem terribly concerned about an invader. In fact, a strong case can be made about how utilization of all tax dollars for peaceful and economic purposes would actually strengthen the country. There must be a clue here as to what to do about large defense budgets. Just think, if no country had a military, then no country would be threatened. There must be a simple solution here, somewhere.

## Is World Peace Possible?

The Bushmen of the Kalahari live with no internal or external violence. In fact, there are at least 25 societies around the world today with little or no warfare.[292] In ***Beyond War***, Douglas Fry demonstrates how war can become obsolete.[109] He differentiates between human frailty towards personal problems and warfare. The former is natural, the latter, can be controlled. The bottom line, from studying aboriginal societies, is that fighting wars is not an essential attribute of society. Warfare is not inevitable.

Ironically, waging peace has not been a safe task. Mahatma Gandhi and Prime Minister Itzhak Rabin were assassinated seeking the peace. The Dalai Lama proposed a Team Nobel to prevent wars, an inspired, but hazardous, idea.

The Matsunaga-inspired U.S. Institute for Peace has found a home in Washington, D.C., and is a think tank with a goal towards resolving conflicts through peace, not war. A partnership with similar organizations throughout the world, the religious sector of society and the United Nations seems hopeful as the structure for the future.

While not exactly world peace, there are various humanitarian and environmental missions that can serve as pathways to amity. Certainly, military units throughout the globe have assisted during major natural disasters. That's a given. Also, too, there seems to be a calling for adding environmental remediation as a complementary task. There are many more examples worthy of consideration, but just one, providing shelter for the homeless, should be underscored as an opportunity. Military bases become obsolete and navy ships are mothballed. Each base commander should be urged to reach out to the community. The advantage of involving the armed forces is that they also have the capability to provide re-training. A little irony, but in Chapter 5, it is suggested that each church also become engaged in this mission, for they too have the means to link with jobs through their congregation. What better partnership than war and peace to assist humanity?

But to the purpose of this section, one surefire way for the world to cooperate is from a threat to the entire Planet. We saw this in ***Independence Day*** and ***Mars Attacks***, movies where aliens try to conquer us. An interesting point was made in the fourth "Body Snatchers," this one in 2007 called ***The Invasion***: where one of the aliens tries to persuasively argue that there would then be no war in Iraq, no genocide in Darfur…no conflict in general. This would mean that everyone would become a Stepford Human. There is something missing in a society without any conflict. Do we ban the Olympics for being too internationally competitive? Little League Baseball?

In any case, there must be something better than what we have today, and Herman Wouk has been quoted to say: "War is an old habit of thought, an old frame of mind, an old political technique that must now pass as human sacrifice and human slavery have passed." As Kenneth Boulding, a speaker at one of the workshops I early co-directed, said, "anything that exists is possible." Yes, worldwide peace is most definitely possible as our civilization matures. It's only a matter of time.

## Is Democracy Working?

Without getting into the debate of whether the U.S. is a democracy or republic (*the **Constitution** says it is the latter*), let us simplify the government form called democracy (*or republic*) as a sovereignty of the people where the majority rules with minorities protected. The system provides for basic human rights, fair elections, equality before the law, constitutional limits on government and general pluralism. Both Democrats and Republicans function in our democracy, so any government form of the above that is not authoritarian or a monarchy qualifies in this book as a democracy. Democracy is the institutionalization of freedom.

Democracy might have been invented in India before the 6$^{th}$ century BC. India today is the world's largest democracy. However, the history books tend to write that this form of government was started around the same time in Athens, Greece, where it was practiced. North Korea's constitution describes the country as a democratic state, but it does not operate on those principles. Thus, it is not a matter of what a country is called or what its governing document says—the reality is in the performance. There are gray areas, such as social or anarchistic democracy. We will stick with the popular form of liberal democracy as utilized in the United States, which began to gain worldwide dominance only after World War II.

During the past century, about one/third of society has lived in democratic nations. Democracies come and go, with the U.S., U.K. Sweden, Switzerland and Canada perhaps noteworthy as being able to continuously maintain this form of government. Fascism was a problem, but was eliminated. Democracies tend to be immune to communism. Military and assorted coups have overthrown democracies more than 30 times over the past century. Thailand regularly does this.

According to Freedom House (*an American organization*), at the end of 2005, there were 122 electoral democracies, representing 64% of all nations, compared to 40% in the mid-80s.[167] The 2006 ranking for best democracies show Sweden at the top and the U.S. at #17. Why so low? Civil rights have recently been compromised and there is a sense that the government is not functioning. They could be right. The U.K. is at #23, India at #35, Thailand #90, Russia #102, Iraq #112 and North Korea #167.

There is even a new journal on the subject, called ***Democracy: A Journal of Ideas***. It is one year old with their Winter 2008 issue, and, for a rather diminutive edition, the $9 cost might be a bit pricey. One interesting point made is that open-source technology, such as ***Wikipedia***, is making government decision-making more democratic.[225]

Is there hope for democracy in Islamic countries? Interestingly enough, two Muslim countries, Lebanon and Turkey, are similar to U.S. views on favoring democracy over a leader with a strong hand: U.S. at 63%, Lebanon 63% and Turkey 57%. U.S. at 63%?? The other 27% must want something else than a democracy. Anyway, on the question of whether democracy can work in their country, the Pew Research Center reported that:

- Kuwait 83%
- Nigeria 75%
- Lebanon 68%
- Pakistan 58%
- Turkey 50%
- Indonesia 41%

The study further indicated that 70% of respondents from Turkey, Senegal and Mali agreed that religion should be kept separate from government policy. The U.S. result was 55%. That is, 45% in this country think that religion should not be separated from government.[14] If you're wondering about the insanity of some of this, wait till you get to Chapter 5 on the Golden Evolution.

In mid 2007 a poll of Iranians by Terror Free Tomorrow found that 79% supported a democratic system in which leaders are elected through free elections.[338] 78% favored nuclear energy, but only 33% were for nuclear weapons.

Thus, the bottom line is that people of the Middle East feel that democracy can work in their country. They don't like the U.S. telling them what to do, so there needs to be a different approach. A 2005 Gallup International Poll found 78% from the Middle East agreeing that "Democracy may have problems but it is the best form of government." Further, on the prospects of the United Nations becoming significantly more powerful in world affairs, 77% of Indonesians and 70% of Iranians were positive.[179]

## A Simple Solution to Wars

Is total peace just a simple matter of controlling nuclear power and neutralizing China? It is said that the waging of peace will take many turns and be accomplished in small steps. George Shultz, William Perry, Henry Kissinger and Sam Nunn, a bipartisan team of super decision-makers, wrote an op ed (*opinion of the editor, and also opposite the editorial*) article for The

Wall Street Journal in 2007, calling for a world free of nuclear weapons.[118] They remarked that the Non-Proliferation Treaty of 1967 established the foundation for their plea, but the vision of Iran and emergence of global terrorists have changed the rules of the game. Certainly, the control of the atom will be a necessary early step to pave the way to peace.

Second, what about China? The Ford Foundation and Rockefeller Brothers Fund sponsored a study on "Scenarios for the Future of United States – China Relations," looking ahead to 2010.[98] The policy choices recommended were that:

- The U.S. and China needed to go beyond economic engagement and identify common security interests, such as seeking a common ground on Taiwan and sharing capabilities in environmental protection and sustainable energy.
- The U.S. policy should get off their current incoherent mixture of containment and engagement, and instead work mutually towards China as a global power, after all, it has been predicted that the Gross Domestic Products of the two countries will be equal by 2025.
- The U.S. should carefully support human rights reform in China.
- The relationship should not be one of friends, but of family.

But these are lower order requirements to maintain order and progress. Is there a more definitive, and simpler, means of insuring for future peace? I started writing this chapter without a solution.

Early in 2006 I was thumbing through the latest issue of ***Honolulu***, and amazingly enough, there was the simple solution to ending wars forever. Emeritus Professor Rudolf Rummel of the University of Hawaii Political Science Department wrote an article entitled, "Iraq: was Bush right?" He says yes, but more so, pointed out that of all international wars with at least 1,000 casualties from 1816 to 2005, almost two centuries, there have been no wars between two democracies.[268] There were 166 between democracies and non democracies and 205 between non democracies and non democracies. Let me repeat: NO MAJOR WARS BETWEEN TWO OR MORE DEMOCRACIES OVER THE PAST TWO CENTURIES.

Is that a clue to end all wars or what? Maybe President George W. Bush, too, knows this. Maybe that is why he and his aides have jumped headlong into the Middle East. Certainly, their proposing the establishment of the UN Democracy Fund is philosophically consistent. To boot, their Iraq surge in 2007, as faulty as it was because more troops could have been sent if the politics allowed, actually worked, and there is hope now that not winning has become not losing, all for the long-term establishment of a workable democracy.

I subsequently went to GOOGLE, and there was a ***Wikipedia*** section just on Rudolph Joseph Rummel. Then I remembered that his wife, Margaret, was a high school classmate of mine, but that I had not seen her in half a century. Emeritus Professor Rummel has published 24 scholarly books and over 100 professional articles. He also coined the term democide, or murder by government, claiming that six times as many people died of this act in the 20$^{th}$ century than all wars. His book, ***Power Kills***, published in 1997, was largely available on the internet, so I read it and began communicating with him. He said his hearing was going, so it was best for us to converse by e-mail.

The CATO Institute published their Ninth Annual Ranking of Economic Freedom in 2005, stipulating that economic freedom is almost 50 times more effective than democracy in restraining nations from going to war. Professor Rummel reacted with sadness, pointing out in blogger Democratic Peace, that not only was this wrong, but incompetent. The basic argument: if the study uses data showing zero wars between democracies over almost two centuries, how can economic freedom be 50 times better? The point, of course, is not to refute Professor Rummel's contention, but, only so, to underscore that our present government's policy to promote peace in the Middle East and other regions through democratization is of questionable worth. It should be remembered, of course, why these organizations push a cause. The CATO Institute happens to be a libertarian public policy research foundation. Libertarians want to limit the role of government and they love free markets. Rummel, a libertarian on domestic issues, still felt compelled to respond.

So I now had a solution to end wars, courtesy of Professor Rummel. Clearly, the U.S. is only a necessary participant in the process, and is not in any position to coordinate the larger peace.

Searching my soul, the only final stage solution I could formulate was for the United Nations to be provided enhanced powers to insure for the phase-out of wars by:

- Creating a World Peace Institute (*WPI*) to train peacekeepers. While every major country has academies to train warriors, the time has come to produce the leaders who have the mentality, attitude and capability to engender peace.
- Set up a peace equity fund by assessing companies/governments exporting war equipment of any type. It is reported that the U.S. alone sold abroad more than $142 billion dollars worth of weaponry in 1992. This amount has dropped since then, but, world-wide, remains in the range of $50 billion/year. This fund will be used to establish and operate the WPI. The rate can be determined by need. This so-called investment (*also known as a tax*) for peace should serve an enhanced role by reducing the market demand, sort of like how significantly increasing gasoline taxes would lower consumption.

Well, Reagan's Star Wars strategy bankrupted the Soviet Union, so we conveniently were able to win the Cold War for the cause of freedom. About China, well, let's see what we can do to steer them towards a democracy. Step one has been successful, which was to introduce free enterprise into their economy. Of course, Taiwan, a splinter we support, is a representative democracy. Where is Chiang Kai-shek or the next one, to unify the entire country? Or, more sensibly, future leaders of China might someday succeed in courting Taiwan into accepting some form of governmental partnership, which could well provide the Trojan Horse to long-term democracy. Macau and Hong Kong are already partly serving this function.

Or, there is the theory that China will go the way of the Soviet Union and split into a bunch of smaller nations, as soon as the period immediately following the 2008 Summer Olympics, for their over spending on this spectacle in combination with the internationalization of the country, could well catalyze something monumental. Whatever, the SIMPLE SOLUTION strategy is clear: to end all wars for a long time, steer China into democracy.

Thus, the simple solution to ending wars forever is simply to:

1. Establish the World Peace Institute under UN auspices.
2. Broaden the UN Democracy Fund to convert all countries to democracies.
3. Financially support the above by placing a peace incentive surcharge on exported armaments. The rate will be determined by the amount required to progressively carry out tasks #1 and #2. This fund will over time drop to zero because of the following monumental breakthrough.
4. Whether they be world conditions or inspired leadership by the major countries, it is conceivable that the G8 Nations can someday simply agree to total disarmament over, say, a 10 year period. This time, all nuclear weapons should be immediately and terminally dismantled. If at the height of the Cold War the U.S. and USSR found it possible to agree on philosophical disarmament, it should be easier and almost predictable for the G8 to take this grand step for the future of humanity. Can you imagine the benefits if the entire budget of all countries can subsequently be focused on benefiting people and our planet? This is partly why Japan and Costa Rica can be so economically competitive already, for the former has minimal defense expenditures and the latter has no military. If crime and drugs can also become obsolete, allocations for police, the judiciary, prisons and the like can also be shifted to the 7 R's of education, the environment and a sustainable world.

How long will this all take? Maybe never if you're a pessimistic, or realist. But only three generations would be about a century, an infinitesimally minuscule period considering that we have 5 billion years left before the Sun expands and engulfs Planet Earth.

Yet, to be truly simple-minded, it is not impossible for all this to occur in a decade. How? Say Peak Oil and Global Warming (*details are provided in **Book 1***) begin to show cataclysmic reality. The only solution possible to minimize global economic and political collapse would be for the G8 Nations to provide emergency powers to the United Nations to solve the problem.:

- In the 2009 G8 Summit, President Clinton or Obama calls for immediate and total world disarmament, starting with the U.S. halving our defense budget, and other nations, likewise. A Republican will philosophically not be able to take this colossal step. We can afford to be so magnanimous because we are so dominant that this first step should not cripple our ability to defend our nation, if other countries also comply. The defense budgets would then be applied to fix the energy/environment problem, plus engineer the peace. The military units themselves would be re-assigned to the task at hand, then phased out over time. They are already trained to do so in natural disasters. The military-industrial complex would merely shift their thrust to renewable energy and environmental remediation.

- Pick 2020 as the year in which hydrogen would be made free. GoCo's (*government-company partnerships*) would be formed to insure that the technologies and infrastructure would be available to provide for free renewable hydrogen by that date. Of course, the tax structure will likely need to be adjusted to actually pay for this FREE energy. (*See Chapter 3 in **Book 1, Simple Solutions for Planet Earth**.*)
- As it might be difficult to develop an all-hydrogen system in a few short years, it would be wise to provide for a parallel pathway: biomethanol. Methanol is the only bioliquid that can be directly processed through a fuel cell, so a comprehensive effort should also be focused on the direct methanol fuel cell, gasification and catalysis of biomass into this fuel and retrofitting of supply lines. (*See Chapter 2 of **Book 1**.*) As windpower has more recently become competive, a major effort should be focused on offshore windpower, where bladders in the ocean can be fed electrolyzed hydrogen for export. As utility companies today do not trust the winds supplying more than 20% of their demand, this bulk storage also can be tapped to provide electricity when winds are low, thus eliminating this handicap from wind power. Details can be found in Chapter 2 of ***Book 1.***

Can all this be accomplished in a dozen years? Well, the Hoover Dam was built in five years (*early 30's*), the Atomic Bomb took five years (*early 40's*), Man on the Moon was pronounced by JFK in 1961 (*with Neil Armstrong monumental step occurring in 1969),*, and the largest aquarium in the world was built in Georgia in four years (*2001 to 2005*). Mankind, or individuals, when challenged, can meet difficult goals. Ironically enough, the fortuitous double hammer of Peak Oil and Global Warming could well be that "Attack of the Aliens" requirement for humanity to set aside conflicts to arrive at a simple solution to end all wars.

## The Simple Solutions to Crime and Wars

The two key leaders to bring an end to crime and wars are the United Nations and the United States. The following scenario can be projected:

- In January of 2009 a Democratic is inaugurated as the 44$^{th}$ President of the United States. A Republican is too beholden to the military-industry complex to take the world leadership against wars.
- By the end of 2011 Peak Oil and Global Warming show all the signs of total disaster that the G8 Nations in 2012 agree to totally disarm over the next decade and provide the United Nations a mandate to eliminate crime and war. Yes, why not add crime to the goals, including three strikes and you're dead.
- The glorious vision of 2020 is then of Planet Earth again being secure and Humanity at Peace.

If not 2009, 2011, 2012 and 2020, then, some sequence within the following decade. The only requisite is for that monumental cataclysm, whatever form it might take.

A Democrat, however, will not be able to even mention "Three Strikes and You're Dead." A Republican would be more inclined to do so, but only if there is a groundswell of national fervor for this draconian solution. This could take a long time to build, and most probably will never gain any major foothold. It is incredible that our society, as flawed as it is to make necessary decisions, is better conformed to end wars forever, but because of ethics and morality, might forever be afflicted with crime. Maybe there will be no simple solution for crime.

# CHAPTER 2: DIAMONDS—ETERNAL LIFE

## Diamonds

"A Diamond is Forever," is what the Diamond Trading Company advertises. ***Diamonds are Forever*** was a 1971 James Bond flick with Sean Connery. ***Wikipedia*** spends 19 pages on the subject, and reports that $9 billion worth is annually mined, mostly in Africa, is the hardest known naturally occurring material and is a transparent crystal consisting of tetrahedrally bonded carbon atoms. When carbon forms a rhombohedral crystal, it is graphite, which is soft, opaque and dark gray.[352]

One carat of diamond weighs .07 ounces and costs around $7000, but the cost/carat increases with size, as a 5 carat piece now wholesales for $115,000, or $23,000/carat. The largest one was the Cullinan Diamond, owned by Queen Elizabeth II at 3,107 karats (*it was made into other cuts*), however, in 2007, a 7,000 carat greenish diamond, about the size of a coconut, was purportedly found in South Africa. The largest ruby (*an aluminum oxide*) is 2,475 carats (*about a pound*) and largest emerald (*silicon oxide*) 1,686 carats. These two gems have no carbon.

Scientists have mimicked nature, and artificial diamonds will someday not be readily distinguishable from the real ones by the human eye. Anyway, rubies and emeralds are rarer than diamonds, but both can also be artificially produced.

Alas, diamonds are not forever, as they can burn at 800 °C (*might make a nice counterpoint title to **Fahrenheit 451**, the temperature at which paper combusts, and also the title of a novel by Ray Bradbury*) and over a long period of time (*maybe even the age of the Universe*) decay into graphite. But the carbon nature of diamonds links to human life, which is also carbon-based. There is, of course, the notion that life could just as well have been silicon (*atomic number 14, element found in the popular photovoltaic cells, glass and breast implants*) based, and sand (*another compound of silicon*), too, lasts a long time. In any case, diamonds are symbolically appropriate for a joyful eternal life, for it refracts with brilliance, is full of color and lives forever.

## The Fountain of Youth

The whole concept of immortality started, murkily enough, in the 4th century BC, involving Alexander the Great and the Water of Life. Spanish explorer Juan Ponce de Leon searched for it in Florida during the early 1500s, but failed. In St. Augustine, Florida is the Fountain of Youth National Archeological Park, where de Leon was supposed to have landed. Tourists come to drink the waters, even though no one believes it has any powers of longevity. But there is a secret society in this city claiming to be protectors of THE fountain. Las Vegas illusionist David Copperfield, it is reported, has a fountain of youth on his island of Musha Cay, and has promised to have biologists test it. It would be pathetic if some scientist actually takes this on with some seriousness.

You can improve your odds to live longer through the luck of good genes and by: having a strong social network (*your family*), more education (*which is correlated to a better health plan*), dedicated flossing (*gum disease affects the heart*), good bowel movements (*to reduce colon cancer*), not smoking (*although an unexpected number of really old people smoke a lot*), getting married but not having children, living in a healthier environment, eating smart and less, maintaining an elevated level of high density lipoprotein in your blood, minimizing inflammation, exercising and minimizing stress. ***Wikipedia*** has an entry for immortality, but much of the 23 pages dally on spiritualism and fictional works. But, in this chapter, I plan to take it to the limit: real, scientific, eternal life. One can go back to the Egyptians and wander through religion (*which will be covered in Chapter 5*), but the only focus of this chapter will thus be to explore the scientific validity for immortality. How did I first get interested in this field?

## My Early Years in Biotechnology

In 1968, I found myself in the chemical engineering department at Louisiana State University with a need to come up with a PhD topic. I can still remember my wife, Pearl, reading LIFE magazine, and casually mentioning, why not use a laser? The invention of the **laser**, which stands for **l**ight **a**mplification by the **s**timulated **e**mission of **r**adiation, goes back to 1958, when I was a freshman at Stanford University. Arthur Schawlow (*who was at Bell Labs then, but later came to Stanford when I was a junior*) and Charles Townes (*who was then at Columbia University, but later, ended up at the University of California at Berkeley*) wrote the seminal paper that year, "Infrared and Optical Masers (*the M standing for microwave*)" in ***Physical Review***. Townes shared the Nobel Prize in Physics in 1964 and Schawlow obtained the same honor in 1981. Townes returns in Chapter 4 on Search for Extraterrestrial Intelligence.

Sir Chandrasekhara Venkata Raman, founder of Raman spectroscopy, actually published the first paper on the possibility of lasers. Later in his life, he was asked, "isn't it a shame that you are not given credit for inventing the laser?" "No, no, no," he said. "Many of us come up with many ideas. It is he who takes it to that identifiable level that deserves all the recognition." I can identify with that attitude, and for that, I will no doubt get credited for nothing. But, like Sir Raman, I can live with that.

By 1969, I was able to help convince Milk Proteins, Incorporated to provide $10,000 towards building a tunable laser to sterilize milk. Professor David Greenberg was my major professor, who was instrumental in securing the grant. Why tunable? Because if all the laser energy can be focused at one coherent frequency unto a contaminating cell, where life-determining bonds can be split, that would be an elegant and efficient way to sterilize milk. There were several problems. One, a tunable laser was not sold, so I had to build it from scratch. Then I had to sterilize some bacterium. In those days, the late 60's, only visible frequencies were possible. Visible laser light is very inefficient for sterilization. It was one of my most depressing periods of my life when I couldn't get the laser to work and a chemistry professor laughed that I could use a blow torch to sterilize *Escherichia coli* in a heat resistant test tube. Why bother? He was joking, but it still hurt.

In a real tragedy, two of my young nephews drowned, so I flew from Baton Rouge to Southern California to attend the funeral. On the way back, while dozing on the plane, it suddenly occurred to me that I could use a diffraction grating to produce monochromatic laser frequencies in a manner that could be focused unto a micro drop of *E. coli* in solution. Let's see, was this a miracle, a vision or the product of a dream? Maybe they're all the same thing. A laser monochromatically producing all the colors of the rainbow just by adjusting the grating angle. Wow, color, and potentially so vivid (*coherent*), too. Was this the genesis of Rainbow Visions? For sure, this was the principle that linked me to Professor Townes in Chapter 4.

As the power was relatively low, what about using exogenous photosensitizers, more colors, that is, a dye that could transfer the laser light indirectly to vulnerable links in the gene? This combination worked, providing discretely tunable frequencies from 440-460 nanometers using 7-diethylamino 4-methylcoumarin and 570-600 nm using rhodamine B and 6G, allowing sufficient energy to be transferred to jiggle the DNA and RNA bonds in the vicinity of 265 nm. When toluidine blue at specific wavelengths in the blue spectrum was used as the sensitizer, growth catalysis was experienced in the bacteria sample, and when acridine orange dye and red laser light were combined, sterilization occurred. I was planning to frequency double to directly get to the ideal ultraviolet frequencies, but had run out of money and time, and had done enough for my dissertation, anyway. I never did take that next step, but it should be interesting, and useful, to do this today, a third of a century later. Excimer lasers can now accomplish this task. Anyone reading this and wanting to carry on the research can contact me for details.

Thusly armed with a PhD in biochemical engineering, in 1971 I began teaching at the University of Hawaii. This story continues in the chapter on education.

## The Middle Years

One can logically conclude that planning your life in a cohesive and purposeful manner should optimize success. My life, conversely, mostly appears to resemble Brownian Movement adventures of a misguided soul. However, whether it was pure luck or genius, just by focusing on the search for the ultimate technology, a few good things happened.

In the 1970's I virtually stumbled unto hydrogen at that first Miami gathering of the Hydrogen Romantics, jumped to NASA's Project Orion (*which will lead to Chapter 4 on SETI*) associating me to Carl Sagan, skipped over to the Lawrence Livermore National Laboratory to work for

Edward Teller, and then on to Washington, D.C. to become U.S. Senator Spark Matsunaga's Special Assistant on Energy. All this occurred in less than a decade. In the early '80's, Paul Yuen and I invented the Pacific International Center for High Technology Research, which was described in the Blue Revolution chapter of ***Book 1***, paving the way for what to me had the potential to be the greatest research program brought to the University of Hawaii, the National Science Foundation Marine Bioproducts Engineering Center (*MarBEC*), for the sum of money I set aside in the middle to late '80's to develop biological techniques to produce the ultimate form of energy from the sea, drew to Hawaii the individuals who became the prime supporters of the Center.

In this period from the 80's into the 90's, our attempts to secure an NSF Engineering Center failed every time. We were very close in the early 90's, for we gained a site visit. All of this was written about in ***Book 1***.

A year later, in 1993, I visited NSF and they said, why don't you focus on one area of ocean technology. That's it! No one at NSF suggested that we hire Oskar Zaborsky, for this input came from Neil Rossmeissl, the hydrogen program manager from the U.S. Department of Energy.

But selecting marine biotechnology was not a slam dunk certainty that we could prevail at the national level. The University of Hawaii had a chemistry department which was recognized as a pioneer in natural marine products, but the College of Engineering, which had to spearhead the effort, did not have even one person who researched this area.

Credibility comes from performance, not necessarily producing anything all that useful, but garnering the dollars to do the work. Mind you, a Nobel Prize and pathfinding results are worth more, but very little of what most university researchers produce is recognized in current time as all that important. It is the compounding of effort, over years of toil that someday brings worth. In the meantime, you teach, educate students, publish and get more grants. Thus, by the mid '90's all the ingredients were in place for something I began to refer to as the M Curse.

## My Waning Years in Biotechnology

How does one mourn the death of a grandchild? There is an Oriental proverb that says one's responsibility to family is not completed until the grandchildren are successful. I thus have, in part, failed, for there has been a premature death, of a promising young child.

I have no real children, but I can point to a number of visions in various stages of attaining reality, or not. In most, I am a generation removed from actual parenthood. That is, I planted a crucial seed. In 1990, when I chaired the World Hydrogen Energy Conference held in Hawaii, I was referred to as the grandfather of hydrogen—U.S. Senator Spark Matsunaga was the father—for I had, a decade previously, drafted the very first legislation on hydrogen introduced in the U.S. Senate. I was all of 50 years old when called grandfather. I few years later, at a biohydrogen workshop in Tokyo, the speaker, David Hall of the UK, showed a slide of a project on which we had worked together, and pointed out I was a collaborator, and he referred to me as the grandfather of the field. This was partly, too, because I had chaired the first three international biohydrogen workshops a decade earlier mentioned in the previous section. Having written the first Senate draft of the bill on hydrogen, which became law, I take particular pride in serving as the grandfather of biohydrogen, and, perhaps, hydrogen in general (*Chapter 4* ***in Book 1*** *treats this subject.*) Yes, Henry Cavendish, in 1766, discovered hydrogen, the most abundant element in the universe, but call him an early great grandfather.

### The M Curse

To make a very long story short, in 1997 we finally were awarded the National Science Foundation Marine Bioproducts Engineering Center—MarBEC—one of my grandchildren. But to best appreciate the promise and tragedy, I need to go back to the beginning. Let me share one person's view of the elements that had to be put in place to establish the groundwork to bring to the middle of the Pacific, at the University of Hawaii, a National Science Foundation Engineering Research Center (*NSF ERC*), one of the most coveted jewels in academia, for involved was funding of $5 million/year for ten years, or more, in an emerging technology to bring supreme eminence in the field for the selected university, while boosting economic development for the community and nation. Selection as the NSF ERC designated your institution as the national, if not world, leader in that particular technology, and provided the foundation to initiate a new industry in your state.

So, let us analyze what went right and wrong, for both the development and demise can teach lessons for the next generation. Also, MarBEC, as some visions do, and, perhaps, livings things too, morphed into another biotech center, this one somewhat linked to a new high priority area for the campus, medicine. More and more, I'm beginning to visualize what appears to be a great grandchild. So is this a tragedy? Maybe not. A curse? Yes, maybe still.

## Origins of the Curse

There is, of course, no such thing as a curse. However, in attempting to pull together the threads forming the fabric representing one of the greatest achievements attained by the University of Hawaii, one can't help but notice the significance and preponderance of "M's," that is, people whose last names started with an M. I call it a curse because many M's died for the cause.

There was, of course, U.S. Senator Spark **M**atsunaga, whose authorship of bills ranging from peace to hydrogen to ocean thermal energy conversion, set the stage for **M**arBEC. His administrative assistant in Washington, D.C., Cherry **M**atano, ran the office with a velvet hammer, and, in ways she did not realize, contributed to the foundation of the curse, or opportunity. She lived to a riper old age, but at this writing is not doing well.

Professor Akira **M**itsui was a University of Tokyo graduate who married a citizen of the United States, and thus, eventually ended up teaching at the University of **M**iami. He became director of the International Research Center for **M**arine Bioscience and Technology. We met at various technical gatherings and formed a good relationship. "Pat, Pat, he screamed late one night to me on a call, Nejat is trying to steal my money." By the 1990's I had chaired the Secretary of Energy's Hydrogen Technical Panel and the 1990 World Hydrogen Energy Conference, and had gained a reputation as one who could help people in need, especially in hydrogen related matters. At any university, the leader of a national grant is faced with a myriad of shortfalls, and virtually his only option is to tax the people doing the research. Generally, this director was instrumental in securing the funds, so he had a rightful imperative. I, of course, tried to help by reaching Professor Nejat Veziroglu, Director of the Clean Energy Research Institute, and usually ended up commiserating with him on the agony of research administration, but the wonderful promise of hydrogen. But Professor Mitsui felt I did the best I could, for the all the funds were not, in fact, stolen.

Professor **M**itsui collected, and fiercely protected, a large number of **m**arine **m**icroorganisms, mostly from the Caribbean. An influential post-doctoral (*a one to two year period that many technical researchers devote after obtaining a doctorate to better prepare them for the real world*) student of **M**itsui's in the early 1980's was Tadashi **M**atsunaga, who went on to become editor of the ***Journal of Marine Biotechnology***, dean of the College of Engineering at Tokyo University of Agriculture and Technology and is now headed towards the presidency. I spent a sabbatical period on Matsunaga's Tokyo campus during a crucial period just after we were notified of the NSF **M**arBEC award. Professional **M**atsunaga also, earlier, spent some time in Hawaii, and was the first International Professor for the Blue Revolution.

Professor Shigetoh **M**iyachi, a fellow student with **M**atsui in Japan, after a fruitful University of Tokyo career, left academia in the late 1980's to become the director of the Japan **M**arine Biotechnology Institute. Professor **M**iyachi, then, was the foremost authority in marine biotechnology, and, as will later be described, was an important partner in the formation of **M**arBEC. He came to the first PICHTR biohydrogen workshop earlier mentioned.

Dr. Jun **M**iyake was a prominent biotechnologist in the Japan Ministry of International Trade and Industry (**M**ITI) at Tsukuba. I met him in the early 80's at a Beijing gathering chaired by Professor Veziroglu. I'm tempted to acronymize "the early 80's" into TE80's because this term will be used a lot—for pieces of the **M**arBEC puzzle all formed in that period—but won't.

Professor Kazuhisa **M**iyamoto of Osaka University post-doc'd at the University of California in the early 80's, joining a team supervised by another young researcher, John Benemann, who as of this writing, is completing our overview draft on biohydrogen. **M**iyamoto in the nineties served as the lead scientist in a visiting review group sent by **M**ITI to evaluate the potential of a joint Japan-U.S. venture in biotechnology. You will note that all these individuals have names starting with **M**.

Unknown to me during this formative early '80s period was a threesome at the Engineering Directorate of the National Science Foundation: Oskar Zaborsky, Harvey Blanch and Lynn Preston. No M's here, but, what is a curse without a conspiracy. All three were keys to the **M**arBEC success story: Zaborsky, at the University of Hawaii, was the principle investigator; Blanch became chairman of the University of California at Berkeley Chemical Engineering Department and deputy director of **M**arBEC; and Lynn Preston served as the NSF coordinator for the ERC. A cold case can be made that these three, with their Japanese connections, planned and orchestrated a future Pacific engineering research center in biochemical engineering to feature international cooperation. Is this legal? This is called good vision and careful planning. On the other hand, perhaps **M**arBEC was all purely coincidental. This just goes to show that irrefutable evidence is not necessarily germane to cause and effect, just like there is no such thing as a curse.

But back to that hypothetical Curse, the American side suffered. The original director of **M**arBEC, the very young Oskar Zaborsky then, had escaped with his family from East Germany around the time when the follow-on director, Alexander **M**alahoff, and his family, escaped from Russia at the end of World War II. Let's see now, the Soviet Union and East Germany now had an inside track to American biotech secrets. No, that's not the conspiracy or genesis for the curse, but, one can't help but wonder if this similar experience affected their psychology, as we shall see. Lorenz **M**agaard also emigrated from Europe (*West Germany*), and his first connection to **M**arBEC was when, as acting dean of the School of Ocean and Earth Science and Technology, he signed the approval letter to hire Zaborsky, and, later, went on to serve as director of the **M**arBEC educational program under **M**alahoff.

Kenneth **M**ortimer was selected president of the University of Hawaii in 1992 during a period of declining budgets, because of poor economic conditions in the State. He was an "expert" at reducing expenditures, and became by the nature of the times and task a very unpopular president. However, he believed that **m**arine biotechnology offered a promising hope for a future new industry in Hawaii, and his key contribution was that he overrode his staff by providing significant cost-matching. Had he not made this command decision, the school would not even have submitted the **M**arBEC proposal to NSF.

Kelton **M**cKinley grew up in Ohio and found his way to Hawaii after he obtained a PhD in ecology from **M**ichigan State University, and taught for a period at a small college in **M**aryland. At a low point of his career, while on the Porsche sales staff in Honolulu, I hired him to become the coordinator of the biohydrogen research effort at the University of Hawaii. In academia, one cannot just hire anyone. If any position opens up, or funds are secured to add staff, a selection committee is formed, and there is a range of Equal Employment Opportunity, gender equity and other factors that rightfully affect the process. The reality, though, is that the preferred person will be selected, with, maybe, some excessive paperwork necessary. The process to hire professors, deans and directors is similar, and leaves much to be desired at public universities.

Even if you have been dozing off, you should have noticed that virtually everyone thus far has had a last name starting with the letter **M**. The ingredients for the curse are being positioned, and all these **M**'s were influential in helping develop pre-**M**arBEC resources. To take some of the mystery away, as of this writing, as long as these Japanese citizens kept their primary household in their country, they not only survived, but flourished. The curse applied only to **M**'s in the United States. These seeds of "**M**" were thus germinating for at least a dozen years.

## The M Curse Begins

On May 31, 1994, at the age of 65, Akira **M**itsui died of cancer related complications. He had lived in Key Biscayne, Florida for 22 years.

What to do with the **M**itsui collection? The University of **M**iami seemed ambivalent about maintaining the lot. Both Japan and Germany expressed interest in taking it over. Three thousand samples with 928 known strains. The value was estimated to be $1 million, but the potential for biotechnology applications was priceless.

In a Department of Energy hydrogen review meeting held at Coral Gables, Florida, the program manager, Neil Rossmeissl, asked, "do you think the Japanese would pay half the cost of moving and taking care of the **M**itsui Collection, if we transferred it to Hawaii?" Ever the opportunist, I said, "yes, that would be possible, and yes, Hawaii would be an excellent home for the **m**icroorganisms."

In November of 1994, the Research Institute of Innovative Technology for the Earth (*RITE*) hosted a follow-on meeting in Tokyo to the various gatherings held in Hawaii from the mid-80s. Another University of Tokyo professor, Yoichi Kaya, had served on the board of the Pacific International Center for High Technology Research, original sponsor of the biohydrogen meetings, and was director of RITE. Professor Kaya was also a key leader for the Kyoto Protocol regarding global climate change. This particular workshop featured continuous presentations for two days, where speakers spoke in a dark room. No one knew if you were there or not, so I went back to my room and took a nap from 2PM-4PM, for the talks, to me, anyway, were mostly too, too boring, and were followed by dinner, with various small groups going out to karaoke bars at the end. Typically, sleep came after midnight, and the whole thing re-started the following morning at with breakfast at 7:30AM.

I was looking for an opportunity to bring up Rossmeissl's request, when at the end of the second day, Professor Tadashi **M**atsunaga and I found ourselves as the only two left in his favorite karaoke bar. He was asleep more than awake, but asked me, "we don't think that the American government would allow the export of the **M**itsui Collection to Japan, even though we paid more for that collection and sent many of our best students to help. We would like to provide $50,000/year to share the Collection in Hawaii. We can also send one of our young scientists to take care of the collection. What do you think the Department of Energy would say?" Not sure if he was fully awake, but appreciating this incredible good fortune, I sort of repeated what I mentioned to Rossmeissl, "yes, that would be possible, and yes, Hawaii would be an excellent home for the **m**icroorganisms." There was a lot of luck floating around, but, certainly, this is another example making your luck.

The following morning, a select group of individuals were invited by RITE to participate in a discussion to agree on cooperative research. Chairing the meeting was Jun **M**iyake, who appeared to have forgotten to comb his hair, and was doing this primarily because Kazuhisa **M**iyamoto, the moderator, had overslept, and came rushing in a few minutes into the discussion, apologizing profusely. As I said, these past few days were strenuous and most of them had not had not had much sleep. I was the only person in good awake shape. Sitting across from me was Tadashi **M**atsunaga, who, very early in the meeting, keeled over, hit his forehead on the table and had an obvious red welt all morning. Of course, they were all **M's**, but I bring this up because all three of them no doubt had sat through two whole days of lectures, went out at night (*where, as I indicated, all the really important discussions occur*), and had only a few hours of sleep. I've noticed this syndrome in dedicated scientists, and early in my career found a simple solution: take a nap in the afternoon.

As **M**itsui was a jealous guardian of the collection, no one previously had any access to it. Only later did I learn that many of the Japanese researchers sent to work on the **M**itsui collection took the more useful ones back home just by stuffing a test tube in their pocket. They probably would have been able to officially request and obtain anything they wanted, but by the mid-1990's, the shipment of bioorganisms was becoming a problem. Native countries were beginning to appreciate the value of their indigenous microbes and, conversely, governments were getting worried about dangerous germs entering the country.

There, too, is the attraction of Hawaii. Everyone wants to spend some time here. That really is an unfair advantage for us. On the other hand, most government program managers look upon any visit, any conference, in Hawaii, as a boondoggle and unjustified. So, there is a kind of wash here. In Tadashi **M**atsunaga's laboratory (*of approximately 50*), there is a group known as the Hawaii **M**afia, which controlled everything. They were the ones who were carefully selected to spend several months to more than a year at our laboratory in Hawaii.

On December 8, 1994, I wrote to Neil Rossmeissl about ***An Urgent Need to Resolve a Crisis with Opportunity for Cost-Matching***:

> *As you know, Catherine Gregoire, Paul Weaver and I participated in the Tokyo Biological Hydrogen Production Workshop last month. Maybe the hotel was not quite up to my standards, but the whole event was well planned and the discussions went very well. Approximately 100 attended, and the participation of the private sector was strongly evident. The group resoundingly endorsed rotating this gathering every 18 months or so among Japan, Europe and the United States, with the next meeting most probably in Italy sometime early in 1996.*
>
> *The value of these sessions, of course, is in the after hours unofficial discussions. A proposal was expressed by the Japanese to bring Dr. Nemoto and the entire Mitsui collection to Hawaii. Japan would provide 50% cost-matching for maintaining an expanded repository, sharing the information and carrying out related research, where focus would be on marine biological microorganisms.*
>
> *One of the interesting developments at the workshop was the growing attitude that the ocean might well be the key to both large scale biological hydrogen production and remediation of global climate change. This international partnership would, quite appropriately, then, begin to focus on marine biotechnology. The article that Kelton McKinley and I wrote a couple of years ago for the charter edition of* ***The Journal of Marine Biotechnology,*** *which turned out to be the only U.S. publication in that issue, no doubt provided some confidence that the University of Hawaii was ideal for this*

*purpose. Secondly, in terms of proximity and cultural similarities, Japan is clearly more comfortable interfacing in Hawaii.*

*From all indications, there seems to be a scramble on to gain samples from the Mitsui collection. While a few researchers from scattered laboratories might benefit, there must be a better alternative to what is looming as general dissolution of a potentially valuable resource.*

*As McKinley and Weaver are closely involved with the subject, have the appropriate backgrounds and are personally familiar with the key researchers in the U.S. and Japan, I have asked them to follow up with you and Catherine to lead the task to come up with a more intelligent solution and look into creation of an international biological hydrogen repository. Eli Greenbaum might also be included in an advisory capacity.*

*It is essential for steps to be taken now to take advantage of this opportunity. We think that Hawaii is the logical site for this activity, but we stand ready to act for the national welfare should another location become obvious or necessary. I look forward to your comments.*

*Aloha.*

Copies were sent to various national labs and Department of Energy decision-makers. Weaver worked for the National Renewable Energy Laboratory and Greenbaum was from the Oak Ridge National Laboratory. Nemoto was a post-doc under Mitsui at that time, and, after a stint in Hawaii, he joined Professor Matsunaga's department.

In record time for national consensus, I was able send Matsunaga the following letter on January 24, 1995:

*Dear Dr. Matsunaga:*

*You will be very pleased to learn that your unofficial suggestion that Japan would be interested in cost-matching the relocation and operation of the Mitsui collection from Florida to Hawaii has been very strongly endorsed by key officials within the Department of Energy and National Renewable Energy Laboratory. Also, the University of Miami has blessed the transfer.*

*There are a few important logistical and legal hurdles to overcome, but we are beginning to resolve them. As a first step, the USDOE will provide continued support for the individuals managing the project until the summer. We trust that the actual movement of the organisms can occur later this year.*

*Catherine Gregoire-Pardo (remember, Tsukiji?) will be attending the hydrogen conference in Japan next week and has been briefed by the USDOE to work out an agreement. Can you please arrange the appropriate meetings for her to discuss this cooperative effort?*

*It might be of interest to you that there is new leadership in our U.S. Congress, where early and strong enthusiasm has surfaced for hydrogen. The chairman of the key House committee on Science and Technology just introduced a $100 million hydrogen bill and has been asked by the Secretary of Energy's Hydrogen Technical Advisory Committee to provide a keynote address at our next gathering in March.*

*Good luck on your discussions with Catherine.*

*Aloha,*

What also helped to move this along was that I was at that time the chairman of the Secretary of Energy's Hydrogen Technical Advisory Panel, and that I was the one who had written the original legislation 15 years earlier. Plus, I had by then taken at least 50 trips to Japan and learned the system. Unfortunately, I never learned the language, which was no doubt a psychological hang-up to being a Japanese-American growing up in Hawaii during World War II.

International agreement was reached: $100,000 per year from Japan, and the same from the USDOE. Plus, we bring to Hawaii the Mother Lode of marine biotechnology, at a time when we were thinking about proposing an engineering research center focused on this topic. No local staff, but the beginnings of an international collaboration, building critical mass to our efforts.

## The Curse Continues

Kelton McKinley was assigned to meet with the quarantine people to determine how best to have the Mitsui Collection sent to Hawaii. Little did we know that the biological scientists at the university had had a long and bitter struggle to import anything resembling bacteria into the State. Even simple teaching samples were a problem.

Kelton presented his case to Larry Nakahara and Amy Higa of the Plant Quarantine Branch of the State of Hawaii Department of Agriculture. As I am told, Kelton then asked, "how long will you need for your approval?" Larry responded, "maybe two or three years." "Two or three years for only one specimen?" Asked Kelton. "Do you have more than one sample?" Amy inquired. When Kelton said "maybe 3000 species," they promptly kicked him out of the conference room.

Now, it is possible that Dr. McKinley was a bit angered. He was very bright, quick-witted and, well, short-tempered. Kelton had grown up in Ohio, and, he told me, watched his father, a union organizer, get beaten. Ohio, furthermore, has odd enclaves of religious cults. He was divorced from his wife, but was very protective of his daughter, who must have been about 7 years old at that time. His wife had recently written that she would be sending their daughter to one of those religious schools in that state that did not believe in evolution. Kelton was already in a troubled mental state when he walked into the quarantine office.

With no particular confidence, we arranged a second meeting, and, just as I was about to enter the conference room, a person who looked very familiar, walked by, who also recognized me. He was Dr. Glenn Takahashi (*no relation*), and he was Nakahara's and Higa's supervisor. We had last seen each other, maybe, half a century ago, when, as kids, we played. He decided to sit in. Also, there was Dr. Lyle Wong, higher up in the organization from the Division of Plant Industry. I don't know if my friendship with Glen was it, for in the totality of things, anything or nothing can make an important difference, or if Dr. Wong was the key, but, in effect, we were constructively instructed to meet with the director of the Department of Agriculture, who would gain the governor's approval, and go to the State Legislature, as they were being difficult only because the laws forced them to be conservative. We also had to gain the approval of the Board of Agriculture.

On March 23, 1995, Kelton McKinley instantly died of a heart attack, at the age of 45. HNEI did not have another micro-bio person, so, we asked Dr. Kathleen Baker, someone with approximately the background of Kelton, and who was hired to do some lab work for Kelton, to take on a leadership role. She had just the right unassuming personality (*unlike Kelton*) to take on the task, so I made her Interim Director of the Bioresources Laboratory at Kewalo Basin, where the repository would be located.

We made the rounds of the Ag offices and the State Legislature. They all loved what we were proposing: the basis for a new industry in marine biotechnology for the State of Hawaii. We then faced the Board of Agriculture. We were, again, in luck. One of the members was a former distinguished professor with my Institute and another was a long-time collaborator on environmental matters. The Board not only approved our application, but also determined that a new law was not necessary, for there are provisions for permitting the importation of the type of microorganisms on our list. They were mostly sensitive to larger organisms, like unagi, a type of freshwater eel, which is a Japanese delicacy. So, magically, from a two to three year ordeal, per specimen, to almost total approval of the entire Mitsui Collection, we had come a long way in a few short weeks. Actually, there were several bacteria on a restricted list, which we had to still work out, but that was relatively trivial.

## Not All Curses Turn Out Bad

Within a week of Dr. McKinley's death, the SOEST dean's office, procedurally, began to retrieve the position. In some desperation, I wrote to Dean Barry Raleigh, to recapture that position and begin a search for Kelton's replacement. He agreed that we could advertise, and an ad was placed with a deadline of June 6.

By the summer of 1995, the Mitsui Collection Project was going well. We decided to host a dedication, and with input from Professor Matsunaga, we named it the Mitsui-McKinley International Marine Biotechnology Culture Collection.

During this period, the University of Hawaii was in the throes of huge budget shortfalls. There was a rumor that a freeze would be placed on hiring. Unless you try to hire an important football coach at a university, it is essentially impossible to quickly bring on board anyone in any timely manner. Acting deans sometimes stay on in that role for years, maybe even up to a decade. It took all of one week for the University of Hawaii to hire coach Gregg McMackin in 2008. We succeeded 23 years earlier with Kel's replacement. There is an amorphous cloud obscuring what really happened that summer because I can't seem to find all the legal paperwork, but in July:

- o I vaguely remember a memo dated July 18 from Dean Raleigh telling me there is a freeze coming so don't hire anyone. I interpreted that to mean if the freeze is announced.
- o I recall asking Associate Dean Magaard the following day, for Dean Raleigh had left on his summer vacation, to please approve hiring Oskar Zaborsky, for there is not now a freeze, but there could be one tomorrow.
- o Magaard signs.
- o Then a month later, Raleigh, back from his vacation, sends me a sarcastic letter for selecting someone like Zaborsky, although maybe it was because I had hired someone when there was a freeze, which had, in fact, occurred. I accepted the blame for some misunderstanding or procedural uncertainty.

Sometimes one has to bumble into things to avoid the specter of insubordination. I could not help, though, responding to Dean Raleigh's deserved sarcasm with:

> *Thank you for your memo of August 21, 1995. Yes, I too noticed some imperfection in Oskar Zaborsky's publication record, but there were important intangibles that made him by far the best candidate. I look forward to meeting with you tomorrow afternoon to discuss these strategic points.*
>
> *To begin with, your statement that "we don't have the scientists to do the necessary research, except for one in the Chemistry Department," is much too pessimistic. For example, when we first initiated the hydrogen program nearly a decade ago, we had no researchers with a proven background in this field. We were able, however, to largely recruit faculty from throughout the campus, and during the past three years of annual reviews—and these are tough three-day sessions involving a panel of about a dozen from industry and academia—have been ranked #1 among universities. In fact, I'm pretty certain that we are at the top in the whole world with respect to a totally integrated academic program, as now and then I'm asked to evaluate these research programs in Japan and the European Union.*
>
> *To set the stage for Zaborsky, we have already begun to form a team of potential contributors from SOEST, Pacific Biomedical Research Center, School of Natural Sciences, Cancer Research Center, College of Tropical Agriculture and Human Resources and various national laboratories. I've been told that during the next fifteen months the best universities and a few companies in Japan would like to send six post-docs to work with us for one and two year assignments. At the local level, we have been meeting not only with elements within the UH System, but also organizations such as the Oceanic Institute and Cyanotech to gain their participation. A report of our state-wide capabilities in natural products will be presented to Vice President Smith next month. We have the basis for forming leading programs in biopharmaceuticals,*

*biological energy production and agribusiness. What we do not have is a leader to bring together this potential critical mass. That person is Zaborsky.*

*We have succeeded in gaining control of the pre-eminent marine biotechnology culture collection (with an estimate worth of about $1 million, even though the true value is inestimable), and are talking to curators of other international collections for possible transfer here. The Japanese and U.S. governments have agreed to cost-share the transfer and maintenance of the repository at our Bioresources Laboratory. Perhaps most enticing of all is that discussions have been initiated for each country to contribute $1 million/year to support research on the International Marine Biotechnology Culture Collection. This will open the door to industrial contributions. However, to be realistic, I wonder if we can pull this off with our current reputation and paucity of proven capabilities. We need someone like Zaborsky to insure that current talk becomes true substance.*

*When I initially inquired with key funding agencies about who they might recommend for this position in question, the feedback was nearly unanimous. Both the Japan Ministry of International Trade and Industry and the U.S. Department of Energy recommended Zaborsky for this role—not merely endorsed, but recommended him. We can now add the National Institutes of Health to this list of supporters. Follow-up discussions have reinforced our selection.*

*With respect to other options, there is no one else with the credibility Zaborsky brings to develop an integrated multi-million dollar research program at the University of Hawaii in marine biotechnology, especially since the bridge to early funding needs to be linked to biological hydrogen production and environmental remediation. There are some top scholars and consultants we know who have published extensively, but each has some major flaw in personality, motivation or leadership ability. We subsequently were careful in the search process—for some of them review our proposals, and we couldn't afford to alienate key individuals in the field. If Oskar declines our best offer (and his acceptance is far from certain under any affordable circumstances) we should be able to find an outstanding researcher who probably will need a lot of help and a decade to build a strong program in this area.*

*However, the timing is now, as the current State and University budgetary conditions are such that if we miss on Zaborsky, it is doubtful that we will be able to marshal any support for a second try, thus forfeiting our chance for attaining greater international prominence in the area of natural marine products. We will also stand to lose:*

*a) much of the above;*
*b) the $250,000 contribution from Hawaiian Electric Company to support an individual in hydrogen systems;*
*c) a golden opportunity to gain a leadership position in international biopharmaceuticals, with good potential for funding from the National Institutes of Health and the private sector; and*
*d) the momentum towards our quest to bring to the University of Hawaii both a National Science Foundation Center for Bioproducts Development and U.S. Department of Energy Hydrogen Technology Center.*

*The campaign for Zaborsky is, thus, much larger than the position previously occupied by Kelton McKinley. You assisted Kel build-up the Bioresources Laboratory, the base from which Oskar will operate. Without this foundation we would not be able to take this next step. But indeed we can compete, and I trust that you will appreciate the timing of this incredible conjunction of personalities (living and otherwise), budgets (where hydrogen, biotechnology and sustainability appear to be surviving well) and geopolitical circumstances (the Americans and Japanese want to work together in Hawaii in this field) so that we can leverage what we now have up to world class status.*

*Mahalo.*

A copy was sent to the Vice President of Research, Dean Smith. Four days later, I sent a memo to Smith, with a cc to Raleigh:

*"Since our meeting last week with President Mortimer, I had long discussions with Barry Raleigh and Oskar Zaborsky and I feel comfortable in saying that Dean Raleigh is now supportive of Dr. Zaborsky as the leader we need to raise the University of Hawaii to a leadership role in marine biotechnology. .....*

*Mahalo.*

So Oskar was hired, but primarily because he was especially gratified about being named the **M**atsunaga Fellow in Renewable Energy Engineering, a program funded by the Hawaiian Electric Company, headed by **M**ichael **M**ay. The double **M**'s worried me a bit. Oskar was part of an intricate web involving the National Science Foundation and Akira **M**itsui, and the details might be shared in a more complete publication on this matter in the future. In the meantime, it did truly bother me that soon after accepting, Zaborsky's wife, **M**arcia, yes, another **M**, was diagnosed with cancer and remained in the D.C. during Oskar's relatively short reign in Hawaii.

## The Curse Mutates

To summarize, then, the two most important researchers, **M**itsui and **M**cKinley, have died. I then retired, but as a "T," in my mind, I was never in jeopardy. President **M**ortimer resigned and moved to the State of Washington. But a short two weeks after official notification by NSF of the award, Dr. Zaborsky resigns and is replaced by Alexander **M**alahoff. Yikes, **M**alahoff directing **M**arBEC. A double "**M**." I shared my **M** Curse theory with Alex, and, I understand, that might have spooked him. Well, after a relatively brief stint, he resigned and left for New Zealand on sabbatical, where I heard that he was incapacitated by some severe heart condition. As far as I know, though, he is still alive, and, perhaps, is well. Maybe he left just in time.

What began as the greatest hope for the future economic development of Hawaii became a Ship of **M**adness. I would rather not go into the details, but the National Science Foundation served as God and killed **M**arBEC after a period of five years. Worse, soon after leaving the

University of Hawaii, Oskar was hit with an incurable degenerating nerve disease, and recently passed away.

I began writing ***THE M CURSE*** as a docu-novel soon after I retired, but was warned by the University of Hawaii lawyer, Walter Kirimitsu, who later went on to become the President of Chaminade University, that there might be some legal ramifications if I were to continue. Warned is too severe a statement, it was more me asking and he playing the role of a protective university lawyer. Thus, I sanitized the whole thing and insert it here as a condensation. This is a good a time as any to now approach the matter of eternal life itself.

## But First, Let Us Look at Other Related Life-Issues

Appendix A in **Simple Solutions Book 1** covered life expectancies and risks towards life. Here we will run through an assortment of popular health and life topics.

The Center for Disease Control and Prevention lists the top ten public health achievements (*from 1990 to 2006 in per capita improvement*):

- *Vaccination (47%* increase in immunization coverage)
- Motor-vehicle safety (40% *decrease in motor vehicle deaths*)
- Safer workplaces
- *Control of infectious diseases (45%* decrease in infectious diseases)
- Decline of deaths from coronary heart disease/stroke (*20% decline*)
- Safer and healthier foods
- Healthier mothers and babies (*35% decrease in infant mortality*)
- Family planning
- Fluoridation of drinking water
- Recognition of tobacco use as a health hazard (*30% decline*)

Most of these achievements are significant, but yet, sorely deficient. Let us closely look only at motor-vehicle safety. Of the major developed countries, the U.S. remains the worst, with 15.5 deaths per 100,000, nearly three times higher than Sweden. But it is 5 times worse in Mexico and 20 times even worse in the Bahamas. Worldwide, more than 1 million are killed on the roads every year and up to 50 million injured. The number one killer of tourists is not crime or terrorism, it is motor vehicle crashes. But this is a chapter on bio-issues. What about safer and healthier foods?

### You Are What You Eat

I can still picture in my mind a bumper sticker during Thanksgiving with a turkey carrying a sign: *You ares what you eats.* For those who actually missed this joke...you don't want to become a turkey, do you?

There have been fruit alerts. The Great Alar Scare of 1989 tarnished the reputation of red apples. Alar, or daminozide, a plant growth regulator and apple color enhancer, is a carcinogen.

But you need to drink 5000 gallons of apple juice per day to get close to laboratory animal effects. Alar was taken off the market anyway, and, in some ways, is symptomatic of public overreaction, later shown in airport security and the bird flu. More recently in 2007, Europe went through a period when pesticides on a variety of fruits caused some concern.

There was the North American ***E. coli*** outbreak of 2006 in lettuce and spinach. There are safe ones and the deadly 0157:H7. I sterilized this microorganism with a tunable laser for my PhD dissertation. Scarily enough, just washing these vegetables might not help, as the bacteria could be inside the plant. Three died and several hundred were hospitalized. Generally, the problem comes from irrigation water contaminated with animal feces.

Remember Mad Cow Disease? I was in London during the height of this crisis, and gave their cattle industry a vote of confidence by consuming what must have been the largest hamburger I had ever seen in my life.

Castleberry Food Company's chili recall resulted in my wife finding four cans of it at home, so she returned them to Costco, to learn that she was credited for six, so we must have eaten two cans. Somehow, we managed to avoid botulism. Good thing I don't consume pet foods, for that scandal resulted in at least 16 dead dogs and cats and a trace to the bustling Chinese city of Xuzhou…and wheat gluten.

What is wheat gluten? When you wash dough made from wheat flour, the starch is rinsed away, leaving something called gluten. Yes, gluten was first used in ancient China. This noodle-like tendon is popular for macrobiotic diets as a meat substitute.

Wheat gluten is a perfectly safe food base. The danger comes when melamine is accidentally or purposefully added to supposedly increase the protein content. Melamine is an organic base with a molecular formula of $C_3H_6N_6$, and is used to combine with formaldehyde to produce melamine resin, which you have no doubt used as a plastic dish, countertop, glue, fertilizer or flame retardant. Yes, you have also eaten some of it, as melamine was patented as a feed for cattle to provide non-protein nitrogen. In 1999, the Environmental Protection Agency proposed to remove this compound as a test for meat and poultry because "it is no longer considered a residue of concern." Melamine-contaminated feed has subsequently been detected in pork, chicken, fish and shrimp, which were cleared for human consumption. The bottom line, evidently, is that melamine in small doses does not harm us. The largest melamine factory in the world, at 120,000 tons/year, is scheduled to open on Hainan Island off the Chinese Mainland in 2008. So, if anything, you will ingest more melamine in the future.

Diethylene glycol (*DG*) [313] is a particularly troublesome chemical. Remember when cats used to lick antifreeze and die? That was ethylene glycol. Now a bittering agent is added to this chemical, which is still used. But DG has recently made the news as counterfeit glycerin (*G, a natural byproduct from soapmaking*) because DG is cheaper than G, and companies in China have substituted small amounts (*up to 5%*) of DG for G to cut costs, for used in toothpaste. No one dies if the toothpaste is not eaten. However, added to cold medicine, several hundred have succumbed in Panama. There have also reportedly been mass poisonings in Haiti, Bangladesh, Argentina, Nigeria and India.

Did you know that Colgate fluoride toothpaste contains: sodium monofluorosphosphate, hydrated silica, propylene glycol (*this is okay, but diethylene is not*), tetrasodium pyrophosphate, sodium bicarbonate, sodium saccharin, pentasodium triphosphate, sodium lauryl sulfate, carrageenan (*from seaweed*), a host of flavors with exotic names, sodium hydroxide and calcium peroxide?[160] On this note, have you taken a close look at some of the chips sold in bags? First, those chemicals make no sense at all, so don't bother.

Which brings us, then, to any import from China. The Consumer Product Safety Commission banned 28 imports in June of 2007—17 were from China. My first knee-jerk reaction harkens back to conspiracy and the American Japanese in World War II and American Muslims in the War of Terror. Is there something about China that brings out an inherent paranoia? Chinese recalls ranged from hammocks to toys to jewelry to tires to toothpaste to medical drugs to, of course, food. Seems like lobbyists were having a field day trying to knock out the competition, and Federal officials were only too accommodating. Well, there are no safety standards, apparently, on these imports, and, my gosh, we need to protect our pets.

**Diets and Obesity**

The diet of 2007 is Wu-Long slimming tea. Oprah swears by.... Whoops! That was an ad. When it comes to diet, it's best to know what not to do. All diets work to some degree. Some, though, can kill you, and most will not work because of you. These advertisements try to sound as medically sanctioned as possible, tossing in very fine print Food and Drug Administration references to exhibit an aura of respectability.

It is said that 75% of those in the U.S. are concerned about being overweight.[119] ***Fat Land: How Americans Became the Fattest People in the World***, written by Greg Citser, was published in 2003. From 1976 to 1991 fatness increased by 31%, then another 24% between 1994 and 2000.[157] Lost productivity amounting to $75 billion per year has been shown. Worse, this trend is continuing, and being overweight is said to be our second leading preventable cause of death, responsible for as much as 365,000 casualties each year.

Yet, the Center for Disease Control and Prevention (*CDCP*) changed their earlier position and reported in 2004 that packing on the pounds can only account for less than 10% that figure. Here we go again, the medical profession reversing itself. Then, in 2007 CDCP, really did it, as they described some advantages for being overweight.[302] While being fat increases risks associated with diabetes and kidney diseases, being slightly overweight does not affect cancer and heart disease. <u>In fact some extra pounds protect the body from DEATH</u>.

There is something called the Body Mass Index (*BMI*), where an obese person is classified as anything over 30, and overweight is from 25 to 30. The example provided is that a 5-foot-4 woman is overweight at 145 pounds and obese at 175. Whew, I'm male, but 160 pounds and about 5-ft-9, placing me with a BMI in the 23 to 24 category, definitely, then, NOT overweight. I can now stop trying to lose weight and enjoy life a lot more. A 5-ft-9 male becomes obese at 200 pounds. Obese is not good.

How to calculate your personal BMI? Easy:

- o Weigh yourself in kilograms (*or pounds divided by 2.2*)
  160 pounds / 2.2 = 72.7
- o Measure your height in meters (*or inches divided by 39.37*)
  69 inches / 39.37 = 1.75
- o Calculate your BMI, which equals your weight (*kg*) divided by height (m), and, again, divided by height (*m*)
  72.7 / 1/75 / 1/75 = **23.7**

In any case, contrary to popular opinion, Americans are NOT the fattest people on Earth. Qatar, with 45.3% of all women being obese and 34.6% of men ranks as #1. Lebanon, with 36.3% men (*38.3% women*) is next worst, and the U.S. is #5 for males (27.7%) and #8 for females (34%).[368] People in the Middle East appear to be the fattest. Here, I thought Muslims had a sparse and healthy diet. Some stewed sheep, dates, water. Not so in this global economy. In another part of the world, 13.8% of males in Mongolia are considered to be obese. Yes, there are fat people there, too. So eating less is probably good, but being subsequently skinny is not.

Eating just normally, apparently, might not be optimal, as rats on a subsistence diet have been shown to live 30% longer than those free to eat at will. So do skinny people live longer? Well, vaguely yes, except that being underweight could well pose an even greater risk as you age. Osteoporosis (*disease of the bone*), for example, can be controlled by body fat. For those 55 and older, an extra 5 to 10 pounds actually improve your chances for a longer life.[30]

There must be a contagious obesity virus in fat countries, as there is at least one medical study showing that adenovirus-36 does tend to infect fat people.[38] Whether this true or not, the chances are that genetics, lifestyle, attitude and other factors weigh more heavily. The bottom line is that if you don't smoke and are healthy, being really fat is bad for your longevity, but being slightly overweight might not be all that bad, especially as you get older.

Finally, can you help control your weight by sleeping more? At first glance, you might wonder if this is also some kind of joke, for sleeping is the most sedentary of all activities. But, yes, obesity is linked to lack of sleep.[143] Children sleeping 10 hours/night were 3.5 times more apt to become obese than those who slept 12 hours/night.[16] Go to these references and read about the leptins and ghrelins, for me, I noticed that when I went to sleep later, I tended to get hungry and had a snack.

The body weight of a person is a simple matter of energy/mass balance. If you eat more caloric food and exercise less, you will get fat and probably be unhealthier. Like most things in life, you need to strike that proper and enjoyable balance. A very simple solution for anyone with diet on your mind is to just remember that cutting 150 calories per day, like a can of soda everyday, can result in 2 pounds less of you by the end of the year. In ten years, you should be 20 pounds lighter, unless you've then reached the age of 55, when you might want to think about increasing your weight. Stay tuned to any changes to the current medical belief that older people should be a little overweight, plus the advent of those anti-obesity pills (*three are already on the market*).

**So What is Safe to Eat and Drink?**

Let me start with a standard disclaimer. These are not my recommendations. The following bullets are culled from the popular written media:

- First butter was bad, now margarine can be worse. The trans fats (TF) in margarine were the killer, literally. You can now purchase zero TF margarine, and, while this product still has as many calories and fat as butter, has less of the saturated variety and is easier to spread (and the healthier ones can be poured), while others can be kept at room temperature longer. Liquid margarine is recommended by the Cleveland Clinic over butter.[306] Ah, but they say, there is something about real butter and cooking. And the dairy industry keeps reminding us that margarine is one molecule from being a plastic.
- Eggs were once to be avoided. Today, they might be back in the diet, for, while it is indeed high in cholesterol, eggs do not increase your personal cholesterol level. Same for shrimp, which has more recently been shown to lower your cholesterol. Some early medical researchers actually got confused between high density lipoprotein, which is good, and the low density version, which is bad. Thus, the latest advice, if you don't have diabetes, is that there should be no guilt to eating eggs.[266]
- Red meats? Bad! Beef tends to cause cancer, their fat concentrates toxic chemicals and eating too much could increase your weight (*I spent a week in Buenos Aires, where I had at least 10 steak meals, gained 4 pounds, and NEVER was able to lose this weight*), plus, cattle is said to be worse for the environment than auto emissions.[162] Red **processed** meat, like bacon and sausage? Terrible! Just 1.7 ounces/day increases the risk of colorectal cancer by 21%. Why? Smoking, nitrates and high sodium. However, don't totally sacrifice on living, as one pound of steak per week is permissible.[137]
- High cholesterol does tend to harm the cardiovascular system, but too low a count has negative effects.[258] An increase in violent deaths is associated with lower cholesterol levels. Serotonin, bad temper and over-aggressiveness, too. Anyway, high density lipoprotein is good for your circulatory system.
- Stop eating tuna to avoid mercury poisoning or drink more coffee to reduce the risk of diabetes…or perhaps these warnings and recommendations only apply to pregnant women. The most expensive of sashimi, the blue fin tuna, is about as bad as it gets, for tests as high as 6.1 parts per million (*0.4 ppm seafood can be banned*). Very few of you are pregnant, so, as you can't afford the fatty part of tuna anyway, everything in moderation seems like a good recommendation.
- A high fiber diet will prevent colorectal cancer. Nope, says the American Medical association.[41] But roughage up to 35 grams/day does tend to give you regularity (*in bowel movement*), lower cholesterol, aid diabetics and help those who suffer from heartburn. Thus, do eat fruits, vegetables, bran muffins and cereals.
- Too much tofu induces brain aging…that was the bombshell headline from a ***Honolulu Star Bulletin*** article on November 19, 1999, written by Helen Altonn, reporting on the preliminary work of Lon White of the Pacific Health Research Center. Sales of tofu dropped, significantly. Nearly a decade later, tofu sales are up and soy is still generally looked upon as a gift from God. What happened? Nothing much, except, below the

marketing horizon seems to be a dark side hinting that there might be something naturally toxic about this bean.[120] This is not the end of this controversy.

- o Boiled peanuts bring out up to four times more disease-fighting phytochemicals (*they reduce cancer*) than dry or oil roasting the nuts, or leaving them raw.[27] Maybe this is why Hawaii people live longer, as this is a standard item at football tailgate parties and the like.
- o Is it true that if you are a Japanese American (*that's me*) who drinks fruit juice just every other day, you reduce the risk of Alzheimer's by 76%? Amazingly, the answer appears to be yes, from the Kame Project, headed by Qi Dai, reported in ***The American Journal of Medicine***: 2006, Volume 119, pages 751-759. Wine is included, so I am very well covered. Why only Japanese Americans? Because the study was of 1836 Japanese Americans living in King County, Washington. Doctor's are, in this sense, conservative about these things.
- o Will eating curried rice reduce prostate tumors? I love curried foods and, being a male of advancing age, am happy to report that the answer, again, is yes.[174] Curcumin is found in curry as the active agent. Cauliflower and broccoli also are good, but for the phenethyl isothiocyanate. These studies were made on rats, but there, apparently, is reasonable correlation to humans.
- o But working the graveyard shift is not good for your health, as the World Health Organization reported that there is a higher incidence of breast and prostate cancer for those who work after daylight. This has something to do with the circadian (*biological clock*) rhythm being disrupted, reducing the natural production of melatonin, which can suppress tumor development. Also, the body's immune system becomes more vulnerable with an uneven sleeping schedule.[48]
- o Is the Chinese restaurant syndrome—consuming food with monosodium glutamate, or ajinomoto—a myth?[190] Yes, it is a myth!
- o Salt is bad for your health. Yes, the American Medical Association warns us to watch out for salt in the most innocent of foods, and cutting consumption in half could save 150,000 lives each year.[216] The Institute of Medicine says the 2,300 milligrams of sodium/day standard set by the Federal Government is too high, and should be 1,500 mg/day. However, we consume up to 4,000 mg/day, an equivalence of about two teaspoons. Over the past three years, the sodium chloride (*salt*) content of cheese has increased by 35%. So it is not a simple matter of adding only so much salt. You must watch what you eat, and processed food has a lot of salt.
- o However, is it true that, if you have a normal blood pressure, you are 37% <u>less likely to die</u> of a cardiovascular disease if you consume <u>more sodium</u> than less?[45] Again, the answer is yes, which is totally contrary to popular belief.
- o Does green tea help prevent cancer and heart disease? Well, various medical studies are available showing clear benefits. Unfortunately, Ito En, a Japanese company, in 2005 petitioned the Food and Drug Administration to allow them to claim that drinking at least 5 ounces of green tea/day could lower the risk of heart disease. The FDA responded in 2006 that there is no credible evidence.[273] So who's right? Who knows! I guess the moral of this story is, don't ask unless you are sure that you will get the right answer.

- o What about those who take a handful of vitamins or one large dietary supplement? The record is mixed, and you need to be a bit careful about any long term effects on various organs, especially your liver, but, for example, some combination of B (*12 more than 6*) complexes and folic acid (*another B*) seem to fend off Alzheimer's and is supposed to maintain nerve and red cells, plus help make DNA. However, only 3 ounces of clam provides 14 times the recommended daily value of B12.[308]
- o Then there is the container. How safe are plastics, especially when used to microwave food or freeze drinks? This almost sounds like one of those urban legend hoaxes, but polyvinylchloride is definitely not recommended for this purpose and bisphenol-A (*BPA*), used in the synthesis of plastics, is more and more appearing on watch lists. Cancer, chromosome abnormalities, memory and a full range of symptoms have been suggested. While there was no comprehensive medical report on this subject at the time of this writing, a sensible rule of thumb is to use glass for microwaving, and I'm not sure what to do about freezing. The difficulty is that there are more than 20 million registered chemicals, and the FDA has more important problems to tackle.

You can chalk it up to the benefits of advancing medical research and sway with the latest scoop or more probably conveniently lose confidence in those medical recommendations that compromise your lifestyle.

Red wines deserve a category of their own:

- o Is it the resveratrol in red wine that helps the heart? Probably. Better yet, champagne contains high amounts of polyphenols, which are also conducive to better health, so red champagne (*from pinot noir and cabernet sauvignon grapes*) could well be even better for your health. I actually invested in a start-up company to import sparkling red wine from Europe, but mainly because I thought RED CHAMPAGNE could be marketed in China with that description (*in Chinese*). Red is symbolic with celebration.
- o Wine is supposed to promote longevity, slow brain decline, and lower heart disease, diabetes, stroke, cataracts and colon cancer risks, but much of this is published in wine magazines, as for example just in ***Wine Spectator*** for 2007:

  - o ***The Journal of Agricultural and Food Chemistry*** reported that the University of Pavia in Italy found both red and white wine prevent the growth of streptococci associated with tooth decay and sore throats (*October 15*).
  - o ***Neuroscience*** indicated that researchers from the University of Porto determined that rats given heavy doses of red wine did not suffer memory damage, compared with those given pure alcohol. These red wine rats performed as well as those only drinking water (*October 31*).
  - o ***The Journal of Carcinogenesis*** featured an article from the University of Alabama showing that red wine protected the prostate (*November 15*).
  - o ***The Journal of Neuroscience*** reports that one or two glasses of wine per day improves memory.[93]

Here the wine industry is not necessarily funding the study, this wine publication just selectively reports the information. I give wine the benefit of any possible doubt because it's trendy, tasty and makes you high. Soon, a test will be available to steer you away from red wines that cause some the red wine headache.[362] It's all in the amines, which are found in wine and sake, but not much in beer. Of course, there are winos, and any responsible person would know that anything to excess can be bad. How much is just right? Well, the consensus seems to be ten ounces (*2 glasses*) per day as being good for a typical male, and a lower amount for females who are proportionately smaller. A bottle in the U.S. is 26 ounces.

### Other Longevity Factors

Sleep is important for a longer life, and, apparently, the more the better. Newborn babies and many convicts on death row sleep around 16 hours/day. Teenagers are supposed to get 9 hours/night. The optimal hours for adults range from 7 to 8 hours, but more if you're pregnant and less if unusually conformed. I remember when I once worked for U.S. Senator Spark Matsunaga and a ***Washington Post*** article headlined the "Senator Who Never Sleeps." He boasted that he could get by with only a couple of hours per night. However, he tended to doze off in many hearings.

Medical studies have indicated that:

- You lose memory and weaken your immune system through sleep deprivation.
- Working the graveyard shift tampers with the sleep cycle and is reported to cause cancer and other ailments.[54]
- Driver fatigue causes 100,000 motor vehicle accidents/year in the U.S.[359]
- Women might have a higher life expectancy (*seven years longer*) because they sleep better. This might have to do with learning how to cope with crying babies.[68]
- Poor sleep may raise the risk of diabetes.[272]

Of course, sleep depends on genetics, the quality of sleep and timing. For example, naps are returning as a good thing, even in certain companies. One of the benefits of retirement is that you can sleep as much as you want, and for that reason, people like me should thus be healthier and skinnier (*see obesity section above*).

There is the matter of stress. In a nutshell, the less the better. Not sweating the small stuff helps people live longer.

Inflammation, the biological defense response of your body to harmful stimuli, was once not an item considered as important for long life. Now it is. You have experienced swelling, and redness. Your body is at work protecting you. Chronic inflammation can lead to tissue destruction and other ailments. Drug and herbal companies try to sell you products to reduce inflammation. Be careful, but there are benefits. Aspirin reduces inflammation. An all-purpose anti-inflammatory pill could well someday control diabetes, cancer, heart disease and dementia. Details will come in the next section, but a simple blood test for C-reactive protein (*CRP*) can detect inflammation in blood vessels for it is twice more likely than high cholesterol to cause a heart attack.[257]

There is something about incubation periods or long term health problems that are disturbing. I recall sitting in on a talk a long time ago—maybe 20 years—about a viral terminal ailment, somewhat similar to mad cow disease, which you contract from eating organ meats. The problem is that if you ate a contaminated meal, you will die 20 years or so later. Wow, any day now! Good thing that the only exception I make is foie gras, for goose liver is not a particularly suspect example. But even something so simple as *E. coli* is troubling, for a decade or two later, you can be stricken with high blood pressure and kidney damage.[217] Then there is lead. Higher lead exposure (*such as inhaling leaded gasoline fumes and the product of combustion in the 60's and 70's*) appears to correlate with accelerated aging of your brain.[260] Well, don't get paranoid…there isn't much you can do about this now, although, no doubt, to be announced, will be nanobots to rid your body of that virus or advanced chelation (*too absorb out the lead*) treatments and the like.

Finally, do you want to live 14 years longer? According to the University Cambridge, all you need to do is to eat copious amounts of vegetables and fruits, not smoke, exercise and drink alcohol, albeit in moderation.[55]

So, then, if you sleep enough, reduce stress and check inflammation, how long will you live? Try Thomas Perls' Longevity Calculator to indicate how long you will live. Go to www.livingto100.com. It is supposed to take about 10 minutes to complete, but I got kicked out the first time. I tried again and learned I will live to between 96 and 98, meaning I have thirty years to go.

**The End of Diseases**

No one in the world died this past year from smallpox. A couple hundred succumb each year to polio and the plague, plus a couple of thousand from yellow fever and cholera. We are doing very well in neutralizing some of these classical diseases, for the Black Death killed up to 30 million in Europe 700 years ago and cholera took the lives of 500,000 in the 1830's in New York City alone. However, one child dies of malaria in Africa every 29 seconds…one person is infected with HIV every 6.4 seconds…someone in the world dies of TB every 18 seconds.[322] The major disease deaths come from HIV/AIDS (*up to 3 million*), malaria (*up to 2 million*) and tuberculosis (*less than 2 million*). But 56 million people annually pass away and 130 million are born, with the world population continuing to increase.

There were up to 6 million cases of malaria in the U.S. in the 40's, which dropped to almost nothing by the 50's through the spraying of DDT (***dichloro-diphenyl-trichloroethane***). Similar results occurred worldwide. Paradoxically, DDT was said to be the spur for Rachel Carson's ***Silent Spring***, which initiated the environmentalist movement, ultimately resulting in banning DDT use. After being prohibited for thirty years, the World Health Organization, though, began to again use DDT to control malaria, but in 2007 remarked that it is committed to phasing out the use.

More DDT, less malaria deaths. Less DDT, more malaria deaths. What to do? You say, why not use something else. Well, there is no something else today. They say vaccines are getting close, but this has been touted for several decades now.

In the U.S., heart disease and cancer account for more than half of all deaths. In the world, heart disease takes only 12.4% and cancer comes in at tenth place. Why? Because those in the developing world die earlier from HIV, diarrhea, tuberculosis and assorted other maladies.

The Gates Foundation has, perhaps, the ideal balanced goal. Do what you can today by providing vaccinations to save lives, while sponsoring research to eliminate those diseases in the future. The Foundation has about $66 billion to spend, almost half coming from Warren Buffet. It allocates about 5% of its worth each year, meaning that 95% gets invested, sometimes in controversial areas.

Perhaps a more sensible development area is to take the positive approach, that is, one whereby the body is strengthened to prevent diseases. There is exercise, of course...good diet, surely...reasonable body weight, certainly. But vaccines to prevent obesity, smoking and illegal drug use? They will all probably come because of demand, and a lean gene has already been detected in worms, flies and mice.

The same can be said for raising IQs and changing the body physique. The modern Wonder Woman or 21st Century $6 Million Dollar Man will begin to merge with machines. Transplants are now ordinary and totally non-biological body parts are routine. Artificial blood, cancer-killing nanobots, and immunotherapy treatments are just around the corner, if not tomorrow, than certainly in the 22nd century.

In 1907, Alois Alzheimer, a German neuropathologist, first identified certain protein clumps in the brain of patients with dementia. A polymer of a peptide, or a neurotoxic molecule called ADDL, has more recently been targeted as the culprit causing nerve cell (*neuron*) death or disruption. In a few years, a simple blood test will be able to predict whether you will contract Alzheimer's in six years.[142]

There is also the matter of inflammation, a little known immune-system response partly to blame for Alzheimer's, cancer, diabetes and heart disease. If you can control chronic inflammation—which is stimulated by things like stress, overeating and smoking—you will be well on your way to a long life. How do you know you have this ailment? Simple. Talk to your doctor about a blood test for C-reactive protein (CRP). The higher your CRP, the worse the inflammation.

I served on the board of Hawaii Biotech during its transformative years, and observed the debate between developing vaccines for third world diseases such as dengue fever versus focusing on astaxanthin, a carotenoid (*a kind of biological pigment*) that can be extracted from microalgae, and is said to prevent inflammation. The result was a sensible split into two companies to do both.

As I have been jokingly critical of oil companies and my president, let me add one more target, the medical professioin. But first, an internet joke: 700,000 doctors supposedly cause 120,000 accidental deaths each year, so there is a 17% kill rate/doctor. There are 80 million gun owners in the U.S., with 1500 accidental deaths/year. That is a rate of 0.002%/gun. Are doctors more dangerous than guns?

For one, there is a tendency for doctors to prescribe too much medication. You can't help but wonder about how much influence the drug companies really have. Second, on the matter of immunotherapy, when, for example, a child has a fever, there is a propensity to recommend Tylenol or aspirin, the purpose being to lower the temperature. Yes, perhaps, the child will then feel more comfortable and go to sleep, but it's probably more for the mother who feels something has been done. However, the evolution of our body has engineered a reason for fever, which is mostly, I would gather, to combat viruses and bacteria. Then, too, hit with a cold and a runny nose, we take a variety of pills to reduce this condition. If anything, we should help our body by doing everything possible to eliminate this waste. Same for diarrhea. We tend to focus on short term comfort at the expense of long term resolution. I'm not a medical doctor, but I wonder about the illogic of many standard medical treatments.

Well, anyway, when will medical science totally eliminate all diseases? The easy answer is that this will just be a matter of time. The reality could well be apocalyptic, as there have been rumors of a "Black Pox," some genetic combination of small pox and Ebola, with a 100% casualty rate. Thus, with a few retrogressions now and then inspired by nature, war and deviants, the more pragmatic answer is, sometime after finding the clue to eternal life, as the aging gene might be easier to identify and re-program than finding a cure for the totality of human diseases.

**Are We Overreacting to the Avian Bird Flu?**

Bird, or Avian, flu, particularly strain H5N1, was first seen in Hong Kong in 1997. The 1918 Spanish flu, which killed 40 million people, was an avian flu virus. According to the World Health Organization (*WHO*), 150 million birds have been affected, but chances are the number is even higher. Humans can thus far be infected only by direct contact with the sick fowl.

Let us get the human and cost factors making some sense:

- On September 29, 2005, David Nabarro, the Senior UN System Coordinator for Avian and Human Influenza, warned that this deadly virus could kill 150 million people.
- On November 3, 2005, the Asian Development Bank warned that the economic damage from a pandemic affecting 20% of the region's populace could be $282 billion. [221]
- On November 7, 2005, World Bank economists reported that a worldwide epidemic would cost $800 billion, with 100,000 to 200,000 dying in the United States alone. [172]
- CNN reported on February 19, 2006 of a study reported by the Lowy Institute of Australia that as many as 142 million people around the world could die in a worst case scenario, causing global economic losses of $4.4 trillion. [247]
- On March 27, 2006 Reuters reported that bird flu could cost insurers $53 billion. Fitch Ratings indicated that 400,000 deaths could occur in Europe and 209,000 in the U.S. [253]

Well, at least there is some consistency that, perhaps, 200,000 might die in the U.S. But the financial loss ranged from $282 billion to $4.4 trillion.

However, during the past decade, only 321 cases have been confirmed, with around 200 deaths, although none in Europe nor the U.S.[42] You cannot catch this flu by eating the flesh of a tainted bird nor from another individual who has this ailment.

A first generation vaccine has been developed. That is the good news. Hate to say this, but the volume of the very large injection is more than ten times the dose of a regular flu shot, and only half of you will be protected.[219] Your home state has begun to purchase this vaccine with your tax contributions, but to inoculate health workers. The quest for a better vaccine, which will take a lot of money, makes sense, but to significantly stockpile something that will soon become obsolete is close to being dumb. The problem, of course, is that you can't develop a vaccine if you don't know what the strain will be.

All this sort of reminds me of the town fool, walking through downtown Chicago (*or anywhere*) banging a cymbal all day. When asked why he was doing this, he said he was trying to scare away marauding elephants. The remedy was effective, but was there a problem?

In counterpoint, every day, more than 3,000 people are killed in car accidents, where during the past nine years since this bird flu was first detected, more than 10 million have died in traffic—versus about two hundred bird flu deaths, versus 200 million sacrificed chickens. Kind of reminds me of shark against mankind. They get, oh, 5 of us every year, but we kill 100 million of those marauding predators (*and mostly for their fin*). It has been reported that 150 people die each year from falling coconuts…almost ten times more than succumb to the dreaded new avian flu/year.[254, 286] Any talk of outlawing vehicles or cutting down coconut trees? Finally, ***Time*** reports that 430 babies die each year from sudden infant death caused by secondhand smoke.[223] Anyone doing any research to find a vaccine to prevent smoking? Actually, from the previous section…yes.

A growing concern is the superbug, methicillin-resistant ***Staphylococcus aureus*** (*MRSA*), pronounced as mersa. In 2005, MRSA killed 19,000 (*and made 94,000 seriously ill*) Americans, a year when 17,000 died from AIDS complications.[195] Hospitals and medical treatment centers are mostly responsible for this problem. But that's another subject.

On May 31, 2006, it was reported that the H5N1 bird flue killed six of seven relatives in remote village in Indonesia, so, maybe, the virus had finally mutated. No, just poor sanitary practices did in this unlucky group. In the weeks following the quarantine from May 22, no additional cases were reported, and a genetic check on the virus indicated it had not mutated. There was a further quip that Indonesia is just, basically, screwed up as a government and can't seem to organize anything. Now with 100 avian flu deaths as of 2008, Indonesia has leaped past Vietnam's 48 fatalities.[358]

So what is the big deal with H5N1? I don't know. The only way this specific avian flu can cause a pandemic is if the virus mutates, and while I've read reports stating that very few bird flu viruses have ever done this to infect humans, I saw an unsubstantiated newspaper report implying that flu viruses are prone to genetic mutations. What is the reality? Is this yet another example of airport security overkill? Don't get me started on that one.

My simple solution is to be vigilant, but stop overreacting. You might be one of the more than half a billion or so slated to catch the flu this year, but the odds are infinitesimal for you being nailed by H5N1. Okay, it would be smart to avoid chicken farms in the Orient, and don't prepare any dead fowl found in the woods for dinner, but don't let this scare affect your eating habits. About all this money being spent as a precaution? Spend a small percent of it on educating the public about pandemics and continue researching the baselines for a future vaccine, but let's not get carried away by something that almost surely will not happen.

### A Primate Virus: HIV/AIDS

Acquired immune deficiency syndrome (*AIDS*) is caused by a human immunodeficiency virus [288] which weakens the body for tumors and infections. There is no cure and the retrovirus (*not worth explaining*) is transmitted by direct contact of mucous or blood from the infected carrier. Up to 50 million are now affected, but as less than 1% of the population of Africa, where the ailment initiated, has been tested, who really knows the extent of the severity. More than 25 million have expired through this illness since first recognized in 1981, and of the 3 million annually killed, half a million are children.

As the avian flu came from birds, AIDS probably originated with primates, although there are various other theories. As early as 1959 a case was recorded in the Belgian Congo. Thus, Zaire and Rwanda might well have been the primary source. However, no monkey or chimpanzee has ever been found with this virus.

Economists estimate that an investment of $27 billion could avert 30 million new infections by 2010. The U.S. Congress is considering a $5.4 billion HIV/AIDS budget for fiscal 2008, which would bring the U.S. contribution to $18.3 billion. There is no simple solution for HIV/AIDS.

However, recent reports have indicated that the problem is being exaggerated to gain more funding. Over the past decade, global spending to treat and cure this disease has increased 30 fold and is now up to $10 billion/year. The United Nations in 2007 lowered its estimate of AIDS cases from 40 million to 33 million, still a high total.[321] But the larger question is, if Peak Oil and Global Warming will be devastating the global economy in a few years, which problem deserves the higher priority? Remember, the annual U.S. Department of Energy budget for renewable energy has averaged less than $1 billion over the past decade.

## The Science of Eternal Life

Before delving into the realm of eternal life, let us first explore how life began...according to scientists. Quasi-equal treatment of more biblical beginnings will be found in CHAPTER 5. In CHAPTER 4 on Search for Extraterrestrial Intelligence, is a term, $F_l$, representing the percentage of planets where life could have originated. There are, of course, theories that comets or aliens brought life. See the SETI discussion for those alternatives. So if life was initiated on Earth, how?

Starting with energy, water and elements, there is a range of likely environments where life could have begun:

- o Aristotle (*Greek philosopher*) in the 4th Century BC said that life occurred abiogenetically, that, is, spontaneously.
- o Louis Pasteur (*French microbiologist*) proved Aristotle wrong in 1862.
- o Joseph Dalton (*English botanist*) in 1871 suggested that life began in a "warm little pond, with all sorts of ammonia and phosphoric salts, lights, heat, electricity, etc, that a protein compound formed."
- o How close to right he was, for Aleksandr Oparin (*Soviet bioscientist*) and John Haldane (*Scottish geneticist*) organic soup theory pretty much exhibited in 1953 by Stanley Miller and Harold Urey at the University of Chicago, just about did that. Miller was a graduate student of Urey, who by then had already won a Nobel Prize in Chemistry (*1934*) through his work on deuterium and heavy water. Water, methane, ammonia and hydrogen, compounds of primordial times, were heated and sparked in a flask for a week, producing more than 10% organic compounds, 2% being amino acids, including 13 of 21 used to make proteins in living cells. Clearly, though, they should have also added hydrogen sulfide and some phosphate compound. Hmm...sounds like another good experiment.
- o J. Brooks and G. Shaw (*UK bioscientists*) in 1973, though, surmised that there was no soup, for nowhere on Earth are there any massive sediments of these compounds, also more recently stated by David Abel and Jack Trevors (*U.S. and Canadian bioscientists*).
- o Graham Cairnes-Smith (*Scottish bioscientist*) in 1985 postulated the clay theory, that complex organic molecules are formed over time on clay crystals in a process of exaptation, a form of biological adaptation.
- o Then there are theories about life starting at the bottom of the ocean through chemical genesis, in deep rocks in the form of archaea (*a microorganism somewhat like bacteria*), and at bubble interfaces.

The Origin-of-Life Foundation (*life@us.net*) will give you a million dollars if you can explain how the original genetic code arose. There is, yet, no winner.

## Germs

There is no scientific meaning for germs, which are single-celled and commonly thought of as bacteria. Also add archaea, only discovered in the ocean in 1977. Even if viruses are supposedly not alive, throw this group of microorganisms into the germ pot. There are single-cell fungi and protozoa, so they can be added, too.

These microscopic life forms appeared as long as 4 billion years ago, represented the only life for up to 2 billion years, and, actually, still rule Planet Earth, as it is reported that there is more mass in "germs" or micro-life than all the macro-life (*humans, other animals, trees, whatever you can see that lives*). There are studies showing that there is about the same amount of plant biomass as bacteria (*about 2 billion tons each*), but there is very roughly the same mass in archaea and viruses compared to bacteria, so germs still dominate. For the record there are 700 million tons of domesticated animals, 500 million tons of krill (*those small shrimp-like creatures eaten by whales and fish*) and 250 million tons of us humans.

Just in a liter of seawater live more than 20,000 different kinds of bacteria.[370] A milliliter of saliva can contain as many as 40 million bacteria. There are about a billion different kinds of bacteria. If a virus had the shape of a baseball, a bacterium would be the circle around the pitcher's mound and a human cell would be in the range of the ballpark.[299] As a virus requires a host, it has to invade a microorganism, human or any life form, to survive.

Most of you don't realize that:

- You harbor 100 trillion bacteria in and on you, but have only around 10 trillion cells of your own, thus, you host many times more germ cells than your own. Before you get too revolted, you should know that your cell is much larger than a bacterium.
- You have probably up to three pounds of bacteria in your gut. Yes, this is most disgusting.
- Some of your personal cells have formed a symbiotic relationship with these germs, and, there are growing theories that they, in fact, now affect the nature of genes.

That said, 99% of germs are good. While viruses exist only by attacking and nourishing themselves on living cells—thus, they are the natural predator for bacteria and you—there are no known pathogenic archaea. You will more and more see these beneficial germs in your diet. From baby food to yogurt, there are now more than 150 probiotic and prebiotic products in your supermarket.

**Artificial Life**

While the term, artificial life, coined in 1987 by Christopher Langton at his first "International Conference on the Synthesis and Simulation of Living Systems," seems more linked to computer systems, I will focus only on the bio-option. In Chapter 4 on Search for Extraterrestrial Intelligence, we will return to the matter of what is intelligence and whether life on Earth is all that there might be.

J. Craig Venter—high school dropout, surfer, and Navy veteran of Viet Nam, who went on to gain a PhD from the University of California at San Diego and become head of Celeria Genomics, a private group that sequenced the human genome in a dead heat with the international, government-supported project—announced a new partnership with the U.S. Department of Energy in 2003, this time, to create a new type of bacterium using DNA (*deoxyribonucleic acid*) manufactured from basic chemicals. They also had hoped to produce hydrogen, sequester carbon dioxide and clean up the environment, like of nuclear wastes. This organization, the Institute for Biological Energy Alternatives, includes Nobel laureate Hamilton O. Smith, an expert on genetic science. Their engineered microbe could well be dual purpose: make hydrogen and absorb carbon dioxide. They are dealing with the matter of creating life itself

Venter's team selected *Mycoplasma genitalium*, whose habitat is in the genital tract of humans, not because this is where life begins, but more for the microorganism's simplicity and fragility.[249] They don't want a super bug to escape into the environment and eat up the world. Emblematic is that the very first attempt at formulating artificial life will be a genetic microorganism to produce hydrogen.

Success was attained in 2003 with the creation of an artificial virus. Venter said they only took two weeks to accomplish this task. What they did was fashion a synthetic genetic map, or genome, of an existing virus and implanted it into a cell. The virus supposedly became biologically active and reproduced.[343] But is a virus alive? No.

In October of 2006, Venter filed an application to patent this first artificial microbe. The U.S. Patent Office published on May 31, 2007, the application (*#20070122826*). This man-made organism was called ***Mycoplasma laboratorium***. But, almost predictably, the field went somewhat berserk with challenges from those worried that God now had a competitor to others with scientific and ethical concerns. A more apt tag was also stated regarding Venter's venture: the Microsoft of synthetic biology.

## On Genomes, Stem Cells and Cloning

Many can recall the double helix adventure of research fellow James Watson and graduate student Francis Crick in 1953 at Cambridge University. However, the notion of nucleic acid was discussed as early as 1872 at the University of Basel by Friederich Miescher. In 1943, an American, Oswald Avery, proved that DNA carried genetic information. In the late 40's and early 50's, people like Linus Pauling and Erwin Chargaff provided the foundation for the helix and nitrogen base pairs, and Rosalind Franklin of King's College in London first "saw" the coil in x-ray diffraction images of DNA. Maurice Wilkins, also of Kings College, "leaked" this information to Watson and Crick, and all three went on to win the Nobel Prize in 1962. Franklin had passed away by then.

One can only wonder how Watson, who was once more interested in birds, and Crick, who designed naval mines in World War II, both with little training in microbiology, went on to become Nobel Laureates discovering what has been lauded as the most important piece of biological work this past century, if not ever. So, my adventures into crime, war and religion might still, in time, be justified.

Watson in 1988 became the first head of the National Institutes of Health Office of Human Genome Research, which, with the U.S. Department of Energy, initiated the Human Genome Project (*HGP*) in 1990. 1992 was a tumultuous year, as James Watson resigned and J. Craig Venter also left the NIH. Venter formed Celera in 1998 and said that he would sequence the human genome in three years at a cost of $300 million. After a series of collaborations and squabbles between the federal and private competitors, they split at the end, only to both publish their successful findings: HGP in ***Nature*** (*February 15*) and Celera in ***Science*** (*February 16*).

A gene, a DNA sequence containing the template for the synthesis of a protein or RNA product, is the unit of heredity in living organisms. A genome is the set of genetic material of an organism. The human (*homo sapiens*) genome is composed of 24 chromosomes with approximately 3 billion DNA base pairs containing as few as 20,000 genes (*but as much as 25,000*), a number which has been revised down from the initial 100,000 prediction. A mouse has about the same number of genes, of which 99% or so are similar.

All living things have cells—as reported earlier, approximately 10 trillion in a human—with the primary genetic materials being deoxyribonucleic acid (*DNA*) and its partner, ribonucleic acid (*RNA*). DNA is always a double stranded coil and RNA is single stranded. There are only four components to DNA: **a**denine, **c**ytosine, **g**uanine and **t**hymine. Thus, while we have 26 letters in our alphabet, DNA has only four: A, C, G and T. These four letters are combined in three-letter words to produce 20 amino acids, which are sequenced to make proteins. Life could have been a lot more complicated.

Why are we so like rodents? Evolution indicates that we split off from them only 75 million years ago, and this is but a flash of time in the realm of genetic mutation. Interestingly enough, the mouse DNA actually has shown a higher order of hybridization, but mostly because they have a shorter lifetime. Another way of looking at this in the extreme is that we need 5 million years to pass through 300,000 generations. Bacteria require only 25 years. Thus, germs mutate quickly away from current treatments and can more easily adapt to changes in the environment if, say, global warming becomes the Venus Syndrome.

Of these couple hundred different genes, rodents have developed a few to give them a better sense of smell. The whole basis of evolution is that our DNA now and then makes a mistake and the product turns out different—usually worse, but sometimes better—adapting to the changing environment. This is called evolution.

We are genetically closer to the apes, as there is about a 98.77% (*or 99.2%, depending on time and report*) similarity pattern between humans and our earlier ancestors from which we diverged 6 million years ago. We actually have one less chromosome than these primates, as it appears that our chromosome 2 represents a fusion of two mid-sized ape chromosomes.

Here it gets a bit complicated, but if DNA insertions and deletions are taken into account, we only share 96% that of chimps. A comparison shows these genetic differences:

- 60 times less between human and chimpanzee than between human and mouse
- 10 times less between human and chimpanzee than between mouse and rat
- 10 times more between human and chimpanzee than between human and human

In a nutshell, some might be comforted that we are, indeed, more like a monkey than a rat. ***Book 1*** talked about our common ancestor from Africa who lived about 3.2 million years ago, **Lucy**, named from a Beatles song, ***Lucy in the Sky with Diamonds***, which was playing on the radio when Donald Johanson and his team were celebrating the find. Chapter 5 on religion will glance at Adam and Eve, say, 6000 years ago, but here we'll go back much further in time, to find **Luca**.

## The Search for Luca

Suzanne Vega composed and sang a haunting song about a battered child in 1987 called ***My Name is Luca***. In some ways, Luca, the acronym for the Last Universal Common Ancestor, way before Lucy, is the scientific equivalent of a battered child. The scientist who finds Luca, who it is estimated to have appeared between 3.6 and 4.1 billion years ago, will win that million dollar prize mentioned earlier. All life derived from Luca. However, Luca was not probably the very first life form. Nature experimented, and Luca survived. Earlier than Luca was Lua, for last universal ancestor. Thankfully, Luca prevailed at that historic gathering of 1996 in Provence, because lua in Hawaiian is outhouse.

There are three branches of life: bacteria, archaea and eucaryotes. The first two are simpler, called prokaryotes, having no nucleus and with all genetic material in a single filament of DNA. *E. coli* is a typical bacterium, and, well, you wouldn't recognize one archaea from another. Algae are eukaryotic, and so are amoeba and paramecium, microbes you all saw in your high school microscope. Eucaryotes have a nucleus containing genetic material. As they are more complicated, it was earlier thought that bacteria and archaea were first to come, especially archaea—which was only identified in 1977 by American microbiologist Carl Woese and American chemical engineer George Fox—and mostly consists of extremophiles, those organisms that live in extreme environments. There is one line of reasoning, called fusion, where archaea and bacteria combined to form eucaryotes. This is beginning to lose favor.

Others have advanced an argument that eucaryotes were the first of the three, and, therefore, Luca was one of them. It turns out that the prokaryotes are more efficient than eucaryotes, representing a kind of natural selection, so instead of fusion, the three domains of life resulted from fission. Then, too, what about viruses? But life is not all that simple, for there are at least five tribes of beliefs representing one organism or the other, or something in between, or, perhaps, none of them at all. I'm leaning towards viruses as the precursors to life, as DNA first came from them, which are, nevertheless considered by most biologists to be non-living.[379] A good book covering this subject is by Robert Hazen.[136]

Well, in any case, how do you find Luca? There is the bottom-up approach, starting with early Earth conditions, and building up to Luca, or the top-down approach, using genomic data. You can also identify possible universal genes and assemble them into a Luca genome, sort of the Miller-Urey experiment brought up to date.

But you ask, like dinosaurs, why don't scientists just measure the oldest living thing by carbon dating or something more advanced? Well, can't be done for these microbeasts. Radiocarbon dating is good only for specimens younger than 60,000 years, plus anything billions of years old and that small is hard to find. Radiometric dating (*measuring decay of radioactive isotopes like rubidium-strontium, with a half-life of 50 billion years*) can go back to the beginning of time, but only things like rocks.

After Luca, how did these single-cell organisms become animals and plants? Something happened 540 million years ago, when the Big Bang of biology created most multi-cellular life, in a relatively short period of 10 million years. Then came Lucy 3 million years ago and, finally, the at Dawn of Humanity, us, as recently as 200,000 years ago, and most probably in Africa. Can we bypass evolution by living forever? One next step is through cloning.

## Stem Cells and Human Engineering

### My Experience with Biotechnology

I feel particularly blessed because I was there in the very early stages of genetic engineering, or recombinant DNA technology, for the Bay Area of San Francisco is where the industry really started. My PhD interest in the DNA/RNA of *E. coli* no doubt was seeded here.

Yes, in Genesis 30:25 – 43, selective breeding of sheep was practiced, wheat was carefully developed from wild grasses 10,000 years ago, and we know of Gregor Mendel, Austrian Augustinian priest, and his pea plants about 150 years ago. But I remember sitting in on some lectures by biochemist Arthur Kornberg while at Stanford in the early 1960's, where there was excitement of molecular re-design. It was not until 1972, though, that Paul Berg, from the same department, succeeded in combining the DNA of two viruses. Both Kornberg, who passed away in 2007, and Berg, are Nobel Laureates, and Roger Kornberg, son of, and another biochemist at Stanford, was awarded that Prize in 2006. In 1973, two more biochemists, Herbert Boyer of the University California at San Francisco and Stanley Cohen of Stanford University, produced the first recombinant DNA organism, establishing the foundation for the industry. Cohen went on to win the Nobel Prize and Boyer in 1976 co-founded Genentech, the first true biotechnology company, although Cetus, differentiated as a biological engineering firm, out of Berkeley, was started in 1971.

In 1980, the U.S. Supreme Court ruled that life forms could be patented, and Wall Street came calling. Soon thereafter, Genentech had an initial public offering (*IPO*) and gained $35 million. Cetus followed with a $107 million IPO. Just in the Bay Area alone, there are now 800 biotech companies employing 85,000 people, generating annual revenues approaching $5 billion. And this is just the beginning.

In contrast to the Bay Area success story, my attempts at marine biotechnology in Hawaii, as we shall see, largely failed…yet, perhaps I have planted a few seeds that might yet germinate over time. When I first joined the University of Hawaii in 1971, I teamed with Sidney Gaines of the Medical School to refine my PhD dissertation on "Tunable Organic Dye Laser Irradiation of *Escherichia coli*." The student researcher was William Bow, who now runs his engineering consultant firm, and, of all the coincidences, more than a third of century later, was sitting amongst the Pearl Harbor Rotary listening to my first public presentation of ***Simple Solutions, Book 1***. But in the early 70's, the environmental and energy crisis arrived, and I moved on to other priorities.

Much later came the adventures of MarBEC, where Hawaii was supposed to become the Silicon Valley equivalent for marine biotechnology. In parallel I helped start a firm to conduct R&D on a high value bio-product at the Natural Energy Laboratory of Hawaii Authority. This pearl venture was reported on in ***Book 1***.

But a real opportunity came when, at the turn of the Millennium, I was asked to join the board of Hawaii Biotechnology Group, Inc., a company founded by colleagues at the University. I helped them accomplish three things. First, the name was too unwieldy, so I suggested Pacific Biotech. The change was made to Hawaii Biotech, Inc. Early in my directorship of the Hawaii Natural Energy Institute (*HNEI*), I recommended a change to the Pacific Institute for Oceanic, Natural Energy and Environmental Resources (*or PIONEER*). I was accused of trying to take over the university, so I relented. I've always thought Hawaii in a title was too limiting, and, if you're going to have a name, if at all possible, make the acronym meaningful.

But a company can't waste its time on small grants from the National Institutes of Health, so, second, I helped point the way to larger Department of Defense funding. Homeland security was becoming an important then, so what better than to have U.S. Senator Daniel Inouye assist them get bigger bucks to counteract bio-terrorism. This worked. But the larger problem was the company itself.

HBI was twenty years old and still competing for research through federal grants to stay alive. This is necessary for a university unit, but not what real companies should be doing. There was a sense of slow death. So I assisted in the transition to make HBI entrepreneurial. It is a very trying process transforming a company led by research professors, but, ultimately, even they took this chance.

In 2001 David Watumull was hired. It was unfortunate that he knew scant little about biology, had not even graduated from college and was involved in a lawsuit from his previous company, Aquasearch (*which is another interesting story in itself, having been founded by Mark Huntley, for a short spell a researcher at HNEI*), but David had the smarts, financing experience and local contacts. Six years later, Cardax was spun off to produce an anti-inflammatory compound, and he became its first CEO, and HBI continued in its quest for recombinant vaccine development, led by a team of high-powered alien (*not from Hawaii*) investors. Here I was waiting for the IPO to cash in my stock options, but got a reality check when Stanford Ovshinsky, who invented amorphous silicon products, told me that, by the time the financiers got through with it, a few bones were tossed his way. So much now for me ever getting rich.

I remain optimistic, however, about Hawaii ultimately gaining a foothold in this business, as the Medical School shows promise, marine natural products are ideal for development and our presence between East and West surely must be a plus. We did have that mouse, Cumilina, cloned by Ryuzo Yanagimachi, and, Hawaii Biotech is still alive. Marine biotechnology will someday, I predict, become the tool for next generation clean energy and natural pharmaceuticals…and maybe Hawaii will yet play a crucial role.

### Nanobiotechnology

One of my final tasks as a University of Hawaii faculty member was to chair a search committee for three MarBEC positions. We had the freedom to select any field we wanted, so the committee chose protein engineering, bioinformatics and bionanotechnology. I actually wrote the requirements for bionanotechnology. We found good candidates for the other two, but never did recruit anyone for the third. We hired Guangyi Wang, a post-doc of Jay Keasling in the Cal Berkeley Chemical Engineering Department, who went on to lead a team gaining a majestic grant of $42.5 million from the Gates Foundation to design molecules capable of doing what is usually in the province of microorganisms. I asked Jay how close he was to patenting the cure for malaria and how I could buy stock in his company. He just laughed. The chemical engineering of synthetic biology should someday prevail over the natural process because these drugs could then be produced ten times more cheaply. During this process I was also on the PhD committee of a political science candidate doing his dissertation in nanotechnology. Alas, he never graduated.

Nanotechnology deals with the study of very small things from 1 to 100 nanometers. A nanometer (*nm*) is one billionth, or $10^{-9}$, of a meter, which is like comparing a marble to Planet Earth. A DNA double-helix has a diameter of about 2 nm and a bacterium is in the range of 200 nm. Hair grows faster than one nm/second. Japanese scientist Norio Taniguchi coined the term in 1974 and American engineer Kim Eric Drexler wrote a book describing molecular nanotechnology in 1986. The notion of nanorobots to scavenge, say, cancer cells, has received some science fiction press, but no obvious way has been advanced on how to manufacture these nano-critters.

The solution might rest in the synthesis of nanotechnology and molecular biology into a branch called nanobiotechnology. I thought I was inventing the term, only to learn that a National Science Foundation Nanobiotechnology Center was being established in 2000 at Cornell University, as a partnership with Princeton, other universities and industry. Microfabrication is just about becoming real. Nanomanufacturing will be 1000 times more difficult.

### Stem Cells

Stem cell research is all about human engineering. Is it morally right to do this? James Watson of double-helix fame has been quoted to say: "If you are really stupid, I would call that a disease…so I'd like to get rid of that…People say it would be terrible if we made all girls pretty. I think it would be great."[347] Needless to say, there are contrary opinions from moral purists.

Well, what is a stem cell? It is a cell found in all multi-cellular organisms and has the ability to differentiate into a diverse range of specialized body parts. In other words, certain human cells can initiate a process to create muscles, a heart or whatever, regardless of where it came from. Bone marrow, a particular stem cell, for example, has been transplanted to treat a wide variety of diseases. Or, someday, a doctor might be able to inject a few stem cells into your failing heart, leading to a complete cure. It is reported that 100 million Americans living with incurable diseases from diabetes to heart conditions to Alzheimer's to Parkinson's to ALS to MS…can be helped.[326] You can add broken bones, brain damage, severe burns, some cancers, hepatitis, and stroke.

Would the ethical concern be tolerable if an empty cow egg is utilized to fuse human DNA? U.K. universities (*King's College London and the University of Newcastle*) were given the green light to proceed in 2007. What about from human skin?

How did all this get started? Glass was invented around the year 100 AD, and lenses were formed not long thereafter, but the earliest mention of eye glasses for improving sight was not until the 13th century. The father and son Dutch team of Hans and Zaccharias Janssen in 1590 carefully placed several lenses in a tube, inventing the microscope, leading to Italian Galileo Galilei, looking from the other end, building a telescope just after the turn of the century. In 1665, Englishman Robert Hooke published ***Micrographia***, reporting on some of his biological observations through a microscope, and coined the term, cell. Dutch Antonie van Leeuwenhoek, who lived to the ripe old age of 90, was inspired by Hooke's book and shifted using the microscope from improving textiles into the natural world. He later became known as the "Father of Microbiology."

In the early 1900's, European scientists reported that blood cells came from one particular stem cell. In 1963 Canadian cellular biologist Ernest McCulloch and biophysicist James Till at the University of Toronto discovered stem cells in blood forming systems and in 1998 a group led by developmental biologist James Thomson of the University of Wisconsin isolated and grew stem cells from human embryos, which led to the ethical concerns of today.

There are three categories of stem cells: embryonic, adult and cord blood. Embryonic stem cells are the most valuable, for they can differentiate into 220 cell body types (*which accounts for the whole body*) and have an unlimited capacity for self-renewal. They are obtained from the inner cell mass of a 4-5 day old embryo. That is the controversy. It is a moral, and, usually, religious issue. You are killing a human being. A simple solution might be to agree that life begins at one week instead of at conception.

For all intents and purposes, federally funded research in this field is limited. The religious factor sways Republicans, especially President George W. Bush, to be against embryonic stem cell research. In 2008 the Democratic U.S. Congress might pass a pro-research bill, but this will be vetoed by the President, and will not be overridden. But science is moving forward faster than politics, so there will be other options to neutralize politics.

Adult stem cells are not much of an issue, and reports keep surfacing that they can now be extracted from human skin, ordinary cells, human amniotic (*liquid in which the fetus subsists*) fluid, and more. Geneticist Shinya Yamanaka of Kyoto University has mixed a chemical cocktail of four ingredients to treat adult cells for this purpose. In November of 2007, ***Cell*** reported Yamanaka's team is now able to make patient-specific stem cells for therapies without fear of immune rejection and ***Science*** featured an article from the University of Wisconsin similar to the Kyoto development, in effect reprogramming implanted skin cells to convert them to stem cells. Furthermore, it was reported in ***Nature*** that an American group had found a way to extract embryonic stem cells without killing the embryo.[262] Yes, this was a mouse embryo, but something new pops up weekly.

In any case, the private sector and states can themselves fund stem cell development. California has earmarked $3 billion (*$300 million/year for 10 years*) and New Jersey $270 million. However, court challenges from mostly religious groups have stalled progress. Yet, it is reported that Stanford's human embryonic stem cell lab, the California Institute for Regenerative Medicine, has already received the largest grant, $26 million.

Private donors have contributed more than $150 million in California alone, and Mayor Michael Bloomberg donated $100 million to The Johns Hopkins University, where he went to school and obtained a science degree, largely for R&D in this field.[115] When you add the rest of the world to any undercover research, this field is booming.

The entire human embryonic stem cell research budget for the National Institutes of Health this past year was $40 million. A particular irony, is that more human embryos now are available for research than if President Bush had not imposed any restriction.[22] The U.S. Department of Health and Human Services indicated that 2002 data showed $270 million supporting 1000 scientists in 30 firms in industry. That was in 2002!

In polls:

- **CNN/Opinion Research Corporation Poll from May 4-6, 2007**

  *Do you think the federal government should or should not fund research that would use newly created stem cells obtained from human embryos?*

  Should = 53%    Should not = 41%

- **USA Today/Gallup Poll from April 13-15, 2007**

  *As you may know, the federal government currently provides very limited funding for medical research that uses stem cells obtained from human embryos. Which would you prefer:*

  No Restrictions = 22%
  Ease Restrictions = 38%
  Current Restrictions = 20%
  No Funding At All = 16%

- **ABC News/ Washington Post Poll from January 16-19, 2007**

  *Do you support or oppose embryonic stem cell research?*

  Support = 61%    Oppose = 31%

- **Newsweek Poll from October 26-27, 2006**

*Do you favor or oppose using federal tax dollars to fund medical research using stem cells obtained from human embryos?*

| Favor | Oppose |
|---|---|
| Republicans = 34% | Republicans = 54% |
| Democrats = 62% | Democrats = 27% |

In mid-2006, President Bush used the first veto of his Republican presidency to block a Democratic congress's act lifting the 2001 Republican ban on federal funding for most stem cell research.

- **Newsweek Poll from August 24-25, 2006**

*Do you approve or disapprove the way Bush is handling federal funding for stem cell research?*

Approve = 31% Disapprove = 52%

These results are, actually, surprising, as Chapter 5 will show that Americans are a highly religious group, and most of the opposition to stem cell research is from religious groups. The Republican opposition and Democratic support would be expected. In any case, there is something about President Bush that should change the national priorities with the next president in 2009.

From the religious perspective, a poll commissioned by the Secretariat for Pro-Life Activities of the U.S. Conference of Catholic Bishops in May of 2006 showed the following results:

- Stem cells are the basic cells from which all of a person's tissues and organs develop. Congress is considering the question of federal funding for experiments using stem cells from human embryos. The live embryos would be destroyed in their first week of development to obtain these cells. **Do you support or oppose using your federal tax dollars for such experiments**:

Support = 38.6%
Oppose = 47.8%
Don't know = 11.9%
Refused = 1.7%

The results were just the opposite. Just goes to show it is in how and who you ask. Also, therapeutic cloning appears to be gaining in support, as two-thirds of Americans are in favor to produce stem cells for this purpose.[252] In any case, stem cell research will thrive into the future as scientists sufficiently adjust to overcome religious discomfort.

## Cloning

Clone comes from the Greek word for twin, and for this section, cloning will refer to the manipulation of a DNA sequence within the cell to obtain multiple copies. While the technique is complicated, this allows for replication into an exact copy. Grafting of a grape plant also can be considered to be form of cloning.

There is a kind of natural cloning beyond single cell division called asexual reproduction or parthenogenesis. This is relatively common in a few species of reptiles, fish and birds. Apparently, it is possible for the female hammerhead shark and Komodo dragon to conceive without the help of any male, the offspring turning out to have a genotype exactly of their mother, but not identical.

Hans Spemann, a German embryologist, who was awarded a Nobel Prize in 1935, wrote of his 1928 salamander nuclear transplant experiment in his 1938 book entitled, ***Embryonic Development and Induction***. However, he never himself ever attained a successful clone. The first reported actual human induced cloning, was that of northern leopard frogs in 1952 by two American scientists, Robert Briggs and Thomas King. Tong Dizhou, a Chinese embryologist, in 1963 produced a clone of a carp. The Briggs-King technique was used to create, 6LL3, or Dolly—after Dolly Parton, because the cloning was of a mammary cell from a Finn Dorset lamb—the sheep, in 1996. Dolly apparently died from accelerated aging, caused by shortening of telomeres (*located at the tips of a chromosome, which could well be the vital clue to eternal life*).

There is, however, considerable controversy as to who should get credit. English embryologist Ian Wilmut was the supervisor, but English biologist Keith Campbell did most of the lab work. In 1997 came Cumulina by Ryuzo Yanagimachi at the University of Hawaii, and Campbell, in 1998, cloned Polly, another sheep, from genetically altered skin cells containing a human gene. Since then, clones of a rhesus monkey, cattle, cat (*Little Nicky, 2004*), mule, horse and dog have been created.

There was ***Frankenstein*** by Mary Shelley, but that was just a fabrication from assorted human parts, and ***Jurassic Park***, the novel by Michael Crichton and film by Stephen Spielberg, which featured clones of dinosaurs. Can this actually be accomplished? Apparently yes, as a team from Japan and Russia are trying to extract the DNA from a frozen woolly mammoth to bring this beast, at least the clone, back to life. The San Diego Zoo stores frozen tissues from the most endangered of species, awaiting the day.

Human cloning is the generation of a genetically identical version of a person. Identical twins are clones. The controversy has to do with cloning yourself. Animal stem cells are one thing, while embryonic stem cells are another. This distinction is amplified when it comes to animal cloning and human cloning. Cloning will develop into one option for eternal life.

How can a human be cloned? Basically, copying the Briggs-King technique: take an egg cell from a donor with the nucleus removed, then fuse on your cell with the proper genetic material.

Has there been any success? In 2002, Clonaid claimed victory with Baby Eva, and in 2004 returned with announcement of 13 additional clones. However, this organization is the medical arm of a religion called Raelism, which believes that aliens introduced human life (*see Chapter 4*). Absent any genetic confirmation, dubiosity runs rampant. In a nutshell, the field has been riddled with hoaxes and scientific frauds, including the incident out of South Korea, later described.

Notwithstanding, human cloning is now just about a given. In 2008, Stemagon, a company in La Jolla, California, announced it had cloned Samuel Wood, their chief executive.[345] Wood, himself, indicated their firm had no interest in cloning humans as such (*although, this is a wise thing to say today, not necessarily indicating ultimate intention*). Their primary purpose was to grow the clone of a patient from which stem cells can be harvested to grow replacement tissues and organs.

The following polls show public feelings (*all of these are virtual as of August 2007, except as indicated*):

- **From Explore More poll on genetic engineering:**

*Do you think cloning should be legal?*

| | |
|---|---|
| Yes | 55% |
| No | 45% |

*What are your feelings about human cloning?*

| | |
|---|---|
| Doubtful | 15% |
| Fearful | 41% |
| Hopeful | 44% |

- **From About.com on Agnosticism/Atheism:**

*Should research into human cloning be permitted or banned?*

| | |
|---|---|
| Permitted | 49% |
| Banned | 44% |

*Should actual cloning of human beings be permitted or banned?*

| | |
|---|---|
| Permitted | 34% |
| Banned | 59% |

- **From the United States Conference of Catholic Bishops (May 2006):**

*Should scientists be allowed to use human cloning to try to create children for infertile couples:*

Yes 9.7%

*No 83.4%*

*Should scientists be allowed to use human cloning to create a supply of human embryos to be destroyed in medical research?*

Yes 11.4%

No 81.2%

It's pretty clear that Americans have a negative opinion of human cloning, especially if a religious organization runs the survey. Most of the earlier traditional polls, actually, showed a negativity factor in the 80-90% range for actual human cloning.

In a poll of undergraduate students in Indonesia, Kenya, Sweden and the U.S., 10% were positive to human reproductive cloning, while 74% were negative. Muslims were the most negative and Hindus least. Non-religious respondents showed about the same overall average.[129] It's all in how you ask the question, but, even in Europe, disapproval of cloning prevails.[293] Strangely enough, this same poll hinted that the views from both Mexico and Turkey had only a 50% disapproval figure.

The UN General Assembly in August of 2005 did adopt a declaration prohibiting all forms of human cloning. The vote was 87 in support, 34 in opposition and 70 abstaining or absent. But the edict was non-binding. The European Convention on Human Rights and Biomedicine prohibits human cloning, but has not been ratified by most countries. There is, further, a Charter of Fundamental Rights of the European Union, which bans reproductive human cloning, but it has no legal standing. Cloning is largely unregulated in the U.K., but a therapeutic cloning license was issued in 2004 to the University of Newcastle. Human cloning, actually, is legal in the U.S., but there are Federal prohibitions against research.

Some countries have observed the American reluctance to support human cloning research and have taken definite steps. South Korea made a quick entry, but fell by the wayside in the scandal involving Professor Hwang Woo-Suk of Seoul National University (*SNU*), who announced in 2004 that his team had cloned human embryos and would someday be able to grow genetically matched tissues to repair anything in your body that broke down. His monumental breakthrough was published in ***Science***, the most prestigious of scientific journals. It turned out to be a hoax. He did not produce even one stem cell line, while endangering the lives of junior female researchers who were unethically coaxed to donate their eggs for this research.

But Korea plugs along, as in 2006, a collaborator of Professor Hwang, Lee Byeong-chun, also of SNU, succeeded in cloning the first female dog, Snuppy, an Afghan hound, using 2000 eggs to make 1000 embryos to produce one dog. Snuppy's surrogate mother was a yellow Labrador. Professor Lee, though, remains in jeopardy because of the earlier scandal.

Singapore, a former British colony of 4.5 million people, has also entered the competition. For all intents and purposes, while a democracy, it is about as close to a benevolent dictatorship as there exists today. The government decides what is best and gets the job done. Education is one area, which is reported in the next chapter. Biotechnology is also a priority area. They have created Biopolis, a $300 million, 2 million square foot research center focused on biomedical development. They have recruited world class scientists who are fed up with national politics in their own country. Singapore is trying to establish a world sanctuary for stem cell research. While first inaugurated in 2003, Biopolis is already home to scientists from 50 nations.

A prime attraction is that Singapore allows stem cells to be drawn from embryos up to 14 days old. I keep reading that human cloning will be banned with a fine of $60,000 and five years of jail time, but I haven't yet seen the actual law. Perhaps the benevolent dictatorship group is mulling over the humanitarian prospects of someday becoming the site of choice for therapeutic cloning, as depicted in a former CBS television drama, ***Century City***.

What about China? University of Connecticut animal cloning director Jerry Yang Xiangzhong told ***The Standard***, China's business newspaper, that China can jump ahead of the U.S. in three years if their scientists were given the green light to proceed.[375] His contention is that in much of the developed world scientific progress in this field is hindered by political and religious debates. There is also the moral problem with something called human dignity. Apparently, these difficulties would not be experienced in China.

So where is the USA on human cloning? Harvard initiated efforts to clone human embryos in 2006. They are funding this work with private donors without any government assistance. Mind you, they are not cloning humans, they would like to harvest stem cells to fight leukemia and diabetes. On the West Coast, the University of California at San Francisco announced a similar pursuit. There are also companies, such as Advanced Cell Technology of Massachusetts, pursuing human embryonic stem cell cloning. The ethical issues, however, will determine how quickly this effort develops. Well, now on to the next logical step beyond human cloning: eternal life.

## Eternal Life

### Background

All living things today are essentially already immortal. We should be able to, someday, trace ourselves back through 50 billion DNA copyings over 4 billion years to determine our Luca. Our DNA has, thus, had everlasting life. Of course, we live through our children and their children. Then, too, the products of our life, such as books and statues, live for a very long time. However, Woody Allen has expressed a sense that he was not satisfied living forever through his works, for he wanted to live forever by not dying. Conscious eternal life, if not rejuvenation and reversal, then, is an ultimate goal on the level of world peace and universal happiness. Sounds a bit like Heaven.

It has been speculated that someday, through human cloning and the transfer of your memory to this new body, eternal life can be attained. Computer technology now exceeds 100 trillion calculations per second (*$10^{14}$ cps*), and should reach $10^{16}$ cps in a decade, at which size the brain can be simulated. Such a computer should only cost about $1000 in 2020. Then there are algorithms and biological interfacing challenges. This should all be possible in 25 years. However the focus in the following discussion will be on biological immortality.

The search, thus, is for the aging gene. Science is on to finding it and stopping the tick of this biological clock. The human genome table offers this opportunity. As chemists once tinkered with the periodic table of elements (*there are 115 elements, although one atom of 118, Ununoctium, guessed to be a colorless gas, was first found in 2002, leaving 113, 115 and 117 still undiscovered*) bioscientists are today just beginning the quest with many thousand times more "elements."

There is a difference between life expectancy and life span, with the former the number of years something is expected to live, and the latter referring to the maximum age possible. Some animals, such as alligators and female flounders, apparently, have no limit. The Turritopsis nutricula jellyfish can transform itself back into a child. There are definite clues here.

Our early humans had a life expectancy of 18, although averages as high as 33 have been reported for limited periods tens of thousands of years ago, which, actually dropped back down to 18 during the Bronze Age (*3500-1200 BC*) with more crowded conditions causing infections and lack of proper nutrition. During classical Greek and Roman periods, the lifespan was 28, which improved back up to 33 in Medieval England. The average today is 67, with females at 69.5 and males at 65. Andorra, in the Pyrenees Mountains has the highest at 83.5, with Japan #2 at 82.6. The U.S. is #39 at 78.2.

The oldest human ever was Jeanne Calment of France, who quit smoking at the age of 117 and passed away in 1997 at the age of 122. As of this writing, the oldest man is Tomoji Tanabe of Japan, who is only 112 years old, taking over from Puerto Rican Emiliano Del Toro, who died in 2007 at the age of 115. The oldest person is 114 year old Edna Parker from the state of Indiana, USA. Since 1955 there have been 54 oldest humans, so, on average, there is a new oldest person about every year.

In 1964, Donald Currey, a graduate student from the University of North Carolina, received permission from the U.S. Forest Service to cut down Prometheus, a bristlecone pine growing at altitude on Wheeler Peak, and by counting rings, determined that it was 4862 years old.[78] Currey died in 2004 at the age of 70. What a tragedy, the death of Prometheus! Can we learn from trees?

The life span for the Galapagos tortoise is 193, Bowhead Whale 211 (*harpoon of 1790 attached to body*), giant aldabra tortoise 250 years, and Icelandic Cyprine mollusk 374. However, in 2007, it was reported that Ming, an ocean quahog clam, was at least 405 years old, making this the oldest animal who ever lived[166] Incidentally, guess what, to determine the age of Ming, British scientist had to count the rings of its shell. By doing so, they also killed the clam. We did it again.

Medical researchers studying animals have determined that a 50% caloric intake can increase mean life span by 65% and anti-oxidants MLS up to 30%. There definitely are clues here.

**Telomeres**

The telomere is a protein (*ribonucleoprotein*) complex found at the edges of a chromosome, and a little bit is lost, or shortened, every time the cell divides. Depending on age and site, a cell then dies after between 20 to 100 divisions. The concept was envisioned by Cornell cytogeneticist, Barbara McClintock, although she was a faculty member of the University of Missouri at Columbia when she published her paper in 1939 on the subject. She primarily worked on maize, and went on to win the Nobel Prize in 1983 at the age of 81.

Telomerase is an enzyme found in the telomere region, and was discovered by Carol Greider in 1984, working, it is said, on Christmas Day. Telomeres can be lengthened by the activation of telomerase, and could be the key to immortality. However, while aging is thus slowed, there is an increase in vulnerability to cancer. Geron Corporation granted a license to TA Sciences Center to market a telomerase activator agent extracted from the Chinese Astragalus plant. Human trials for extending lifespan are expected within the decade.

The bottom line is that research for curing cancer or heart failure is a necessary step towards finding the secret for immortality. Get to know your telomeres and telomerases.

**Notables in the Search for Eternal Life**

Leonard Hayflick, a dragon twelve years older than me, is a professor of anatomy at the University of California at San Francisco (*UCSF*), and is previously from Stanford University. He is known for the Hayflick Limit (*most cells divide 20-100 times before dying, as a limit for humans*), which directed research towards the cell as the controller of aging. Importantly, he determined that the capped telomere enzyme region appeared to be the key to aging. He effectively found this biological clock in 1961. Every time a cell divides, a small segment of telomeric DNA is lost, so, the telomeres shorten, or age, like a burning fuse. Cancer cells have found a way to ignore this process. However, we now know that this mechanism, the shortening, could well be the body's mechanism for eliminating cancerous cells. Thus, if we can find out how cancer cells do this, or otherwise prevent this shortening, life should go on forever. The attraction of stem cells, too, is that they appear to be able to regenerate new cells as long as the organism lives. Thus, finding out why stem cells are so different, combined with deactivating this natural shortening, if not lengthening them, while still having the capability for eliminating cancerous cells—as perhaps using nanotechnology robots to root them out—are three areas worthy of exploration.

Elizabeth Blackburn, from the UCSF biology department, originally from Australia, was a co-discoverer of telomerase, for Carol Greider was using Blackburn's lab at the University of

California at Berkeley when the enzyme was found. She won the Lasker and Gruber Prizes for her work on telomeres and telomerase, a nice pathway to a potential Nobel. She might best be known for her firing from the President's Council on Bioethics in 2004 for her "non" conservative views on the subject. A firestorm of protest came from the scientific community. The council was created in 2001 to monitor stem cell research.

University of Colorado behavioral geneticist Thomas Johnson, in 1988, extended the life of a worm called *Caenorhabditis elegans* by 60%, thus introducing this nematode to the scientific world. He chaired two Gordon Conferences on the Biology of Aging.

A third UCSF faculty member, biologist Cynthia Kenyon, MIT PhD associated with Lenny Guarente, holding the Herbert Boyer (*who was earlier mentioned*) Professorship, and who previously worked for Nobel Laureate Sydney Brenner, wants to live to be 150. She has increased the life span of *C. elegans* by a factor of six, meaning the equivalent human life of 400 years.[92] She has merely suppressed the regulator gene, daf-2. *C. elegans* is a good lab model because it only has about a thousand types of cells and is translucent, so you can see the organs. She helped found a company, Elixir, with Guarente, raising $37 million to find a Fountain of Youth pill. Kenyon believes it is in the realm of possibility that just changing the right human gene could double our lifetime. Then, who knows?

Aubrey de Grey a biomedical gerontologist from the United Kingdom, has been working on "strategies for engineered negligible senescence (*SENS*), or, finding a cure for human aging. He lists seven types of aging damage, but I've compressed them into five:

- cancer
- mutations
- junk molecules
- death of cells
- loss of elasticity linking cells

He co-founded the Methuselah Mouse Prize (*MMP*), with a sum of $4.5 million to fund researchers to extend the lifespan of mice. Methuselah reached the age of 969 years in ***The Bible***. However, there are arguments that the secrets for aging will come from a fruit fly or worm, rather than a mouse. Grey has been quoted to say that people will start living ***thousand year lives at any selected age in 25 years. MMP and Technology Review of MIT sponsored a $20,000 ($10k each) prize to the first scientist who could show that SENS was so wrong that it was unworthy of debate. Preston Estep and his colleagues proved to be the most eloquent, and were given the TR share, but not good enough to blow SENS out of the water.***

Michael West offers a personal journey in his ***The Immortal Cell***.[346] He was initially a creationist, devoted to dispelling evolution, but made a full reversal after witnessing the death of his father, shifting from Greek and Hebrew to biology, gaining a PhD degree, and turning to immortality science. He co-founded Geron in 1990, the first to biotechnologically treat age-related disorders, becoming a pioneer in stem cell R&D. Very simply, their goal is to take the patient's own cells, rejuvenate and modify them, and insert them back in the person to treat diseases. Specifically, telomeres would be lengthened. Their experimental cells now double more than a 100 times. Macular degeneration and atherosclerosis (hardening of the arteries) will someday thusly be treated. He is now president and CEO of Advanced Cell Technology, which is the only American company pursuing human therapeutic cloning research, and serves as Adjunct Professor Bioengineering at the University of California at Berkeley. West, no doubt, came full circle when President George W. Bush denounced the intent of West from the Rose Garden of the White House.

Among the other pioneers:

- o Michael Rose, evolutionary biologist from the University of California at Davis, has extended the life of the fruit fly.
- *o* ***Stephen Helfand, biology professor at Brown Medical School, discovered an aging gene called INDY** (for "I'm not dead yet")* ***in fruit flies.***
- o Valter Longo, molecular geneticist at the University of Southern California, has deleted the SIR2 gene from yeast, extending the life span by a factor of six. He suggests that the SIRT1 gene might be the mammal analog.
- *o* ***SIR2 was co-discovered in life extension studies in Lenny Guarente's** (with Elixir)* ***lab at MIT by Matt Kaeberlein, who now is at the University of Washington.***
- o Richard Weindruch, professor of medicine at the University of Wisconsin, seems to have shown that rhesus monkeys eating 30% fewer calories lived longer.
- *o* ***The interesting link was a possible connection between restricted diets and SIR2, for the increase in yeast life span occurred only when SIR2 was present.[267] Further, SIR2 was dependent on another molecule, nicotinamide adenine dinocleotide, or NAD, but this is getting too scientific.***
- *o* ***David Sinclair, a post-doc of Guarente, now at Harvard, showed that fat mice fed resveratrol** (yes, trans-3,3,4'-trihydroxystilbene, that compound found in red wine)* ***lived 15% longer. Sinclair has founded Sirtris, a company dedicated to finding polyphenyl drugs to affect the SIRT1 gene, basically mimicking caloric restriction. Remember champagne and polyphenyls?***
- o The same effect was seen in yeast, worms and fruit flies, but there have also been contrary reports that resveratrol has no effect on SIR2 activity.

Sirtis and Elixir are companies currently focused on finding FDA-approved drug pathways to combat diabetes and neurological disorders, one step towards immortality. There are many more scientists exploring the boundaries of this field, and, like in string theory, the best is hopefully to come.

**Bioethics of Immortality**

Science fiction has long reported that, someday, we will be able to live forever. A simple matter of using the best of the above techniques to improve our current bodies should someday be available, and, perhaps, in a decade or two or slightly more. However, a second mechanism in case science is late or bioethical attitudes prevail to delay development is to store your memory in a computer for later transference to either your clone or, even, better body, for all of us are deficient in some way. How can you store your memory? Its amazing how quickly the field of electronics and, soon, bioelectronics, is advancing. In your lifetime, for some, this capability should be possible.

But what of human clones, superbabies, the Boys from Brazil, Adolph Hitler, playing God? The public will support therapeutic cloning, but will it ever allow federal funds to allow focused research, and, ultimately, the open marketing of immortality? Do we need the federal government?

As I will cover religion in Chapter 5, let me close this discussion by referring you to the following books:

- ***Merchants of Immortality***, Stephen Hall, Houghton Mifflin, 2003.
- ***Aging, Death and the Quest for Immortality***, C. Ben Mitchell, Robert Orr and Susan Salladay, editors, William B. Erdmans Publishing, 2004.
- ***The Scientific Conquest of Death***, Immortality Institute, 2004
- ***The Geneticist Who Played Hoops with My DNA***, David Ewing Duncan, Harper Collins, 2005.

Frank Tipler has written ***The Physics of Immortality***, which will be relegated to Chapter 5 on religion.

There is no way I will be able to influence anyone on the bioethics of immortality. You can do it yourself.

## The Simple Solution to Immortality

Clearly, a few master genes regulate the process of immunotherapy. The ticking of your biological clock appears to be related to the shortening of your telomeres. The combined fields of stem cells, nanobiotechnology and anti-aging—involving lengthened telomeres, sirtuins (*those SIR genes*) and nanobots—will someday all come together to check aging, if not even, reverse the process.

The solution? Await the coming. Some will fight it, but they will, ultimately, falter. You just need to live long enough.

# CHAPTER 3: TEACHING RAINBOWS—THE 7 R'S

## Rainbows

Iris, meaning rainbow in Latin, was a messenger of the Olympian gods and the goddess of this optical phenomenon. Chinese, Indian and Norse mythology also relates the rainbow to gods. Aristotle mentioned the moonbow. In ***The Bible***, the rainbow is the covenant between God and Man. The Irish leprechaun found a perfect place to hide his pot of god because you can never get to the end of the rainbow. But, then, that in itself is a fatal flaw to the concept because they, too, could not get there, unless they were supernatural, which, I guess, they were, if they were real.

But getting to reality, Euclid's ***Optica*** (*300 BC*) and Ptolemy's ***Optica*** (*140 AD*) both tried to formulate a law of refraction (*you might recall that science project where the prism separates sunlight into colors of the rainbow*). However, rainbows first began to be seriously analyzed much later in the 13$^{th}$ Century by Persian and English scientists. The earliest theoretical explanation was reported by German Theodoric of Freiberg in 1307. In 1637, Descartes experimented with sunlight through a glass sphere.

It was Isaac Newton, though, who, between 1666 and 1672, used a prism to refract the transparent light of the Sun into the full visible spectrum: red, yellow, green, blue and violet. The mnemonic, Roy G. Biv—or red, orange, yellow, green, blue, indigo, violet—is commonly used to remember Newton's later addition—in 1704 from his ***Opticks***—of orange and indigo (*420 to 440 nm, see the **Colors** section in the **Intro****duction***) to equate with the seven notes of the musical scale. I've long been waiting a computerized all purpose keyboard of the seven colors to finally learn how to play a piano.

There is, of course, no definitive line of demarcation. The rainbow is a continuous spectrum from red to violet. There are more colors, but the human eye cannot see infrared, ultraviolet, X-rays or Gamma Rays, although our bodies can feel them.

Poet John Keats, nearly two centuries later talked about Newton unweaving the rainbow,[330] destroying the beauty of nature by analyzing light with a prism and splitting it into colors. Two centuries again later, Richard Dawkins, in his ***Unweaving the Rainbow***,[82] chides Keats about being a very young man who (*died at the age of 25*) did not appreciate that mysteries don't lose their poetry because they are solved. Here I disagree with Dawkins, for the mystery is what keeps religion, for example, functional. Once humanity determines there is no magic to miracles, religion will either become unnecessary or evolve into a more realistic culture, and maybe even spur the Golden Revolution, depicted in Chapter 5. The poetry, in some respects, will be gone, but like life in general, things do change. Notwithstanding, Richard Dawkins was singularly influential on my views in the chapter on religion.

Without getting into the real science, the rainbow is a virtual (*unreal, cannot be captured, maybe like a ghost or God, but wait until Chapter 5*) image caused by sunlight shining through water droplets, like rain, with you in the middle. Thus, you cannot see a rainbow while facing the sun (*except for very rare fourth harmonics...but forget this*). A direct line connects the Sun through the back of your head to the center (*middle of the circle*) of the arc. Red is always inside, but, conversely, outside in the double rainbow. If you are on the ground, and 90 degrees is straight up, morning and afternoon rainbows can only be seen when the sun is lower than 42 degrees (*just below the halfway up and down points*). I now and then saw a circular rainbow from our former apartment, and thought I saw a side by side rainbow while golfing earlier this year, but did not have a camera. Maybe I was dreaming, for this has to be impossible, as both were of the same size and intensity. Of course, you also see rainbows in sprays from sprinklers, falls and waves.

***Over the Rainbow***, music by Harold Arlen and lyrics by Yip Harburg, sung by Judy Garland, won the Oscar as the song of the year in 1939 and was named the top American song of the 20th Century by the Recording Industry of America and National Endowment for the Arts. Hawaiian Israel Kamakawiwoole recorded this song in 1993, combined with ***What a Wonderful World*** and ***Rainbow*** was released by Jack Johnson, also of Hawaii, in the same year. Another ***Rainbow*** by George Hamilton IV was popular in 1961. The opening song of the 1979 ***Muppet Movie*** was ***The Rainbow Connection***. ***Rainbow*** by Mariah Carey in 1999, with a ***Rainbow*** Interlude, and by Neil Diamond in 1973, without anything close to a song by that title, are two of many rainbow albums. Sammi Davis (*nope, this one is a female*) starred in Ken Russell's ***The Rainbow*** in 1989. Then in 2008 there was Radiohead's "In Rainbows" album.

Jesse Jackson had his ***Rainbow Coalition***, Greenpeace's ship is the ***Rainbow Warrior***, hippies gather at ***Rainbow Gatherings***, and the rainbow is the universal symbol of the lesbian, gay, bisexual and transgender people. The University of Hawaii, it is reported, switched from rainbows to warriors, perhaps for this reason, but, more so, to better market black colored uniforms.

China had a rainbow bridge made of bamboo in the 12th Century, while Japan now has a suspension bridge crossing northern Tokyo Bay, which is white in the daytime, and sort of red, white and green in the evening, using lights powered by stored solar energy. Sort of, because from any distance it still looks white at night. I gave a talk to a high school group in Japan and tried to inspire them to work with Hilton—as this hotel chain at one time used the rainbow in its advertisements—to make the Rainbow Bridge truly rainbow colored, becoming yet another of my failed ideas. The cover of ***Simple Solutions for Planet Earth***, Book 1, featured a rainbow bridge. For this chapter, that cover would be more appropriate.

The Discovery Channel sponsors the Rainbow Education Media and there are various rainbow education systems. I would like to propose the teaching of rainbows, not the virtual image, but the full spectrum of the seven R's, to match Newton's color music wheel. However, I will first describe my educational experience.

## My Life in Education

### The Early Years

A rainbow is virtual, again, something you can't touch...it is not real. There are so many inculcation theories, that for all practical purposes, they, too, are virtual. Our schools today focus on **r**eading, w**r**iting and a**r**ithmetic, the three **R**'s, only a small part of the rainbow. We need to expand the spectrum to at least seven.

School boards are fixated on the budget and standardized tests. The White House does not want to leave a child behind. An early national commission wondered if our Nation was at risk because of our educational system. All are noble and worthy foci, but limiting.

But hey, I've got good news, we are doing okay! The USA is the greatest country in the world. Yet, we can do a lot better, and must, as the world is catching up in various ways. While K-12 teachers are given all the formal tools, professors, like myself, are never told how to teach. Which way is better? The jury is out, which is another way of saying, it almost doesn't matter. How many of you took a course on how to be a good parent? Anything works, but nothing is good enough. Such is the nature of education.

I remember when I was a four year old in pre-school when World War II was still raging, and in Honolulu, we had experienced Pearl Harbor and went through blackouts every night, fearing another attack. Gas masks were prevalent. I hated being in this virtual prison, that year in nursery school. The tomato juice was just awful and the hot chocolate was not hot chocolate. The problem with me in those days, and many people today when they even grow up, is that you don't appreciate your life. I could easily have been starving or with a bunker mentality in Hiroshima or Dresden, but, here I was, in Hawaii, and bemoaning my misfortune on the hard floor in a sleeping bag being forced to take a nap when I could have been playing.

One day I decided to do something about my confinement, and, somehow, before nap time in the afternoon, escaped. I don't remember the details, but do recall walking around the neighborhood as a free boy. At some point I got bored and went home. There was a policeman talking to my mother. The daycare center had reported my absence and I had become a fugitive or kidnapee. Bear in mind that this was wartime. I've forgotten the consequences, but in hindsight now can pinpoint my life from that afternoon, chapter by chapter, as always being on the edge of the envelope. Apparently, this experience did not frighten me into becoming a better citizen, but, instead, set the tone for the rest of my life, until I retired and again became a free man, with peace of mind. So what do I do? I begin to write ***Simple Solutions***, again saturating my life with controversy.

In real kindergarten, at Pohukaina Elementary School, my only memory was fighting over a nametag with someone named Pauline. We pulled in opposite directions, and it ripped in two. Unfortunately, because Patrick and Pauline were similar to two five year olds, my Patrick was the casualty, and I spent all school year with a Scotch-taped nametag, for it was, it turned out, my tag. I learned that being right was not necessarily good or sufficient.

In first grade, my most vivid recollection was a girl, just outside our room, throwing up... worms. I can still see them squirming on the ground. There are some memories that never go away. I should delete this paragraph, as it has no redeeming virtue.

In the second grade, on the last day of class, the instructor picked a student to carry the records, with the group following, to the third grade room to meet the teacher for the following year. This selected individual stood up and made the usual thank you for teaching us speech, and, being next to her, as she began to sit, I got the sudden urge to pull her seat. She fell to the floor. Well, I think I might be the only one who has ever spent an hour disciplinary period on the last day of school. But this was not the end of this type of punishment. I think it was just mischievousness, and I learned something that day: don't be so stupid. This is called gaining maturity.

The only thing that comes to mind about the third grade is that the teacher made cinnamon toast and sold them to us; in the fourth, that we drew pictures of Hawaiian flowers and shrubbery; in the fifth when we painted pictures and sang songs; and sixth, yikes, spitting out the window from the second floor and hitting the school principal, who just happened to walk by. This was not malicious, but the lesson I learned was that you need to be careful about where you spit...or whatever you do, yet another step towards maturity.

I learned to do well with what you can—like being on time—for there are so many other factors over which you have no control. I remember missing school one week while I was sick in bed, when fractions were covered, and for the longest time, never really understood the concept. Most of us have flaws in something or another because we were not there when the lesson was being taught. The biggest lessons, the other four R's, are never really covered in our schools, so we all suffer, especially society.

Well, I graduated to Central Intermediate School and the seventh grade, which was another war zone for me. There were fights and bullies and I was never really all that comfortable in this arena. How can I forget David Kakalia, who regularly borrowed a quarter from me through pure intimidation. A couple of decades later, I read that he had died, and only then felt relieved that he wasn't going to come after me, again. As I think about it now, he probably only "borrowed" from me a grand total of a dollar, probably less, but the fear factor was everything. I'm not sure what I learned from this experience.

I do recall that I did okay in math, but in the eighth grade, scored in the bottom ten percentile in the verbal portion of some standardized test. We walked to school, which was half an hour away, at least, and barefeet. How we got by is a mystery, because there were glass shards everywhere we went. In a sense, I can better understand how dogs and lions can survive without wearing any kind of protective footwear.

I graduated, to McKinley High School, but we were wearing shoes by then. However, growing up, you exist in gangs. Ours was about ten strong, and the process of getting to school was exasperating. The person farthest away walked by the next, and by the time they came to me, we were still at least twenty minutes away from the campus. Invariably the group had to wait for someone, so we were perpetually tardy. Doing so meant you had to report to a room at the end of the school day. We held the world record for being kept after school, but the psychology of being friends is that you just accepted all this.

In those days, and maybe so today, too, students in English/Social Studies were placed according to how smart you were. In my sophomore year I was in the second level class, with some not so bright students, but above the truly dumb and unmotivated ones. Around this time, though, the Kakaako area was being re-developed, so my family moved to Kalihi, really not that far away from Farrington High School, another tough public school. To maintain continuity, I caught the bus to McKinley and was on my way to becoming a model citizen, for I was never again kept after school. The bus was always on time.

The turning point in my life was during this transition period. My focus and grades began to improve, to the point where I was placed with the best students in my junior year. Does the environment and who you hang out with make a difference? It certainly did in my case. Most of my gang never went to college. I still see them every so often, for some have in most ways remained my closest friends.

There were two crucial factors in my junior year of high school. First, I had Mildred Kosaki as my English/Social Studies teacher. She quit teaching soon after my class—nothing to do with me, I hope, for she did go on to become an important planner and served on the board of Hawaiian Electric Company. Something she did as a teacher woke me up on what I wanted to be. The low aptitude I had in verbal ability was confirmed early in this junior year of 1956 when I took the practice college board exam, did well in math, but, again, scored in the bottom percentiles of the English portion.

Second, in the spring of 1957 I broke my wrist playing basketball. In those days, many, during the summer months, labored in the pineapple cannery. This I could not do, so I decided to extend what Mrs. Kosaki kept preaching, and memorized the vocabulary words in a red and blue colored (*I vividly can remember what it looked like*) college board preparation book. They say that you cannot improve your test scores much, but I am living proof that you can. My high 200's verbal score more than doubled into the 600's when I took the real college entrance exam early in my senior year.

During the spring of my junior year, though, I recall, for a reason that still mystifies me—for I never before had the guts to run for any office of any kind, and never have again—I campaigned for Senior Class Vice-President, and faced three female opponents. I guess it was more the gender ratio advantage, but the cast I wore possibly served as an identifiable macho symbol, and I triumphed. My VPship put me in charge of graduation exercises, and I somehow prevailed in having Mrs. Kosaki's husband, Richard, who was a fresh political science professor at the University of Hawaii, as our Commencement Speaker. Normally you provide a really old important person this privilege. Much later, when I joined the faculty of the UH, Professor Kosaki had become an influential administrator. Just as I am writing this, I received in the mail the Commencement Program from Richard, showing him as the keynote speaker and me as the chairman. He even sent me his speech.

You see where this is headed? One thing leads to another. I would never have been accepted into the California Institute of Technology had I not improved my Scholastic Aptitude Test scores; probably not into Stanford University if I did not show any leadership skills; and perhaps not have been as successful a professor without Mildred's and Richard's assistance. Thus, breaking my wrist catalyzed a whole range of opportunities. I've particularly noticed that the best comes from the worst.

**My University Years**

Stanford was my first retirement. I had studied so hard and was relatively burnt out by the time I made it to this college campus in September of 1958, that it was fortunate I was here, for many of the top schools actually flunked out people. That "look to your left and look to your right" lecture on opening day to determine whether it was to be only one-third who would be forced to leave or graduate (*this range varies from school to school*) did not apply to Stanford. There, they figured you were worthy of something, so almost everyone graduated. The only exception I remember is a friend, a really nice guy, who, at the end of the first quarter (*at that time we had three quarters of school and one quarter of free summer*), went around, shook our hands, and told us that he was called in to determine why he was doing so poorly, and was told that the admissions people made an embarrassing mistake. He should not have been accepted in the first place. He was asked to voluntarily leave. I can still see his face and the agony he was facing of going back home.

The second good thing was that I majored in chemical engineering. Why I did this had something to do with facing a challenge, for I never did all that well in chemistry in high school and did not know much about this field, but it appeared to be an exciting unknown. I think it is in my blood to head in the direction of the challenge. What I did not realize then was that, year after year, chemical engineering B.S. students always received the highest pay of anyone graduating. Even in 2006, when liberal arts majors garnered $30,828, business administration grads got $39,850, and computer science majors received $50,046, chemical engineering degree graduates received an average starting salary of $55,900, more than $3,000 over those in electrical engineering. [356]

That one-third ratio, actually, was much worse in chemical engineering. While there were 75 or so who appeared to be majoring in this field as freshmen, my graduating class 45 months later was 8, or about 10%. But I don't know of any who flunked out. They mostly transferred into economics and the social sciences, and no doubt are making a lot more money than I ever earned. Eight seems like a small number, and should be below the minimum to attain any kind excellence. In our junior year, the chairman of the department, David Mason, rushed into one of our lecture classes, and proudly announced that our department had gained accreditation. To our general astonishment, no one had ever before mentioned that we were NOT accredited. Yet, a decade after I graduated, the Stanford Chemical Engineering Department attained #1 status, as tiny as it still was in size. It by then had moved out of chemistry into engineering.

Funny, but I was more concerned at the beginning when I arrived on campus that Leland Stanford Junior University was a real university, and not a junior college, rather than the department I joined being accredited. Such is ignorance and youth!

***Book 1*** described some of my history, including my five years in the sugar industry, and the fact that I graduated in less than four years each from both Stanford and LSU, as again indicated in Chapter 7 on Eternal Life. Armed with a PhD in biochemical engineering, I went back home to teach at the University of Hawaii in 1971.

The first college course I taught was FORTRAN, a computer language. I was given the text the day before my first class, had not ever taken the class and I barely knew anything about the subject. Let's see, should I confess to the class that I would be learning with them, or wing it. As I walked up to the podium I chose the latter. Questions came up that I did not understand, but I deftly side-stepped them with the response, "we will take up that subject later in the semester. I don't want to confuse the group."

There were a hundred or so in that first class, from freshmen to graduate students. After the course was over, streams of students, including those in graduate school, came by to tell me how much they enjoyed the semester. This never happened again in such numbers in my 28 years in academia, although I only taught for a few years. The lesson learned was that if you don't know what you are teaching, but must, you actually make the course easier to understand. This state of semi-panic evokes humility. From then, in all my courses, my problem was not to visibly laugh at the elementary nature of student questions. This kind of arrogance hurts teaching. I became an administrator not long after that first experience, but now realize that I really should go back and teach teachers to teach. There is an important educational clue here I should be developing. However, as this is about all I'll ever do, I hope some educational professor or influential higher education administrator is reading this.

I also taught an elective (*meaning it was not mandatory*) called "Technology and Society." Dean (*of Engineering*) John Shupe was a man of the world and was very supportive of my attempts to teach technology to non-technologist, and, conversely, the real world to engineers. He and I even teamed one semester. In a typical class of a hundred, one fourth each were engineers, natural scientists, humanists and social scientists. I never used a text and covered everything from the environment to politics. Much of the course dealt with what was happening that day or the long term future. They needed to form teams to perform a service in the community.

I sometimes gave a final exam where there were four columns of students, representing each of the major areas, and they were provided the option of completing the exam as an individual, or forming a team of up to four students, one from each column representing the four study areas. Usually, the better students went solo, but the exams were so long that only the teams did well, and, as a warning, I underscored this point. The whole point of this exercise, of course, was to begin to change the attitude of those top scholars, which is, it is sometimes better to work with others.

I almost always gave a final essay question everyone had to answer on their own where I picked three topics I could not imagine were in any way related, and asked them to spend no more than 10 minutes to develop one paragraph linking those words. Every one did spectacularly, with answers beyond my expectation. I learned a lesson here, that everyone has the potential to be creative when absolutely necessary. I'm not sure if this kind of final exam would survive today, as grievances would almost surely be filed.

One class in particular was noteworthy. There were 75 students. Instead of doing things in the community, teams of half a dozen wrote one chapter of a book on energy self-sufficiency (*this was the period between the first and second energy crises in the 70's*), and produced a play for presentation at an upcoming energy conference. We had sufficient connections to extract some funding from the National Science Foundation to publish the book, which was adopted by the Hawaii public school system for their use. One problem was that each chapter used a cartoon from the popular media. We got a letter at one point from Sidney Harris of ***American Scientist***, who said, if you use my cartoon, I will sue you. How he found out about our plagiarism is a mystery, but he eventually settled for a $100 fee. Maybe he was doing this in jest, but the initial letter seemed so angry that I suspect he was serious.

The energy play was presented to a NSF Science for Citizens audience at the Hawaii State Capitol. The conferees (*including mayors and legislators)* enjoyed the message so well that the group received funding to take the show on the road. During the summer, the class presented this energy self-sufficiency play (*with dances and songs*) on all the major islands. Battle of the Bands in Naalehu, depicted in ***Book One***, was one of my singular public accomplishments. The phenomenal success of these 75 students can be added to my top ten.

I learned several other lessons from "Technology and Society." As mentioned before, it is difficult to get people to work together. Engineers are probably the worst at this. Success comes from influencing and working with people. The know it all quickly descends, and becomes bitter. We need to change our educational objectives. I've lost count, but this is another of my failures. I was never able to convince even one faculty member or administrator that we had a faulty educational system. Granted, I did not try too hard, for I was busy doing energy and environment things.

**Serteens**

It is said that the top 2% in any community do half the work. Well, interestingly enough, it is reported that the richest 2% own half the wealth.[333] Conversely, the poorest half of the world's population own 1% of global assets. American schools spend more than $8 billion annually to educate the mentally retarded, while spending less than $800 million on gifted programs.[64] While this can be understood, and is the only humane thing to do, is it smart?

In 618 BC child prodigies were assembled by the Tang Dynasty to the Imperial Court for specialized training. Today, China provides more than half a billion dollars each year to Key High Schools for science and technology. Plato, circa 400 BC, wrote about specialized training for the gifted. The Renaissance saw a wide variety of gifted provided special education in the arts. In the U.S. the shock of Sputnik in 1957 no doubt inspired me towards engineering and helped create a higher interest in science and engineering as a matter of national security.

Now, not faced with a competitive enemy, we are today failing our geniuses, as the highest achievers are challenged the least. You would expect those with superior intelligence would at least stay in school longer, but the dropout rate is similar to other students. America's gifted, furthermore, score significantly lower than the gifted from Japan, Hungary and Singapore, because we basically ignore our top students.

Ex-Air Force officer living in Honolulu, George Carter (*now, author,* ***The Splintered Rainbow****, AuthorHouse—who was the individual who talked me into publishing* ***SIMPLE SOLUTIONS*** *with this company*), in the 1970's, formed a chapter of SERTOMA (*from SERvice TO MAnkind*), a service club first started in Kansas City in 1912. SERTOMA focused on promoting freedom and democracy, plus assisting with hearing disorders. There is usually some association with the military, for patriotism is a motto. How I ever got involved with this organization is a real mystery, for only today, decades after leaving them, do I now appreciate the value of freedom and democracy, from the first chapter of this book, and am beginning to lose my hearing.

Clearly, the top 2% of students, the ones that go on to our best universities, then go on to get a PhD degree or an MBA, will have a greater influence on the future of the world. Partly with this thought in mind, George formed the Serteens Club of Hawaii to enhance the future success of gifted and talented intermediate and high school students who tested in the top 2 percentile. It became his passion.

Part of my joining SERTOMA could have been to assist George with Serteens. I recall participating with him in an early planning meeting with the Hawaii Superintendent of Education. I came away stunned. Here was this highly respected educator (*and father of someone who later became a valued staff member of the Hawaii Natural Energy Institute, an organization I directed at the University of Hawaii*), who essentially refused to cooperate with George. The attitude portrayed was that one shouldn't spend extra money on the elite. We needed to treat all students equally. However, it would be permissible to skew the budget towards the needy, as the gifted will somehow find their way. This is the American way of life. While I could live with this form of sympathy, I was nevertheless troubled that we were missing an opportunity.

This is the problem. The gifted, especially, tend to focus on themselves. They do extremely well in achievement tests and inordinately focus on their studies, for the rewards of current acclaim and future scholarships steer them towards personal success. Then, someday, they find themselves in the real world and discover that only looking out for yourself does not work. You need to be able to influence people. You are part of a total system of systems. You don't learn leadership in any of your courses, unless you took ROTC or were part of team sports. On the contrary, mathematics, science and language in the past taught you to NOT cooperate. Serteens promoted people relationships and becoming involved.

George, nevertheless, plugged on and, over time, gained a measure of the State Department of Education's confidence. His students were terrific, and will go on to become societal leaders. In 2004, the current crop renamed themselves the George B. Carter Serteens Club of Hawaii. After two decades, I have on my schedule participating in their annual Hawaii Volcanoes National Park camp out, the week after I submit this book for publication.

Regarding education, of course, you can't prioritize everything, for the budget is limited. As a simple solution, though, I would like to suggest that $8 billion continue to be annually appropriated to improve education opportunities for the mentally retarded. However, instead of $800 million, we need to increase this figure by a factor of 10 for the gifted to optimize the prospects for the future of humanity. In consideration of crime and Chapter 1, I can add another $8 billion (*wincing that the annual Department of Energy budget for renewable energy has averaged less than $1 billion*) to the edification of those individuals who show signs of becoming our future career criminals. So how will this sum of double digit billions magically become available? Read on.

## History of Education

Education began with the first child, as the family is the most important component in the total pedagogical system. It does take a village, and some formal or sensible structure can help, but from before birth (*as there is evidence that "feeding" the womb information can help and providing the wrong nutrition can hurt*) to the first real school day, and throughout the process and lifetime, parents, certainly, but siblings and relatives, too, are crucial. The word education, from the Latin, means to nourish or raise. I am the fortunate product of my upbringing.

That said—and appreciating the necessary focus on the budget, standardized testing, application of new technologies and politics—I will then proffer only one observation for consideration: we need to expand the teaching of the three R's, by incorporating four more R's. But, let us first look at the U.S. and education.

### Education in the United States

Education in Colonial America was private, excluded and focused on reading, writing and arithmetic, plus Latin. Around the time of the birth of the nation in 1776, 75% of males and 65% of females were literate in the New England colonies, but lower elsewhere. There were colleges, but only for males. There is nothing in the Constitution about education.

The Common School Movement began in the mid 1800s to broaden opportunities, partly, but also to preserve social stability, reduce crime, Americanize foreigners and reduce poverty. Sounds like today, actually.

The Morrill Act of 1862, sponsored by Vermont Congressman Justin Morrill, providing 90,000 acres to each qualified state, brought higher education into prominence. His Act in 1890 extended land grants to 16 southern states. Effectively, the legislation allowed states to sell and use this land to establish engineering, agriculture and military science colleges. This is the genesis of American superiority.

By the early 1900s, universal education at all levels arrived. However, in 1900, only 5% graduated from high school and 1% went on to college. During this period, southern states made up 34% of the U.S. population, but received only 3% of the education funding. The NAACP (*National Association for the Advancement of Colored People*) was formed by a diverse group representing all colors to advance the cause of African Americans in 1909 to coincide with the centennial of Abraham Lincoln's birth year. It was a painful struggle fighting legalized racial discrimination, finally coming to a kind of climax in the middle 1950s with the unanimous vote of the U.S. Supreme Court in 1954 striking down separate white and black schools and in 1955 by Rosa Park's refusal to give up her bus seat.

There has been a century of good progress, as 25% of all Americans are today in school (*private schools teach almost 7% of them*) and 85% graduate from high school. We now have a literacy rate of 98%. At $11,000/student/year, Switzerland and the U.S. rank #1 in world-wide spending for public schools. Yet, the District of Columbia, at $13,000/student/year, about the highest nationally, shows about the worst student results. Thus, it takes more than money to educate a child. Success begins with the family and extends into the village, or 'hood."

Why go to school? The average annual salary of a college graduate exceeds the national average by more than $10,000.[52] College graduates in 2003 will earn $409,959 more over the lifetime than someone who did not.[208] Or, adults with a master's, professional or doctoral degree earned an average of $79,900 in 2005, compared with $19,900 for those without a high school diploma. To this financial advantage add productivity, prestige, status in society and lifestyle.

How should schools be governed? States run their system, but the Feds can hold funding if certain requirements are not met. There are some who feel that schools should be nationalized, and others who home school. The two primary issues today are, then, the No Child Left Behind Act pulling towards national standards and decentralized charter schools, born as recently as 1990 to minimize bureaucracy, allow for vested management by those who care and provide focus on curricula of choice.

Hawaii always compares unfavorably with the nation in standardized exams and we have the highest percentage of schools missing No Child Left Behind benchmarks. In many ways, this is analogous to the U.S seemingly falling behind the rest of the developed world in comparative tests. These conditions bring an inferiority complex to the State and general anguish on part of national educators and decision-makers.

Actually, 36% of the Hawaii population represents immigrants and their children.[125] No doubt it is this transitioning group that is skewing the low scores. Yes, 68% of incoming freshmen to the University of Hawaii require remedial English, and, worse, 89% need remediation in math,[35] but this group has made an important leap into higher education, on which our future depends.

Similarly, the seeming mediocrity shown by our students at the national level compared to countries like South Korea and Singapore might not be as grave as is portrayed. I will later describe why.

At the local level, educator James Shon has passed on to me books and papers on education, and we have had discussions on various aspects of the subject. I had breakfast with him in September of 2006, the day after the newspapers announced his firing by the Hawaii Board of Education. Dr. Shon, a former state legislator and a long time ago on my staff at the University of Hawaii, was executive director of the Charter School Administrative Office. He was incredibly at peace with the process and felt he had done all he could to steer the 27 charter schools, with 6,000 students and a budget $1,880/student/year less than the public schools. He was ready to move on. He believed in the charter system, and to a good degree, I agree that this concept has a lot to offer. While there are aspects of this system that provides some of the flexibility provided in No Child Left Behind, in most ways, NCLB focuses too much on government control and the traditional R's.

Charter schools reportedly do not outperform their public counterparts, which I find surprising because they do generally involve stronger family involvement. I suspect, though, that this comparative analysis focuses on the 3 R's, leaving out the other 4 R's, which I have not yet identified, the strength of charter schools.

In my opinion, charter schools are safer than home schooling, which socially handicaps the child. The parent probably provides superior 3R teaching, enabling the student to score higher on standardized tests, but I would worry about long-term life success. Yet, just getting into college might be more important than anything else, so, there are advantages to home schooling, for we will later learn that our superior national advantage is based on our world-class post-secondary education system.

## No Child Left Behind

Public Law 107-110 of 2001, the $22.5 billion No Child Left Behind (*NCLB*) Act, the reauthorization of the Education Act of 1965, was signed into law by George W. Bush in 2002. NCLB increases funding for education, provides for teacher recruitment / principal retention and gives added flexibility to school districts, but under the pressure of losing Federal funding if they fail. Local accountability, more testing, attention to minorities, incentives/penalties and school choice are featured. In general, many of these objectives make sense.

Maybe that's the nature of media, but I mostly hear and read of how NCLB is failing. My problem is that the law only attempts to improve English and mathematics, with science to be added. This 3R focus is the wrong objective. What about the other 4 R's (*which I haven't yet detailed*)?

Ruben Navarrette, nationally syndicated columnist with the Washington Post Writers Group, wants to give NCLB a better chance, and offered:[214]

- The deceptively named Civil Rights Project at Harvard University advances an agenda that is dangerous and backward.
- The National Education Association (*NEA, largest teachers' union*), after five years trying to undermine NCLB, has decided to live with it, as long as "standards are lowered and accountability measures watered down."

- o The problem is that, like all unions backing its constituency, the NEA is not concerned about students or schools, but, only about its members, the teachers.

***Time***, in 2007, gave a report card on NCLB:[304]

| | |
|---|---|
| o Informing the public on school failure | A |
| o Helping schools improve | F |

So this is another problem. The public now knows how bad schools are, but the Department of Education admits that any remedies are not working. With a Democratic Congress, NCLB could well get a name change, and will likely become gentler and kinder, with more money.

A more telling gripe comes from a teacher at Mililani High School in Honolulu, who wrote a newspaper commentary (*regarding NCLB*):[264]

- o He no longer waits eagerly for school to start, as "teachers and principals will be berated for failing to do the impossible."
- o He contends that the disparate socio-economic levels create and maintain the achievement gap...and there is nothing teachers can do about that.
- o Of course, this is because most parents don't care enough, or are too busy.
- o Further, there is no student reward for taking the Hawaii State Assessment, that is, grades are not affected, et al, so there is no incentive to do well.
- o State educational policies are not helpful at all.

In short, he pleads for a more realistic approach, as the inconvenient truth is that teachers and schools cannot eliminate the achievement gap.

## Let Us not Leave the Teachers Behind

There is no more important profession in our society than education. Yes, policemen are necessary, secretaries are important, computer programmers are essential and the military is vital. But we entrust our children and the future of the world to teachers. You want the very best people for this task.

According to at least one 2007 study, teachers put in 15.5 hours per workday.[71] That is, double most occupations. Yes, there are long summers, or at least there once were, in Hawaii. Plus teachers don't toil and sweat, like a construction worker, although very few college graduates do, anyway.

Then, too, when I once taught in college, and that was about thirty years ago, the State Legislature became concerned that professors only taught about 6 hours per week, so we had to undergo a comprehensive review, providing a log of our personal activities. I don't remember how many hours the report indicated we spent on educational activities, and we all of course padded as appropriate, but, nothing came of it and we have not since then been bothered by such nonsense. I do vaguely recall, though, that the average faculty member did not spend anywhere close to 80 hours/week, as our teachers now do.

How well are we paying them? Read the book, ***How Does Teacher Pay Compare?***, written by Sylvia Allegretto, et al.[312] It says that recruiting has become a serious problem because teachers are moving into higher paying, or less stressful, means of livelihood. Further, the claims of the National Compensation Survey—showing that teachers, in consideration of their fringe benefit bias, are actually well compensated—are prejudiced.

The National Education Association (*NEA*) reports that in the 1940 to 2000 period, teachers lost ground and status:[20]

- For college graduates, in 1940, male non-teachers earned 3.6% less than male teachers, and female non-teachers earned 15.8% less than female teachers.
- In 2000, male non-teachers made 60.4% more than male teachers and female non-teachers made 16.4% more than female teachers.

Lost ground is a gross understatement, for from male teachers earning 3.6% more than their fellow graduates in 1940 to now earning 60.4% less, who would want to enter teaching? So you say, 75% of K-12 teachers are female, and they earn only 16.4% less than their counterparts, with the advantage that these teachers have schedules better suited to being good mothers, and you kind of know why this occurred. As an average, those who go into teaching earn 53.5% less than their classmates, which actually understate the gap, because many teachers go on to earn master's degrees. Women with some graduate education now earn about 40% more than female teachers with a master's degree. Should their pay rate be increased? Heck yes, and by at least 50%, if not doubled!

Where was the NEA during this tragic transition? Well, they kept bringing up this crisis, but no one listened. They kept publishing the sort of information you read above, and the public just did not care enough. I kind of relate this toothlessness to my warning decision-makers (*in **Book 1***) that the sky could be falling regarding Peak Oil and Global Warming, but I can't seem to convince anyone. K-12 teachers, or certainly those at the K-6 levels, have a compelling wild card to use. If they don't teach, something has to be done about taking care of all those children suddenly abandoned. But I guess most educators are above it all, or are satisfied enough, which is somewhat my take on why nothing has been done about the coming energy crisis. Our political and governing system is influenced by voters and the public at large. We get what we want!

Finally, I would like to share a lament:

- There is an emergency in education—140,000 teachers left the profession during the past year. They were replaced by young or incompetent teachers.
- The great majority of those who left did so for better pay, reflecting ambition, intelligence and progressiveness.
- The only solution is better pay for teachers.
- Children—our future men and women—deserve our best efforts and unstinted help.

This was written by W.C. Canterbury, Secretary of the Oklahoma Educational Association, on May 6, **1920**.

You might say that nothing has changed today. A successful teacher, nevertheless is confident, enthusiastic and imaginative. Self-assuredness is easy as you know more than the student. Some people have more passion than others, but all can lean in the direction of being energized, for learning can become contagious with the right approach and style. While we don't pay our school teachers enough, a sufficient number of them exude the above attitude that our products turn out to be okay. This is almost a terrible statement, but if society never gets around to improving teachers' salaries, our national future might still be secure. We'll later see why.

## U.S. versus the World on Education

Somewhere between 82% and 85% of the world adult population is literate, depending on the study and parameters. Europe is at 99%, U.S. just below that and Africa 73%. But literacy is but a step towards competency.

The Organization for Economic Co-operation and Development (*OECD*) brings together the governments of 30 countries committed to democracy and market economy. It is headquartered in Paris and exchanges views with 70 countries. Their Program for International Student Assessment surveys 15-year olds in the principal industrialized countries. In 2003, the poll (*a free 471 page report can be obtained through the internet*) showed that the U.S. ranked (*out of **38** countries*):

| | SUBJECT | RANK | TOP THREE COUNTRIES | | |
|---|---|---|---|---|---|
| o | Mathematics | 24 | Hong Kong | Finland | South Korea |
| o | Science | 19 | Finland | Japan | Hong Kong |
| o | Reading | 12 | Finland | South Korea | Canada |
| o | Problem Solving | 26 | South Korea | Finland | Hong Kong |

China, India and Singapore were not surveyed. Germany and France did better than the U.S., but were not in the top ten.

Was it government support? The Czech Republic, in the top ten for math, spent only one third as much as the U.S. per student. Teacher's salaries? The average American teacher is paid about $40,000/year. The pay for a Finnish teacher is about $33,000.

In just another of innumerable comparative tests, the Progress in International Reading Literacy Study reported that Russia, Hong Kong and Singapore topped 45 countries in a fourth-grade reading test. Even with No Child Left Behind, which stresses reading competency, the average for U.S. students dropped, and we ended up in 18$^{th}$ place. To accentuate this decay, reading scores on the Scholastic Aptitude Test (*taken by high school students*) declined to a thirteen year low in 2006.[169]

The ***New York Times*** reported on December 7, 2003, "Economic Time Bomb: U.S. Teens are among the worst at math." Nation at risk? Blue ribbon panel convened by the President? Nope! Nothing. We are awaiting the 2007 report, to, no doubt, still do nothing.

USA Today sponsored a debate on improving education, and two points drew my attention.[325] First, it was shown that teachers and unions were fighting a plan by President Bush to build an adjunct teacher corps of 30,000 experienced scientists and mathematicians to assist schools. The unions resisted by saying that teacher pay had to be increased and working conditions improved. There are two sides to this question, so let me just say that there must be a way to justify higher salaries, plus use this cadre of citizens.

Second, it was shown that, in the U.S., 15% of undergraduates received degrees in science or engineering. The figures for our competitors, courtesy of the National Academy of Sciences, were: Singapore (*67%*), China (*50%*), France (*47%*) and South Korea (*38%*). This is not to say that only scientists and engineers are important to a society, but this wide discrepancy has to be of some, if not a lot, of concern. But is all this crucial to the future of the Nation? Maybe not.

**The South Korean Example**

You will note above that South Korea scores well. This is good and bad. During his presidency in the 1980s, Chun Doo-hwan (*mentioned in Chapter 6 about my dinner with the Kims*) banned hogwons, or private cram schools. This prohibition was lifted in 1990, changing the life of a South Korean student.

Always, there was the parental goal of their child getting into the SKY universities, the acronym of the three top schools, **S**eoul National, **K**orea and **Y**onsei Universities. Jobs with the chaebols (*big business groups*) and government are predicated on being a graduate of a SKY college, as, for example, 12 of the 18 top ministers in the federal government today are graduates of SNU. Suitable marriages and assured success are also drivers.

How best, then, to gain acceptance? First, you must get into the right kindergarten, then complement regular school with more intensive lessons that could well mean arriving home after midnight. The UN Committee on the Rights of the Child complained that children in South Korea were having their right to play violated. The size of the average Korean class is 37 students, more than 50% larger than the 24 for the typical OECD nation. There are thus perceived gaps in the public school system. Thus, the rise of cram schools, which could cost up to $1000/month/child. It is estimated that parents spend at least $16 billion per year for this service. Remember that outrageous $16 billion per year sum suggested to raise the bar for gifted students and convert a potential criminal into a model citizen? South Korean parents pay at least that amount just for cram school.

All this begins to reach a peak as the time comes for the national College Scholastic Ability Test. Nearly 700,000 students seeking entrance spend a day determining their future life. American college boards are tense. In South Korea it is pathological, or certifiably nuts.

Daechidong (*location in Seoul where the cram schools are located*) moms spend up to 100 days before that date praying in a church for an hour and a half every afternoon, chanting for success and bowing to Buddha a thousand times with a photo of their child at their feet.[151] You think the child will not be affected by all this effort?

That day, the entire country delays the start of work until 10 AM so that these students will not be inconvenienced by traffic jams. The exam itself starts at 8:40. Emergency vehicles are available if necessary by calling 119, honking is prohibited, aircraft takeoff and landing times are rescheduled, sellers of good luck charms make a handsome profit and the cheerleading junior class sings comforting words of encouragement. There is a slight exaggeration here, but not much.

In Korea, moms were asked about their educational system, and the general response was that their children were too lazy and there was insufficient homework. In the U.S., the complaint was there was too much homework and more should be done about boosting student pride. Huh?

Well, is homework bad? Two American books actually back up the U.S. mom. ***The Homework Myth*** (*Alfie Kohn, Da Capo Press, 2006*) and ***The Case Against Homework*** (*two mothers, Sara Bennett and Nancy Kalish, Crown Publishers, 2006*) argue that homework torments families and serves to turn students against learning. Further, cited is a study by Duke University showing that homework does not measurably improve academic achievement for grade school students. And, even further, those who study 2 hours or more in high school tend to get lower scores.[334] What? Oh course, most of us don't realize that we had it easy. Since 1981, homework has gone up by more than 50% in the U.S. And we are still doing so poorly in those comparative surveys? That is, indeed, a concern.

Shouldn't childhood be fun? Yes, of course, so, perhaps, achievement is being overdone in South Korea. Also, cheating has become a problem. Bribes, just to have your child accommodated in regular classes, are not uncommon, because, in addition to the test score, you must also do well in school. Plus, during the past few years, it was reported that nearly 500 students committed suicide as a result of this process. Frighteningly, nearly 50% of students, it was found through a Ministry of Education survey, actually contemplated this act. Thus, success is coming at a price.

### Then There is Singapore

Singapore, with a population approaching 5 million and more than three-fourths third generation Chinese, is the closest thing to a benevolent dictatorship that calls itself a parliamentary democracy. First colonized by the British in 1819, it became an independent republic in 1965. It is the smallest country in Southeast Asia and the 18th wealthiest nation with an area about 3.5 times that of Washington, D.C. By all standards, Singapore is a remarkable marvel and deserves its reputation for order, prosperity and modernity. Like in Norway, everything works and is clean.

How did this happen? Lee Kuan Yew was its first prime minister in 1959, and his reign prospered until 1990, when he willingly stepped down at the age of 67. There is a president, but the PM runs the country. Lee's eldest son, Hsien Loong, in 2004 became prime minister. The People's Action Party has always controlled the politics. That continuity, clever planning and some ruthless control made the country. They set and meet goals.

Singapore Airlines is the #1 airline, Changi Airport is always #1 or #2, the World Bank rates the country as #1 out of 175 in "doing business," Foreign Policy Magazine ranks it #1 of 62 countries in globalization and Transparency International gives it a #5 (*meaning good*) rating among 163 countries in corruption.

While Singapore did not participate in the above evaluation of 15 year olds, there is no great surprise, then, that their fourth and eighth grade students, in both math and science, ranked #1, followed by countries of the Orient: South Korea, Hong Kong, Chinese Taipei and Japan. The U.S. made it to #9 in $8^{th}$ grade science. Maybe there is hope for the younger generation.

However, there is a reason why ***The Economist*** ranks Singapore as #84 out of 167 in their Index of Democracy and Reporters with Borders ranks them as #146 out of 168 in the Press Freedom Index. Singapore also has the highest execution rate per capita. Reference can be made to the tip of the iceberg represented in the Michael Fay case reported in Chapter 1.

There is a way any country can become the best, and Singapore has found a way to not only survive, but excel at it, through their form of government, whatever you want to call it. A book to read to gain understanding about the country is ***Economic Growth and Development in Singapore***.[357] Singapore, certainly, is worthy of consideration as the best place in the world to live, if you are willing to sacrifice some alienable civil rights.

**Finland Works**

In the latest (*2006*) Programme for International Student Assessment of the Organsation for Economic Co-operation and Development, Finland ranked #1 in science (*Hong Kong #2, Canada #3*), #2 in reading literacy (*Korea #1, Hong Kong #3*) and #2 in math *(#1 Chinese Taipei, #3 Hong Kong*). Singapore did not participate. The U.S. ranked in the 30's. Interestingly enough, there are generally no end of year tests to measure progress. There is an expectation that students will be successful. No child left behind? The U.S. does it in just the opposite fashion, and seems to be paying for it.

In Finland, the family brings up the child to the age 6, and reading literacy is ingrained into the daily life. Most go to day care at the age of 1, as most mothers work. Education is compulsory between the ages of 7 and 16 and there is no separation of the smart from the stupid in all classes. Students, though, spend among the fewest hours in school. Meals are free. After the age of 16, students generally continue schooling, but take separate academic or vocational paths. There are no fees for any of this, but Finland spends the second highest/student of OECD nations.

Only 8% of those who apply can major in teaching. Teachers at all levels must be highly qualified with at least a master's degree, and, this is very important for any society…educators are highly respected. You want a prescription for success? Look closely at Finland, which also is doing very well economically (*#11 in GDP/capita, ahead of Canada, U.K., Sweden, Japan, Franc and Germany*).

## What is Wrong with Our Schools Today?

Wow, I can list a hundred things wrong with our educational system. But in the totality of things, all the hand wringing and anguish might not be worth all the concern, as we'll learn in the final section. The good news is that we are, actually, depending on what you consider to be important, doing fine.

In any case, the scary thing about my whole attempt to introduce additional R's into the educational process, is that schools apparently aren't doing all that well with only the existing 3 R's. You can go into any business community and get scolded that their entry level employee can't write nor communicate. Its worse where I'm from, as the National Association of Education Progress rated Hawaii #47 out of 50 in our report card.

There is also a disconnect on perceptions, as 77% of those who graduated and did not go to college seem to blame the high school for not demanding more of them.[36] A comedy writer can live for years on just this theme.

Our schools are not perfect, but the larger question, really, has to do with **what is wrong with our society** today:

- The nuclear family has not disintegrated, but is not the same as before, and this is generally not good for education and life in general.
- The male half of our population is going to the dogs, as boys:[329]
- when I was going to college, accounted for nearly 60% of the students; we now are down to 44% of undergraduates;
- are 33% more likely to drop out of high school than girls;
- score 16% lower on reading tests; and
- are 30% more apt to use cocaine.
- Television and video games have made it difficult to focus on homework.
- Unions have become counterproductive, but are necessary, for, as much as we tend to mouth the importance of education, were it not for their single-minded zeal to improve the lot of their constituency, teachers' salaries would be even worse today.
- Of course, parents don't care enough or are just too busy. There is some involvement in grammar school, but this totally disappears in high school.
- Yes, classrooms are inadequate, books are too expensive, drugs are prevalent, security is becoming a crisis and teachers are overworked.

This book is not going to solve these problems, so let me just say I mentioned them.

Regarding school itself, longer hours and more days/year are becoming a trend. Merit pay is gaining in support. Schools are being re-designed. But the reality is that some things just **won't** happen in our lifetime, and many more to come, as for example:

- Teachers will be put on a pedestal and rewarded with double their current salaries because they have the critical responsibility for guiding our future, the next generation.
- We are the greatest, so American students will become #1 in science, math, reading and analysis in world-wide standardized tests. Can we possibly even hope for a top ten finish in anything academic, as we are still winning Olympic Gold Medals?
- Parents, business, government and political foes will, together, take on the challenge to make their school system the best in the nation. There will be, here and there, exceptions. Bless them and try to replicate the process.

I can go on, but you, again, get the point. I just hate to leave this section with a negative note, so would like to point out that I have two simple solutions at this stage of the discussion: don't overreact to the negatives and keep an open mind to more than teaching only reading, writing and arithmetic.

## *What, Then?*

In 2005, the U.S. Department of Education formed the Commission on the Future of Education. However, the main task was for the group to recommend a national strategy for improving our universities, probably because 30 years ago, 30% of college students were in the U.S., versus the 14% of today. Of course, two corresponding charges were to provide guidelines on how high schools should prepare students for post-secondary education and, also, for the 21st century marketplace. Yet, in their first report on September 26, 2006, the Commission said they would be focusing on:

- Access (*to universities*).
- Affordability (*for non-traditional students*).
- Standards of quality in instruction.
- Accountability of institutions of higher learning to their constituencies.

So this Commission will not solve our K-12 (*kindergarten through high school*) public education system, which many say is the root of our problem. But, aha, this blue ribbon commission probably knows something that will become obvious by the end of this chapter. The punch line to this entire section comes then.

In 2005, Bill Gates, in a keynote address, told a meeting of governors and policy makers that our high schools were obsolete, and that they should be redesigned to meet the challenges of the new century. The crux of Gates' argument was, though, that we should use better technology. He further advocated online courses. What would one expect from the Chairman of Microsoft? Who am I to chide the richest man in the world, but I think he only has part of the answer. Yes, the world is changing and technology with it, but the problem with our students is that they tend today to be too attached to computers, and online courses would only further separate them from other people.

"Our schools were designed fifty years ago to meet the needs of another age. Until we design them to meet the needs of this century, we will keep limiting—even ruining—the lives of millions of Americans every year," he further said.[211] I agree with this statement, but, perhaps, not in the manner he perceives. Again, I'm being negative, but I do have a positive solution.

In December of 2006, the independent New Commission on the Skills of the American Workforce, partially composed of former congressional members, cabinet secretaries and state governors, and funded by private foundations, released their report, ***Tough Choices or Tough Times***, a follow-up of sorts to Nation at Risk, the 1983 epistle which scared the country, but did not do much about improving K-12 education. This new Commission called for drastic revisions to school structure and raising teachers' salaries up to $110,000. Chairman Charles Knapp, former president of the University of Georgia, said "the United States has one of the highest costs of education, but produces mediocre results."[135] A price of $60 billion was attached to the 15 year implementation plan, and the hope was to change laws, stimulate cultural shifts and alter political will. In a kind of insult, the report recommends recruiting future teachers from the top third of high school students rather than the bottom third. But, I guess this must be true of the present, else why would they so state? Said William Brock, former Secretary of Labor in the Reagan Administration: "This proposal is radical? Yes. Hard to achieve? Of course. Essential? Absolutely. Our nation's schools are failing to educate our children, and that has to stop—else we condemn our own kids to even lower incomes. We must act—now!"[367]

Strong language from a blue-ribbon and conscientious group charged with a monumental task. Like Nation at Risk, though, I can predict that nothing much will change in our educational system, but mostly because of the above reasons, plus, maybe things are not all that bad, anyway.

## Teaching Rainbows: the 7 R's

There are, of course, the 3 R's: Reading, 'Riting, and 'Rithmetic. Motivational speaker John Blaydes promotes Resiliency, Renewal and Reflection for educators. The Democratic Party, setting the foundation for a new educational philosophy, came up with the Public Education Reinvestment, Reinvention and Responsibility Act. These R's are all important to support the student.

As we all know, the students we are currently producing, first, cannot compete with those from other countries, at least in how to read, rite, do rithmetic and science, and solve problems. Businesses complain that recruits can't read nor communicate.

Furthermore, I've said this before, and I'll say it again. We go through the first 18 years of our life looking out for ourself. The educational system provides rewards only for grades, graduating and getting into the college or job of your choice. Sure, there will be team projects, but these you will manage to get by with minimal effort without incurring the animosity of members. The academically gifted, especially, will focus on their studies, for what better way is there to attain your goals? Some will nevertheless become class officers, newspaper reporters, whatever. The less driven will turn to sports and extracurricular activities. This latter group could well become more successful in life, but chances are, if you do both, you will be even more prosperous.

Let's follow a typical child from K-12, with some going on to college. You toil in school, year after year, take tests, study, play, then, finally, one day, find yourself, hooray, most of you, anyway, a graduate, whether with a high school degree or PhD. You enter society, get a job and continue doing what you always did. You keep looking out for #1, you, as that is all you know.

You don't realize that it is not how successful you are in what you personally do, but, more, how people around you flourish. Success is attained not by hogging the limelight or taking credit for everything that happens. In fact, just the opposite happens. You alienate yourself from your colleagues and wonder what went wrong. You haven't yet learned that it is in how well you sacrifice, sell and give credit that work best. Of course we all eventually learn the true game, some faster than others, and many not at all.

So we have this sub-optimal educational system where we score worse than most developed nations, end up working with the wrong attitude and where teachers, employees and parents are not very happy. Yet, we are doing quite well economically and continue to be, by far, the most powerful nation, ever. How come? What went right?

Maybe the 3 R's are not that important, after all. Maybe that credit we get for teaching creativity over rote learning should be explored more carefully. Perhaps the smart alecks we produce are the keys to real success. We are doing something right, and not realizing it, or at least, not optimizing from it.

So let's go back to square one in education. Yes, do teach the 3 R's. They are fundamentally necessary. With computer/information technology, it should be easier and faster to inculcate the basics. I've always felt, for example, that any engineering course can be taught in half the time, with the now extra sessions available to go into what good this information is and how best to apply it to the real world. Thus, there is now more time for analysis, problem solving and the all important 4 extra R's.

**The Four Added R's of Education**

On first thought, one might ask, why change anything when our educational system has made the USA #1. However, we are leaving children behind (*not as preached by the Bush White House, but in a marshmallow sort of way, still to come*) and are sub-optimizing the process when the world, indeed is catching up. It would be foolish to keep the status quo.

A simple solution is to add four more R's:

**R**igor. My sense is that something is missing today from the curriculum, or the teaching methodology. I haven't been to school in a long time and I might be totally wrong, but, hate to say this, there is not enough suffering. You remember best when challenged with sacrifice. How to attain this level of rigor? I don't know and am willing to discard this R if in any way pressed. Times have changed and, perhaps, the lack of rigor can be called progress.

**R**espect. A student from Laos in my first year of college teaching called me honorable professor. Well, he turned out to be the last one to do so, but walking across the campus recently with a South Korean faculty member, one of his students smiled and called him honorable professor. In the U.S., and, perhaps, much of the developed world, there is no respect for teaching and teachers. It is not that it is necessary for a teacher to be lord over his flock, but I keep hearing complaints that they are today more baby sitter, enforcement official or cowed servant than anything else. Again, this is the 21$^{st}$ millennium, and respect is earned, so the issue cuts in two directions.

**R**elevance. There are numerous papers on relevance for or of education. That is not the problem. Education is relevant. The teacher cannot make the student learn. The student learns best when something is relevant. It is internal motivation that creates the drive. How then to connect fundamentals to reality. The student learns best when the equation or graph or issue is important to her. With the advantage of current technology, there comes the need for someone to connect lesson to life. That is the role of the teacher. Harvard University in 1945 produced the Red Book standards and in 1978 established the Core Curriculum, changing education. In 2007, Harvard announced new guidelines for their general education curriculum, linking courses to problems, issues and questions students will encounter later in life. Or, in other words, introduce relevance.[205] Students will now better think, then apply knowledge.

**R**elationship. This R is the most important one of all. Rigor can be eliminated, and mankind will not be lost. Respect might well be an anachronism. Relevance is in the eye of the beholder. Each teacher is smart enough to understand relevance, and there are innumerable ways to do this in a classroom and out. But relationship goes counter to current policy. Today, we focus on math and reading, give standardized tests and, at the end of the school year or semester, grades, which determine the future of a student. That's okay, in fact, necessary. We, simply, must find a way to, **in addition**, produce a graduate who is more valuable to the community and more capable of succeeding in the real world.

What these R's do is to level the playing field for those students who are not particularly gifted academically, but have other skills and talents equally important to success in life. These new R's can lift the impulsive and unmotivated to a higher plateau, or, perhaps even, sway the potential lawbreaker towards good citizenship.

### Relationship

Sometimes called emotional intelligence (*EI*), on occasion social intelligence (*SI*), Daniel Goleman in the 90's, then a science writer for the ***New York Times***, wrote on both subjects. A more recent treatment, by Karl Albrecht, ***Social Intelligence***, appeared in 2006. ***Wikipedia*** has ten pages on emotional intelligence and two on social intelligence, so that very well summarizes the field, which is what relationship is all about.

In 1920, Edward L. Thorndike of Columbia University used social intelligence regarding the skill to understand and manage people, while the first use of emotional quotient could have been as recently as 1985, when Wayne Payne had a doctoral thesis on the subject. The first published article appeared in 1990 and Goleman's book, ***Emotional Intelligence***, in 1994.

In the science of EI, there are four emotions: perception, utilization, understanding and management. Like an IQ aptitude test, there is a social quotient *(SQ)* test, but it has an acronym of MSCEIT (*Mayer-Salovey-Caruso Emotional Intelligence Test*). Further, those in the field dismiss this test as one of intelligence. In general, both IQ and MSCEIT show inheritance (*60 to 70%*) more dominant over the environment. From all indications, that more familiar measurement, IQ, is NOT a good predictor of job performance.

Goleman, a psychologist, claims that his EI test is a better predictor of workplace success, and is based on: self-awareness, self-management, social awareness and relationship management. Albrecht, a business writer, proposed 5 parts to his SPACE model: **s**ituational awareness, **p**resence, **a**uthenticity, **c**larity and **e**mpathy.

The difference makers were abilities such as handling of frustration, control of emotions and getting along with other people. With respect to professional success and prestige, social/ emotional abilities were four times more important than IQ.[56]

## The Stanford Challenge [138]

University President John Hennessy in 2006 announced The Stanford Challenge. I even got what looked like a personally signed letter of appeal, dated, September 2007. He intimated that there comes a time in the course of an organization when critical decisions must be made to have a monumental impact on their future and the world. Stanford is not that old, as the first student in 1891 was our 31st President, Herbert Hoover. Hennessy cites Frederick Terman and Wallace Sterling as laying the groundwork for Silicon Valley, and bemoaned the fate of GM, Ford and Chrysler for their apathy and IBM for its focus on mainframe computers. Not unlike horse and buggy or typewriter firms of their day, the world changed and they did not. Stanford will, he says.

Stanford will marshal University resources to address some of the century's great challenges in the environment, peace and health through genetic mechanisms. Interesting that ***Simple Solutions for Planet Earth*** (*or, **Book 1***) takes on the environment, Chapter 1 of this book does peace and Chapter 2 genetics. It's almost like I was there when the plan was crafted. I'm sure I did not contribute a bit during my nearly four year stay there almost half a century ago.

As Stanford is an academic institute, Hennessy also indicated that the other half of their efforts will be on education (*this chapter*). Clearly, I'm going to have to send him a copy of this book to congratulate them for their perspicuity. More so, their commitment will be on K-12 education, and, in particular, starting a new charter school. He didn't quite say that relationship was an important 4th R, but when they read this chapter, certainly, they might reconsider. Oh, they plan to raise $4.3 billion over the next five years to support The Stanford Challenge. To close, he quoted Jane Stanford: "our children's children's children" will thank us for the courage of that vision. Evidently, that is from whom I borrowed when I co-directed a NASA public education program on "Earth 2020—Visions for Our Children's Children." No, as I think of it, I contributed Earth 2020, it was Hans Mark, then director of the Ames Research Center (*located down the road from Stanford*), and later, Chancellor of the University of Texas System, who used Jane Stanford's vision.

Now, the following experiment came way before this Challenge was announced, but if with more than $4 billion they can even approach the significance of these results, wow! I then give you...

## ...The Stanford Marshmallow Test

The Stanford University marshmallow longitudinal (*retest over time*) study was run by Michael Mischel, and remarkably demonstrated how **self-discipline** can lead to success. The beauty of this experiment is that any parent today with a 4-year old child can determine how she will score in her scholastic aptitude test in high school, and, how well she will succeed in life. This would even apply to males.

In the 60's, four-year old children were taken one at a time into a room and shown a marshmallow. The child was told he could eat it now, or wait until the experimenter came back from an errand, when he could have two. Some ate it immediately, but others waited as long as 20 minutes until that person returned. Fourteen years later, these same children took the SAT test, and those that immediately ate (*impulsive*) scored 1052 combined on verbal and math, while those who received two marshmallows (*impulse controlled*) scored 1262, a 210 point difference! The adolescents were then observed to have the following attitudes and capabilities in high school:

| **1262 Group** | **1052 Group** |
|---|---|
| Assertive | Indecisive |
| Could cope with frustration | Overreacted to frustration |
| Worked better under pressure | Overwhelmed by stress |
| Confident | Gave up easily |
| Dependable | Provoked arguments |
| Academically competent | Poor students |
| Could concentrate | Impulsive |
| Eager to learn | Sharp temper |
| Followed through on plans | Still couldn't delay gratification |

Of course, a quick check of student backgrounds might well have explain some of this, for, chances are that the impulsive came from a lower income group, where that was the prevailing mode of action. Of course, too, an individual who knows the child cannot conduct the test because there is generally some trusting relationship, and the subject will almost surely be swayed not to touch the marshmallow.

***The whole point, though, is that we then try to train these impetuous individuals mostly how to read, write and do math, when what they really need is to learn the four other R's.*** The notable lesson to be gained is that these one marshmallow children are NOT doomed. ***This is what education should be all about. Read on.***

## Principles to Improve the Fate of a One Marshmallow Child

Goleman suggests classes, with parental involvement, in:

- Self-science
- Emotional literacy
- Social competence and development

In addition, include the following:

- Identifying feelings
- Decision-making
- Impulse control
- Anger management
- Conflict resolution
- Empathy
- Relationships
- Problem solving
- Temptation resistance

## Learned Optimism

Martin Seligman, psychology professor at the University of Pennsylvania, is known to be the father of "positive psychology." He wrote the book, ***Learned Optimism***, on how optimism enhances the quality of life, and how it can be learned.[280] The debate is on whether the pessimist is better grounded and the optimist deluded. Certainly, there is a link between pessimism and depression. Seligman says that pessimism played a role in the survival of our species, but might now be partially obsolete.

Everyone fails at something. The optimist has a way of bouncing back, while pessimists are defined by their failures. Optimists have less illness and recover more quickly. Read ***Learned Optimism*** for details.

For sure, optimists are more successful, as in the insurance industry, where optimists, in his survey, sold 37% more than pessimists. Seligman studied 500 freshman at his university and found that how well they did on his test for optimism were a better predictor of actual grades than their SAT scores or high school grades.

Thus, the bottom line is that optimism is better than pessimism, and that optimism can be learned. But are our schools teaching these attitudes? No.

## Kagan Structures and Cooperative Learning

Spencer Kagan in 1968 began an effort to promote interaction among students. He says its all about engagement, has about a dozen books listed in Amazon.com on the subject and has an active web site for educators. His Kagan Structures transform how content is taught, producing positive outcomes in academic achievement, thinking skills, character virtues, race relations, emotional intelligence and affirmative attitudes toward learning.

He is involved with learning centers and workshops, promoting grouping strategies and cooperative learning. It is in the mechanism of teaching, not the content. For the student, learning becomes more fun and social skills are enhanced.

## Tony Wagner and the Change Leadership Group

Tony Wagner has been a leader in educational innovation, and his book on ***Making the Grade: Reinventing America's Schools*** (*Routledge, 2003*) and ***Change Leadership: A Practical Guide to Transforming our Schools*** (*with Robert Kegan, et al, Jossey-Bass, 2006*) stand out as prime movers. He is co-director (*with Kegan*) of the Bill and Melinda Gates Foundation Change Leadership Group at the Harvard Graduate School of Education. Having served as teacher, principal and educational professor, but, more so, inspiration and vision, he certainly has the credentials and personality to lead the charge.

As he has on occasion come to Hawaii, I certainly would like to discuss with him how to best re-educate the one marshmallow child and upgrade gifted and talented programs. I wonder, too, how he feels about the "theory" that the future of the country is in good hands because our post-secondary educational system is so superior.

## High School Courses in Relationship

Thus far, all the relationship ideas have come from PhD's with impressive credentials. I would like to balance these inputs with "The Young View" column written by Katie Young, from ***MidWeek***, published in Honolulu on November 16, 2005.[374] She writes that high schools should teach courses in:

- Divorce—How to Deal
- Why Dad Wants to Tell You All His War Stories and Why You Should Listen
- They'll be Dead Some Day, So Show Them the Appreciation They Deserve Today
- How to Treat the Ones You Love

There were more, but you get the point. She covers rigor, respect, relevance and relationship. Young goes on to say that "school is supposed to prepare us intellectually to find the career most suited to us, but as far as I can remember, there was no course offered in emotional intelligence to help us maneuver through our relationships." Further, "how do we become good partners when all our lives we've been taught to be strong individuals?" I couldn't have said it any better.

**What then about the New 4 R's?**

There are many, many more good ideas about what to do about the new R's. What about Edison schools? Saving school dropouts (*30% will leave without graduating from high school, and many from this group will earn less than $20,000/year, or become criminals*)? I just scratched the surface.

Finally, we should not dismiss cognitive factors, that is, IQ, for you need some smarts to just get into college or graduate school. IQ could be almost half determined by your environment, like school. Thus, basic knowledge helps, and reading, writing and arithmetic are important. But they are not enough. Once in the work place, your EI will better determine your success in life, and, hopefully, make you a more responsible citizen of the world.

Relationship more or less covers all added R's, and these key parameters CAN BE TAUGHT AND LEARNED. Are our schools adequately covering the 4 R's? A simple, loud, no. Yes, of course there are pioneers and steeples of excellence, as indicated above. Plus, there are dedicated teachers and administrators doing their best. I can only express my admiration for their devotion and commitment. But they are the exception.

This, then, is a potential area for pursuit by someone wanting to become famous in education. The world seeks the next Ben Franklin or Horace Mann or John Dewey or Martin Luther to galvanize that critical change. Maybe, even, you might be that individual to initiate the first step to make that crucial difference.

## An Additional Suggestion Regarding Early Childhood Education

As barely mentioned earlier, yet another opportunity not being embraced, mostly because of budget priorities, is early childhood education [249]. Government can only do so much, and ECE has historically been looked on as a free baby-sitting service, when applied to 2 to 4 year olds. There is also the important matter of mothers being with their children at this early age, so it was not necessary for the ruling party to take on this responsibility.

I scoured the literature, and found innumerable papers and books on the subject. Most of the treatment reflected standard nursery school practices. That is, provide an opportunity for pre-school youngsters to play and learn how to relate to people and society, allowing the parents to, frankly, work. Unfortunately, this is where the child learns to become a model citizen and loses that innate creativity.

There is that special twinkle in the eye of many children in the 2-4 age category, some who talk too much and many who arrive at ingenious solutions. Parents, in preparing their child for formal schooling, feel compelled to teach good citizenship, which begins the process of destroying this imaginative spirit, and schools provide the death blow. Most never recover this out of box character later in life.

Maria Montessori, in the early 1900's began to develop in Italy a teaching methodology for forming the whole person where children direct their own learning. Teachers provide materials, but maintain a silent presence. If you've ever wondered what the Montessori Method was, this is it. She ultimately upgraded the concept to apply even to universities. There is something to this technique that can preserve creativity.

In 1972, Margaret Thatcher, as the UK Secretary of State for Education, proposed that education be provided by 1980 for 50% of 3-year olds and 90% of 4-year olds. While her motivation might not have been to protect inventiveness, the opportunity was at had to make difference. Alas, economic recession hit, and the plan was never implemented.

The best way to maintain inspiration and resourcefulness in the 2-4 year old is through some mandatory process. The budget and space hurdles will make this concept a difficult sell, but all available data show that such an effort will return several dollars per dollar invested.[47] Even programs like Early Head Start cannot seem to get going. For this Really Early Head Start Program, the beginning will need to be one day per week, probably on a Saturday, so that space will be available, and at least one parent will need to be present to make the effort effective.

## One Final Suggestion: Virtual Libraries

Hopefully this will not irritate yet another sector of society, but I think **libraries are obsolete**. Every education budget attempts to take care of maintaining a progressive book collection system. In particular, at universities, students will virtually riot if they perceive any library service cutbacks. However, this is not because they are protecting the sanctity of knowledge. Students use libraries to study, sleep, get out of the heat or cold, and, of course, now and then search the stacks.

That was fine and necessary a half century ago when I was in college, but beginning now, all libraries should as soon as possible be converted into virtual learning centers. I am in engineering, and maybe we are an odd lot, but I know of no faculty associates who depend on the library for any services. Everything today is done on the computer using the internet.

Google and a host of other dot.com firms are quickly converting all journals, books, maps and anything a library shelves for electronic access. The library of the future will be virtual, and if your library hasn't yet begun the process, it is never too late.

The upside is that those immense structures can now be utilized for other needs. What will be the fate of all those books? Well, people collect them, and a gigantic book sale can be held to clear the stacks, while creating an endowment.

I recall a dozen or so years ago being on a campus improvement committee. At some point I recommended that the new library currently under construction become a virtual library, and certain floors instead be used to support technology development initiatives, allowing companies to use them in partnership with the university to commercialize our research results. In those days, the concept was relatively new, and I felt, with some confidence, that we might have the inside track through our Stanford University connections linking with Google and a couple other companies in Silicon Valley to serve as the first wave of electronic centers.

While it was not particularly surprising, the reaction of the committee was swift and condemning. This was particularly invective from the humanities side of the aisle, and from students. I was effectively blackballed from the committee and lost any respect I previously might have had. I still kick myself today for backing off and not being any more convincing, for, at the least, I could have orchestrated a presentation from Google. However, like most people on campus, I was too busy to focus on this dubious need, so the world swept by the University of Hawaii, again.

Now many years later, I'm writing this passage in my hotel room in Vancouver, Canada. There is an ongoing municipal strike that has affected the city for two months. Garbage collection is a pain and libraries are closed. Interestingly enough, people are mostly complaining that they are being deprived of using the free library computers. No one is missing the book borrowing part. If this is not a sign of things to come, I don't know what can be.

The beauty of a virtual library is that all of the budget item called libraries will continue to gain public support, so, transitioning to an all-electronics version should start with plentiful seed funds, and, over time, save a lot of taxpayer money. Thus, even college students will be supportive, for actual space can now be set aside for their dozing off use, but more so, for conveniences such as wireless internet access, video-conferencing, use of next generation digital media facilities and the like. The greater benefit, of course, will be the cost-effectiveness and enhancement of the educational process.

## The Simple Solutions to Education

So is the U.S. in trouble? Is the strongest economy ever a generation or two away from mediocrity? **Nope.** There is one area where we still lead in education: higher education. The total expenditure per student in the U.S. is $18,570, compared to Denmark at #2 with $11,600 and Britain at #3 with $8970.[366] Having only 5% of the world population, the 2007 Academic Ranking of World Universities indicated that the U.S. has (*www.arwu.org/rank/2007*):

- o The top three universities (*Harvard, Stanford and Cal-Berkeley*).
- o Eight of the best ten (*Cambridge and Oxford were also here*).
- o Seventeen of the top twenty (*add Tokyo University at #20*).
- o Thirty seven of the best 50 universities.

**As a nation, we have, apparently, decided to focus on the few who will lead and produce. Who said there is no gifted children program in the U.S.? We have, it's just that it is limited to higher education. Something is working, and this could well be the answer.**

Our university system, though, can be better.[53] We rank #13 to Sweden (*#1*) and Finland (*#2*) in college affordability, and #4 in accessibility to the Netherlands. Plus, our net cost after tax expenditures of $11,283 is next to Japan (*$14,040*) for developed countries.

It would be callous and careless to say that it might not matter if every citizen is perfectly educated. Certainly, educate to minimize the development of the criminal element. Of course, provide every opportunity to all children. We should, though, initiate the optimization process at the K-12 level with a more progressive program for the potentially gifted. The able should be even more outstanding in college to determine who will rule the corporate world and lead and produce in the public sector, whether it be government or academia. The finest will succeed with greater capability. The Nation and World will benefit. I just hope that the next generation will have a higher appreciation beyond profits and power. We lack a basic humanitarian trait and don't have sufficient appreciation for the environment. The 4 R's beyond the classical 3R's are advocated to insure for this more responsible future.

In any case, this chapter is incomplete. It represents certain thoughts that entered my brain somewhere back in time and remained. However, these are seminal educational opportunities worthy of pursuit that I bequeath to the educational world and humanity at large:

- Initiate formal teaching at the age of 2. However, stress imagination, not civil obedience. A child at that age has an incredible ability to visualize the unimaginable. Human societies extinguish that flame to maintain order and sanity. This inspired impulse rarely returns when quenched. How to teach the student to be a progressive citizen, while nourishing this creativity, will be an important key to the future of our civilization. How to afford this luxury? Well, maybe we can end wars and spend some of these defense savings for education.
- Spend these early years, 2-5, identifying the one and two marshmallow children, so that we design an optimal educational pathway for them. One strategic must would be to work with the village to direct the potential mental case, drug addict or delinquent—and usually all three characteristics are blended in these individuals—towards a more productive life. All the signs might not yet be evident, but this is that influential period when education can, indeed, make that crucial difference.
- Teach the full **Rainbow** spectrum: **R**eading, '**R**iting, '**R**ithmetic, **R**igor, **R**espect, **R**elevance and **R**elationship. There seems to be a sense that an American education actually does make our graduates more creative and assertive, and we must nurture the positive aspects of those attributes and improve on them.
- Begin converting all libraries into virtual ones. Go to Bill Gates and Google for help. This will save a lot of trees and make information access much more efficient and cost-effective.
- Double the education budget. Take money away from war.
- Maintain a superior higher education system. As a corollary, recognizing that universities can serve as the economic engine for a community, the business sector

and local legislature should recognize the wisdom of partnering and contributing to the greatness of their college campuses.

Science and engineering got a jolt of support nearly half a century ago, thanks to the Soviet Union and Sputnik, leading to landing Neil Armstrong on the Moon. A decade later, in the mid-70's, the U.S. ranked #3 on percentage of undergraduates in engineering. Today we rank #17. This sounds familiar, but I'll say it again: it is not that we only need engineers to save the world, but this plunge is symptomatic of a dangerous trend in a world more and more dependent on technology. Sure we need engineers, but clearly with more heart and sense, plus the range of associative specialties to provide balance and imagination.

We react to crises. Peak Oil and Global Warming looms as the next peril. Alas, the prevailing attitude seems to be, what crisis? Maybe that's just the nature of human society today. Thankfully, someone, or a discerning group, some time back in our history, crafted a total educational system that has worked. The World might not this cycle react in time, and the consequences will be dreadful, but I would not be surprised if the USA subsequently rebounds to maintain our dominance.

Thus, the simplest solution to education in the USA is to maintain the course, but, by gosh, strive to do even better, as suggested above. Certainly, don't unnecessarily anguish, as we are doing fine, in fact, terrific!

# CHAPTER 4: SEEKING THE LIGHT—SETI

## The Search for Extraterrestrial Intelligence (SETI)

### In the Beginning...

...There might have been nothing, or something, but what? One theory is that a vacuum fluctuation (*this is an even bigger leap of faith than most religious miracles, but let me leave this Intelligent Design-inspired creation to the next chapter*) triggered an event called the Big Bang. That was about 13.7 billion years ago. This mysterious beginning is at the heart of the debate regarding God and science. Today, we do know that the universe is vast, but, to even further confuse you, it is reported that there is six times more dark matter *(stuff no one has yet seen, but astrophysics declare must be out there so that their theories can make a little more sense*) than "regular" atomic matter (*like stars, trees, us, etc.*).

Our galaxy, the Milky Way, where Earth is in the very outer suburbs, has, maybe, 400 billion stars. Yes, we don't know for sure how many. The Hubble Telescope was capable of detecting 80 billion galaxies, or so, perhaps each with its 400 billion stars. But who knows how many more were outside the capability of Hubble. The European Space Agency calculates $10^{24}$ stars out there in our universe (*galaxies make up our universe, but, there might be other universes*), most you can't see.[373] If you spent one second counting each one, it would take you 30 million billion years. Remember, the Universe is less than 14 billion years old. Even the National Aeronautics and Space Administration (*NASA*) reports there are zillions of uncountable stars.

On the basis that light travels 186,282 miles in one second (*671 million miles per hour or about 6 trillion miles in one year*), if it were possible to design a spacecraft to travel at that speed (*and the best we've done is Voyager 1 moving away from the Sun at 38,600 mph*), it would take about four years to reach our nearest star, which is Proxima Centauri. With that in mind, you should appreciate that light would take about 100,000 years to travel from one end of our Milky Way (*which, again, is a disk-shaped galaxy*) to the other end.

Or, using another analogy so that you can visualize all this better, if our solar system were the diameter of a quarter, the Milky Way would be about as large as the continental USA. The farthest object the human eye can see in the sky is the Andromeda galaxy, a mere 2 million light years away. We're changing scales here, but if our Milky Way were the size of a CD, Andromeda, about the same size, would only be 8 feet away. So, if it takes 100,000 years for light just to traverse across our galaxy, it then would take 2.56 million years just for light to travel from our galaxy to the next closest one, and there billions and billions of galaxies, according to Carl Sagan (*actually, he said 100 billion galaxies*).

In 2004, the combined power of the Keck Telescopes on Mauna Kea and the Hubble Telescope discovered what was reported to be the most distant galaxy 13 billion light years away, but earlier in 2002, a galaxy 13.6 billion light years was also supposedly seen, and now gamma-ray bursts suggest distances close to the time of the Big Bang. Thus, there is some sorting out still going on in the field.

Conversely, in the direction of really small, in ***The Elegant Universe***, Brian Green writes that the fundamental particle is a string, a one dimensional vibrating loop. How large is this string? Well, if an atom has the diameter of our entire solar system, then a string would be about as large as a tree. As you know, an atom is almost infinitesimally tiny—about $10^{-8}$ centimeter—so this piece of string is estimated to be $10^{-33}$ centimeters.[224] Interesting to note that ***Book 1*** speculated that your odds of being born a human being was $10^{-34}$, an even smaller number. And, while you live in a three dimensional world, String Theory starts with 10, and probably more, dimensions. So let us simplify this chapter by merely looking outwards from Planet Earth for life in space and stick to three dimensions plus time.

What you once learned in school has been updated. Do you know, for example, that there are 137 known moons in our solar system? Wait a minute, one more was added yesterday. Jupiter alone has 60 of them, while Pluto has three. One of these, Charon, has also been added to the list of new planets, with Ceres and Xena (*now officially named Eris*). So, there are now 12 planets. Well, then, again, no, as a dissenting group of the International Astronomical Union fired off a rebuttal, contesting that Pluto itself should be a "dwarf" planet, and they prevailed, dropping the elite planetary number to 8. Being plutoed was chosen as the 2006 word of the year by the American Dialect Society, meaning, being demoted or devalued. Grown men and women are serious about all this. Your tax dollars are partly responsible. Anyway, there are a lot of moons out there, but at least one of them was absolutely critical, for one theory has it that life could not have begun on this planet if we had no moon to stabilize our orbit.

The first seed for the Search for Extraterrestrial Intelligence, or SETI, might have been planted as early as 700 BC when Indian astronomer and mathematician Aryabhata is known to have visualized heliocentricism (*Earth revolves around the Sun*). In the fourth century BC, Greek philosopher Metrodorus of Chios, wrote in his book, ***On Nature***, "to suppose that Earth is the only populated world in infinite space is as absurd as to believe that in an entire field sown with millet, only one grain will grow." However, Ptolemy, around 150 AD, still viewed Earth as the center of the Universe, the prevailing theory then, until Polish astronomer Nicolaus Copernicus, actually also trained in medicine and law, in the 1500's, founded modern astronomy, placing Planet Earth as a mere object revolving around the Sun. He also advanced the possibility of other earths revolving around other suns. Copernicus survived the clergy because his first book on the subject was not published until the last day of his life. Much braver, but maybe not so smart, was Dominican Monk Giordano Bruno, who suggested that there might be an infinite number of suns with inhabited planets.[19, 289] Alas, he was arrested in 1592, condemned, and burned at the stake in 1600.

Not long thereafter, German astronomer Johannes Kepler wrote that the moon might be inhabited by beings with large bodies to withstand the long, hot lunar days. He expanded his habitats to include four moons of Jupiter, recently discovered by Galileo Galilei, the father of modern astronomy and modern physics, who because of his scientific discoveries, was, at the age of 69, convicted by the Inquisition and sentenced to life imprisonment. He, though, had religious connections (*Pope Paul V and Pope Urban VIII*), and served the equivalent of house arrest. Three hundred fifty years later, Pope John Paul II rehabilitated Galileo.

In 1728, Bernard du Fontenelle [105] of France expounded on the subject and a few years later, English poet Alexander Pope, in his ***Essay on Man***, wrote:

> *He who thro' vast immensity can pierce,*
> *See worlds on worlds compose one universe,*
> *Observe how system into system runs,*
> *What other planets circle other suns,*
> *What vary'd being peoples ev'ry star,*
> *May tell why Heav'n has made us as we are.*

In 1834, a century later, Britisher Alexander Copland published ***The Existence of Other Worlds: Peopled with Living and Intelligent Beings*** [70]. Also during the middle 1800s, German mathematician Carl Friedrich Gauss tried to initiate a project to plant a gigantic forest in the shape of a right triangle so that astronomers from other worlds who saw it would realize that Earth was inhabited with an intelligence that was familiar with an unnatural geometric shape. But in general, there was an attitude of caution in this century and extraterrestrial speculation was discouraged.

While the Mars observations of Italian astronomer Giovanni Schiaparelli back in 1877 suggested something called "canali," or channels, American astronomer Percival Lowell in his 1908 book, ***Mars as the Abode of Life***, reported on his theory about intelligent beings responsible for the crisscrossing canals. These canals proved to be an optical illusion by the Mariner spacecrafts in the 1960s. In 1919, Italian inventor Guglielmo Marconi of wireless fame caused a public stir by suggesting that some unusual radio signals came from Mars. Around that time, Albert Einstein recommended that light rays might be an easily controllable method of extraterrestrial communication.

The fear of Martian invasion grew for decades, and when Orson Welles in his 1938 Halloween radio broadcast dramatized H.G. Wells' novel, ***War of the Worlds***—even though there was a warning at the beginning that this was a re-creation—too many took the message too seriously. This was a period when Hitler was advancing in Europe. When the first movie in 1953 appeared, the Korean War and communism were in the minds of the populace. The 2005 Spielberg version came on the heels of our war on terrorism, so the threat of extraterrestrials seems to work best when civilization is somehow being threatened.

The religious-SETI love-hate relationship continued in 1952 with a statement regarding the new science of radio astronomy by Oxford cosmologist, E.A. Milne:[203]

> *"In that case there would be no difficulty in the uniqueness of the historical event of the Incarnation. For knowledge of it would be capable of being transmitted by signals to other planets and the re-enactment of the tragedy of the crucifixion in other planets would be unnecessary."*

In 1959 two Cornell University physicists, Philip Morrison and Giuseppe Cocconi, wrote [66] about the basic concept of a search for extraterrestrial radio waves, which inspired Frank Drake, then a young radio astronomer at the National Radio Astronomy Observatory, to in 1960 search Tau Ceti and Epsilon Eridani to determine if they might be sending coded signals. In his autobiographical history of the SETI movement, Drake remarks [291]:

> *"I have been waiting for this moment nearly all my life. Indeed, if there is anything unusual about my otherwise normal childhood, it is that I started tracing my ties to alien civilizations of intelligent life in the universe at the age of eight."*

He went on to say:

> *"I fully expect alien civilization to bequeath to us vast libraries of useful information, to do with as we wish. This Encyclopedia Galactica will create the potential for improvements in our lives that we cannot predict. During the Renaissance, rediscovered ancient texts and new knowledge flooded medieval Europe with the light of thought, wonder, creativity, experimentation, and exploration of the natural world. Another, even more stirring Renaissance will be fueled by the wealth of alien scientific, technical and sociological information that awaits us."*

Called Project Ozma—the Queen in the ***Oz Books*** by Frank Baum, from which came "The Wizard of Oz" in 1900—Drake's project survived into the 70's. As an aside, I was surprised to learn in 2006 that there was a 13-minute film based on this book in 1910 and a later 1925 full length silent version before the 1939, colored, song-filled blockbuster featuring Judy Garland.

Work on Communication with Extraterrestrial Intelligence (*CETI*) began in the former Soviet Union in 1964, and the following year, scientists announced that they actually detected signals. It turned out that they were measuring quasars, very bright centers from distant galaxies. While that was at least mildly embarrassing, the field recovered enough so that in March of 1974, the Academy of Sciences of the USSR, approved CETI as a research program, for the logic of that day was, what if the Americans are gaining a Cold War advantage through this weird scheme. The Soviet Union even hosted international SETI conferences in 1971 and 1981.

The logic of SETI is sound: interstellar space travel is expensive and way beyond our current engineering ability. The fastest man-made object travelling in space needs to go about 17,000 times faster to approach the speed of light.

Cost of current space activities? Just NASA's Deep Impact project, that relayed back to Earth the flash of a probe hitting comet Tempel 1, perfectly timed to draw the attention of the nation on July 3, 2005, cost $333 million. Spectacular? Absolutely, as to track for 172 days, after travelling 268 million miles, and hit a Manhattan sized comet 82.5 million miles away moving at 66,880 miles per hour, is amazing. Purpose? To answer basic questions about the origins of the solar system. Ulterior motive? Perhaps hype up funding for NASA. Coming on the eve of Independence Day, the effect was newsworthy. NASA has a way of orchestrating these events, for good reason. I worked for them once.

The entire Apollo Project to send Man to the Moon would have cost $140 billion today. Unknowingly, this extravagance did help to bankrupt the Soviet Union, resulting in the end of the Cold War, so it was worth every penny. Remember from Chapter 1, the Afghanistan-Iraq war will probably cost somewhere in the realm of $3,000 billion, or $3 trillion. Today, with no obvious world threat, each Space Shuttle flight continues to cost around $1.3 billion, more than what the Department of Energy annually spends on renewable energy development. The matter of significance and priorities continue to challenge our nation and world.

Not to really rub it in, but a few disasters of course would be expected: NASA's 2002 Comet Nucleus Tour, or Contour, to explore comets, went missing at a cost of $159 million, and the 1992 Mars Observer stopped communicating in 1993, for a loss of $1 billion. The next bold new mission for NASA is Project Juno, to, in 2010, robotically orbit Jupiter, for only $700 million. NASA launched The Mars Reconnaissance Orbiter, a $720 million mission, on August 12, 2005, the Phoenix Mars Scout in search of organic chemicals on Mars in 2007, and in 2009 will hurl the Mars Science Laboratory into space. Thus, it can be argued that setting aside a small percentage of these sums, say $10 million/year, should be a justifiable token to continue the research to detect signals from space. But NASA is today forbidden by Congress to do any obvious SETI work.

U.S. Senator Spark Matsunaga, in his book, ***The Mars Project*** [194], advocated the U.S. working with the Soviet Union to get to Mars. Matsunaga's two great legacies, the U.S. Peace Academy (see *Chapter 1 of this book*) and hydrogen (*as reported in Chapter 3 of* ***Book 1****, as he was the originator of the national hydrogen fuel R&D program*), will prevail over planetary exploration because the Cold War soon ended and cooperation with Russia became a given. I was working in Senator Matsunaga's office when the Mars Project was initiated, and worked closely with the ghost writer, Harvey Meyerson, on several projects. Meyerson later fashioned an interesting career himself, promoting international cooperation in space, and might yet someday amalgamate SETI with Herman Melville, his twin passions, although I guess *Star Trek* has already saved a whale in time, so Harvey needs to amplify his creative reflexes.

In 1989, President George H.W. Bush's "Space Exploration Initiative," with its $500 billion price tag, targeted Mars, but was never fleshed out. The International Science and Technology Center, created in 1992 through an agreement among the European Union, Japan, the Russian Federation, and the U.S., headquartered in Moscow, produced a 13-volume study blueprinting how best to send an expedition to the Red Planet. Cost for putting Man on Mars? $20 billion, much cheaper than the Apollo Project. Russian space experts, though, reported in 2004 that they could send a six-man crew to Mars within a decade for only $3.5 billion (www.msnbc.msn.com/id/4720408/). The world scoffed, and the retort was that such an effort would actually cost a trillion dollars. President George W. Bush in 2004 did hint of a Moon + Mars plan, but, like his father, just planted a seed. University of Illinois engineer Cliff Singer [133] estimates the price of 1 million person-centuries to send a manned space ship to another star. Cost? $10 trillion.

Against these numbers, SETI looks like a bargain, especially as you don't need to actually travel long distances to pick up the message, for all you need to do is detect and encrypt signals from space. I'm beginning to sound like those naysayers criticizing Cristoforo Columbo (*that Italian credited with discovering America in 1492*) but, under current conditions, SETI makes a lot more economic sense than sending Man into Space.

SETI has been regularly reviewed as good science, and additionally, hopes for real answers to ultimate questions, and communication by radio waves is elegant and relatively cheap. Narrow band frequencies traveling at the speed of light in the microwave portion of the electromagnetic spectrum would carry long distances (*in the range of 500 light years with current technology*) with minimal power and signal interference, and would not be absorbed by cosmic dust. What if signals are coming from civilizations Out There far more advanced than ours? Drake's ***Encyclopedia Galactica*** could be ours to use.

We, Earthlings, did, actually, in 1972, launch Pioneer 10 featuring a gold anodized aluminum plaque with a pictorial message from humanity with our location to the red star Aldebaran via the Planet Jupiter. However, the estimated date of arrival is still 2 million years away. In the meantime, our television signals have been beaming out since the 1930's.

The key vocabulary of SETI speak, so that the reader can understand the jargon and comprehend the immensity, might include:

- one astronomical unit (*AU*): the 93 million mile average distance of Earth from the Sun, which is a distance measurement;
- one light year: 5.88 (*call it 6*) trillion miles—multiply the speed of light (*186,282 miles per second*), times 60 seconds in a minute, times 60 minutes in an hour, times 24 hours in a day, times 365.24 days in a year to get the distance traveled by light in one year, which, again, is a measurement of distance or length, not time;
- 4.2 light years: the distance of Proxima Centauri, our closest neighbor, a distance the 1977 Voyager would take 70,000 years to reach, where it is humbling to appreciate that Jesus Christ was only 2,000 years ago;
- there are about 1,500 stars within 50 light years from Earth, and these solar systems all have now received our regular TV signals (*which travel at the speed of light*), except that with our current technology, we today might be able to detect this same signal only if it emanated from about a light year away, meaning that we would not be able to detect a similar TV signal originating anywhere outside our solar system;
- SETI typically searches for alien signals from as far away as 150 light years, so for detection, the signal must be really, really powerful and largely pointed to us;
- however, Frank Drake was quoted in 2000 that "the power of our search system is 100 trillion times what it was 40 years ago [188]," so technology is growing with incredible speed; and

- Drake formulated the seminal equation (*promise, this will be my only equation*):

  $N = R^{*} F_p N_p F_l F_i F_c L$

Where:

| | | |
|---|---|---|
| $N$ | = | number of technological civilizations in our galaxy |
| $R^{*}$ | = | average annual rate of star formation in our galaxy |
| $F_p$ | = | fraction of stars having planets |
| $N_p$ | = | number of suitable planets per planetary system |
| $F_l$ | = | fraction of planets on which life starts |
| $F_i$ | = | fraction of life that evolves to intelligence |
| $F_c$ | = | fraction of intelligent species to develop communication |
| $L$ | = | longevity in years of the technological phase of this society |

Of course, you need to provide reasonable figures for each term, and workshops of intelligent minds have resulted in the values of N ranging between 10,000 and 1 million possible intelligent societies capable of sending and/or interpreting radio wave signals. To my surprise, in the discussions with my involvement, men of the cloth were the most comfortable with the potentiality of a receiving such a message.

We can write books on each term, and in Chapter 2 I already analyzed $F_l$, how life can start from elements, water and energy. But let us here examine one more, $F_c$, or the matter about intelligence, for this is the one that, like $F_l$, needs something close to a miracle. Well, perhaps not, for it has been reported that the simplest of life, the single cell bacteria, has intelligence.[275] I think this is ludicrous, but scientist have been known to disagree.

**SETI in the 70's**

In 1971, Bernard Oliver of Hewlett-Packard and John Billingham of the National Aeronautics and Space Administration (*NASA*) Ames Research Center (*ARC*) conducted a summer workshop, and the group picked 1.42 GHz, the spectral line caused by interstellar hydrogen, and 1.66 GHz, caused by hydroxyl ions, called the "Water Hole," as the ideal portion of space to conduct the search. For one, water symbolized life, and that band was relatively quiet. There is now that transitional link, for ***Book 1*** featured a chapter reporting on hydrogen. Maybe there is something about hydrogen that goes beyond mere utility.

In 1972, Oliver and Billingham authored a NASA study proposing an array of one thousand 100-meter telescopic dishes to pick up television and radio signals from neighboring stars. Project Cyclops was projected to cost $10 billion, but was never seriously considered.[161] At this point in history, the U.S. Congress was not aware, or cared, that NASA was doing SETI work.

As an assistant professor of engineering, I then teamed with the resident futurist at the University of Hawaii, James Dator, and the Ames Research Center, on "Earth 2020: Visions for Our Children's Children," where in the summer of '74 we brought to Hawaii noted lecturers of national stature in topics related to Planet Earth, the environment and space, and weekly filled a two thousand seat auditorium. We also conducted a workshop for forty or so secondary and university faculty. Having been thusly enlightened with this course, many of them went on to become principals, a university president, a provost, and elected public officials. Professor Dator later gained fame as Secretary General, then President, of the World Futures Study Federation. Identical summer workshops were held at San Jose State University and San Diego State University, with the advanced planning final report prepared by faculty from all three workshops. There was also a lot of cross-fertilization with the leaders of Project Cyclops. The information and curricula we generated became the standard instructional tools for a large number of teachers in Hawaii and California in the growing field of environmental consciousness. Remember, this was more than a third of a century ago.

Having thus been exposed to the SETI field, in 1976 I joined 19 other university faculty members from across the nation at NASA ARC in Mountain View, California, on Project Orion, to detect an extrasolar planet *(or exoplanet, used interchangeably)*, that is, a planet revolving around another star, spearheaded, of course, by Oliver and Billingham. The first question asked of Cornell Professor Frank Drake was: "Extraterrestrial intelligence? How do you know there are even other planets outside our solar system?" So the faculty group was tasked to design a system to accomplish this feat. Why me? Well, I had an idea on how to do this, plus I long harbored visions that the cure for cancer and the solution to world peace might be beaming unto Planet Earth from advanced civilizations.

Originally, in the mid 1800's, stars were classified by hotness (*Class I for white and blue, down to Class IV for red and Class V*). Early in the 1900's, the Harvard classification was adopted, ranking stars by luminosity—O, B, A, F, G, K, and M—**O**h **B**e **A** **F**ine **G**irl, **K**iss **M**e.

F and G type suns seem best suited for planets. Our Sun is in the latter category, and the guess is that there is a 7% chance for a solar system, while the former is 1.3 to 1.5 solar masses, with a 10% chance of planets. Planets do not form in binary star systems, and have a higher probability of creation in galactic arms where heavy elements are located. There is a 20-30% chance towards the external portion of a galaxy, where we are located.

How does a planet form? Well, more and more, astronomers are seeing disks surrounding stars. Very simply, the dust agglomerates into planets.[380] Thus, first find a planet, any planet. Then, find planets where life is possible. These sites should be:

- o older than 3 billion years;
- o with a star smaller than 1.5 times our Sun mass;
- o having a stable location between galaxy spiral arms; and
- o in a solar system which is singular, that is, without a binary star.

While most of the team went on to design an interferometric system to **indirectly** do the job, a few of us were allowed to pursue other directions. Indirect means to measure something else. That is, as you can't see that extrasolar planet, the starlight being so intense relative to the reflection from the planet, measure the orbit wobble of the star, with the pattern mathematically being fitted for possible planets. Direct means somehow block out the starlight and see that extrasolar planet, or, better yet, actually measure and track something, anything, from the planet itself. I was the only one to take this latter option, for I like to see what I'm doing, and the optical spectrum was my choice.

That same previously mentioned (*in Chapter 2*) Charles Townes, who had won the Nobel Prize for the laser, and who will later be mentioned in Chapter 10 for being awarded the 2005 Templeton Prize (*generally given to a noted scientist who has religious predilections*), happened to just arrive at the University of California Berkeley from the Massachusetts Institute Technology in 1976, and had published a paper speculating that planetary atmospheres lased (*that is, flashed a well-defined color like in a typical laser, representing the gaseous molecule undergoing this phenomenon*).

As an aside, there is something karmic coupling the afterlife with SETI, as ***Science Digest***, in its October 1985 issue on "The 20 Greatest Unanswered Questions of Science," featured on its front cover, English-born and Princeton professor Freeman Dyson, the 2002 Templeton Prize awardee. Dyson was asked the question, "Are We Alone in the Universe?" He responded, "engaging in mathematical calculations on the probability of intelligent life elsewhere in the universe is not a worthwhile exercise. The universe may be crawling with life. The answer is: Wait and see." Dyson had previously worked on a different Orion Project, but that was around 1960, and it had to do with using nuclear pulse propulsion for space-flight.

Anyway, returning to the discussion, a Jupiter-size planet cannot be seen revolving around a typical Sun-size star tens of light years away because the starlight is so much brighter than the reflection from such a planet, by 5 to 10 orders of magnitude (*meaning 10 to that power, or in the inverse, the light from an extrasolar planet is from 1/100,000 to 1/10,000,000,000, or one ten billionth that of the star*). However, if the planetary atmosphere lased, then these spiked discrete frequencies, first, might well be detectable because you would know exactly which monochromatic colors to check (*the lasing frequency of those gases that would be found in planetary atmospheres*), thus, also, this would accordingly give the atmospheric composition. Conversely, if no lasing is detected, then that planet has no atmosphere, and can summarily be deleted from future consideration regarding the potential for harboring life. My PhD dissertation experience, which included building a tunable laser before you could purchase one, provided this spark of imagination. I went to see Professor Townes, and he graciously provided encouragement.

My final report to NASA was called "To See the Impossible Dream: the Planetary Abstracting Trinterferometer (*note the acronym, PAT*)," with a Man from La Mancha symbol on the cover. I of course quoted Miguel de Cervantes:

> *To Man, the Don Quixote of the universe*
> *May he succeed in his impossible dream.*

At first I thought David Black, the NASA coordinator, reacted to my paper as being some kind of joke, but I now understand that optical searches were not company policy. That is, as it makes a lot more technical sense to measure the microwave spectrum for actual alien signals, NASA seemed wedded to focusing only on that particular technology, even for detecting extrasolar planets. Till today, I still can't quite grasp the reason for this shortsightedness, for the two missions are totally different. Anyway, he surmised that the Hubble Telescope would be soon fly and find such exoplanets. Hubble was actually deployed 14 years later, has yet to directly detect an extrasolar Earth-sized planet, and might never directly measure an exoplanet with life potential. This telescope is expected to be serviced one final time later in 2008 for operation until 2013, when the James Webb Space Telescope is expected to be launched. However, without an orbit reboost, the Hubble could plunge to Earth sometime soon after 2010. In any case, the prevailing convention then, as now, was to explore and receive the microwave band, so anything resembling optical searches did not meet the accepted requirements.

Either way, there is a timing concern, as, more and more, new commercial communications satellites will cloud the radio spectrum, especially in the range of the most promising detection channels. Thus, SETI will soon need to move into outer space if the focus is to continue traditional interferometry measurement techniques on Earth.

Two final bits about the '70's, in 1975, the U.S. Congress published "The Possibility of Intelligent Life Elsewhere in the Universe." In 1978, Senator William Proxmire (D-Wisconsin) selected NASA's SETI program for one of his famous Golden Fleece Awards. The following year found me in Washington, D.C. as U.S. Senator Spark Matsunaga's Special Assistant on Energy. Little did I know that while helping to solve our second energy crisis, one of my more interesting tasks would be related to SETI.

**Exoplanetary Search and SETI from the 80's into the 21st Century**

You will note that I have added exoplanetary search to SETI. There is a reason for this.

In 1981, Senator Proxmire sponsored an amendment to eliminate SETI from NASA. One of my side efforts was, with others, and also the considerable personal suasion of Matsunaga with Proxmire, help Carl Sagan, a colleague of Frank Drake at Cornell, reinstate funding. The involved team set up that fateful meeting with Senator Proxmire, who was of the Dyson school of thought that it was a silly waste of government funds to search for extraterrestrial intelligence. I had met Sagan when he served on a panel during my NASA Ames stopover, where he was in a group commenting on the first Viking photos to arrive from Mars. We were the first to see these photos, line by line, being posted unto the auditorium screen in Mountain View before they were released into TV land. Who knows, maybe fuzzy Green Ladies could have shown up. I still remember Sagan pontificating as to why the color of Mars had a salmon-tinge, and commented so in fine scientific detail...except, well into his elocution, a technician sheepishly commented, "Dr. Sagan, we haven't yet applied the correction filters." That's the only time I saw Sagan visibly embarrassed. It turned out that the addition of the filters did not change the salmon hue.

The story has become almost legendary, as Carl Sagan was so successful in his conversation with Senator Proxmire that the following year Congress funded SETI at the level of $1.5 million. This support very slowly grew to a point in the early 1990's when a ten year, $100 million program, was announced by NASA. A sum of $11-12 million was annually expended through three fiscal years in the early 90's. The web page (www.setv.org) on "A Scientific

Search for Visitation from Extraterrestrial Probes," is 58 full pages long, with references, abstracts and a fair mix of both SETI and UFO related documents and articles. I should underscore, of course, that the two acronyms should not be confused to be themselves related. SETI is good science, while UFO's belong in the realm of the twilight zone.

Then, Congress summarily terminated the program in 1992. Explained Stephen Garber of NASA:[113]

> *On Columbus Day, 1992, the National Aeronautics and Space Administration formally initiated a radio astronomy program called SETI (Search for Extraterrestrial Intelligence). Less than a year later, Congress abruptly canceled the program. Why? While there was and still is a debate over the likelihood of finding intelligent extraterrestrial life, virtually all informed parties agreed that the SETI program constituted worthwhile, valid science. Yet, fervor over the federal budget deficit, lack of support from other scientists and aerospace contractors and a significant history of unfounded associations with nonscientific elements combined with bad timing in the fall of 1993 to make the program an easy target to eliminate. Thus SETI was a relative anomaly in terms of a small, scientifically valid program that was canceled for political expediency.*

Why did Congress kill SETI? Proxmire was no longer in the Senate. Neither was Matsunaga. The identified assassin was Senator Richard Bryan (*D-Nevada*), who largely avoided discussion with SETI researchers, and even NASA representatives, but it also was the combination of SETI being only a $12 million program, with no major aerospace contractors *(this was an efficient effort where equipment was bootstrapped*), in a field that bridged subject areas with no effective scientific constituency, with a high giggle (*green men*) factor, when there was a serious national budget deficit, and at a time when NASA was fighting bruising battles over much larger programs (*SETI was one thousandth of the NASA budget*). SETI also could only report on the fact that, after decades, it still had not even detected one small promising signal.

The private sector then stepped in to help. In a sense, if the foundation and industrial funding process works, the program will maintain some continuity without the vagaries of Congress. In one parting shot, SETI supporters remarked, "what can you expect from a deliberative body represented by one scientist and four undertakers?" This was true of the 103rd Congress.

Thus, while NASA could continue with search for exoplanets and do astrobiology, it had to completely abandon SETI. NASA hosted two workshops during this period and published *TOPS: Toward Other Planetary Systems*, which is a good source for information on detecting exoplanets. Thus, I should again explain that, as it is today accepted that there are planets revolving around some stars, the next logical step is to find potential Earth-like planets, so that those microwave dishes can more efficiently detect intelligent signals. NASA is involved with the former, while being careful not to hint that the purpose is SETI-inspired.

The non-NASA SETI people in 1992 then went to the rich, corporations and foundations. The SETI Institute (SETII,www.seti.org) itself had been formed in 1984, a year after original congressional funding, to explore, understand and explain the origin, nature and prevalence of life in the universe. Today, in Mountain View, it employs 100 scientists, educators and support staff. There are two scientific leaders:

- Center for SETI Research, where the Bernard Oliver Chair is held by Jill Tarter, and
- Center for the Study of Life in the Universe, where the Carl Sagan Chair, originally held by Christopher Chyba, is now occupied by Scott Hubbard, past director of the Ames Research Center.

Thomas Pierson has served as Chief Executive Officer since the founding, and Frank Drake still serves on the Board of Trustees.

The primary effort of SETII has been Project Phoenix, which was begun in 1995 with private financing, but, equipment "borrowed" from NASA. Congress was cruel, but, either permissive or not too watchful.

Along the way came the 1997 movie ***Contact***, from the book by Carl Sagan, starring Jodie Foster. All the elements were there: God, the afterlife, SETI, attack by religious terrorists. Sounds like ***Simple Solutions, Book 2***. The film starts with the Arecibo dish in Puerto Rico listening to space for signals. As is the tradition of SETI, funding was terminated. Jodie Foster sort of played Jill Tarter of SETII, plus there was a blind researcher, Kent Clark, who in real life was Kent Cullers, director of R&D for Project Phoenix. Measurement then shifted to the Very Large Array in New Mexico, a more photogenic site representative of dish systems, where signals do arrive and get de-coded. The movie then jumps into the hyperspace of the improbable, but, in many ways, that's part of why politicians are wary of SETI.

The Targeted Search System of NASA was upgraded in 2002 by SETII to the New Search System, based on a modular architecture and programmable integrated circuits—a bit quicker, with the same search power, but only 20% the room space. In addition to the Arecibo and Jodrell Bank (*U.K.*) observatories, the initial 42 dishes of the new Allen (*financed by Paul Allen of Microsoft fame*) Telescope Array, located 290 miles northeast of San Francisco in Hat Creek, California, a radio-quiet zone, was added to the mix in 2007. Do you need an expensive 350 dish array, as has been brought to the hypothetical table by the Allen Array? If you can afford it, sure, as Paul Allen has committed $25 million to the effort. There are some cost-matching factors delaying full implementation, but these should someday be worked out.

**What about the Optical Spectrum?**

To be frank, the early focus, plus Project Cyclops, carried so much eminence that the microwave searchers dominated from the beginning and continue to today. Thus, indirect techniques prevailed for the detection of extrasolar planets, while the capability of distinguishing signals from longer distances solidified the case.

There are two types of optical SETI researchers: those employing incoherent photon counting and others utilizing coherent (*like a laser light*) heterodyne detection. I was advocating the latter as an exoplanet detection concept more than twenty years before the optical approach for exosignals began to be accepted by atrophysicists in 1998. However, the second energy crisis arrived in 1979 and I turned my efforts toward crusades like Green Enertopia and the Blue Revolution. A third of century went by and I have finally returned. I missed the 2001 SETI gathering in San Jose where Charles Townes presented a paper entitled, "Reflections on Forty Years of Optical SETI—Looking Forward and Looking Backward," but look forward to participating in the next one.

At that California conference, Stuart Kingsley talked on "Optical SETI Observatories in the New Millennium: A Review." Kingsley valiantly pursued the subject with his Visible Optical SETI Observatory associated with Ohio State University at Columbus. He was mostly self-funded and in 2007, after 26 years of general futility, moved to Bournemouth, England. His attitude is that the scientific community went in the wrong direction because of mistaken assumptions.[168]

In any case, over the next few decades, I would think that the optical spectrum will gain in respect, especially in the search for exoplanets. The next section will provide some details to this historical sketch. If it can be shown that coherent signals can be sent efficiently over reasonable distances, then even the detection of actual optical extraterrestrial intelligence signals might gain in prominence, too. Hmm…a career reborn?

**To See the Inevitable Dream: Earthlike Exoplanets**

The SETI field, while always seeking to detect and encrypt actual communications from aliens, has been plagued by not yet being able to pinpoint even one suitable extrasolar planet where life could exist. In many ways, this was then an impossible dream because it never had been done, yet. My interest during those early days of finding an Earthlike planet circling another star has, shockingly enough, still eluded the experts. But this dream is no longer impossible, it is now inevitable. Drawing together some of the historical threads previously mentioned, let us now focus on task #1: find Earthlike exoplanets.

Remember, NASA does fund these searches. However, astroscientists mostly use INDIRECT methods to hunt for exoplanets, like astrometry (*measure a star's position in the sky—if there is a planet, then the orbit would be affected*), radial velocity (*determine variations in the speed at which the star moves from or to our planet, the change surmised to be caused by a planet—this has been the most productive method*), pulsar timing (*detect anomalies from the precise radio pulses, which must be caused by a planet*) and a host of other esoteric techniques. In short, wobbles are measured and programmed for computer matching with a possible planet or more.

The direct means used involve the transit method (*when a planet crosses in front of the star, the brightness drops—you need to be really lucky for this one*), circumsteller disks (*where space dust can more easily be detected, with any features suggesting a planet*) and others. Some of these direct techniques could probably also have been utilized by Galileo.

Take one direct technique, planet dimming. Searchers are focusing on M-dwarfs, faint red stars, which make up 70% of all stars. In these solar systems, it is possible to obtain light reduction of up to 1% when a planet passes across the star, as compared to 0.001% dimming if you were viewing from many light years away and Earth blocks the light of our Sun, a G2 star.[185] But life prospects are not exciting for M-dwarf systems. So why? We already know there are planets outside our solar system.

When was the first extrasolar planet truly detected? This remains somewhat controversial, but it was in 1988 that Canadian astronomers Bruce Campbell, G. A. H. Walker and S. Yang, using radial velocity observations, first cautiously claimed success. The first published and confirmed paper appeared in 1992 when Polish astronomer Aleksander Wolszczan and Canadian radio astronomer Dale Frail announced the discovery of planets around a pulsar. In 1995, Swiss astronomers Didier Queloz and Michel Mayor saw a planet orbiting a typical star, using high resolution spectroscopy.

At the end of 2005 there were 150 exoplanets identified, doubling by 2008. On November 7, 2007, the W.M. Keck Observatory reported on a fifth planet orbiting 55 Cancri, a star about the same size as our Sun, and just 41 light years away. But none of them would qualify to harbor life as we know it, for most of these exoplanets are Jupiter-sized with very short orbit periods. But, of course, that is because the current techniques can only find these, except for those lucky dimming observations.

Absent really useful data because all the planets unwobble-ized, as of 2007, are too large, a planet orbiting the red dwarf star Gliese 581, could be at a probable surface temperature where liquid water might be possible. Discovered on April 24, 2007 by a Swiss team using a radial velocity technique in La Sill, Chile, the speculation is that this exoplanet is not good enough because Ymir, still officially called Gliese 581 c, has about five times the mass of Earth, an orbital radius only about 7% that of Earth (*but the red dwarf is cooler than our Sun*) and a period of only 13 days (*that is, it takes 13 days to revolve around the star*). When you look up into the night sky, you can't help, though, but be impressed with how in the heck astroscientists can glean so much information from a rotating body so far away.

**Hawaii and SETI**

There were several astrophysicists at the University of Hawaii Institute of Astronomy and Physics Department who I've met with to talk about SETI. All of them, to my knowledge, came and went over time.

I first became involved when I sent a letter[315] to Mayor Dante Carpenter of the Big Island of Hawaii, dated March 1, 1974. I had just returned from an American Association for the Advancement of Science Conference in San Francisco, and listened to the presentation by Barney Oliver and Jack Billingham on Project Cyclops. They had proposed spending $5 billion (*later expanded to $10 billion*) over the next 15 years just to listen to the Universe. Mind you, this was in 1974 dollars, so that would be equivalent to a scientist today proposing a $25 billion SETI project today. I wrote to Mayor Carpenter to meet with Jack Billingham, who was into snorkeling in Hawaii, for the Big Island surely had some worthwhile sites, both snorkeling and a possible location for Project Cyclops.

Like most things I have proposed over time, nothing happened. But, as reported earlier, I did join the Billingham group at the Ames Research Center two summers later to test out some of my ideas. Thus, it was in 1976 when I first advised NASA on my plan to cost-effectively detect an extrasolar planet using Townes' laser light theory. After being ignored by them over the past few decades—well, actually, interest was lacking from both ends—I have toyed with the idea of helping a high school student beat NASA at directly finding an Earth-like planet revolving around a star. I never found time to do this, but was partly daunted by a fear that the concept made no real sense.

But on the Big Island, detection potential was rapidly expanding. William Myron Keck was a self-educated oil worker who founded Superior Oil Company and became very, very rich through drilling and offshore exploits in the field. The Keck Foundation, started in 1954, received an infusion of $43 million in 1979, and now has assets greater than $1 billion. A sum of $144 million went to the California Institute of Technology and partners to build the Keck Telescope and Observatory on Mauna Kea. More than ten years ago I remember driving one of his sons, who I believe was also called Bill, with his new second or third wife, through a whiteout, a true blizzard, to inspect Keck I. At 13,796 feet (4205 meters), and all that snow, I was convinced that this was not a place I again wanted to visit.

In 2001, the W.M. Keck Observatory and NASA jointly announced their "outrigger" project to link Keck I and Keck II with six 1.8 meter (6 foot) new telescopes to provide sufficient resolution to detect these planets. Unfortunately, this came at a time when Hawaiians and environmentalists were in a strengthened mode, and thought that enough was enough. There were already too many telescopes on the mountain. If my street smart geothermal staff got derailed when environmentalists were weak, there was not much hope for the astrophysicists.

Yet, in 2005, NASA officially selected Mauna Kea for the Outrigger Telescope Project because no alternate site matched the scientific capability of Mauna Kea. There was some passing mention of the Wekiu bug, found nowhere else in the world. This insect, actually, is interesting, as its blood has an anti-freeze like substance. Well, Mauna Kea Anaina Hou (*People who Pray for the Mountain*), a local organization, was watching, and pointed out that:

- Mauna Kea is sacred to Native Hawaiians.
- The summit is home to divine deities, the meeting place of Earth Mother and Sky Father, and the temple of the Supreme Being.
- The cinder cone where the outrigger telescopes were scheduled to be built is where Lilinoe, the wife of the deity for fishermen, Kukahau'ula, was buried.
- The Hawaii State Historic Preservation Division is planning to propose that the entire summit be listed in the National Register as a historic district/cultural landscape.
- There are eleven indigenous anthropods living there, with, of course, the Wekiu Bug, a candidate for listing as an endangered species.
- The highest lake in the country, Lake Waiau, is located in this area.
- Mauna Kea is part of Hawaii's ceded lands trust that belongs to the Hawaiians.
- In 1998, the Hawaii State Auditor issued a report criticizing the management of their mountain.

NASA did offer $1.86 million towards Native Hawaiian causes. A sum of $15 million to $20 million was spent to prepare the documentation.

In June of 2006, NASA announced that they were pulling out of the Outrigger Project, saving $50 million. That same month, acceding to a Natural Resource Defense Council's suit, U.S. District Judge Florence-Marie Cooper issued a temporary restraining order barring the use of any sonar in the annual rim of the Pacific naval exercise (*Rimpac*) around Hawaii, involving 19,000 servicemen, 35 surface ships, six submarines, and 160 aircraft and amphibious forces of the navy and coast guard from the U.S., Australia, Canada, Chile, Peru, Japan, UK, and Korea, severely compromising their activities.

So, the thought from the intelligentsia then was that Hawaii might well have eliminated itself from playing significant roles in the romance of space, defending freedom and developing renewable energy, all because environmental and cultural factions prevailed over technological progress. The irony is that much of this effort involved the research of clean energy technologies and high tech jobs for tomorrow. Well, there, too, is the evidence of a pod of 200 melonhead whales frightened into Hanalei Bay, Kauai in the 2004 Rimpac.[97] In 2008, our Commander in Chief, President George Bush, override the judiciary by exempting the Navy from this nonsense, but permits for this planet seeking project were rescinded.

But, still alive is The Thirty Meter Telescope (*TMT*), ten times more powerful than any other, to watch planets orbit distant stars. Let's see now, it will take at least three years to complete a needed archeological survey, then there will be a need to establish an acceptable plan for re-burial of potential findings. Operational date is supposed to be circa 2015, with a site to be chosen very shortly. In contention are Mexico, Chile and Mauna Kea on the Big Island of Hawaii. While Hubble is still operating, who knows, it might not get a reboost, and TMT is almost a decade in the future, so perhaps a high school science fair project might still be a worthwhile endeavor.

So I went to one of the most innovative public high school in Hawaii, Kapolei, principled by Alvin Nagasako, a very progressive educator. My primary purpose was to gain a sense of where the field was for my chapter on education. However, I thought I might as well also try to find a high school student to beat NASA at directly discovering a planet outside our solar system. The teacher coordinating science courses, it turned out, had a son, who already had directly found an extrasolar planet. He used a masking technique and actually succeeded. So much for trying to interest him in something as prosaic as an optical coherent technique for what he had already accomplished. I nevertheless introduced this student to my contact at the Institute of Astronomy, and waited to help. Nothing happened. The student has since graduated from high school and the astrophysicist has left Hawaii. I think I've heard this song before.

Reviewing in hindsight, thirty years later after my Ames stint, I should have learned from an even earlier experience not to joke around when it comes to scientific proposals. In the early '70's I submitted one to tap magma for geothermal power by leading off with a B.C. cartoon on power from volcanoes…and got thrown out for irreverence. The combination of PAT from La Mancha was not smart.

Thus, the field still is mostly confined to measuring star wobbles and finding giant sized (*meaning no chance for life*) planets. Notwithstanding TPF, NASA's main-line detection architectures seem not to be close to directly measuring an Earth size planet and determining its atmosphere.

Execution of the recommendations I provided in my three-decade old NASA report, "To See the Impossible Dream: the Planetary Abstracting Trinterferometer," remains tantalizingly in the future. If this book ever gets published, perhaps I will be contacted by some high school student [*PTakahas@Hotmail.Com*]...or NASA.

## The Other Side of the Story

There is the Fermi (*Nobel physicist Enrico Fermi of the Manhattan Project*) Paradox: Where are they? Why are no aliens or their artifacts evident? Why haven't we detected even one example of anything resembling intelligent life beyond our own?

A second problem is that two way chats are not feasible, as the more promising stars are just too far away. For example, if the best sites are a hundred light years away, should we receive a signal, send a response, and expect anything back, that would be a 200 year wait. However, some others say that it is possible that we will be able to detect the atmosphere of life-bearing planets within the next decade or two, and some could be as close as 30 light years away. Even then, 60 years between messages would stretch anyone's patience. The three Alpha Centauri stars are only a little more than 4 light years away, but they do not show any potential for life. In any event, just the confirmation of any signal should be the story of the millennium and the spark compelling religion to be even more creative, or accept the inevitable.

In addition to some in Congress, there are scientific detractors, so, reverting back to the Drake equation:

$$N = R^* F_p N_p F_l F_i F_c L,$$

Russian Astronomer Iosef Shklovskii and Carl Sagan assumed R* to be 10 stars/year *(that is, 100 billion stars formed over the past 10 billion years*), the N and all the F's to equate to 0.1 and L, the longevity of the average technological society, to be 10 million years, resulting in a million advanced civilizations (*0.001% of all stars*).

Michael Hart surmised that only spectral class G (*such as our Sun*) stars had the right properties to support life, reducing star formation (R*) to 0.001 start/year, thus dropping the Shklovskii-Sagan million to 100 civilizations. But only 10% of G stars are single and only 10% rotate slowly enough to have planets. Soon the number magically drops to one...Planet Earth.

Two other skeptics, James Trefil, a physics professor at George Mason University, and Robert Rood, an astronomy professor at the University of Virginia, calculated that the chances of other life in the Galaxy at 3%, and these would become so advanced that within 30 million years they would be able to colonize the entire Galaxy. If so, parroting Fermi, where are they?[327]

Professor Rood, actually, has gone on to conduct SETI research himself, in the belief that, while it is unlikely anything will be found, it is still worth looking for, since theorizing can't prove or disprove their existence, not unlike the quest for God. Even Professor Trefil appreciates the value of technological spin-offs from SETI.

Finally, people confuse SETI with UFOs, or unidentified flying objects. Those associated with the former loath to mention the latter. Yet, there was a time when even I believed flying saucers were real, maybe even into my college days. This is similar to the Santa Claus Syndrome (*read the next chapter*), but UFOs can still be believed at a more mature age than the man in red. Some never get over it. About 90% of Americans believe in some afterlife (*again, read the next chapter*). Think X-Files. At some point, though, the logic should kick-in, and one generally should mature into a non-believer, like the U.S. Department of Defense, with particular reference to Project Blue Book and the U.S. Air Force. Yet, of the 12,618 UFO sightings investigated, 701 remain open to speculation, not much unlike any attempts to scientifically explain religious miracles. UFO, miracles, the afterlife—this mystery, that unknown...they all appeal to the human emotion, and maybe they have a point there. But isn't this all so obviously deluding?

Stanford engineering professor Ron Bracewell, who, as one of the speakers during Project Orion in 1974, provided convincing arguments why human intelligence could well have had some extraterrestrial origins. Definitely X Files stuff, and counter to classical evolution. Said he, if you travel only at 10% the speed of light, with the universe just so large, it is conceivable that we could have been visited many times, and, perhaps, 3 million years ago, to be fertilized. They might well drop by again, maybe a million years from now, to check on the damage, or good, done. Daily flights? Unlikely. What about the energy to tool around? Well, that is a dilemma, but there are black holes and time warps and immortality and stuff. Who really knows? The best is yet to come.

A related mode of thinking was offered by Fred Hoyle, the coiner of the "Big Bang," who, in his book, *Intelligent Universe* [147], speculated that panspermia is the origin and evolution of life on Earth, that is, we were seeded from space; not spaceships, but the building blocks of life, and maybe even bacteria. At around 450 BC, Greek philosopher Anaxagoras paved the way for the atomic table and thought of these space seeds, but Aristotle prevailed for two millennia with his spontaneous generation theory, that is, frogs came from mud. It took Louis Pasteur in the late 19$^{th}$ Century to disprove Aristotle. A few years later, British physicist Lord William Thomson Kelvin and German physicist Hermann von Helmholtz extended Pasteur's logic with the notion that microbial life might be ubiquitous in the universe, and in the early 1900's, Swedish chemist Svante Arrhenius (*yes, the same scientist who suggested that a doubling of our atmospheric carbon dioxide would lead to a temperature increase of 5°C*) theorized that bacterial spores propelled through space by light pressure were the seeds of life on Earth.[212] More recently, comets have drawn attention as particularly good hosts for these biological seeds.

Can panspermia or the Bracewell supposition explain what happened in a period of 10 million years between 500 and 600 million years ago when, suddenly, after only bacteria, algae and plankton for the first 3.4 billion years of life, creatures appeared representing the beginnings of the entire animal kingdom? This was biology's Big Bang.[99]

The key point being made by Bracewell and Hoyle is that, while evolution, of course, has been occurring, the seeds of life might well have been initiated by biological remnants and higher evolution by intelligent control from extraterrestrial civilizations. There are two critical leaps:

- The formation of life from chemicals and energy is maybe the most difficult, so bacteria from space conveniently skips that most intricate of steps, and we all know that bacteria can survive extremes of temperature, pressure and irradiation.
- Intelligent life from bacteria is quite a jump, so, perhaps a few bridge species, including humans, were planted by advanced civilizations. Maybe reptiles were first tried (*which says something about some aliens*) 100 million years ago, which did not develop well, so a later invader looking like us planted an early form a couple of million years ago. There might have even been an extraterrestrial Noah's Ark, for there is no foolproof way to determine that bacteria came before, say, dinosaurs, as carbon dating does not function beyond 62,000 years.

Cosmic ancestry (Brig Klyce, www.panspermia.org/intro.htm) could well be at the heart of extraterrestrial theories, and, while mostly antithetical to current science, nevertheless has been strengthened by science:

- Two scientists at Cal Poly in 1995 showed that bacteria can survive without any metabolism for at least 25 million years, and are probably immortal (*see CHAPTER 2 on Eternal Life*).
- A team of biologists and a geologist on October 19, 2000, announced the revival of bacteria that are 250 million years old.
- A NASA working group on December 13, 2000 demonstrated that Mars meteorite ALH84001 showed biological evidence.
- Geneticists in June of 2002 reported evidence that the evolutionary step from chimpanzees to humans was assisted by viruses.
- On August 2, 2004, NASA scientists showed evidence of fossilized cyanobacteria in a meteorite.

Details can be found in the panspermia web page identified above. Whether from natural biological evolution or intelligent control from aliens or, horrors, a supreme being, both theories can support the existence of extraterrestrial life.

However, David Morrison of the NASA Ames Research Center informed me that suggestions of extraterrestrial interference in evolution are incompatible with modern genetics.[209] I would tend to agree with him. That is probably not an official NASA position, for he also indicated that NASA has not officially taken a position on the evidence of biological life in the Mars meteorite, even though the operative scientific consensus is that there was no life in that rock.

I did suggest that to remain silent is as good as confirming the possibility, for the media play is overwhelmingly pro-life. But, then, that might well explain how NASA works.

## The Future of SETI

The major player for SETI into the future will need to be NASA. President George Bush in 2004 identified the search for Earth-like planets in his new vision for space exploration. But that is already what NASA does. No money, though, for SETI.

NASA's Ames Research Center reported on plans for a four-year, $400 million space mission to hunt for Earth-size planets,[204] hopefully to be launched by 2009. But this is legal, for it is science in search for exoplanets. Called space telescope Kepler, it will watch 100,000 stars and look for a dimming of signals that might be caused by an Earth-size planet. The expectation is to, by 2011, find a few dozen Earth- and Mars-size planets. The odds? It is compared to seeing a firefly hovering next to a lighthouse searchlight 3,000 miles away, also appreciating that 99.5% of the possible planets will not be detected because they need to just pass directly in front of the star. That's certainly a lot of money just for this purpose. Why not use the Townes atmospheric optical lasing concept?

Another ambitious mission is the Space Interferometry Mission (*SIM*), now called SIM PlanetQuest, at a cost of $1.4 billion, just to monitor the position of 10,000 stars, but with precision.[331] The launch is now expected to occur in 2015, and the extent of star shimmy will provide clues as to target priority. Let's see now, the 2007 budget for renewable energy at the Department of Energy is less than this amount, so a fair question would be how just to do this specific mission can compare with the incoming asteroid called Peak Oil and Global Climate Warming. And, why be so fixed on indirect techniques or pure luck?

NASA's Terrestrial Planet Finder (*TPF*) mission envisions, over the next twenty years, at a cost approaching $1 billion, the deployment by 2014 of two space telescopes—a coronagraph operating at visible wavelengths and an interferometer in the infrared—capable of detecting molecules such as water vapor, carbon dioxide, methane and free oxygen in the form of ozone, initially within 30 light years and to then, over the follow-on decades, out to 45 light years. The European Space Agency will cooperate. But in 2007, Congressional action all but killed this project.[354]

Another terrestrial capability is the interferometric imaging $120 million Large Binocular Telescope of Germany and Italy, with American partners, located on 10,400 foot Mount Graham in Arizona. "First light" was seen in 2005, but "second light" will take a couple more years. It is reported that LBT will finally make direct observation of extrasolar planets possible, but only of Jupiter-sized objects.[228] Why bother?

Finally, the Square Kilometre Array (SKA) could become operational by 2020. SKA would be the most powerful radio telescope, 50 times more so than existing facilities, and theoretically could pick up television signals from a planet several light years away. [276] China, Argentina,

Australia and South Africa were in the running for this $1 billion project, but the latter two countries appear now to be the front runners. Why not the USA? Well, according to the reporting article, we withdrew from the competition because of a lack of funding to prepare a decent proposal.

Thus, you can appreciate the NASA logic of first determining where Earth-like planets might be located, an acceptable mission. Then, someday, when the political setting is more favorable, perhaps contributing to the real search, which is to detect incoming signals. Having by 2025 detected potential Earth look-alikes out there, Life Finder might be initiated to use a space telescope to look for signs of life on exoplanets.

All this leads to the future of NASA, for the science portion has become the equivalent of a ping pong ball, with no SETI money. NASA Director Michael Griffin, himself, when he was first appointed, told the disorganized and new NASA science advisory panel that he made commitments in advance that he could not honor, leaving the actual budget to the whim of Congress.[182] The White House request for FY2008 funding was $17.3 billion, about half a billion dollars higher than FY2007, with $5.5 billion for the Science Missions Directorate. The Planetary Society, founded by Carl Sagan, Bruce Murray and Louis Friedman, has been reasonably effective speaking out for the field.

About $6.8 billion is earmarked for Space Operations, with the Space Shuttle budgeted for $4 billion. A CBS News poll of 1,222 adults about continuing the Space Shuttle Program showed that support has declined:[314]

- 2005 59%
- 2003 75%
- 1986 80%.

But, The Gallup Poll in 2006 reported that two in three Americans say that the NASA budget should not be decreased.[51]

So if any money is to be spent on space, should there be some tangible reward for us taxpayers? Not necessarily, as science is based on the search for fundamental knowledge, which is fine, and should, to some degree, continue to be supported. But the argument could be made about what use might come of knowing how the solar system started. At some point, some congressman, or the president, might demand value to society, as we have seen all too often. SETI at least has potential for providing some ultimate solutions for humanity.

## Are You Interested in Becoming a SETI Contributor?

There are various websites available for anyone interested in being part of the SETI program, for it has, in a way, sadly, but in other ways, gratifyingly, taken on a warm, fuzzy, peoples' mission. Brochures can theoretically (*my messages never received a response*) be obtained by writing to join@setileague.org, and information at info@setileague.org. There is a membership fee of $50/year. Their Project Argus is a real time microwave SETI project linking 5,000 small radio telescopes from around the world to monitor the entire sky. You can participate by building your very own telescope for around a thousand dollars. There are only 121 currently operational.

There are four more microwave SETI projects: Project Beta (*Planetary Society, Paul Horowitz*), Project Phoenix (*SETI Institute, Seth Shostak, info@SETI.org*), SETI@home (*UC Berkeley, et al, Dan Wertheimer, www.setiathome.ssl.berkeley.edu/*) and Southern SERENDIP (*SETI Australia Centre, et al, Frank Stootman, F.Stootman@uws.edu.au*). In particular, SETI@home is reportedly linked to 2 million computers from 225 countries, making it the world's largest supercomputer. They all predict their chances of success as unknown.

There are more than 1500 members from 66 countries involved in SETI. Among some of the user group pages are from:

- SETI.Germany,
- Baha'i SETI,
- Let's Kick Some Alien Butt Team,
- Yahoo SETI Club,
- AOL Beta Team,
- Team Truth Seeking,
- WeAreNotAlone Team,
- SETI@Taiwan,
- Very Big Ear Team, and
- SETI Turkey Team,

just a few of the hundred odd organizations dedicated to the sport.

Incidentally, if you are able to individually design, build and operate a system that actually receives an ETI signal, you will no doubt win a Nobel Prize. So what do you do if you score a hit?

- First, contact the Central Bureau for Astronomical Telegrams (*CBAT*) operating out of the Harvard-Smithsonian Center for Astrophysics. CBAT is the clearinghouse for new space discoveries and was created in Germany in the 1880's, which eventually moved to Cambridge, and is currently directed by Daniel Green. You will be faced with at least a minor problem because no one has yet reported an ETI signal. You will thus need to hurdle some bureaucratic-computer interface hurdles. So, after the necessary interval of frustration, send an e-mail to cbat@cfa.harvard.edu to log your entry with all the relevant details. If you are absolutely sure of your luck, you can cc your local media.
- Then, contact your most trusted observatory to see if they can confirm your finding. However, telescope time is booked months in advance, so don't hold your breath. At this point, if you truly detected something real and alien, turn on your television, for the world should already be stunned by news from CNN or Fox. But if not, yet, proceed.

- o Re-check your information and, if still viable, try the International Telecommunication Union, which reports to the United Nations, and is headquartered in Geneva. The Secretary-General is Hamadoun Toure of Mali. Well, at least ***Wired*** magazine suggested this pathway. A phone number is 41 22 730 511, with itumail@itu.int for general inquiries. Lots of luck. Have you ever tried working with the UN on anything which has to be swiftly managed? However, Dr. Toure has a PhD from the University of Electronics, Telecommunications and Informatics of Moscow.
- o Failing all the above, go to your favorite local TV station, or, better yet, talk them into coming over to film your monumental breakthrough, for you simply will have the greatest discovery of this millennium. If you've instead detected something not quite so epochal, well, that was in the spirit of this follow-up guide.

As you explore the field, though, as of today, NASA does not do SETI. Only private organizations do. Perhaps your effort should be focused on the Federal government, for, in consideration of the trillions to be spent on Afghanistan/Iraq and billions for farm payments to the dead, a few million, maybe even hundreds of millions, to develop the foundation that could be our lifeline to the future, certainly sounds like a cost-effective way to spend our precious tax dollars. Go lobby the U.S. Congress.

## Simple SETI Solutions

The bottom line is that NASA will continue to flounder until the next space race begins, when, say, China decides to send a team to an asteroid or the Moon to mine some desirable exotic mineral, or some equivalent mission. Sputnik woke up America, and the combination of military rivalry, national pride and occasional need for international one-upsmanship have been shown to be necessary factors for any major space budget upgrade.

Simple solution for SETI advocates: stimulate a Chinese connection, for this sort of strategy succeeded for hydrogen R&D (*with respect to perceived Japanese and European priority advancements—see Chapter 3 of **Book 1***). That is, governmental decision-makers (*people in Congress and the Administration*) do get concerned when a serious international rival begins to spend more money on something that could potentially affect the national psyche or security. If Senator Spark Matsunaga were still around, he might have inspired the sequel to ***The Mars Project*** (*advocating U.S.-Soviet space cooperation on Mars*): ***The Milky Way Project*** (*to first bring China into the International Space Station, then find a way to have them develop a trinterferometer—the Station plus two other satellites in geosynchronous orbit, maintaining an equilateral triangulated formation with the Station—to detect the first true Earth-like exoplanet, hinting that their next step would be to detect actual alien signals*). Perhaps, now, that could be my ***Book 6***.

Absent any compelling external force, NASA, and SETI development, will plod along to maintain a dull edge, producing useful science and, now and then, cleverly announcing some potentially significant finding to remain in the public eye. Some unmanned craft will someday, possibly by 2050, actually discover microscopic life in our solar system, probably a moon associated with Saturn or Jupiter. That should be sufficient to continue funding for another century.

Then, a discernible signal will be detected from an earthlike planet, and the glorious mission to communicate with extraterrestrials will capture the imagination of the world for a millennium. This, however, could be centuries or millennia away…unless someone or some thing steps up to make a crucial difference…or that intelligent message arrives. While you await this possible inevitable, to maintain hope, keep watching, at regular intervals, ***Contact***, the movie.

# CHAPTER 5: THE GOLDEN EVOLUTION

## Gold

God and Gold have been with us from the earliest of time and both connote power. Even ***The Bible*** in Genesis mentions this precious element. Gold was sacred in what today are Iraq and Iran 7000 years ago, and till today remains as the universal standard of trade. It says something that the Aztec word for gold, is teocuitlatl, meaning excrement of the gods. At least one society had it right, or at least a sense of humor.

The first Gold Rush in the U.S. occurred—no not San Francisco—but in the State of Georgia. That was in 1828, with the last frenzy occurring along the Klondike River in Canada during the end of the 19th Century. Centuries before Columbus, though, the Incas and Aztecs refined gold, leading to the mythical Lost City of Gold, El Dorado, which hasn't been found, yet. Then there is the tale of General Tomoyuki Yamashita, who commanded the Japanese army in the Philippines during World War II. It is said that he buried gold worth many tens of billion dollars. The American CIA, Emperor Hirohito and Ferdinand Marcos weave into the intrigue. Much of gold lore has been well mined by the media.

Gold has the atomic number 79, does not corrode and is the most malleable and ductile of metals. The density of gold is twenty times that of water and almost double of lead. One pound can be drawn into 50 miles of 5 micrometer (*one-tenth that of human hair*) diameter wire. When beaten into a thin sheet, the translucent color is greenish blue, and in glass imparts an intense red color. Placed in nitric acid…nothing happens. This was early on referred to as the acid test. A liquid suspension treats rheumatoid arthritis, for this element somehow acts as an anti-inflammatory. Contrary to popular scientific opinion, base metal <u>can</u> be transformed into gold. Soviet nuclear reactors produced some (*where the base metal was uranium*) and John Bockris insisted he did (*see his religion section*).

The measurement of gold is arcane. Read the following only with trepidation:

- One troy ounce (toz) = 1.097 ordinary or avoirdupois ounce = 480 grains = 31.1 grams.
- There is also the tael, a Chinese measurement of gold, where one tael is 1.2 ounce. Thus, one tael has about 10% more gold than one toz, which has about 10% more gold than one ounce.
- Further, 24 karat represents 100% (really, 99.9%) gold, making 18 karat only 75% gold, but this is popular in jewelry because the other metals make the piece stronger.

- o Finally, the carat (*note, this starts with a c*) applies to gems like diamonds, where 1 carat = about 0.2 gram. Thus, a 5 carat diamond weighs about a gram. A 24 karat gold bar has a value depending on the weight.
- o For the record, platinum is about twice as expensive as gold.
- o Anyway, gold is measured in toz, except, to further confuse you, it might still be referred to as oz, although they really mean toz.

The price of gold was maintained at $19.39/toz from 1800 until:[101]

- o 1814, when it jumped a few dollars, but returned to
- o $19.39 in 1817, spiked to
- o $57 in 1864, dropping to
- o $20.67 in 1878, jerking upwards to
- o $35 in 1934, when the U.S. Congress devalued the dollar, holding steady at
- o $35-$44 until 1971 when the price floated upwards when President Richard Nixon ended U.S. dollar convertibility to gold, until it reached an all-time high of
- o $850 on January 21, 1980, when the Soviet Union invaded Afghanistan and the Islamic Revolution occurred in Iran, then further to $875, but declining to the
- o $300-$700 range over the next quarter century, until there was a spike to
- o $730 in 2006, floating up into the
- o $800/oz realm in 2007 and
- o $900+ in 2008.

The scary part about $900/toz gold is that knowledgeable people buy this precious metal in anticipation of a severe economic downturn. In 2008, with rising unemployment, a continuing downturn in the housing market, malfeasance of a French trader and growing car repossessions, plus the prospects of Peak Oil and Global Heating, one can only hope that the R (*recession, which occurs about every 6 years when the stock market drops by about 25%, with the previous one being after 9/11*) word does not become a D (*depression, and there have been six since record keeping began in 1867, with 1937-8 being the previous D*). Of course, the Federal Reserve System and congressional stimulus packages will help to forestall the economic downturn, but the combined pressure of all the above will not be overcome.

I thought $800/toz would do it, but $900/toz is ominous. Of course, compared to the $875/toz peak of 1980, which today, would have a value of $2,250, this is certainly not monumental. However, the year 2012 is, indeed, looming as a fateful year, especially if the value of gold continues rising.

Approximately a fourth to a third of the known gold is kept in the Federal Reserve Bank of New York, having a rough value of $250 billion today. The U.S. Geological Survey says that there are about 160,000 tons (*a little more than 5 billion troy ounces*) of gold circulating today, but the ocean has 10,000,000,000 tons.

While sprinkled on fine cuisine and flaked in sake, it nevertheless can be toxic to the human body. Bacteria might well be responsible for concentrating this metal into veins. All the mined goal can be shaped into a 20 meter (*66 feet on each side*) cube and a ton of gold would be about 37 centimeters (1 foot three inches) on each side. Most of gold today comes from South Africa. Three parts per billion of the Earth's crust is gold, while the ocean is at one-tenth part per billion, and could well someday become a major source of this precious metal.

There is a richness and a sacredness associated with gold. Thus, the ultimate Golden Evolution might well be a religious one.

## There is No Afterlife...However

As we get older, the notion of eternal gloom more and more becomes terrifying for some of us. This is the 21st Century. I'm an educated person. Yes, there are a lot of things I don't understand, but something so fundamental as an afterlife surely should have been resolved by now. Why haven't our best minds come up with some proof? Will another billion years of progress add to the information base? Chances are, the answer will be no! Thus, I have come to believe that there is no Afterlife, and, furthermore, no life controlling Supreme Being. The notion that in the beginning God was created by Man, as we also invented the family structure, agriculture and television, is sounding more and more plausible.

This attitude, historically, has always been dangerous to your health, and remains so today. If this book ever gets published, could I rather suddenly be placed by any fervent Muslim on some Fatwa (*decree calling for your termination*) list? There are religious fanatics—make that, really true believers—in virtually every religion that could well share similar sincere views. For anyone contemplating the internet for this unnecessary call to action, I urge you to read through this chapter and consider three grounds for reconsideration. First, I could be wrong. Maybe you can first try to convince me of my ignorance. Second, there are other more radical and insensitive authors out there, perhaps more deserving of your attention. Third, the whole point of this chapter is to arrive at a simple solution for religion. I am trying to be constructive.

A great majority of people, even Americans, believe in God and the Afterlife. Just look at the three most popular newly born boys names in the country: Jacob, Michael and Joshua, all straight from ***The Bible***. Hawaii, of course, where I grew up, is different. Our top three are Joshua, Jacob and Noah. Whoops, maybe this re-education solution is something I should take more seriously. This I actually did, as the following will reveal, although I kept changing my allegiance, and remain stably fluid.

## How Did Religion Start?

You either believe in God, or some version of Him, or not, or, like me for most of my life, something in between. If you do, you are in the high majority and can stop reading here for you already "know" how it all began. Unless, of course, you wish to be entertained, then certainly read on. If you are an atheist or a general non-believer, generally like me today, you wonder about the rationality of how religion really got started.

The natural law of the jungle is cruel. Only the fittest survive. An animal does provide for family, and perhaps immediate clan, but it's a war out there. Homo sapiens eventually formed nuclear families, then colonies of them. Some were more successful than others. The cunning cheater should prevail in a Darwinian culture. How to minimize those acts could have led to a belief system where there was a supernatural enforcer to maintain control for the common good. A telling experiment occurred at the University of Newcastle where there was an honor system for the coffee pot.[344] When a picture of eyes was placed above the payment box, collection more than doubled from a background of flowers. The eyes provided the enforcement factor.

A workable religion induces cooperation and honesty, which, in turn, would strengthen that clan or society. The notion of an omniscient, all seeing, force to watch over everyone helped maintain the order. What better than a God that was responsible for mankind? Thus, soon after the beginning, Man created God. It was the clever thing to do.

This form of early social justice could well be optimal, resulting in groups that best survived. Religion might have been the simple solution leading to the triumph of our species.

So, where does this leave religion today? Well, it got us this far. But one line of thinking leads to the conclusion that all hell could well break loose someday when people stop believing. A second more dominating wisdom applies to people like me, who don't believe, yet are law-abiding citizens. It just makes good sense to utilize most of the practiced morality.

In my conclusion, then, religion was a necessary bridge to establish our society. It might not be needed in the future. Is that time today?

## Introduction to God and the Afterlife

To better understand religion, you can read ***The Bible***, ***The Koran*** and, literally, millions of other publications. Keep in mind that the temporal (*time*) scale is amorphous and events metaphorical (*symbolic*). The problem is that religion usually insists on precise interpretations even though definitions have changed over the past few millennia.

There is the series, ***Conversations with God*** **(Books 1-3)**, by Neale Donald Walsch, and scads of similar drivel. All these books I have read purporting to have any kind of connection with God and the Afterlife are, by my standards, works of fiction. If they say their tome is creative writing, fine. But, as in religion itself, the immorality is in the reality. How can any person or church promise a heavenly afterlife without a shred of proof?

As you don't have time to read them all, to ease the burden, for the afterlife is at least a potential measurable parameter, let me recommend the following to satisfy your need to at least try:

- J. Lewis, ***The Death and Afterlife Book [TDAAB]***, Visible Ink Press, Detroit Michigan, 2001. An encyclopedia, from Adventism to Zoroastrianism, it comes with a complete index. I found surprising inner peace when I read the paragraph on "Anatta," which comes from the Buddhist scriptures, but has a Sanskrit counterpart, anatman, a clue that they, and most religious writings, had a common source. To interpret, life is full of tension and pain. When you die, you only gain pleasure and attain eternal bliss. "Yes," I thought, "it's all in how you approach the end, for this sure sounds a lot better than eternal gloom." There is no proof of an afterlife here, but the terms soothe the psyche.
- F. Tipler, ***The Physics of Immortality [TPOI]***, Pan Books, New York, 1994. In the forward, it is reported that Frank Tipler is a Professor of Mathematical Physics at Tulane University. He has published in ***Nature, Physical Review and the Astrophysical Journal***. He indicated that he began as an atheist, but reasoned that: "There is a God. There is a Heaven. We are all immortal." Tipler cites a Gallup Poll of 1989 showing that from 1944 to 1988, from 94 to 97 percent of Americans believed in the existence of God or a universal spirit. This figure is somewhat high, but it is all in whom you ask and the exact nature of the question. Two other tidbits are that our Sun will engulf the Earth in 7 billion ($7x10^9$) years and neutron stars will cool to 100 degrees K in $10^{19}$ years, for he is into last things, the study of eschatology, the interface of science and religion, for this is where the matter of the afterlife can be investigated. While the book uses some geometry, there is a lot of logic. Plus, the final 40% is devoted to notes, all the equations you will ever need to prove the afterlife, with good references. I could not understand the mathematics, and, yes, I merely flipped through the pages, at least a few of them. Five pages.
- G. Schwartz, ***The Afterlife Experiments [TAE]***, Atria Books, New York, 2001.There is a foreword by Deepak Chopra (*who himself has written several books with God in the title*) and the usual encomiums, one by Rustum Roy, Evan Pugh Professor of the Solid State and professor of geochemistry, Pennsylvania State University: "[A] painstakingly assembled hypothesis followed by rigorous experimentation. Dr. Schwartz has made his case—compellingly, in my view." Dr. Roy is from India, a country where the citizens have a very, very high expectation of some afterlife. As a former materials science colleague of his, I'll need to talk to him about the afterlife. I value his opinion, so, maybe he might be able to set me straight. When you think of it, if there is an afterlife, what media of information exchange are there? This book essentially focuses on one: cold readings. Clairvoyants, mystics, telepaths and mediums—all the same—are supposedly gifted with a special sensitivity to that other world, and can serve as the conduit. Great pains are taken to separate those quacks that give the field a bad name from the laboratory experiments of the author and his partners. The basic message seemed to be that the best mediums are at least as good as the 40-45% excellence achieved by Ted Williams and Michael Jordan, who were the best in their game. The difference, though, is that mediums have the skills to take the intelligent guess, the positive response, anything vaguely relevant, from their pigeon, also known as patient, and through their refined sense of recognizing body language and other factors, control the dialogue such that the subject is cleverly zoned to largely recall the intended purpose. This book attempts to make a science of this phenomenon,

for, as the supposition went, if there can be any kind of successful communication, then there must be an afterlife.

- B. Toropov and L. Buckles, ***The Complete Idiot's Guide to the World's Religions [IDIOT]***, Alpha Books, New York, 1997. This could well have been my first and favorite book on religion. I was brought up a Buddhist, attended a neighborhood Christian church because it had a fun summer school program, went through a few months of Catechism in high school, joined a Nisei Methodist Church because that was socially convenient, participated in Presbyterian rituals at Stanford University, went back to Buddhism during my sugar plantation work period because of social pressures and gravitated towards active intellectual searches later in life. But I never took that early religious stuff seriously, and was able to synthesize a knowledge of religion for the very first time because the ***Idiot*** series is written for people like me.
- R. Dawkins, ***The God Delusion [TGD]***, Houghton Mifflin Company, Boston, 2006. Richard, as I called him when we had a small chat in Honolulu in 2007, is my favorite writer on the subject of religion. I revere him, mainly, I think, for his courage. I honor him later with a special section. Professor Dawkins very clearly argues that there is no God. I changed the tenor of this chapter after our talk.
- S. Harris, ***The End of Faith [TEOF]***, W.W. Norton and Company, New York, 2004. A follow-up book called ***Letter to a Christian Nation*** was written as a rejoinder to the criticisms the first effort engendered, but, I thumbed through it and saw how thin it was and superficial it read for the price quoted, so I passed. ***TEOF***, though, was beefy, with a lot of good quotes and analyses. Harris subscribes to faith as the Paul Tillich defined, "act of knowledge that has a low degree of evidence," or, more specifically when applied to religion, as "unjustified belief in matters of ultimate concern." While not at the heart of the matter, he goes on to suggest that oil has made the Islamic terrorist what he is, and, perhaps the most peaceful way we have of diffusing the problem is to initiate a Manhattan Project for alternative energy. We hear more from him during a later treatment on faith. Harris is not a heathen, and suggests that understanding of the sacred dimension might well be our highest purpose.
- C. Hitchens, ***God is Not Great [GING]***, Twelve, New York, 2007.[141] A noted British journalist, who is a visiting professor in the U.S., provides an angry and vitriolic treatment of religion, maybe even sensational. He already indicts religion with his subtitle: How Religion Poisons Everything.
- Tim Leedom and Maria Murdy, Editors, ***The Book Your Church* Doesn't Want you to Read [TBYCDWYTR],*** 2nd Edition, Cambridge House Press, New York, 2007. This is an anthology mostly by contemporaries, but also including Thomas Jefferson, Thomas Paine and Bertrand Russell, commenting on aspects of all religions. The content is obvious.
- Daniel Dennett, ***Breaking the Spell [BTS]***, Penguin Books, 2006, New York, 2006. A non-dogmatic, well-referenced, indexed effort by a Tufts philosophy professor that could well change the ingrained views of many faithful readers away from religion.
- Victor Stenger, ***God, the Failed Hypothesis***, Prometheus Books, Amherst, 2007. A colleague of mine from the Physics Department of the University of Hawaii, his subtitle provides the clue: How Science Shows that God Does Not Exist. Stenger mentions that there has never been any verification of the Israelites and Moses in

Egypt and that the empires of David and Solomon never existed. He also reports that Christians make up 80% of the prison population, while atheists represent only 0.2%. There was a Calabash (*point, counterpoint*) page from ***Honolulu***, the magazine, providing Professor Stenger's belief, as contrasted by the past dean of the College of Natural Sciences at the University of Hawaii, and former chairman of the Physics Department, Charles Hayes.[134] Chuck is of the Francis Collins' school of faith, to be discussed again.

o Tom Flynn, ***The New Encyclopedia of UNBELIEF***, Prometheus Books, with articles by a who's who of atheism, including a foreword by Richard Dawkins. Interesting that this publication costs more used than new on Amazon.com when I last checked, although the cheapest price is still greater than $100.

There are others, such as ***55 Questions to Life After Death*** [140], ***Life after Death in World Religions*** [19] and ***The Tibetan Book of Living and Dying*** [259], but the above list of books should provide more detail that you will ever need to understand and inquire with intelligence. So, armed now with the basic info—and the summary I have provided above actually allows you to already proceed—let us first look closer at religious beliefs, starting with an analogy.

I like to use the Santa Claus paradigm where all children believe in Santa Claus (*or his equivalent*), then, as maturity and reality set in, the truth becomes self-evident. In religion, with family upbringing infused overriding education, the concept of a God always remains an undying belief for most. Why?

**Santa Claus Versus God**

Santa Claus and God are almost eerily similar. In my mind, they are both Anglo-Saxon males who promise gifts or a reward if you are good. Christmas celebrates the birthday of God's only son, Jesus, and the eve is when Santa operates. Many, men in particular, once believed in Santa Claus, then, reached a maturity that told them better, but, not long after that, became Santa Claus, and later in life, looked like him. So goes the joke, anyway.

To recover from that, let me advance the logic one step higher by taking minimal liberties with the response to the following customized exchange in 1893 initiated by Virginia O'Hanlon:

> *Dear Editor—*
>
> *I am 8 years old. Some of my friends say there is no Santa Claus. Papa says, 'If you see it in The Sun, it's so.' Please tell me the truth, is there a Santa Claus?*

Say, in my exercise, I had Virginia asking, instead, whether there is a God. The adjusted (*for God*) reply from Francis Church, editorial writer for ***The New York Sun***, could well have been:

> *Virginia, your little friends are wrong. They have been affected by the skepticism of a skeptical age. They do not believe except that they see. They think that nothing can be which is not comprehensible by their little minds. All minds, Virginia, whether they*

*be men's or children's, are little. In this great universe of ours, man is a mere insect, an ant, in his intellect as compared with the boundless world about him, as measured by the intelligence capable of grasping the whole of truth and knowledge.*

*Yes, Virginia, there is a God.*

*He exists as certainly as love and generosity and devotion exist, and you know that they abound and give to your life its highest beauty and joy. Alas! How dreary would be the world if there were no God! It would be as dreary as if there were no Virginias. There would be no childlike faith then, no poetry, no romance to make tolerable this existence. We should have no enjoyment, except in sense and sight. The external light with which childhood fills the world would be extinguished.*

*Not believe in God! You might as well not believe in Santa Claus. You might get your papa to hire men to watch in all the chimneys on Christmas eve to catch Santa Claus, but even if you did not see Santa Claus coming down, what would that prove? Nobody sees God, but that is no sign that there is no God. The most real things in the world are those that neither children nor men can see. Did you ever see fairies dancing on the lawn? Of course not, but that's no proof that they are not there. Nobody can conceive or imagine all the wonders there are unseen and unseeable in the world."*

*You tear apart the baby's rattle and see what makes the noise inside, but there is a veil covering the unseen world which not the strongest man, nor even the united strength of all the strongest men that ever lived could tear apart. Only faith, poetry, love, romance, can push aside that curtain and view and picture the supernal beauty and glory beyond. Is it all real? Ah, Virginia, in all this world there is nothing else real and abiding.*

*No God? Thank Santa Claus he lives and lives forever. A thousand years from now, Virginia, nay 10 times 10,000 years from now, he will continue to make glad the heart of childhood.*

*Amen!!!!*

While the above rendition has been significantly adjusted, in general, why would a responsible adult go out of his way to fool a child, as was attempted? Well, because everybody does. Clearly, he was espousing a cause for the general public, because the language is way beyond the level of an 8-year old, plus, for how many of them read editorial responses to letters. Church handled all the controversial assignments on the editorial page, especially those dealing with theology. He died in 1906, having had no children, and is best known for authoring the original version featuring Santa Claus of this most famous of editorial responses. Till the end he said that all he did was share the truth. Virginia passed away in 1971 after a fruitful career as an educator. But somewhere along the way, she eventually stopped believing in Santa Claus, I trust, and, perhaps too, God.

I sent this mischievous deed of mine on Christmas Eve of 2004 to some close friends, and there were several dozen. Not one reprimanded me for being sacrilegious and some thought I was being reverential (*incredible!*), although I suspect most did not bother to read and digest it. There is something about family life combined with religion, perhaps assisted by, maybe, a God gene, that obscures reality. With just the replacement of Santa Claus with God, we can somewhat understand how children grow into adults, but generally maintain a belief in God. What gives?

In December of 2007, ***USA Weekend*** provided three modern-day responses to Virginia's letter, and all three news reporters maintained the charade, although one probably got too philosophical (*perhaps he, too, forgetting that he was responding to an 8 year old*) with a statement that, yes, there is a Santa Claus, but not that jolly fat man, for he is you and anyone with hope. At least this kind of makes sense.

The North American Aerospace Defense Command operates a Santa tracking web site, and he can be seen on December 24 moving at warp speed from the North Pole first to New Zealand, then eventually to Hawaii. Nearly a billion hits were received from 181 countries in 2005. The Santa Tracking Operations Center, staffed by 500 volunteers, actually received 55,000 calls that year. The number of calls has increased each year, so our youngsters are certainly not getting any smarter. But, then, even I, at that age, could not comprehend the enormity of Santa and his flying reindeers needing to move at several million miles/hour to get the job done in 34 hours (*yes, think about it*).

Now why would NORAD stoop to all this frivolity? Well, there is a history. It was started by a Sears-Roebuck ad in 1955, with phone number if you wished to talk to Santa. Alas, there was a typo, and the number listed was that of an earlier form of NORAD, the Continental Air Defense Command. All in good fun, and now that we don't have to worry about missiles from the USSR or North Korea, what harm does this do? Also, the military plays Santa around the world and this gentleman is a symbol of good will and cheer. Plus, he's a good poster man for God.

### What is God

"Religion is an illusion, and it derives its strength from its readiness to fit in with our instinctful wishful impulses," said Austrian psychiatrist and Galician Jew Sigmund Freud, the father of psychoanalysis. But Jewish people don't believe in an afterlife, or at least, don't have to, although reincarnation is possible if you are an Orthodox Jew. Yet, there is the notion of an immortal soul, similar to Christianity.

In 1882, said German philosopher Friedrich Nietzsche, "God is dead." So goes the joke, "Nietzsche is dead," said God, in retort. For that past century and more, God has prevailed, for religion has continued to maintain a hold. What are the statistics?

Tipler in ***TPOI*** reported around a 95% average figure over the past few decades for those believing in God in the United States. Surely enough, Robert Mellert[199] mentioned a 96% belief in God number, but, perhaps, they were referring to the same survey, which was probably the Gallup Poll[117] which reported a 96% figure for both 1944 and 1994.

Thinkers/philosophers for millennia have been writing on the subject. French philosopher Rene Descartes in the 1600's provided an elaborate series of proofs for the existence of God. In the 1700's, Scottish philosopher David Hume repeated what various atheists of his day and before said: if God were so omniscient, why did he create such an imperfect world. Therefore, there is no God. Then there is the grand synthesis of French Jesuit philosopher, Pierre Teilhard de Chardin, for whom God is all, not unlike the Eastern Hindu idea of pantheism. Thus, God is a range of images from a concept to a force to an anthropomorphic grandfather.

There is a Darwinian insight, where He listens to prayers, and responds accordingly. Charles Darwin, though, finally opted for agnosticism (*I haven't seen the Light, but please try to convince me*). The Einsteinian view, as his equations, is a bit abstruse: divine immanence is stressed over divine transcendence.

Of course, God means different things to different people. Many in the Western world conceive of that white bearded guy earlier compared with Santa. This one would thus be the omnipotent creator of the Universe. This is the most popular representation, but science is eroding this metaphysical image, for a God beyond molecules and time cannot intervene in the present, so goes the physics. Or, should not, anyway.

Then too, there are many variations of that internet story about how God is seen by many:

> *Noah had struck out in his T-ball game and, in embarrassment and anguish, decided that he had to meet God to seek his help. The next day, as it was to be a long journey, he stuffed his backpack with a can of macadamia nuts and two bottles of deep ocean Hawaiian freshwater (reverse osmosis of seawater from the Natural Energy Laboratory of Hawaii Authority) and started his expedition. But where could he go? After a few blocks in the hot sun, he saw a bench under a banyan tree, and thought this would be a good time to take a break. There was an old lady sitting on one end, so he sat down on the other side and cracked open his macadamia nuts. He felt obligated to offer some to the lady, and she accepted with a smile. As he had two bottles of water, he gave one to that lady. He wanted to ask her if she knew where to find God, but instead ended up talking about her granddaughter who, he learned, was wheelchair bound. It occurred to him that life was not all that bad, for he could walk, and upon departing, made a comment to her about how blessed Lani was to have such a fine guardian angel. At dinner, his mother wondered why Noah looked so happy, and he said, "I met with God this afternoon and she told me a story about how lucky I was." Meanwhile, the old lady's son later that day inquired as to why she showed so much joy, and she said, "I had macadamia nuts with God today, and, you know, he is much younger than I expected"*

God is different things to different people. If God can be seen in anyone at anytime, that certainly can explain why the belief rate is so high.

Is this why the United States percentage hovers around 95%? But then, why do Japan and Israel, seemingly wallowing in religious traditions, report much lower figures? There does not need to be an afterlife in the Jewish religion, so, of course, that provides a partial explanation. Japan supposedly is the country, next China, with the most number of atheists and agnostics, so what you see when you visit are artifacts of a past culture.

**But was there a Jesus?**

Found in the Pyramid Texts occurring around 2400 BC was information about Osiris, King of Kings, whose mother's name was Nut. His coming was announced by Three Wise Men, his birth signified by the star in the east (*Sirius*) and who was resurrected after death. The 23rd Psalm *("valley of the shadow of death")* was copied from an Egyptian text appealing to Osiris. He had a son, in a convoluted way, named Horus.

Conceived by a virgin named Meri, with a foster father Jo-Seph, heralded by Sirius (*the morning star*), born on December 25 in a cave-manger attended by three wise men, with no data about his life between the ages of 12 and 30, having 12 disciples, performing miracles (*including walking on water*), known for a key Sermon on the Mount and self-designated God-man Savior of humanity, he died by crucifixion and resurrected three days later. His name was Horus, supposed son of Osiris. HUH??? He was born in Egypt in 1550 BC (*yes, a millennium or so later, as I did say convoluted in the previous paragraph*), but more than 1500 years before Jesus Christ. WHAT???

In 1027 BC, Beddou was born of a virgin, lived in the desert until the age of 30, performed miracles...you get the idea? This was in China. From India, Virishna (*Krishna*) was born in 1200 BC and Indra in 725 BC of virgins, performed miracles, crucified and resurrected. Much of the above and some of the below were inspired from ***The Book Your Church Doesn't Want You to Read***, by Tim Leedom and Maria Murdy,[210] earlier mentioned.

That's not all. Greek historian Herodotus wrote in the 5th Century BC about Greek God Dionysius, whose mother was a mortal virgin, father Zeus (*King of Gods*), wandered off to India, suffered like Jesus, and likewise was resurrected. In Islam, Jesus is called Isa and considered to be a prophet of God, most definitely not the Son of God, and is expected to return as a Savior. There are those who equate Jesus with Buddha, but only in principle, for the latter died from food poisoning, maybe. Oh, by the way, I should have added above that Buddha, a Hindu from Nepal, was born of virgin Maya, performed miracles, wandered around for a spell, died and ascended into Heaven somewhere between 544 BC and 383 BC. Mexican God Quetzacoatl was born about 300 BC of a virgin, wandered in the wilderness, preached, was crucified and resurrected three days later.

You can look at this in both ways. First, God had a game plan, tried it first in Egypt, and failed, so went around the world seeking other Messiahs. After umpteen failures, He found success with Jesus. But, then, second, if this God was omni-everything, why did he fail even once?

**So, therefore, place yourself back to circa 50 AD. Nothing much can be found about Jesus. Conflicting descriptions can be unearthed about this individual, but absent any**

**miracles and the connection with Son of God. Is it possible that a group, say, the Antioch Jesus Movement, sees an opportunity to spur something called Christianity? So they pick a mortal of those days who might just fit a concept called the Messiah. They borrow selectively from early Egyptian, Indian, Chinese, Mexican (*nah, scratch this, Columbus came 1500 years later*) and Greek writings to create the legend of Jesus Christ around a real-life martyr. He was in his prime at the age of 30, so they choose 30 AD as the founding of Christianity. Could this incredible PR ploy have started it all? Did all this lead to the Catholic Church of today!**

As the story unfolds, Jesus was born a little more than a billion minutes (*if you were born in the mid '70's, you arrived a billion seconds*) ago. It is said that St. Francis of Assisi in 1223 AD embellished the birth site into a Nativity scene, so our Christmas enactments almost surely do not represent an accurate portrayal. Further, this term "virgin," is liberally used in ancient texts as unmarried or young, so we don't need to unnecessarily scoff at the ridiculousness of Mary's condition, for the mother of your Jesus was said to be 12 or 13 when pregnant and unmarried, which, in those days, could have meant death. So, along came Joseph. And, oh, that star was probably a conjunction of planets, not a supernova or comet, for these latter two indicate a coming disaster. Then, again…

By any comparative standard, fictional or real, Jesus is as significant as any human can get, for Christmas, his birth date, is widely celebrated, and the year 2008 means 2008 years since he was born. Yet, this can get complicating, for you will find BC (*before Christ*), BCE (*before common era*), AD (*anno Domini, Latin for "in the year of the Lord"*) and CE (*Christian or common era*) in the literature. Be prepared to be confused, as more and more, you will see BCE and CE, because these tend to be religiously neutral in this day of political correctness. For the record, there is no Year Zero. Also, January 6, not December 25, is probably more accurate as his birth date, and 3 or 2 BCE was probably the year.[353] But, who's counting, since this could well all be a beautiful redaction, anyway.

To add to the confusion, keep in mind that the consensus of biblical historians is that Jesus had six siblings (*who could well have been children by Joseph from a first wife, for he is usually portrayed as much older than Mary, perhaps even 90 years old, as there are some reports indicating that he died at the age of 111*) named Judas (*sometimes called Jude, plus also an uncle Judas, brother of Joseph*), another called Joses (*short for Joseph*) and a sister named Mary. Thus, there were three more Marys in addition to the "Virgin" Mother, another being Magdalene (*Miryam of Magdala...consort, wife, lead disciple, prostitute, companion, who knows...??*) and Mary of Bethany (*teenager who apparently had a crush on Jesus and was present at that Last Supper, but did not make the cut list for the painting by Da Vinci*). Toss in Judas, (*not Jesus' brother nor uncle*), who was the chief financial officer for the movement, and whose reputation changes every few hundred centuries, and you now have a real mess of contradictions and misunderstandings.

Jesus of Nazareth (*where he was from*) becomes known as Jesus Christ (*in Greek, "anointed"*) and the Messiah (*Hebrew*). The claim that he rose from the dead and ascended into Heaven is more and more being interpreted as his soul or spirit that was resurrected, not the entire dead body. Joseph, his "foster father," later became St. Joseph, namesake of many schools and cities

(*San Jose is Spanish for St. Joseph*) and much later, the object of millions of statues buried upside down to help sell homes. That was not a joke, but this now is, as it is said Jesus was Jewish because he went into his father's business, lived at home until he was 33, was sure his Mother was a virgin, and his Mother believed he was God.

To make a long story short, then, Jesus was a Jewish mystic and healer. He probably was not a carpenter (*dad Joseph was*) in the tradesman sense, but was so alluded to only metaphorically, ironically and perhaps in sarcasm. He was tried for sedition and crucified on what is now known as Good Friday at the age of about 33. The stories regarding resurrection and such were shared by his disciples through oral tradition and only decades later actually transcribed. If the Antioch Jesus Movement orchestrated the whole thing, they almost botched it, as those apostle tales were not even close to being consistent.

There is, allegedly, a genetic connection to Jesus. No, not from the ***Da Vinci Code***, that book by Dan Brown, and movie directed by Ron Howard starring Tom Hanks, but, the Shroud of Turin, which is a 14 foot long and 3.5 feet wide woven cloth with a negative image of the crucified Christ, with blood, kept in the cathedral of St. John the Baptist in Turin, Italy, home of the 2006 Winter Olympics.[243] [50] Well, actually, one conspiracy theory does have Leonardo Da Vinci, in fact, being responsible for this purported Middle Ages hoax. But, the latest thinking seems to show that the impressions on the fabric reveal the kind of chemical decomposition consistent with that which would occur over a millennium or two. Then, we learn that a 1998 carbon 14 dating showing the age to be during the Medieval Period (*1356*) was in 2005 proved inaccurate, in that a re-woven strand from this age (*thirteen hundreds*) was actually measured earlier, and, the latest evidence from a dating indicates that the cloth could well be 2000 years old. But, the face of Jesus Christ? How can such interpretations, almost surely hoaxes, continue to bear credence and sacredly revered? Sort of reminds you of religion itself.

Speaking of Da Vinci, his painting of ***The Last Supper*** was poorly researched. The utensils, clothes, whatever are representative of his (*Leonardo's*) day (*1500 AD*). It is like an artist today painting the Passover meal using the setting of Ruth's Chris Steakhouse. Yet, religious analysts use every glance, people placement, or symbol as indicative of hidden truths. Leonardo was not there!

Finally, be prepared for annual holy breakthroughs gaining attention just before Easter. There was that bone box in 2003 and in April of 2006, the papers of Judas—thirteen papyrus sheets bound in leather found in an Egyptian cave—were announced, absolving him of betrayal.[79] National Geographic carried an hourly feature on "The Gospel of Judas." As yet another "great" archeological find, James Cameron, of Titanic film fame, was executive producer of a documentary and book in 2007 on the "Lost Tomb of Jesus." Well, maybe not, as the definitive archeological world denounced the discovery as a publicity stunt. [69] The Greatest Story Ever Told is certainly still being written. You can expect a third millennium version of the 1965, 199 minute film, featuring Max Von Sydow as Christ, to have more stars and in three dimensions.

There have been numerous attempts, of course, to critically assess the reality of Jesus. This a mouthful, but nevertheless necessary: in 1982, the Religion and Biblical Criticism Project was founded by the Committee for the Scientific Examination of Religion (*CSER, pronounced Caesar*), a group formed by the Council for Secular Humanism, associated with ***Free Inquiry***, the magazine.[104] In 1985, the Project convened a conference entitled "Jesus in History and Myth," chaired by R. Joseph Hoffmann, a young associate professor of religion from the University of Michigan, where the gathering was held. After participating in the discussions, Robert Funk, a noted biblical scholar, that year, with John Dominic Crossan, brought together 200 or so biblical scholars to vote—more specifically select red, pink, grey and black beads—in a series of seminars for what was probably real about Jesus. Several publications resulted, and you can go to ***Wikipedia*** for the details. The Jesus Seminar said that this itinerant mystic preached a sapiential eschatology, and it really doesn't matter what this means, for it failed to determine if there really was a Jesus. The effort did serve to popularize the authenticity of Jesus, although there was a swarm of critics, including one complaining that this was a tool of Satan. Funk was, after all, a skeptic on orthodox Christian belief. A young audio-visual volunteer for the conference, Tom Flynn, in 2007 published, as mentioned earlier, ***The New Encyclopedia of UNBELIEF***.

Well, R. Joseph Hoffmann is back. After assignments at Oxford, Beirut, Africa and New Zealand, he now directs CSER out of the Center for Inquiry at Amherst, New York. CSER convened another conference in 2007 where the Jesus Project was announced. This time, 50 interdisciplinary scholars will supposedly answer the question: did Jesus exist? Hoffmann says that "The Jesus Project is the first methodologically agnostic approach to the question of Jesus' historical existence."[144] The Project will publish its final report in 2012, which is certainly becoming a particularly symbolic year.

You must understand the psyche of religion to appreciate why so many have expended so much time on something so abstruse. Let me leave this with that. But, wait, a Spielberg-Crichton thriller about the genetic Second Coming of Christ!

**The Second Coming of Christ**

Let's see now:

- Israel was reborn on May 14, 1948.
- There has been a shocking plummeting of morality.
- We are beset with famine, violence and wars.
- There have been more earthquakes, especially in Indonesia. Perhaps that is where he will appear, a Muslim nation, at that.
- Travel and education has vastly increased.
- There has been an explosion of cults and the occult.
- The UN and G8 nations indicate that there is more and more a centralization of world financial and political power.
- There has been a curious combination of apostasy (*renunciation of religious faith*) and an outpouring of higher faith.

My, my, my, aren't those the exact signs that are supposed to foreshadow the second coming of Christ? You can go to JesusSoonReturn.com to receive guidance. Forget the movie, await the real thing!

**How to Become a Saint**

The Catholic Church recognizes special people who demonstrate a life of almost perfect virtue, and more. Generally, the Pope first beatifies that individual, particularly when it can be shown that this person performed a miracle. Six years after her death, Mother Theresa attained beatification. But a book (*see later section for details*) was published showing that she "lost" faith. For sainthood, there must be a second miracle. Thus, miracles are fundamental and necessary for Christianity. Something tells me that Mother Theresa will never attain Saint Theresa status, but not because of an absence of purported miracles.

It is informally reported that 3,000 people have been sainty-fied by the church. Pope Paul II canonized (*process of granting sainthood*) 480 individuals and beatified 1340. His staff must have uncovered a whole swarm of miracles, a subject we will later investigate.

There are, of course, saints in the Islamic world. Saints' tombs are all over the landscape in most Muslim countries.

It is said that India has produced more saints per capita than any other culture. Thus saints can be found in the Hindu tradition.

There are, of course, Buddhist saints. Here is an almost sure way to attain <u>living</u> sainthood, something rather difficult in the Christian world, in fact, impossible. Take the case of Japanese Genshin Fujinami, who, for more than seven years, dressed in white, undertook a punishing quest of starvation, isolation and marathon traveling, featuring:[316]

- o 1000 days of running/walking up to 52.5 miles per day, carrying a shovel, length of rope and short sword, the latter two items to commit suicide if he failed to continue the pursuit, and
- o rituals such as sitting in a lotus position for nine days without food, water or sleep.

In 2003, at the age of 44, Saint Fujinami became only the $48^{th}$ Tendai sect marathon monk.

However, in the Buddhist religion, you can aim even higher, for you can also become a buddha, that is, attain Enlightenment. I've long been seeking some answer as to how many have reached this level beyond Gautama himself, and the best I've been able to find is a statement that there is Amitabha (*monk named Dharmakara*) and 28 buddhas of the Pali Canon. But, of course, there must be many more, whatever attainment of those levels might mean.

But, perhaps, we are getting ahead of ourselves. Let me next provide a quick summary of the major world religions.

## Religions of the World

Religion has to do with the worship and devotion to God or some other supernatural entity. While Hinduism has no established beginning, it has been developing for four thousand years. Buddhism began in 600 B.C., while the concept of the other major religions sort of started a little more than two thousand years ago with Judaism. The numbers influenced by religions are growing because there are more and more people and both China and the Soviet Union, which discouraged such practices, have lost influence over what their population can do.

While China has the most number of atheists, a little more than one hundred million, that represents a tiny fraction of the population.[240] There is a strong cultural belief system, as for example, in the Year 2007, the Year of the Pig, there was expected to be an increase of 3 million babies born that year, a 20% increase from the norm, because they wanted their children to be fat, happy and prosperous, like a pig.[67] That is, an extra birth surplus of three times the total population of Hawaii, because of the symbolic value of a pig. On top of this, pigs are mostly eaten. Can't imagine from where the prosperity part comes.

Christianity represents one third (*2 billion*) the religions of the world, with Islam (*1.3 billion*) at 21%, the second largest and fastest growing. Surprisingly, Hinduism, #3 with 900 million, shows the highest growth rate in the U.S. Approximately three quarters of humanity belongs to Christianity, Islam Hinduism, and Buddhism. Actually, non-believers occupy third place with about a billion. This means that 85% believe in some religion. Scientology is in 22nd place with half a million.

Can you reconcile religion and science? Isaac Newton believed God was responsible for gravity and some of the Hindu religion have used quantum physics to explain some basic theological concepts. William James' pragmatism, perhaps, might be the grand compromise: science predicts in the physical world and religion helps people cope with emotional and moral decisions.

### Christianity

Christianity started 2000 years ago, was derived from Judaism, and was named after Jesus Christ. Christ, in Greek, means the anointed one. Christians believe there is one God and that Jesus Christ is the Messiah, the savior of Mankind. There is supposed to be a Second Coming of Jesus…any day now. There is a Heaven and a Hell in this religion, and ***The Bible*** is the accepted authority, although interpretations vary. The bottom line is that your soul will maintain consciousness until Judgment Day when only the righteous will be resurrected.

Constantine the Great, the first Roman emperor to embrace Christianity, although he did it more for politics than religion, moved the capital city from Rome to Byzantium, and renamed it Constantinople, which is now known as Istanbul. He has been said to have re-constructed ***The Bible***, including the deification of Jesus, through a council he convened in 325 AD. Just because ***The Da Vinci Code*** said some of this does not mean it has to be fiction.

The Protestant Reformation in the beginning of the 16th century, for which Martin Luther (*1519*) of Germany no doubt played an important role, was reinforced by King Henry VIII, who named himself as the head of England's church. Without going into the more interesting excesses of Roman Catholic money-grubbing, concubinage, military alliances and the fact that the Pope would not approve of Henry's marriage dissolution from Catherine of Aragon, prosaically, in 1604, King James I convened the Hampton Court Conference to begin re-translating ***The Bible***. The completed work was issued in 1611, is today the bible of choice, and for the longest time, has been the #1 best seller. So, beginning with Hebrew and Greek history came a Roman emperor, then a British King, who are credited with being the prime movers of the most popular religion today. John Remsburg has catalogued what ***The Bible*** authorizes and defends, and this list is merely a portion: lying, cheating, theft, murder, wars of conquest, human sacrifices, cannibalism, slavery, polygamy, prostitution, ignorance, cruelty to animals and injustice to women.[251]

Christianity is so split that there are 34,000 factions/sect/denominations/etc. There must be something to strength through diversity. Now there is a growing ecumenical movement to promote unity within the Church. That is a good first step towards a simple solution.

Roman Catholicism is the largest single denomination, with half the members, and while the Pope, their leader, operates out of the Vatican, the country with the largest number of Catholics is Brazil, nearly 100% a century ago, but while today losing ground to Protestant evangelicals, remain 74% Catholic.

The evangelicals have more recently made religious life more meaningful. Leaders (*pastors*) have used high technology and mass marketing, and have become quintessentially American. Evangelicals are more intense in their beliefs and tend to be a little more Southern, rural and older. They are self-appointed ambassadors for Jesus. Sexual morality, anti-evolution and being tough on immigration are watchwords. White evangelicals are more conservative, vote Republican and oppose gay marriage (*84%*). Black evangelicals support Democrats. The movement picked up in the later 70's when Jimmy Carter (*D-Georgia*), a born again Christian (*admitted to in a **Playboy** interview*), was elected president. President George W. Bush (*R-Texas*) has been quoted to say: "I also have this belief, strong belief, that freedom is not this country's gift to the world; freedom is the Almighty's gift to every man and woman in this world. And as the greatest power on the face of the Earth, we have an obligation to help the spread of freedom."[10] He stands as the poster boy for the mission, but there are rock bands (*MercyMe, Switchfoot*), recording artists (*Amy Grant*), actors (*Stephen Baldwin*), next door neighbors and family members as devout evangelicals.

Seventy six percent of the U.S. population is Christian, with 13% having no religion, a figure which has doubled over the past decade. Atheists represent from 3-9% of the population. More about this non-belief factor and politics later.

### Islam and the World

In August of 2005, U.***S. News and World Report*** had a special issue on Islam the the World, indicating that Islam is more a way of life than anything else, and is derived from the Syriac word for "making peace." Islam started in 622 AD, more than half a century after Jesus Christ, and adheres to the same God as Christianity. Muslims controlled much of the civilized globe from North Africa to Indonesia and into Europe from the 7th through 1lth Century.

Islam has again become a daily headline item. "Beheadings and bombings leave more than 860 people dead." Baghdad? Afghanistan? Nope, Thailand! More Muslims live in the Orient than the Middle East. Indonesia's Muslim population is twice that of Iran, Iraq and Afghanistan combined. China has more Muslims than Iraq and Afghanistan, combined. With 210 million adherents, Indonesia is the largest Islamic country.

Five million Muslims live in the U.S., half being born here. As much as 9/11, the assignment of women as second class citizens, allowance of polygamy and range of other cultural variations will make life difficult for Muslims in American, strict adherence to the Koran will especially make integration into the general community difficult. Unlike the Bible, the Koran was never created, but has existed with God for all eternity, therefore, making any adjustment to modern life challenging.

The Islamic God or Allah cannot be visualized, but is present everywhere and will sit in personal judgment of every person. Many Muslims pray 5 times each day, facing Mecca, and end each with salaam, or peace. If you follow His commands, you go to Paradise. If not, you face eternal damnation.

***The Koran*** is the first book in the Arabic and includes Mary's Immaculate Conception and Noah's Ark. It was a series of revelations from Allah through the angel Gabriel from which came the ***Koran***. Do you get the feeling that maybe ***The Bible*** was the inspiration for Muhammad? He was born in the year 570 AD or CE, and was an illiterate goat herder, who married an older widow, went on to become a successful trader, married his second wife (*after the first passed away*) when she was 10 years old, and finally rose to conqueror and prophet. At the end, he had 10 wives. Interesting that Abram (*later Abraham*), a paltry sheepherder, circa 1792 BC, more than a thousand years earlier, in what today is Iraq, was contacted by a similar, but Christian, deity, through which today all monotheism flows. Islam and Christianity might well be the same religion from the same source, for they are nearly identical. This similarity might provide a clue to how these religions might unite.

Muslims have an obligation. Once in their lifetime, they must make that pilgrimage to Mecca, but only if it can be afforded. The ritual can be traced back to Abraham around 2000 BC, even though the religion was founded in 622 AD. In 2007, the Hajj began on December 18. But the previous year, 349 people were crushed to death, the worst tragedy since the 2500 trampled in 1990. Normally a crowd of from 2 million to 3 million descends on Mecca. Males wear two white sheets and women wear their hijab, a normal modest dress, and all walk counterclockwise seven times around the Islam, the Sacred Mosque. No perfume, no sexual intercourse, no killing allowed.

There is then the matter of the two sects: Shiites versus the Sunnis. While Shiites are the majority (*60%*) in Iraq, worldwide, they represent fewer than 15% of all Muslims, for in Indonesia, almost all of more than 200 million Muslims are Sunni. Shiites were responsible for the Iranian revolution in 1979 and formed the Hezbollah terrorist group. However, suicide bombers today are mostly Sunni. It is even more confusing when you learn that the only real religious difference between the two is that Shiites believe that temporal successors to Muhammad should come from his family line, while Sunnis believe that this caliph need only be a believer, although the former then feels that the Koran should be interpreted for modern times when the latter doesn't. Shiites do have a fundamental interest in democracy.

Why did the war on terrorism even begin? Say you are truly religious. Add the insult of heathens jerking your country and culture around, and then observing them, through the omnipresence of television, wantonly enjoying life. The thought of sacrificing yourself to live forever among 72 virgins and a river of honey, or insuring for the future fate of your entire family line, can be highly motivational. Our War on Terrorism would not have happened if the hijackers did not believe in the afterlife.

Finally, there is the matter of denial.[19] Islam is a religion of peace. So is Christianity. But the Crusades? It is all in the personal interpretation, and Mohammed Atta, the ringleader of 9/11, in the note he left behind, specifically quoted the Koran. Religion, while providing purpose, can also be a convenient excuse.

**Hinduism and India**

Hindu means Indian, or inhabitant of the Indian subcontinent. This earliest of religions began in India 1500 years before Jesus Christ. The first Hindu bible is the Rig Veda, a collection of 1028 hymns. There are many gods in Hinduism, beginning with Shiva, symbolically depicted in phallus form. Animals are worshipped, with cattle and peacocks being sacred. Thus, vegetarianism is widespread among followers. Yoga is the path to enlightenment, and there is an afterlife, because there is reincarnation. The caste system is part of the religion.

With a population just over one billion, about 82% of Indians are Hindu, with Islam accounting for 12% (*120 million*). Eighty percent of Nepalese are Hindus. While India occupies 2.4% of the world land area, 15% of the world population lives here.

In Pakistan, Hindus only account for 1% of the population, as 97% are Muslims, of which 77% are Shiites. Two percent of Indonesians are Hindus.

Oh, and why is Hindu the fastest growing religion in the United States? First, Christianity declined from 86% to 77% from 1990 to 2001. Second, non-believers, in this period increased from 8% to 14%, with the state of Washington at 25%. Third, Hinduism is <u>not</u> the fastest growing religion, it is Wicca, a Neopagan religion known as Witchcraft, from 8,000 in 1990 to 134,000 in 2001, or an increase of nearly 1600%! But, fourth, of the major religions, Hindu increased from 227,000 to 766,000, or 237% (*Buddhism 170%, Islam 109%, Christianity 5%*).[250] The relatively low number was suddenly increased by Indian immigrants, almost all who were Hindus. There were about 400,000 during that decade, and with the added children plus high rate remaining in the country, this would explain most of the increase.

**Buddhism and Japan**

Japan is a bit more complicated. Seventy percent are Buddhists *(began around 500 BC)*. When you add the numbers following Shinto (*started around 500 AD*), you will surpass the 127 million[237] population, but that is because most consider both to be important. While Buddhism came from India, Shinto is indigenous, is the official national religion, and its priests are state officials. Shinto handles daily life. There are virtually no Shinto cemeteries, for Buddhism is responsible for death. They have long co-existed.

Siddhartha Gautama, a Hindu, attained enlightenment and became known as Buddha, "the Awakened One." He extolled of the Four Noble Truths, all dealing with suffering. His definition of anatta, which, you will recall, supposedly assuaged my fear of death, did not incorporate an eternal soul, for the purpose of life is to ultimately escape by attaining Nirvana, a state at which you become extinct, which sounds awfully close to eternal gloom to me.

As terminal and awful as this might be to some, Buddhism actually portrays a gray ending, because most never get there. There are the interminable reincarnations, a clear afterlife, but, I remember in my early youth asking a Buddhist priest how many people he knew had ascended to Nirvana. Yes, there was Buddha, himself, but he was hard pressed to come up with another name.

This was my "aha, there is no Santa Claus," point of my life, with respect to a Supreme Deity. First of all, if only one person made it, what were my chances? Then, too, maybe this is all made up, anyway. In any case, an earlier section identified at least 30 buddhas, those that attained enlightenment, which remains an awfully small number considering the billions of Buddhists who ever lived.

More recently, I've asked several Buddhist priests, "tell me about the afterlife," and most of the responses approximate, "it's what you believe." I think there is a tendency to provide the fear story to children—be good, or you will return as a cockroach—but to adults, the safer and more readily acceptable message is put in the abstract. So why do most Japanese not believe in an afterlife? My sense is that they have grown up, like me. The bottom line, though, is that Buddhists do not believe in the existence of a God who created the universe, although, depending on sect, there are deities. Further, there is reincarnation and karma, so the door remains open to an afterlife.

One final issue refers to the Yasukuni Shrine, a Shinto memorial to Japan's war dead, a bitter subject to China and South Korea. Yasukuni means nation at peace. It was established in 1868 and is the sanctuary (*there are no real bodies here*) for 2.5 million killed as servicemen, 2.1 million from World War II. The problem is that 14 WWII war criminals are registered here, and the Japanese Prime Minister annually honors them all in a publicized visit. The gripe about this call is that China and South Korea are insulted that the head of state is worshipping these convicts. The problem is that, in Japan, there is an attitude of: "We Japanese will never back down to that kind of Chinese and Korean pressure."[130] Seems like there is a some maturing required, for just announcing the symbolic move of those 14 souls to another place of rest, should eliminate this resentment.

## Secular Faiths

Secular relates to this world and is non-spiritual. Religion delivers on God's Word or Rules, where faith is blindly accepted as a necessary belief, and is further treated in a later section.

There are said to be three great secular faiths, all from the 1800's: Darwinism, Marxism and Freudianism. Marxism (*by Karl Marx, German revolutionary from his* ***Das Kapital****, which was never finished*) is socialism, and appears to be on its way out. Freudianism (*for Sigmund Freud, Austrian psychiatrist*) deals with the emotional and psychological state of mind, but more so, that many (*if not all*) of us are not in full control of our actions, and, too, seems to be losing some favor.

Darwinism (*Charles Darwin, British naturalist, who between the ages of 22 and 27 took one grand boat ride around the world on the HMS Beagle, went home and pretty much stayed there for the rest of his life*) was only about evolution, until time and society forced upon this science: creationism, religion and truth. While ***On the Origin of Species by Means of Natural Selection, or The Preservation of Favoured Races in the Struggle for Life*** (*yes,* ***Origin of Species*** *is only part of the full title*), published when he was 50, rankles those who totally subscribe to every word of ***The Bible*** (*which, as shown in the following section, happens to be 45% of Americans*), there no doubt are a few true believers who can adjust to a prime force engineering life through some more sensible process, like evolution.

Paul Kurtz, editor in chief of ***Free Inquiry***, wondered if it might be sensible to create secular and humanist alternatives to religion.[180] It thus occurred to me that as much of the world seems inclined to worship a supernatural god, mostly because belief and faith have been an important part of their upbringing, further providing a psychological crutch for mental security, would it be possible, in a desperate global emergency, to replace a virtual Supreme Being with another symbol, something, perhaps, more purposeful and legitimate, such as the natural environment or mankind itself. That is, believe in your surroundings and the people around you.

This thought began to take shape in the first chapter where it was suggested that the menacing disaster of Peak Oil and Global Warming might become so serious that the only solution would be for the world to immediately disarm and apply all financial and human resources to prevent a global cataclysm. Praying certainly wouldn't help, so why not devote your faithfulness and energies to the task at hand. That secular alternative could well be Planet Earth and Humanity. Amen.

## On the Matter of Atheism

Theism is belief in one or more deities. Gnosticism is belief in an imperfect god. You add an "a" and atheism takes a position that there is no god, while agnosticism is more an attitude that this matter is unknown. In a way, an agnostic rests somewhere between a theist and atheist, in that a person who believes in a god, but is not sure if a god exists, can be called an agnostic theist, while, if he denies belief without claiming to know for sure if no gods can or do exist, he is then called an agnostic atheist. These definitional exercises plague religion.

In the United States, you cannot be elected President if you are an atheist, and could not even run for any public office in some states. You would be among the most mistrusted of minorities. The Boy Scouts of America (*BSA*) do not allow atheist, homosexual or woman members. Even the U.S. Supreme Court passed judgment in favor of the BSA, but this is the governmental body that picked George Bush over Al Gore, even though Gore received more popular votes.

Atheists and agnostics claim about 1% of the American population each, just below Islam and Buddhism. For all of my adult life I looked upon myself as a neo-agnostic—that I did not know, but actively searched for a Supreme Being, and more importantly, the potential for an afterlife. In the process of writing this chapter, partly because of Richard Dawkins, but mostly because I did not think the search would get anywhere, anyway, I became an atheist. But, later, there was a minor re-adjustment.

In the 6$^{th}$ Century BC, Buddhists were atheists, as they remain today. However, Diagoras, a 5$^{th}$ Century Greek philosopher, is commonly known as the first atheist. Socrates was sentenced to death for impiety, and all throughout history atheists have been subjected to persecution. So much so that it was not until Baron d'Holback in the late 18$^{th}$ Century finally could write on this topic and survive. Karl Marx and Friedrich Nietzsche were similarly honest about their belief. Joseph Stalin was one, but Adolf Hitler either was or was not. Other atheists, from the Time-Life 100 Most Influential People of the Millennium compilation are: Abraham Lincoln, Albert Einstein, Charles Darwin, Benjamin Franklin, Carl Sagan (*Ann Druyan was later quoted to say that Sagan was an agnostic, not an atheist*), Bertrand Russell, Billy Joel, Clarence Darrow, Galileo Galilei, George Bernard Shaw, Helen Keller, James Madison, John Adams, Napoleon Bonaparte, James Watson, Jawaharlal Nehru, John Lennon, Walt Disney, George Orwell, Mark Twain, Thomas Jefferson, William Howard Taft, Thomas Edison, Sigmund Freud. The following were either atheist or agnostic: Woody Allen, Fidel Castro, Michael Crichton, Jodie Foster, Linus Pauling, Mao Tse-tung, Richard Leakey, Francois Mitterand, Stanley Kubrick, Jack Nicholson, Mikhail Gorbachev, Warren Buffet, Richard Feynman, and Marie Curie. For a more complete compilation, go to GOOGLE and type in "esau, celebrity atheist list."

For the record, here is the estimated Atheist/Agnostic percentage top ten:[383]

| | |
|---|---|
| Sweden | 64-85% |
| Denmark | 48-80% |
| Norway | 54-72% |
| Japan | 65% |
| Czech Republic | 54-61% |
| Finland | 41-60% |
| France | 44-54% |
| South Korea | 30-52% |
| Estonia | 49% |
| Germany | 41-49% |

Israel is at #18 (37%) and Taiwan #25 (24%). The USA, of course, is way back, as we will see in the section polling Americans.

Atheists don't have a holiday, but we can watch NFL football on Sunday morning in Hawaii without having family or psychological conflicts. There are no charismatic leaders, commanding traditions nor common literature. ***The God Delusion*** might, though, suffice as a galvanizing document. Oh yes, there ***is The Twilight of Atheism: The Rise and Fall of Disbelief in the Modern World*** (Doubleday, 2004), by Alistair McGrath, also of Oxford University, who does not share similar views with his colleague. In fact, McGrath published in 2007 ***The Dawkins Delusion***.

One of the problems with atheism is that it's so, so negative to say there is no God, nor an afterlife. But the thought is pure and not saddled with the baggage of having to defend the impossible or promise the unattainable. There is no dogma. Just believe in the real truth.

## What do People Believe?

While ***IDIOT*** provided the superstructure, ***TIME*** magazine regularly delivers to me the latest statistics. In a poll of 1,004 adult Americans by Yankelovich (*and most of the following surveys, unless indicated, apply to the United States*) [1]:

- **Do you believe in the healing power of personal prayer?**

  YES 82%
  NO 13%

In a telephone poll of 1,018 Americans taken on March 11-12, 1997 by Yankelovich Partners:

- **Do you believe in the existence of heaven, where people live forever with God after they die?**

  YES 81%
  NO 13%

- **Do you believe you will meet friends and family members in heaven when you die?**

| | |
|---|---|
| YES | 88% |
| NO | 5% |

- **Immediately after death, which of the following do you think will happen to you?**

| | |
|---|---|
| Go directly to heaven | 61% |
| Go to purgatory | 15% |
| Go to hell | 1% |
| Be reincarnated | 5% |
| End of existence | 4% |

Incredibly, only 4% of Americans have my eternal gloom belief. I hope the grand majority are right! Ah, but, that faith part might hinder my entrance. Perhaps my basic goodness will prevail.

To summarize the standard American polls, asking for belief in God:

| | | |
|---|---|---|
| Gallup | 2007 | 95% [80] |
| Gallup (*Baylor Study*) | 2006 | 92% [126] |
| Fox News | 2004 | 92% [33] |
| Harris (Taylor) | 2003 | 90% |
| ABC News | 2000 | 95% [207] |

But there are other polls showing the belief in God figure at around 75% and lower. Here is why. A Gallup poll from May 8-11 in 2006 asked a slightly different question. Which comes closest to describing you:

| | |
|---|---|
| Convinced God exists | 73% |
| Probably exists, but have a little doubt | 14% |
| Probably exists, have a lot of doubt | 5% |
| Probably does not exist, but not sure | 4% |
| Convinced God does not exist | 3% |
| No opinion | 2% |

Thus, if you add the first three, the sum is 92%. A second look would be the 1991 International Survey Program survey. There was only a 63% belief in God figure. This number results from "I know God exists and I have no doubts about it." [297] **In any case, a strong statement can be made that more than 9 out of 10 of Americans believe in God, at least to some degree.**

On the global level, in 2001, the International Social Survey Program polled 1,000 to 2,000 in each of 16 countries:

- **Do you believe strongly in God?**

| Country | 18-29 years old | Over 60 |
|---|---|---|
| Ireland | 28% | 73% |
| U.S. | 55% | 72% |
| France | 12% | 46% |

- **Do you believe in life after death?**

| | | |
|---|---|---|
| Ireland | 60% | 82% |
| U.S. | 68% | 66% |
| France | 53% | 45% |

- **Do you believe in Heaven?**

| | | |
|---|---|---|
| Ireland | 70% | 87% |
| U.S. | 75% | 79% |
| France | 31% | 40% |

Interesting that 28% of Irish 18-29 years of age did not believe in God, but nevertheless, 70% of this same group thought they would go to Heaven. For all three countries, the youth, relative to the more elderly, tends not to believe in God. Many in France must be going to purgatory or hell, for about half believe in an afterlife, but only a third believe in Heaven.

In 2002, the Pew Research Center polled 38,000 people in 46 countries [5]:

- **Percent of people who find religion very important in their life:**

| | |
|---|---|
| Senegal | 97% |
| Indonesia | 95% |
| Nigeria | 92% |
| India | 92% |
| Pakistan | 91% |
| South Africa | 87% |
| Brazil | 77% |
| Turkey | 65% |
| **United States** | **59%** |
| Mexico | 57% |
| Argentina | 39% |
| Uzbekistan | 35% |
| Great Britain | 33% |
| Canada | 30% |
| Italy | 27% |
| South Korea | 25% |

| | |
|---|---|
| Germany | 21% |
| Russia | 14% |
| Japan | 12% |
| France | 11% |

What is it about the French? Maybe their culture is more evolved. About Americans, while many more believe in a supreme being, they seem contented in not having to be bothered by church memberships, as the figure here is 59%, not the 90+% that supposedly believe in Him. Symptomatic of the situation is the fact that there are 3% fewer Roman Catholic clerics in the world compared to 1978, but 20% less in Europe. [61]

Worldwide, the older you are, the more you believe. The type of religion makes a difference. The U.S. figure of 59% in the final list is somewhat understandable, as belief in God does not mean that religion, per se, is important. Similarly, the 65% "importance" rate for Turkey comes from a country just about 100% Muslim. Thus, there already seems to be a sliding from *Koran* strictures even in an Islamic country. In the U.S., one believes what is ingrained from youth, and, while Santa Claus can be set aside as a parental and commercial ploy, there is something sacred about religion that defies common sense.

The Council for Secular Humanism reported from ***Free Inquiry Magazine*** [8] in (www.secularhumanism.org/library/fi/bishop193.html):

Percentage saying "I know God exists and I have no doubts about it":

| | |
|---|---|
| Philippines | 86.2% |
| **United States** | **62.8%** |
| Israel | 43.0% |
| West Germany | 27.3% |
| Russia | 12.4% |
| East Germany | 9.2% |

But to the question about belief in life after death:

| | |
|---|---|
| **United States** | **55.0%** |
| Philippines | 35.2% |
| West Germany | 24.4% |
| Israel | 21.9% |
| Russia | 16.8% |
| East Germany | 6.1% |

As an exception, in Israel, the drop from belief in God to belief in an afterlife is a factor of two, from 43.0% to 21.9%, whereas those other countries did not change much. Books and books can be churned out just analyzing these surveys, and they have been. Noticeably lacking were data from the Middle East. The 90's percentage for Muslim and Hindu countries hints that Saudi Arabia and Iraq might rest close to 100%. But the U.S. in the 60-90% range for all these religious beliefs, with France and Japan closer to 10-40%, begs for explanation. Why is something so fundamental so varied?

I have given many speeches in China, and, early on, for my personal surveys, asked a show of hands on who believed in an afterlife. Typically, the response was close to 1%. Little did I know that to express a religious opinion in public was prohibited. Every one who raised his hand came into jeopardy. Yikes! So I stopped asking. It is said, though, that the present regime is not so fussy, and this question can now again be asked, and that the response will be much higher and more accurately reflect actual beliefs.

For entirely different reasons, do not ask this question in the Middle East and at certain gatherings in parts of the United States. In fact, my wife has warned me about such dinnertime conversation with family and friends.

So, finally, what about the world at large? According to reported polls, the belief in God figure is:

| | |
|---|---|
| 96% | (2000)[271] |
| 92% | (2004)[382] |

So the USA is right up there with the rest of the world in God belief. Okay, then, something went wrong with Dawkins' contention that belief drops with education.

**What About American Scientists?**

First, doctors are not really scientists, even though they are well trained and responsible. World-wide, more parents want their children to be doctors than anything else. It is reported that, in a survey of 1,125 doctors in the U.S., 76% believed in God and 60% in some sort of afterlife [77]. The report went on to say that the 76% figure was close to the 83% previously obtained for the general population.

Then, there is a 1999 ***Scientific American***[361] article, which reported on a survey of the biological and physical science (*including mathematics*) members of the National Academy of Sciences. This survey repeated a study undertaken by James Leuba in 1914, and again in 1933. There were only two questions:

- o Do you believe in a God in intellectual and affective communication with man to whom one may pray in expectation of receiving an answer?
- o Do you believe in personal immortality (*that, is, is there an afterlife*)?

In 1914, Leuba found that one in three of the "greater" scientists expressed belief in God, and only a slightly higher fraction in the afterlife. In 1933, less than 20% believed in both. Leuba's prediction, similar to Dawkins', was that, as there is greater progress in science, religious disbelief should grow. Did it?

In the recent survey of National Academy of Sciences members, less than 10% believed in both. Remember, the general American populace figure is between 59% and 96 %, depending on the question. Biologists had a belief rate of around 5%. **In any case, our top scientists just do not believe in God and an afterlife.** Leuba was right, at least for top scientists. One would hope that there has been an improvement in science education in our schools, but, funny, he was wrong, there, for something else—maybe family upbringing—overrode schooling in God belief. The Takahashi Extension is that, into the future, as the World population becomes more educated, religious belief will dramatically suffer, except maybe in the U.S. because of the reverse Santa Claus Syndrome. Ah, this second part is a joke. I'll stick to this Extension, for if it worked for the best thinking people, it should eventually apply to the masses, too, and I have some ***Time*** statistics to back me:

- In 1976 38% of Americans believed that the Bible was literally true, while in 2006, this figure dropped to 28%.
- In 1976 13% viewed ***The Bible*** as an ancient book of fables, while in 2006, this figure rose to 19%.

While this rise represents almost a 50% increase in rationality, it still means that 81% of Americans believe that ***The Bible*** is NOT an ancient book of fables.

Well, if the Takahashi Extension ultimately prevails, which could take many generations, then kamikaze terrorists will all but disappear. Unfortunately, the July 7, 2005 and subsequent bombings of the London transport system already begins to omen higher longevity, as mere rage might be sufficient cause to continue the terror. The advent of home-grown, clean skin—not necessarily lack of facial hair, though this is also increasing, but good citizens with no previous records—believers to the cause will make prevention much more difficult. Totally unrelated to religion, there will most likely also be a growing incidence of environmental terrorism, for, any form of perceived injustice involving only a handful of dedicated individuals can affect the greater masses through the destruction of symbolic targets.

**What About the Origin of Life?**

In the beginning, there was Adam and Eve, or, depending on your belief, bacteria, or, maybe, viruses or aliens. By evolution, came Man, where *Homo sapiens sapiens* spun off from *Homo sapiens* (*knowing man*) about 100,000 years ago, while the latter transitioned from *Homo erectus* perhaps 300,000 to 400,000 years ago. All signs point to this chain of human life starting in Africa. In scientific classification we follow the chain:

- o Subspecies: *Homo sapiens sapiens*
- o Species: *Homo sapiens (the Homo sapiens idaltu became extinct)*
- o Genus: *Homo (Hominini side has two branches, the Pan Genus for some chimpanzees—where the bonobo, or pygmy chimpanzee, looks awfully like humans, but with more hair—and the sapiens line)*
- o Subfamily: *Homininae (our tribe is Hominini, while the gorilla tribe is referred to as Gorillini)*
- o Family: *Hominidae*
- o Order: *Primates*
- o Class: *Mammalia*
- o Phylum *Chordata*
- o Kingdom: *Animalia*

Our Order is Primates. No wonder that some Creationists take offense. The chimpanzee and Man took different pathways about 7 million years ago. Our genetic sequences are 99% identical over 96% of the lengths.[59] While our DNA base pairs have 35 million differences, this is out of 3 billion pairs. Man and ape came from the first animals, sponges...yes, sponges, when, during the Cambrian Explosion 540 million years, ago, during only a 10 million year period, animal life suddenly advanced from worms and sponges into the seven additional animal body plans.[313] For a 75 year old man, 10 million years relative to the time span of life itself on the planet is equivalent only to about 75 days.

But how old is very early Man? A 13 million old fossil (*Pierolapithecus catalaunicus*) from Spain was identified as, maybe, the last common ancestor of all apes.[76] Generally, though, the primate needs to walk upright and have small canines (*teeth*), to qualify as an early man. According to some accounts [145], a 7 million year old skull of a great ape (*Sahelanthropus tchadensis, Superfamily Hominidae*) was found in Chad in 2002. Lucy, an *Australopithecine* was, perhaps, a million years old, and the *Australopithecus afarensis* specie survived a million years, almost ten times longer than us (*so far*). But these early specimens are linked to *Homo sapiens sapiens* only as equivalents on the family tree that died off, but, maybe not.

The story of the Leakeys is interesting. Louis (*also known as L.S.B.*) was born in Kenya in 1903, his English parents being missionaries. In 1931 he made his first trip to the Olduvai Gorge (*now Tanzania*), but did not return to do serious excavation until the 1950s. Mary Nichols was born in 1913, became an expert of the early Stone Age, married Louis as his second wife, and sired Richard in 1944, who made his first fossil find, a giant pig, at the age of six. Mary found *Zinjanthropus boisei* in 1959 (*Louis was sick that day*) and suggested that it lived 1.75 million years ago. In 1960 Mary and other son Jonathan found what amounted to *Homo habilis*, dated to be 2 million years old. In 1972, Richard found a second specimen of the same, which dated back 1.9 million years. All of this occurred in the Olduvai Gorge.

The upshot of this all was their claim that the *Homo* genus did not evolve from *Australopithecus*. The whole family went on to discover an assortment of other origins, but absent from all this was family harmony.

In 1974, Donald Johanson, an American, found Lucy in Ethiopia. The surprise was that in 1978, Johanson came to a conclusion that Lucy was not an *africanus*, but another species, he named *Australopithecus afarensis*, a possible missing link with *Homo sapiens*. If this is confusing, just know that the field is rife in controversy. As bewildering as the paleoanthropology might be, the field has been well studied and generally logical and scientifically sound in developing origins. The shocker comes in surveys on the origin of human life, that is, the knowledge, or lack of, of the citizenry.

But the field of human origins is, at best, still speculative. In 2006, Wil Roebroeks of the Netherlands and Robin Dennell of the U.K. wrote in ***Discover*** that, perhaps, "we are all Asians."[83] Recent fossil finds in Georgia (*former USSR*) argue this case. Further the purity of Homo sapiens is also called into question, as there is evidence of interbreeding with Homo erectus and other early hominids. But these are mere experts. What do the American people think?

A Harris Poll of 1,000 adults in the United States in June of 2005 showed on the question, "Do you think human beings developed from earlier species or not?"

- Did 38%
- Did Not 54%
- Unsure 8%

More than half of Americans DON'T believe in evolution as it applies to human life!

To the question, "Regardless of what you may personally believe, which of these do you believe should be taught in public schools?":

- Evolution only 12%
- Creationism only 23%
- Intelligent design only 4%
- None of these 3%
- Unsure 7%

About twice the number of Americans believes that only creationism (*meaning, created directly by God*) should be taught than those that believe only evolution should be taught! Intelligent design (*ID*) means creation by a powerful force, so that is just about the same as God.

This 90+% belief in God figure for the Nation has huge implications on the future of education, and certainly, extends to stem cell research and cloning, although rapid advances are being made, and a person's skin might well substitute for stem cells in the future, side-stepping one conservative hurdle.

ID was largely created by a Seattle think tank, the Discovery Institute, and their logic is a lot smarter than that of the Fundamentalists. DI found an ally in President George W. Bush.[15] Between the Pentagon and DI, their notion is that we now have fewer science majors because of atheistic biology beliefs of Christian conservatives, so, we need to change this trend. What Frankenstein hybrid future student can we, thus, now anticipate?

An NBC News Poll conducted by Peter Hart and Bill McInturff from March 8-10, 2005, of 800 adults nationwide, showed, to the question, "Which do you think is more likely to actually be the explanation for the origin of human life on Earth?"

- Evolution 33%
- Biblical account 57%
- Created in 6 days 44%
- Divine presence 13%
- None of the above 3%
- Unsure 7%

In the USA today, almost **half of the population** (*44%*) believes that the world was created by God in **6 days!** In reinforcement, a 2005 Gallup Poll from ***USA Today*** showed that 53% of Americans believed that God created human beings exactly as the **Bible** describes.[112] Then, a 2007 Newsweek Poll reported a 48% figure. Thus, it can generally be said that about half of Americans believe that God created us all in 6 days. This bears repeating: **half of Americans believe that God created us all in 6 days.** Finally, ***Christianity Today*** reports that 66% of Americans believe that God created human beings within the last 10,000 years.[230]

In October of 2007, I stayed with a colleague of mine in Florida, and noted to him in the ***Orlando Sentinel*** that their Department Education had drafted new science standards that for the first time required students to learn about evolution. I asked if this was a misprint, and he responded, no, this state is screwed up. This novel concept will await 2008 for approval and implementation. From all reports, though, 80% of Floridians do support teaching evolution. Huh? I felt that I was in a time warp.

I don't need to go into a state by state comparison, but the trends seem definitely mixed, as, ***Wired*** (*May 2007, pg 61*) reported that:

- a Tennessee Senate resolution inquired on why creationism is not being taught in schools,
- there were four anti-evolution bills in the previous Oklahoma legislative session,
- Kansas approved science-education standards that treated evolution in a scientifically appropriate way,
- Mississippi's House killed a bill allowing the teaching of creationism,

- o Montana's House introduced a joint resolution supporting a sound scientific curriculum and
- o Georgia settled a lawsuit in Cobb County School agreeing in perpetuity not to denigrate evolution.

One would have thought all this was settled in the '20's.

The Council of Europe in 2007 approved a resolution against creationism.[192] So the current concern about the religious principles being applied to scientific understanding is more than a U.S.-only issue.

So, should intelligent design be taught in schools? Yes, of course, but not as a counterpoint to evolution. ID belongs in philosophy or maybe even psychology, but not in a science class. The equivalent would be the teaching of stork theory in a sex education class.

Finally, is natural selection the fate of humanity? Individuals and subsequent families were replaced by groups, for security insured higher longevity, but this controlled order, it might have been determined, could best be enforced through an omniscient God. Well, religion was one escape mechanism we invented to improve the evolutionary process, which, at the beginning was probably too savage and, maybe prone to a dead end. Is that requirement for a God now obsolete? Are we ready to graduate from that Santa Claus mentality?

**The Church on Evolution**

I continue to be amazed at what gets published. But my astonishment here is in the wonderment that there are serious writers out there who reinforce my general point of view that has been on exhibit all through this chapter. Two recent books deal with this subject of science and religion:

- o Lewis Wolpert wrote ***Six Impossible Things Before Breakfast: The Evolutionary Origins of Belief***, suggesting that there is a God gene and goes into the evolution of beliefs.[364] From early motive development through language capability to an ability to create what might not even be true now, the human brain has homed in on religion as a safety mechanism. Religion was earlier mentioned to be one of the reasons why our human species might have survived and dominated, so the logic is consistent with that school of thought.
- o Daniel Dennett wrote ***Breaking the Spell: Religion as a Natural Phenomenon***, telling it like it is, in that, in the U.S., the red states are religious and the blue are generally not.[84] Religion is described as merely a matter of biological fitness to survive and conquer.

***Nature*** magazine reviewed both publications and generally applauded Wolpert's presentation. However, Dennett is described as a notorious non-believer and decries his attitude about religion being all smoke and mirrors.

This leads to what the Church, and for this discussion let us focus on the Catholic Church, thinks of Darwin. From all reports, Pope Benedict XVI is contemplating rejecting intelligent design.[46] He is trying to square religion with evolution. Pope John Paul II de-excommunicated Galileo and declared in 1980 that there was no contradiction between the two…but what did that really mean? Benedict has already said that "we are not some casual and meaningless product of evolution," so how then to reconcile with reality?

Austrian Cardinal Christoph Schonborn said in 2005 that the church does not support creationism and that the idea that the biblical account of the creation of the world in six days should be taken literally.[281] Yet, in the same Catholic News Service article, he said:

- Darwin's theories on evolution deserve to be studied in schools, along with the scientific question marks that remain.
- It is right to teach the science of Darwin, not ideological Darwinism.
- In a 2005 ***New York Times*** article wrote that there is overwhelming evidence for design in biology, which was blatantly pro intelligent design.
- That Darwinian theory and faith can coexist.

If you have been keeping score, you should be as confused as I am.

In September of 2006, Pope Benedict convened a retreat on "Creation and Evolution": to which Cardinal Schonborn was invited. Well, on April 13, 2007, Pope Benedict XVI, in his first official release on the subject, said that Darwin's theory cannot be proven.[96] From all reports, the Church will be further clarifying, or muddying, its position. Stay tuned.

## Personalities in Religion

Those who write on religion mostly fall into two categories: those that tout the virtues and others who are skeptics. ***Free Inquiry***, in particular, with Editor in Chief Paul Kurtz and Editor Thomas Flynn, provide a readable example of the latter. Let us start though with…the Amazing Randi.

### The Randi Factor

Randall James Hamilton Zwinge, or The Amazing Randi, who was born in Canada but became a naturalized citizen of the U.S., offers $1 million to anyone who can show, under proper observing conditions, evidence of any paranormal, supernatural or occult power. For most of his professional life, he was a magician, escape artist and amateur astronomer, and actually has an asteroid named after him, 3163 Randi. He gave up doing magic tricks to become the foremost scientific skeptic and challenger of paranormal claims. In 2003, he received the first Richard Dawkins Award (*for best publicizing atheism; Daniel Dennett won the 2007 honor*).

Between 1997 and 2005, 360 notarized applications were received. No one has passed the formal test. In April of 2007 he began limiting entrants to only those with an existing media profile and the backing of a reputable academic. He was wasting time with mentally ill claimants. This challenge will be revoked in 2010 so that he can do more important work.

Randi debunked the efforts of Uri Geller in NOVA's "Secret of the Psychics," and gets 100,000 hits/day at www.randi.org. He is real, he is a pain to some trying to make an honest living out of chicanery and he is undefeated.

Some things don't qualify as paranormal, according to Randi. Bigfoot (*and other legendary characters*), exorcism, the existence of God and reincarnation fall in this list. About God and reincarnation, the problem is that there are no test protocols to verify. The James Randi Educational Foundation chooses not to debate something that cannot be scientifically demonstrated.

Does religion deserve to be mentioned on the same pages as UFOs, spoon bending and the like? There is a kind of sacrilege here, but techniques for proving an afterlife seems to mostly be accomplished through some so-called medium, ideal for the Randi test. Among the paranormal phenomena defined by Randi include: communicating with the dead, faith healing, the existence of ghosts and the like. Again, no one has shown these abilities to Randi. A tally of ***An Encyclopedia of Claims, Frauds and Hoaxes of the Occult and Supernatural***, by Stephen J. Goodson, reveals a disturbing number of religious-related hoaxes, many dealing with the afterlife and miracles. Ergo, if there can be no validation of the afterlife and miracles, maybe that answers this question.

Oh, yes, in addition, any seer with a paranormal aptitude can also contact B. Premanand of the ***India Skeptic*** (*to win 100,000 rupees; about 44 Rs. to the dollar*), Prabir Ghosh (*Rs. 20,000*), Australian Skeptics ($*100,000 Australian, 1.3A$ to $*) and the Association for Skeptical Inquiry *(£12,000, .45£ to $)*. Just go to Google to get the details.

## The Bockris Counterpoint

I consider Professor John Bockris to be a colleague and friend, until, maybe after he reads all this. Just kidding, John. We met in 1974 at that first hydrogen gathering, and he is credited with coining the term, "The Hydrogen Economy." He has written books on this subject. However, in 2005, he published ***The New Paradigm*** [*ibid, Bockris*], a virtual counterpoint to the Amazing Randi. I think John Bockris is one of the greatest physical chemists of all time, and I was in Professor Rustum Roy's office once, when he fielded a call, talked for a minute or two, hung up, and remarked, that was a call from one of the world's finest chemists, or something like that. On the other end was from John Bockris. Professor Roy is mentioned in ***The New Paradigm***, and earlier in his viewpoint on cold readings.

I read John's book, and again find myself in an awkward position I've been in many times before. I can't believe that human life was created by God, but most Americans do. Almost everything the President of my country, George W. Bush, supports, I don't. And most of what I like, he doesn't, or, at least, I wonder why he is really doing something when it seems reasonable. John Bockris is smarter than me. I don't agree with him on the afterlife, and many other phenomena. What is wrong with me? If anything else, these kinds of contradictions inspired me to write this chapter.

First of all, Bockris and I do agree on many things. We concur on 99% of what science represents. He believes that there will be a coming world catastrophe because USA politicians from around 1980 did not take the responsible steps with regard to resource exhaustion. In CHAPTER 5 of ***Book 1*** I, likewise, suggest so, too. He believes in cold fusion (*CF*). I do, too. In fact, I hired a CF researcher, perhaps, even before he, himself, actively got into the field. His book provides details. Secondly, he has gotten into some academic trouble with regard to trying to convert base into noble metals, that is, lead into gold. Bockris and his team apparently succeeded. My inner mind tells me this should be possible. The problem came in reproducibility, quantity produced and the friends he kept. Again, you can read his side of the story.

But about ***The New Paradigm***, in a nutshell, my view wildly conflicts with his, as Bockris states:

- Unidentified Flying Objects (UFO) are real and much is known by the government about extraterrestrials. This information will be made clear early in this new millennium.
- There is an afterlife.
- Reincarnation is possible.
- Cold readings cannot be discounted by science.
- Human consciousness may in some form survive death.
- There is something about consciousness and spiritualism that current day science cannot explain. All the following could well be valid.
- Out of body and near death experiences.
- Poltergeists.
- Ghosts.
- Parapsychology (*psychic phenomena*) is mostly misunderstood.
- Extrasensory perception, clairvoyance, precognition and psychokinesis are valid practices.
- Psychic healing has been demonstrated.
- The Great Randi can be dismissed.

Now, Bockris does not exactly etch in concrete his beliefs in all the above. They are my interpretation based on what I have determined to be his attitude and logic describing the subject matter. More accurately, he, perhaps, is advocating that research on things such as paranormal phenomena and transformation of base metals be supported. His New Paradigm will allow for this leap forward.

Then there are the gray areas. An important aspect of his New Paradigm is the concept of interconnectedness, that is, everything is connected to all other things. There is something to this. Finally, there is much science does not yet know, and we need a new paradigm to allow the unknown to become known. This, too, makes sense.

But, the Great Randi was so systematically convincing, to me, that I felt responsible to provide a counterpoint. John Bockris does so over more than 500 pages.

**Who is Sylvia Browne?**

Sylvia Celeste Shoemaker (*now Browne, having added an e to the Brown of her third of four marriages*) is a psychic, medium, bestselling author, regular on TV and radio talk shows and purported aide to police and FBI investigations and doctors (*350 of them at last count*) for certain types of treatments. She entertains in Las Vegas and the world over. Her grandmother was a so-called psychic, and her son and granddaughter, too, at least by her mentioning. She has written a book on Heaven (***Life on the Other Side****, Dutton Adult, 2000*), which she says is 3 feet above ground at a higher vibrational level with a constant 78°F (25.6°C) temperature, where there are pets. She has also scientifically proven the existence of an afterlife. Scientifically, mind you.

She has been indicted and convicted of investment fraud and has a long running feud with the Great Randi. She got the latest "laugh," when in 2001 on the Larry King Show she warned Randi about a coming heart attack, which he suffered in 2006. She also foresees prostate cancer for another nemesis, Paul Kurtz, but men of advanced age are prone to this condition. Kurtz remains free of that ailment. All good predictors skew their predictions based on sound statistical evidence.

She agreed three times (*they appear together regularly on TV shows*) to be tested by Randi, but has conveniently provided excuses, including not being able to find him, which drew the obvious response: if she can locate people in Heaven, how can she not find me in Florida?

In 2004 and 2005, on the Montel Williams TV Show, she predicted that troops would be pulled out of Iraq, Osama Bin Laden was dead, Michael Jackson would go to jail, Martha Steward wouldn't, the U.S. would go to war with North Korea and Elizabeth Taylor would die, among some of them. She scored with 25-30% accuracy, but two 4th grade classes in Oklahoma City scored about 50% on the same issues.[100]

She tried again in 2006:

- The weather will be worse than last year (WRONG)
- Hurricanes will hit the northeast U.S. (WRONG)
- Two more earthquakes in Asia. (WRONG)
- Governor Schwarzenegger will lose popularity and reelection. (WRONG)
- The 2008 presidential election will be between Kerry and McClain (*not wrong yet, but will be*)
- The U.S. will not invade Syria (*RIGHT, but that's pretty easy to predict*)

There were 32 issues, and she guessed right on less than 10%, with some of the hits being of questionable nature, like the immediate above.

Her predictions for the next century? Remodeling of face to duplicate any look. People will be able to walk out of their bodies at death. There will be no U.S. presidency, as the country will convert to a Green Senate structure. Tsunamis will wipe out a large portion of Japan. After 2050, the people will turn to spirituality. One planetary government. People will see and speak with deceased ones on the other side. Aliens will begin to appear. There are 40 predictions, and some of them actually make sense.

Her first husband, Gary Dufresne, was quoted in 2007 that Sylvia admitted she had no paranormal abilities, but that the gullibles deserve to be taken.[91] So why am I spending so much time on her? She talks about the afterlife. A lot of Americans believe in her and I worry about why they do.

**About Lenora Piper**

Deborah Blum wrote a book called ***Ghost Hunters: William James and the Search for Scientific Proof of Life after Death***, where a certain respectable Boston housewife, Lenora Piper, while a lot more wrong than right, nevertheless was able to show some unreal, perhaps even, otherworldly, talent.[34] ***The New York Times***, wrote two reviews about ***Ghost Hunters***: on August 14, 2006, by Patricia Cohen, and August 20, 2006, by Anthony Gottlieb.

Alfred Russel Wallace, Charles Darwin's natural selection co-presenter, during the mid-1800s, was particularly impressed with mediums, levitation and the like, which irritated Darwin no end, for he was fearful that the concept of evolution would thusly be tarnished. As a practitioner, you could even be part of high society then, as Daniel Dunglas Home kept duping the audience, and eventually married a goddaughter of the czar with novelist Alexander Dumas as his Best Man.

Yes, William was the brother of Henry, and with others, in 1882, formed the British Society for Psychical Research in an era when belief in the occult swept through Europe and America. The Society, while serious in their intent, did unmask a bunch of frauds, but, they generally wanted to believe. Their membership included Lord Alfred Tennyson, Lewis Carol, Mark Twain and William Crookes, future president of the British Association for the Advancement of Science and discoverer of thallium, chemical element 81, used as rat and ant poison. Skeptics wondered if thallium had a deleterious effect on Crooke's mind.

But, ah, Lenora Piper, who lived to a ripe old age of 93. She was usually wrong, but never truly debunked, although science writer Martin Gardner, who in 1992 wrote "How Mrs. Piper Bamboozled William James," was among the many cynics.

The situation was not unlike religion itself, for perfectly sane and respected scientists and solid citizens then believed in the range of paranormal phenomena. Many still do today, certainly the occult, but also religion and the afterlife. These all belong in the ***X-Files*** (*that Emmy winning TV series that lived on for a decade quenching the thirst for American believers of the occult and spirits*).

## Then, There is Richard Dawkins

Richard Dawkins is a British evolutionary biologist from Oxford and popular science writer, who because of his advocacy of natural selection and Darwin, has necessarily become a critic of organized religion and the reality of God, as earlier indicated. We must be around the same age, for he obtained his first college degree in zoology in 1962 when I gained mine for chemical engineering. He went on to a PhD and a DSci. He was referred to by Charles Simonyi (*who endowed the chair Dawkins holds at Oxford*) as Darwin's rottweiler, and is more popularly now known as the nearest thing to a professional atheist since Bertrand Russell. Dawkins is vitriolic in his comments on creationism and intelligent design, and hates religious dogma. Well, we have very similar views.

In the midst of writing this chapter I chanced to ask him how he could be so brave as to risk an Islamic fatwa or bullet from a crazed assassin, for he has an in your face style and tells it like he sees it, in a nice sort of way. His immediate response was that these potential threats just were not that important, and he doesn't let it bother him. Unfortunately, as I kept gently pressing him on this point, and wondered if he knew if Sam Harris (***The End of Faith**, a truly scathing treatment of Islam*) had any problems, he seemed to begin to become concerned, and somewhat muttered so. If he did, I should feel sorry for this. He did indicate that he knew of no fatwa on Harris, and that he has never had a life-threatening incident, or anything even remotely close. He had no bodyguard on our campus.

What this discussion did, however, was strengthen my resolve to not be so wishy washy and Pollyannaish about the future of religion. I strongly considered changing the Golden Evolution to the Golden Termination, but did not, for while the ultimate conclusion of the Golden Evolution could well be a termination, one simple solution could well blend the positives into an almost utopian answer for humanity.

Dawkins began to doubt at about the age of nine, same as me. He, though, was reconverted, but, at sixteen, learned of evolution, which began to lead him astray of religion, again. I have a sense that Darwin being British had at least a small amount of influence on his beliefs, for, in his lecture at the University of Hawaii in 2007, Dawkins showed a PowerPoint slide of the English 10 pound note with the face of guess who, when he commented that the American bills featured "In God We Trust."

My Bible of Atheism is, no doubt, ***The God Delusion***.[81] In sequence, I provide a sampling of his thoughts:

- While 95% of Americans would vote for a woman as President, and 92% for a black person, only 49% would consider an atheist (*pg. 4*).
- Albert Einstein is quoted to have said, "I do not believe in God" (*pg. 15*).
- The Templeton prize usually goes to a scientist who is prepared to say something nice about religion (*pg. 19*). Winners have included Charles Townes[237], John Polkinghorne (*2002*), Freeman Dyson (*2000*), Paul Davies (*1995*), Charles Colson (*1993, who served for President Nixon, and also served time in a federal prison for Watergate-related*

*crimes*), Aleksandr Solzhenitsyn (*1983*), Billy Graham (*1982*) and Mother Theresa (*1973, the year the award was first bestowed*).

- "The God of the Old Testament is arguably the most unpleasant character in all fiction: jealous and proud of it; a petty, unjust, unforgiving control-freak; a vindictive, bloodthirsty ethnic cleanser; a misogynist, homophobic, racist, infanticidal, genocidal, filicidal, pestilential, megalomaniacal, sadomasochistic, capriciously malevolent bully" (*pg. 31*).
- Why is the U.S., a secular government, the most religious Christian country, while the U.K., with an established church, among the least (*pg. 40*)?
- Thomas Jefferson said, "Christianity is the most perverted system that ever shone on man," and Benjamin Franklin remarked, "lighthouses are more useful than churches" (*pg. 43*). Abraham Lincoln also said, "The Bible is not my book nor Christianity my profession…[187]
- The four gospels (*Matthew, Mark, Luke and John*) made the current Bible more or less arbitrarily, from at least a dozen, including James, Thomas, Peter, Nicodemus, Philip, Bartholomew and Mary Magdalene (*pg. 95*).
- Regarding the 72 virgins to Muslim martyrs, the term "virgins" is a mistranslation of a type of white raisin (*pg. 96*). This simple mistake has probably been the cause of countless tragedies, including 9/11.
- Francis Collins, head of the Human Genome Project, is a theist, but a rarity among top scientists (*pg. 98*).
- Only 3.3% of Royal Society members agree with the statement that a personal god exists (*pg. 102, relative to the 5% of biological National Academy of Sciences members*).
- The higher one's intelligence or education level, the less one is likely to be religious (*pg. 103, and that intelligence parameter might well explain the low belief rate of National Academy members*).
- We do not need God in order to be good – or evil (*pg. 226*).

I had written most of this chapter before reading his books or meeting him, and had already included some of the above examples, so I deleted my statements and gave him the honor of citation.

### The Case for Lee Strobel

Having spent so much time on Richard Dawkins, I thought I would give some almost equal time to Lee Strobel, a journalist who saw the light later in life. From a legal editor for ***The Chicago Tribune*** and spiritual skeptic, he became an evangelical Christian. Like most, he kind of believed, until, at the age of 14, learning about the Stanley Miller experiment was a eureka moment for him, and he kicked God out of his life, somewhat similar to my life when a Buddhist priest could not name a second person who attained Nirvana. In ***The Case for the Creator***, I found his presentation particularly interesting because he provides some scientific facts somewhat reminiscent of my ***Book 1***.[307] His reading of Jonathan Wells' contempt for evolution steered Strobel towards believing in a Supreme Being, exactly in the opposite direction as my discussion with Richard Dawkins inspiring me to admit that I was, in reality, an atheist.

The premise of Strobel's argument is that, as the Universe in its present conformation is essentially an impossibility, then, it must have taken an intelligent designer to create it. He quotes an Oxford *(this campus seems steeped in religion, or the absence of it)* physicist, Roger Penrose, about the precision necessary for the Universe forming being the fraction of a number in the denominator so large that there are more zeroes than the number of elementary particles. Also from James Kastings (*Penn State University*) that the Moon is amazingly the right size in the exact orbit necessary to minimize Earth tilt, while providing perfect eclipses, as the Sun is 400 times larger than the Moon, but 400 times further away. We are the only known planet even close to this designed condition. How can this be an accident?

Well, Paul Doland, a vegetarian agnostic (*so indicated in his profile*) said to rank 5,575$^{th}$ among all Amazon.com reviewers, with 68 of them, reacted to ***The Case for the Creator*** with a 31 page critique: (*go to GOOGLE and type in Paul Dolan, Lee Strobel*):

- o This is just another in Strobel's Intelligent Design apologetic series ***(Cases for Christ, Easter,*** and ***Faith***).
- o While Strobel's PhD interviewees are credentialed, they represent a minority opinion relative to others in their scientific field.
- o If human life was created by God as his unique crowning glory, why did He bother to create the billions of other galaxies?
- o The mere ignorance about the origin of the Universe or abiogenesis does not justify a supernatural explanation.

## Neo Atheists

There is a softer, more humanistic, middle-ground within atheism. On one extreme is anti-theist Christopher Hitchens, who wants to banish God. At the other is Harvard Humanist Chaplin, Greg Epstein, who has zero belief in god or atheism, but nevertheless seeks the best in religion. He advocates being good and living well without god. While there is a lot to applaud in the clarity of atheist fundamentalist Hitchens, I feel more in tune with the humanistic atheism concept.

Yet, damned if you're vitriolic and damned if you're nice, for filmmaker Brian Flemming, in his movie, ***The God Who Wasn't There***—which included interviews with Dawkins and Harris, and is said to be the religion equivalent to fast foods and ***Supersize Me***— in his weblog published a comment by R. Joseph Hoffman (*Harvard graduate mentioned earlier with the Center for Inquiry in New York*) that Epstein was just a secular rabbi who has never published a book nor held a faculty position anywhere, who is shamelessly playing the prejudice card. Hoffman further stated that the Harvard Divinity School would be scandalized at the "cynical misappropriation of the University's national reputation as a way of bottling humanism."[103] He could have further added former lead singer of the rock band called Sugar Pill and the person who in 2007 presided over the "coming out" ceremony of Representative Pete Stark (*D-California*), the first member of Congress who acknowledged that he did not believe in

God. THE FIRST ONE TO DO THIS! But, then, Congressman Stark is 75 and has no plans to run for the Presidency.

A movie based on noted religious skeptic Philip Pullman's ***His Dark Materials*** is ***The Golden Compass*** (***TGC***), starring Nicole Kidman and Daniel Craig, which resulted in a boycott crusade by the Catholic League for Religious and Civil Rights, claiming the film was selling atheism to children. ***TGC*** provides the other side of the story from C.S. Lewis' ***The Chronicles of Narnia***, which now has a sequel, ***Prince Caspian***, as soon, too, will ***TGC***. Chances are, any child, and most adults, will, in their vicarious way, enjoy both series, and come away in much the same way as after seeing any Harry Potter, Lord of the Rings or Star Wars movie. But, now that I've told you that the Magisterium in ***TGC*** is the Catholic Church, that might change your viewpoint.

You can take oppositional stands, but this philosophical interface of Humanistic Muslims, Humanistic Christians, etc., call them Neo Atheists, who, while they don't believe in god, might well be the core to someday unite religion, for theirs is an embracing philosophy. Let me, thus, backtrack a step and now become a neo atheist. Our group might even partner with agnostics, who are skeptics and freethinkers, thus, open to sound logic. In combination, then, also with those who have lost faith and religious leaders who are willing to compromise and cooperate for long-term common good, there is something represented by these new atheists that can contribute to the Golden Evolution.

## Religion, on Balance, is Probably Good

Dawkins provides a reasonably good argument that religion and God, per se, do not make people good or bad. However, my gut sense, especially now that I am a neo atheist, is that religion, on balance, is good. Yes, there were the Crusades and the irritating problem in Northern Ireland, plus those Islamic extremists, but the world is a far, far better place because of the benefits of religion. I am troubled about the basic premises regarding God and the afterlife, and therefore the obvious dishonesty and immorality of it all, but religion has been one of the best social inventions of Man. Early in the development, much of this had to do with power and control, but the fact of the matter is that there are many more plusses going for religion than negatives.

Among the pros (*mostly culled from popular U.S. sources*):

- People who attend weekly religious services live 28% longer.[49]
- For black people, the difference could well be 14 years. Why? The religious tends to use less alcohol, tobacco and drugs, and feel a common bond, reducing life's stresses.
- Praying passes on the problem and stabilizes the psychology.[4] Duke University researchers reported that those 64 and older who attended weekly religious services were 46% less likely to die over a six year period than those who went less often[3].

The religious had lower blood pressures and healthier immune systems. All this is medically proven.

- o Teens who consider religious beliefs to be important are three times less likely to smoke or use alcohol and seven times less likely to use illicit drugs.[6]
- o Religious people are happier than those who are not.[279] After all, what is more important than genuine happiness?
- o If you are caught in a dire emergency, being religious gives you more hope. In the 2003 Bam Iranian earthquake which killed 43,000, a 97 year old woman was rescued after nine days under the rubble, and said that reciting the ***Koran*** kept her going.[7] Prayer, in general, has been well studied,[2] and has been validated as being helpful in affecting the condition of a patient. Then, again, other studies have shown contradictions. But, as for example, that obligatory exchange between the child and Santa Claus, where the parent hears or reads what is being requested, which by some miracle, many times ends up under the Christmas tree. In other words, by mouthing your problems through prayer or confession, someone might hear or overhear and do something to help. The Catholic Church has raised this type of personal communication to a particularly high level, reducing the mental stress placed on its flock and providing the Church with information to develop some useful personal and political response strategy measures.
- o There are religious books equating faith with weight loss,[283] fitness[340] and now, covering almost any subject you want on web logs, or blogs, and even podcasts.
- o Very religious people fear death the least.[278] This was deduced from a longitudinal (*meaning that subjects were followed over time*) study. I've long held this morbid concern that death results in eternal gloom. If I don't think about it, no problem. But I do, now and then.

Rushton Couborn has been quoted to say, "societies become weak when religious zeal weakens."[198] This was way back in 1969. Perhaps this is why we are the only dominant world power with considerable confidence since that period to save Vietnam, attack Grenada, start the Gulf War, eliminate the Taliban from Afghanistan and invade Iraq, twice, all by Republican presidents. Today, faith-based programs receive more than $2 billion from the Bush White House, and, generally with beneficial results.[29] Compared to Israel, Japan and France, Americans today still show all the signs of religious zeal. Plus, we are, maybe therefore, #1. I guess that must be good.

There is, though, a new study that suggests that religion does not produce healthier societies, and, in fact, might have just the opposite effect.[246] Higher rates of belief in and worship of a creator correlate with increasing incidencies of homicide, juvenile and early adult mortality, sexually transmitted disease infection rates, teen pregnancy and abortion. In other words, the more religious a country, the more dysfunctional the society. The question could not be answered whether religion causes dysfunction, or whether they just flourish in these socially disordered areas. So, maybe Richard Dawkins is right. I guess, like in medicine, contradictions abound.

A following section also delves into the economic implications of religion, and the signs are mostly positive. Church attendance provides financial advantages through relationship building.

Finally, whether they like it or not, churches have become the solution for the homeless problem, or should. The space is not used at night and the membership generally wants to do well. A well-organized community effort, moving these dispossessed to the religious "home" of their choice, will spread the predicament, provide contacts with caring members and furnish a second chance. There will be problems, of course—for the homeless are just that because they are on drugs and have a high incidence of dysfunctional characteristics—but, certainly, there should be solutions. Military bases, public schools and other concerns with capabilities, land and a roof to offer should be part of the team, of course, but churches are best. The problem is that most churches are still looking the other way. In time, success stories around the world will galvanize religion to work with government and industry to help solve the homeless problem.

## On the Matter of Faith

The crux of the issue is faith, which is true belief. ***The Harper Collins Dictionary of Religion*** defines faith as the act or virtue or spiritual disposition by which people accept the reality, promises, and love of God. The ***Flip Dictionary*** provides a one word definition for "a person without faith": agnostic.

***Surprised by Faith***[32] by Don Bierle, is about a scientist who shares his personal discoveries about God, ***The Bible*** and personal fulfillment. Can I Believe the Bible and What is the Bottom Line are typical chapter headings. This publication is typical of many that sell relatively well for those who need psychological assurance about religion.

A particularly relevant publication on faith is ***The End of Faith***, by Sam Harris,[132] where, provided is a logical series of arguments portraying the end of religion as we know it. Harris cites that the sacred dimension could well be the purpose of human life. Yet, he indicates that religious belief has a fatal flaw: one can only believe in one God, and only mine. Religion, furthermore, is the modern day equivalent of alchemy. He wonders why so many people can believe in obviously obsolete dogmas. I do, too.

When I originally read this Harris publication, I thought he was just another philosophical type author. It turns out that, at this writing, he is a doctoral candidate at UCLA on his way to a PhD in neuroscience. He is tracking belief and disbelief in the brain using a functional magnetic resonance imager. Someday, he might actually develop a scientific theory of faith.

A few examples of how a lack of faith can compromise your life:

- There have been other faith skeptics: Copernicus, Galileo, Darwin and Ramee Abdul Rahman Muhammad. Who? He is that Afghan who converted from Islam to

Christianity in 1990, but was arrested and threatened with the death penalty in 2006. However, there was sufficient world-wide indignation that the Afghanistan government released him by court action either for his being mentally unfit or for their having a lack of information, and shipped him, his pregnant second wife and children off to Italy, for Pope Benedict XVI had asked that he be spared.[355] The moral of this story? Be careful of a vengeful divorced wife during a child custody battle.

- Lina Joy, born Azlina Jailani in the mid-60's to Muslim parents, became a Christian. She wanted her government identity card to recognize this change. The Federal Court, however, ruled that only the Islamic Shariah Court had that power. She has not taken that step because apostasy is a crime punishable by fines and jail in her country, Malaysia, and is contemplating emigration, for she has been disowned by her family, abandoned by her friends and is in hiding.
- Also, too, there is the voice of Wafa Sultan, who once was Muslim, but not anymore, speaking in Arabic and English via Al Jazeera, criticizing Islam as violent and beyond repair.[339] When she lived in Syria 27 years ago, she walked away from her faith when she witnessed the murder of her professor by members of the Muslim Brotherhood. Good thing she is now living in Southern California, for she would get the Abdul treatment back in the Middle East. She contributes to the website www.annaqed.com.
- Say you're teaching an elementary school class. The semester theme happened to be bears. So, you buy a teddy bear and ask the class to pick a name for this mascot. A student named Muhammad suggested his name, and 20 out of 23 in the class agreed. Each student took Muhammad, the toy bear, home, then wrote a diary entry reporting on the experience. The stories were compiled in a book and entitled, "My Name is Muhammad." Several parents complained, and, incredibly, Gillian Gibbons, the teacher, was arrested and faced six months in jail and 40 lashes, plus a fine. But this was in the Sudan, where 70% are Muslims. Ms. Gibbons was convicted, but "got off" with fifteen days of jail and deportation. Some lesson, of course, had to be taught about not being blasphemous. A well-orchestrated protest followed in Khartoum, calling for her death, by sword or firing squad, with her effigy burned at Martyrs Square.
- The shock of 2007 was Agnes Bojaxhiu, born in Macedonia, a Roman Catholic nun, who became Mother Teresa. She represented the ultimate in sacrifice for God. It came to light in ***Mother Teresa: Come Be My Light*** (*Doubleday, 2007*), that, over a 66 year period, she expressed deep spiritual pain, effectively abandoning faith. One can only speculate on what percent of religious leaders truly believe, but guess that the proportion might not be very high.

They say science can't measure faith or love. Not so. Magnetic resonance imaging (*MRI*) of the brain can detect quantifiable love responses of subjects who describe themselves as being madly in love.[372] The source of all this activity is in distinct areas of the brain. Love is a lateralized brain function, like speech. Arthur Aron, *et al*, published in the ***Journal of Neurophysiology***[18] that functional MRI measurements support their two major predictions:[215] early stage, intense romantic love, is associated with sub cortical reward regions rich in dopamine, and romantic love engages brain systems associated with motivation to acquire a reward.[237] A similar tracing could probably be accomplished for faith, as that same Sam Harris (*previously a philosopher*), now pursuing a doctorate in neuroscience, is doing at UCLA.

But is scientific proof for faith or love significant? Yes, in that science can, indeed, measure profound human emotions. But what has that got to do with the afterlife? Everything! There are some things science will not ever measure, particularly if there is nothing to measure. Go to the Randi test. One of them could well be the afterlife. So, with high probability, the major leap in logic can be made that there is, thus, no afterlife. Certainly, no Creator, no God. God never died, he never even existed.

## What About Miracles?

Most religions feature miracles, especially the Christian ones. In fact, C.S. Lewis has been quoted to say that without miracles there cannot be Christianity.[186] What is a miracle? Merriam and Webster[200] say, "an extraordinary event manifesting divine intervention in human affairs." In many, some scientific law of nature is seemingly being violated, and, therefore, if this "something" actually happened, we should be able to explain why. The incident is a lot more difficult to resolve if it happened two millennia ago.

If an individual with cancer of the liver is given three months to live, but completely recovers, is that a miracle? No doubt yes for a very religious person who knows that his family and friends prayed a lot for his recovery. However, any body, now and then, can cure itself. In my definition, this was not a miracle. Some people are luckier than or genetically superior to others.

### Some Modern Miracles

Just to gauge some reaction as to how many get this far in this book, I have a miracle to suggest. About a year and a half ago, I bought a Schick Quattro razor and wanted to find out how long one razor set would last. A year went by, and my somewhat crudded up system still worked. So, to substantiate the first test, eight months ago, I went out and purchased a Schick Quattro Titanium package, where, if you tried to look behind the razor, you would have sworn that a full complement of 6 new blade-sets would have come as part of the $14 cost. It turns out that only one extra was included, with five blank spaces, but that is marketing for you. However, that was inconsequential, for, while the blue Teflon sheet has peeled off, the razor still worked. Same as the first trial. I got intrigued and went to *Google*. The consensus is that Schick Quattro works for about a month before you need to change the blades. But, they most probably gave up because their eyes told them it was about time to put in a new one. Or, by force of habit.

Gillette, controlling 70% of the market, was purchased by Proctor and Gamble for $54 billion in 2005, sued Schick, which itself was bought by Energizer (*the Bunny*) Holdings for $930 million in 2003, for this four-bladed product. The suit never went anywhere, but these two companies have been squabbling for about a century now for the $1.7 billion/year shaving counter. They also compete on the $2.5 billion/year battery market (*Energizer versus Duracell*).

Anyway, what I'm getting to is that it appears that these razors seem to work forever. That is a miracle! I have a traveling razor with two blades. I think it came from a hotel in Japan. After a year of meandering, the system still works. What is going on? What would happen if everyone suddenly realizes that they don't need to regularly change blades and, thus, stops buying replacements? Will a Gillette share still be worth $54? Now that would be another miracle. I can already imagine, though, some manufactured obsolescence entering the picture. Too bad!

Then, the week I was about to submit this manuscript to my publisher, late at night, I happen to see an infomercial ad for Infinity Razor, "the last razor you will ever buy." For $19.95 you get two razors with double-edges and a fogless mirror, although other ads are known to only ask for $9.95. I checked with infomercialratings.com and infomercialscams.com and saw mostly angry responses on how terrible the product was. Funny, but the first time I used my Schick, I had the same reaction. The shave was so bad that I was set to ditch the razor, but, then, I changed the angle of movement, and I've now been using the same two for almost two years.

A true miracle is that urban legend: a bar of soap between the bedsheets will prevent leg cramps.[201] There is something about getting older and lying horizontal. My wife and I, now and then, no, make it frequently, used to suffer from painful cramps. That bar was placed a few months ago, and, amazingly, no leg cramps. I try to position the unwrapped soap—but under the sheet—at our feet about midway in the bed. Just the act of doing this with my toes in the past would have induced cramps. Ann Landers a long time ago mentioned this solution, and so do some doctors. What is the explanation? No one knows. There is no scientific proof. But it works. It's a puzzlement, or miracle. Maybe there is a God. Hopefully, this crack in rationality will lead me to an afterlife.

The University of Hawaii football team experienced a miracle in 2007. For the first time in history, it went undefeated, and was the only major one to do this that year. There are even religious implications, for the front page of the December 24 issue of ***The Honolulu Advertiser*** article written by Michael Tsai was entitled "Their Spirit Carries Them," extending through much of page two. From Coach June Jones to leaders of the team, terms like salvation, glory, savior and believe permeated the story and season. Well, they were trounced in the 2008 Sugar Bowl by Georgia, but many miracles do come to an end, for Coach Jones left for SMU and the entire state went into depression. But then, a hopeful miracle II: new Coach Greg MacMackin.

Why did I bother to write about shaving, soap and football? First, I just thought those were interesting stories worthy of sharing, not to be sacrilegious, but to see if I can get any reaction to this book. Again, don't sue me if the two suggestions don't work for you. These are not like doctors recommending the fentanyl pain patch, which has reportedly resulted in hundreds of deaths. I'm merely transferring non-lethal personal advice that approaches miracle status.

In the EPILOGUE, ABC broadcaster Al Michaels is quoted to have asked, "Do you believe in miracles?" He responded himself, "yes!" That was the 1980 Winter Olympics hockey victory of the USA over the Soviet Union. The later discussion goes on to suggest that this triumph could well have been the one most important contribution to ending the Cold War and possible thermonuclear annihilation. But was God responsible for this miracle? No, but perhaps one mortal doing the right thing at the right time.

**Biblical Miracles**

What is a great big miracle? What about Moses (*born as Moshe*) parting the Red Sea? First of all, recent publications have trashed the notion that there ever was an Exodus or a Moses. The whole thing seems illogical and historically empty. But, for the sake of analysis, let's say there was the Exodus of 1628 B.C. or 1446 B.C. or 13th century B.C...scholars are still not sure when this occurred. One story is that Moses was born around 1392 B.C., lived to the age of 120 and died just before his people crossed the Jordan River. Here were more than 7,000 Israelites...or was that 603,550...or, maybe, 3 million, escaping the Egyptian army and roaming for more than 40 years. An ABC four hour TV special in April of 2006 on ***The Ten Commandments*** showed what appeared to be only a cast of hundreds, so the 3 million figure must have been considered to be an exaggeration by the program writers because computer simulations can place any number, anywhere on the screen these days. The other disappointments in this latest version were the depiction of standard miracles: walking sticks turning into snakes and, yes, that burning bush that talked. The logistics involved with moving, feeding, housing and maintaining the spirit of this group, through mostly deserts and mountains, were at least an equal miracle, if it happened at all. However, the parting of the Red Sea seems to capture the imagination of biblical experts and painters, so, I've compiled some of the best explanations:

- God.
- The crossing was metaphorical, that is, it did not really physically happen.
- Ah, it was not the Red Sea, but the nearby Sea of Reeds, or Reed Sea, a shallow swamp.
- The great volcanic eruption of Santorini, which is radiocarbon dated to have occurred in 1628/7 B.C., resulted in a 660-foot mega-tsunami, opening up a temporary gap and fortuitously providing a channel for passage, while also explaining all those plagues.[39]
- Doron Nof and Nathan Paldor in 1992 published a theory suggesting that the crossing was in the relatively shallow Gulf of Suez, where gale force winds pushed the waters, lowering the water level by eight feet, creating a passable alley.[197]
- Naum Voltsinger in 2004 reinforced the Nof/Paldor water level setdown concept.[234]

And the winner is...you decide. I'm leaning towards the Sea of Reeds because, as coincidental as that mega-tsunami (*see Chapter 6 in **Book 1***) was, I can't imagine 600,000 or so quickly traversing 15 miles of muck before the big waves came crashing back. Also, the big wind theory provides huge disbelief, for the scientific analogy was a sloshing of a giant bathtub, again not leaving sufficient time for such a mob to cross even the narrowest part of the Gulf of Suez.

Let's next look at one of the more fateful days for Jesus, when he walked on water and fed 5,000 with five loaves of barley bread and two fish. These events took place on the same night on the banks of the Sea of Galilee in probably what is now Syria. John the Baptist had just been executed by King Herod. Facing his followers, Jesus asked out aloud for God to bless the bread and fish and whatever else anyone might have with them. No, this third part is never reported, but, at worst, it must have been implied. At the end of the meal, there were supposedly twelve baskets of leftovers. What's the miracle? People shared. Some would call that a miracle.

Later into the early morning, the Sea was misty, as it supposedly normally is, and the only three people who saw him walk on water were his disciples: Matthew, Mark and John (*the Apostle*). Mind you, those 5,000 followers did not witness this miracle. Written decades after the event, these three had totally conflicting stories of what in actuality happened, which leads to the more sensible reality that Jesus was probably walking along the banks of the sea and appeared to be walking on water. No miracle here.

Yet, Doron Nof of Florida State University, a respected oceanography professor who in 2005 was awarded the Nansen Medal for his fundamental contributions towards ocean research, and his colleagues, including Nathan Palador, returned in 2006 to announce in the ***Journal of Paleolimnology*** that Jesus could very well have been walking on ice.[65] Surely enough, there was a cold period around the time of Christ, where sufficiently freezing temperatures did occur. The team speculated that Lake Kinnerat (*the name today for the Sea of Galilee*) could have formed ice every 30 to 60 years.[89]

Finally, you all have seen magic acts. Some of them are amazing. However, once you are taught how they are pulled off, the exploits become trivial. Analogously, we just don't happen to know sufficient details about miracles. Given all the facts, miracles generally vanish. But what else can the Church offer if not the supernatural?

If I seem skeptical of these hypothetical episodes as real miracles, I am not alone. Benedict Spinoza *(1632 to 1677*) said miracles were impossible, David Hume (*1711-1776*) wrote miracles cannot be imagined, and Immanuel Kant (*1724 to 1804*) contended that miracles never occurred, all with carefully philosophized logic.[116] Me, I just read the listed references.

## On the Matter of a Fatwa

I'm at least mildly concerned about how followers of the Islamic religion might react to this book. The fatwa placed on Salman Rushdie and the harsh reaction to the Danish ***Jyllands-Posten*** Muhammad cartoons, which were supposedly an attempt to contribute to the debate regarding criticism of Islam and self-censorship, can be cited. In this day of the internet, any dedicated fanatic could well file a fatwa, and my life would change.

I have, thus, come up with ten reasons why, in the reasoned judgment of a potential fatwaer, I should be ignored or excused:

- o There are no serious Islamic insults portrayed in any of my statements, but if in your interpretation I have, I am willing to make acceptable adjustments. Please contact me (*ptakahas@hotmail.com*).
- o Nowhere do I say anything particularly sacrilegious about Muhammad.
- o With respect, I have treated Islam with, perhaps, more scholarly perseverance than some of the other religions.
- o As an example, re-read the section comparing Santa Claus with the Christian God.
- o What might be taken as sarcasm is actually general innocence or ignorance, not an excuse, but, nevertheless, a sincere attempt to portray seeming reality.
- o However, while I have mostly been non-religious throughout my adult life, I have been searching, and my recent conversion to neo atheism could well be just another temporary phase.
- o In fact, I remain willing to honestly listen to any compelling arguments that insure for a glorious next life.
- o Before passing judgment on me, any prospective terminator should first read ***The End of Faith*** and ***Letter to a Christian Nation*** by Sam Harris, a fellow alumnus from Stanford University, and someone I look forward to meeting someday.
- o Having done so, and not yet side-tracked, certainly go to ***The God Delusion*** of Richard Dawkins.
- o If that failed, try Christopher Hitchens, ***God is Not Great [GING]***. The subtitle is "How Religion Poisons Everything."
- o Still committed? Have you considered President of the USA George W. Bush?

Yes, just including the above is a kind of sacrilege in itself, but that is in keeping with the tenor of the entire book, which is to maximize happiness. Laughs help.

While there are no Buddhist fatwas or Christian ones, in any hypothetical grouping throughout society there is that unpredictable 1% who might strike for what might be a purely personal and rational reason. For those who happen to fall in this broad category, before taking unnecessary action, send me an e-mail first. Perhaps we can work it out to your satisfaction.

## There is that Delicate Other Immorality Matter

Other sections have or will consider many of the personnel, economic and non-sexual morality issues facing all churches. In particular, the sexual abuse cases distressing the Roman Catholic Church, must to be resolved. It is said that 95% of the 194 American Catholic dioceses have been accused.[108] Not only is this act with children a mortal sin, but also a serious breach of secular law. Equally deplorable has been the shameful manner in which the church hierarchy has dealt with this long-standing tragedy. The vital matter of trust is at stake, maybe more important than the financial liabilities, which are becoming severe. Reportedly, American churches have paid off well more than $1 billion for these cases, as in July of 2007, the Los Angeles archdiocese alone agreed on a $660 million settlement for 500-plus sexually abused plaintiffs. However, no amount of money can make up for the shattered trust. Churches in

Oregon, Washington, Arizona, California and Iowa have filed for Chapter 11 protection or bankruptcy to avoid payments.

Rev. Thomas P. Doyle, a lawyer, twenty years ago warned the Vatican about the scandal to come involving children and sexual abuse by priests. After working with 2,000 victims, he co-authored a book called ***Sex, Priests and Secret Codes***.[318, 320] Doyle's efforts sufficiently irritated the Church that they were influential in his being fired as chaplain only months before his retirement from the Air Force.

First, the problem is not limited to the Catholic Church. Second, it is not an American phenomenon. Third, this has been happening not only since 1984, when the matter came to light, but for millennia. The subheading for the above book is: The "Catholic Church's 2,000 Year Paper Trail of Sexual Abuse."

There was a period early in my life when I, somehow, got talked into participating in a few catechism sessions by a friend. I noticed a somewhat uncomfortable relationship between this person and the priest teaching the course. Nearly a decade later, when we bumped into each other, he was suffering from AIDS, and I, while this is quite a stretch, could only blame the Church for initiating him in his youthful liaison. It is possible, of course, that the interest was mutual, but the trust-authority position of the priest made this indiscretion totally wrong, if it happened.

People tend to gravitate into lifetime positions influenced by personal priorities. For some it is money; others, security; and a few, illegitimate sexual proclivities. It has long been known that the Catholic Church, in particular, virtually condoned this practice. Thus, those with these tendencies would tend to gravitate into this profession. In a not too dissimilar situation, particular fields of entertainment, fashion and even the airline industry, draw certain elements, although much of these activities are generally legal, for children are not involved.

Part of the problem with religion is the attitude towards women. Catholic priests, for example, can only be male, and they are supposed to be unmarried. In the early days, celibacy was not a requirement. By 300A.D. a priest could be married, but had to abstain from sex with his wife. In 1139, mandatory celibacy was imposed.

In 2005, the Center for the Study of Religious Issues published ***The Bingo Report***, linking sexual abuse to celibacy in the priesthood. The scary conclusion is that the longer he remains in service to the Lord, the more likely he will act on his struggles and become deviant or criminal in his actions.[154] Wow, that is kind of condemning!

The problem, too, is the Church. In 1962, through a CONFIDENTIAL Instruction, the Vatican told bishops to cover up sexual abuse.[371] This 69-page document was sent by Pope John XXIII to every bishop in the world in "strictest secrecy."[25] In May 2001, Cardinal Ratzinger, now Pope Benedict, sent a reminder letter to all bishops stating that the 1962 instruction was still in force.

The solution is simple. For the Catholic Church, the Pope needs to accept responsibility, and through his intermediaries, work with laity to once and for all cure this horrific problem. The financial burden will be onerous, but the flock will respond. Short of coming clean and taking action, this practice will continue to haunt the Church.

In the Muslim world, there have been several hundred complaints of sexual assaults against young boys studying in Quaranic schools known as madrassas. There are 10,000 of them with a million students in Pakistan, so the numbers are not staggering, but possibly because very little is discussed. In Bangladesh, where girl students are permitted, there have been reports of teachers raping female students. In 2002, the Irish Church in Dublin provided $128 million in compensation to the victims of childhood abuse. These are just examples of a world-wide and historical problem. The traditional church conspiracy of silence and veil of secrecy appear to finally be coming to an end. Will other similarly obsolete and indefensible practices also soon be sacrificed?

## The Economic Implications of Religion

Churches are not taxed much. Any income they derive is not taxable. Property associated with charitable purposes cannot be taxed. While any land utilized for profitable enterprises are taxed, the influence churches can have on politics and business can be significant just because they own so much prime land. Further, in the U.S. alone, the Internal Revenue Service reports that Americans took tax exemptions for nearly $100 billion in religious donations.

The financial health of churches, of course, is being challenged by those abuse suits just mentioned. In other ways, the decline of religion is definitely occurring. In the U.S., the Catholic Church is finding difficulty recruiting and keeping nuns (*180,000 in 1965, less than 70,000 today, with many older than 70*) and priests. There are companies in trouble with the law on their pensions. The financial shortfall for retirees of all orders will be $20 billion by 2023.[232] Financially, this is could well be a more significant issue for churches than sexual abuse.

Hospitals run by churches are transferring ownership, for the cheap management and labor used for operations is diminishing. Land values are growing, making church/hospital property attractive for development, and certainly, more prone for dual use.

During the past half century, church attendance in the U.S. has dropped from about half to one-third. Between 1989 and 2004, the Catholic Church in Northern Ireland saw a drop in attendance from 90% to 62%.[324] From TruthBook Religious News Blog (truthbook.com/news/2003/_10_01_archive.html):

- o A City University of New York survey undertaken in 1991 showed that Americans who picked "no religion" had doubled over the past decade, and stood at third place behind Catholics and Baptists.
- o 71% of Americans believe in the devil, a 7% rise in five years. What??

- o Republicans are more likely to believe in God than Democrats, but Democrats are inclined towards astrology, reincarnation, ghosts and UFOs.

As a result, churches have gone high tech, embraced business principles and are into marketing, following on the heels of the evangelicals. One convincing fact carefully administered is the apparent survey result by Jonathan Gruber, an economist from MIT, that someone's income can rise 10% by doubling personal church attendance.[128] But the idea that religion can bring material advantages is the basis of the Protestant work ethic laid out a hundred years ago by Max Weber. Gruber posits that church attendance yields "social capital", building a web of relationships that fosters trust. Churches, further, offer a kind of mutual emotional and financial insurance. Finally, belief in Jesus, or his equivalent, can reduce mental stress, allowing for a higher focus on the opportunities for financial gain.

Mega-churches have also blossomed, providing total service seven days a week, from dawn to dusk, and these complexes also house banks, drug stores and schools. They help with real estate needs, medical-lending equipment, and personal counseling. Some of them show a weekly attendance of 30,000 and include entertainers like Randy Travis and skate-boarders jumping over a fire to illustrate salvation.

Shifting from churches to the matter of death itself, there are also changing financial implications. On the pure economic quasi-religious front, there was a time when the funeral industry fought Costco, Chinese imports and the federal government to maintain "fair"—meaning the highest possible—prices for caskets. It now turns out that there is an even bigger problem.

The Cremation Association of North America reports a clear growth, for rates were at only 6% in 1975, increasing to 28% in 2000, with an expectation of cremation being the burial of choice for 43% of Americans in 2025. While these urns today generally are stored in crematoria or like a casket in the earth, so a headstone and the traditional visiting process can be honored, more and more, simple wakes even without a priest, seem to be a growing trend. Then the cremated remains are placed in an attractive covered vase, which can be purchased at Wal-Mart's or Ross's, is then kept at home to show evidence of some close respect. More and more, too, the ashes are just carefully and gloriously released into the environment, as religion itself is facing the dust to dust syndrome. This residual feeling will carry on for generations, but the overall drift, because of economics and general non-belief, will show a continuous slide.

As a result, funeral plans, mortuary firms, casket manufacturers and churches will financially suffer. The typical traditional funeral, with casket, has a cost in the range of $10,000. While the grief factor will maintain some strength for maybe another generation, with higher disbelief will almost surely come this glide towards non-traditional (*dumping the ashes*) methods of honoring the dead.

The financial implications towards religion in general will need to be a high priority matter for those involved with the Golden Revolution. More than the economic aspects of this issue, though, will be the necessity to deal with the very foundation of religion itself.

In most ways, an argument can be made that we miss the whole point of religion when we attempt to attach a monetary value to its existence. Where would civilization be today if not for religion? Could the societies of the past endured and progressed without the partner that was God? If God was not created by Man at the beginning of thought, would be we here today? Well, my simple solution is yes, but the fact of the matter is that He was crucial to our presence today, and how best now to deal with Him without the crutch of an afterlife and the advent of a stronger case for evolution?

## The Future of Graveyards

So how can churches respond to the financial challenge? As cremation will soon overtake burial as the safekeeping technique of convenience, the logical next step will be storage of a small portion of your body which can someday be cloned to reproduce you. While cryogenic safekeeping would probably be best, it should not take much to keep a cubic centimeter of bone marrow, drop of blood or piece of your skin. Further, some technique will be devised at low energy and maintenance expense to preserve your DNA/RNA specimen, making the repository even more efficient.

Remember Michael Crichton, who was the villainous author of ***State of Fear*** in ***Book 1***? Well, he also wrote ***Jurassic Park***. Recall that the blood of a dinosaur, sucked by a mosquito, which happened to be enveloped in amber, kept for a million years at room temperature, became the viable fluid biologically useful to clone the beast. Well, that was an exaggeration of reality, but Japanese and Russian scientists are now in the process of cloning a woolly mammoth using this technique. At least the storage need not be for an infinitely long period, as it will just be a matter of a few decades before science should be able to perfect this process.

There will be fly by night outfits to take your money, but the potential of a credible business succeeding around the world will happen, and soon. What organization already into searching for roots has the reliability, managerial ability, international roots and entrepreneurial capability to capture the marketplace? This "company" would need to have been around for a long time, having endured controversy, but nevertheless remain thriving. The answer, to me, is clear...the **Mormon Church**. What better way, also, of gaining new members? Already, Ancestry.com is taking cheek-swiped cotton swab and $200 to add DNA to your family tree. Yes, Sorenson Genomics, the firm doing the work, is headquartered in Utah.

All their temples will add a repository, which no doubt will resemble a mini crystal palace. The setting will be a comfortable purgatory where the visitor can punch in a code to electronically view a video of the person at rest. Flowers? No. People feel compelled to leave a remembrance at the headstone, so the Church will suggest a small donation instead. The opportunity will be utilized to provide just the right message for you to experience what the Church might offer you.

As the average funeral in the U.S. today costs $6500,[75] and the price tag of sustaining this new enterprise, with amortization and all other costs calculated over the lifetime of the effort should be less than 1% of that expense (*my guess*), a simple one time charge of $1000 will be a financial and recruiting windfall for the Church. Analyzing the long-term total benefits, the future value of tithing, for example, a seeming lost leader charge of FREE, might even be considered. Each year, about 1% of the world population dies. Thus the potential exists for the Church to add 70 million new specimens each year. Every society honors the dead in some respectful manner. If the charge is to be free to secure your loved one, with the additional prospect of perhaps a resurrection someday, oh my, the practice should become universal.

Several billion bodies are already in the ground, and another billion or so as dust in urns. Most of these, while now essentially useless as cloning prospects, nevertheless can be transferred to these Mormon temples to keep the family together.

Now, all this sounds much too sacrilegious and sardonic. But if not the Mormon Church, then perhaps the Mayo Clinic or Rockefeller Foundation or some other organization with the sincere interest and means to carry out this ghoulish imperative for a profit, even. Perhaps every church can participate in some small way. This simple solution would make available land for other uses, reduce the cost of death and make it more convenient and comfortable to visit those who have passed on. Of course, most will merely do this at home through the internet. Amen.

## Religion and Politics in the United States

While the United States has since its founding separated church from state, the election process is deeply influenced by religion. Clearly, the Democrats regained control of the White House and Congress because they neutralized religion in politics by using a trump car, the Iraq War. This is the simple solution and a personal opinion shaped by the Pew Forum on Religion and Public Life 2005 survey on the subject of religion in politics in the United States.[189] The Pew Charitable Trusts fund the Pew Research Center, and while the Foundation was founded by Sun Oil money, sentiment is now mostly liberal. The Pew Foundation's entire executive office is reportedly run by women.[88] Notwithstanding, I think their survey report makes a lot sense.

From this publication, it is no surprise that 44% of the American public thinks that liberals who are not religious have too much control of the Democratic Party, while about the same percentage says that religious conservatives have too much influence over the Republican Party. About half feels that Republicans protect religious freedoms (*versus 28% for Democrats*) and half that Democrats protect individual freedom (*versus 30% for Republicans*). There is thus a definite sense: Republicans for Church, Democrats for the People. Social programs are not enough.

Thus, getting elected in America, a country where, according to this survey, 78% say God created life on Earth, means you must do something about this belief gap. It would be impossible to quickly modify the family structure or teach some higher sense of reality in an educational system which seems to have no influence anyway, so how do you contend with the current public impression where 59% see Republicans as friendly to religion, with the figure for Democrats being 29%?

In a 2007 Gallup poll asking Americans how they would vote on the presidency with candidates having the following religious faith:[159]

- o Catholic 95%
- o Black 94%
- o Jewish 92%
- o Woman 88%
- o Mormon 72%
- o Atheist 45%

An atheist came in last, that is, only 45% of Americans would even think about voting for an atheist. Now you know why Congressman Stark was the first member to say that he did not believe in a god.

Beliefnet, in partnership with ***Time*** magazine, has a web page featuring the God-o-Meter (*www.beliefnet.com/godometer*). Presidential candidates are rated, with ten being perfect (*Mike Huckabee, former Baptist minister, is a 10*) and Barack Obama and Hillary Clinton safely maintain a rating in the range of 8. Interestingly enough, Mit Romney now and then drops below 5 because Beliefnet seems somewhat conservative in philosophy, and I'm not sure if a Mormon meets their test. An atheist would score a 0. Huckabee, former governor of Arkansas, believes in God, but not in evolution.

Read the book: ***How the Republicans Stole Christmas: The Republican Party's Declared Monopoly on Religion and What Democrats Can Do to Take it Back***. The author, Bill Press, says that Democrats are uncomfortable talking about God. Plus, Republicans simply ask, do you want to stop abortion and gay marriage? Most Americans do. They vote Republican. They voted for George W. Bush. Democrats might ask, picture God, or Jesus. Would he be a caring liberal Democrat or a grabbing Republican ultra conservative? There surely must be a marketing plan being refined on this theme, as the Iraq War is soon to be over.

There are 6 to 7 million Muslims living in the U.S. There are 535 members in the U.S. Congress. One is now a Muslim, and he was only recently elected. On a per capita basis, this number should be around 10 members. The problem, of course, is that Muslims tend to be scattered across the Nation and have not yet attained any critical voting mass status. Ethnicity and religion are dominant factors in the election process.

The 2008 presidential elections provide an apt platform for diversity. All Republican candidates are White, Christian and male, even Mormon Mitt Romney. The Democrats have a rare gender (*female*) and ethnic (*Black-White and Spanish*) mix. The U.S. has never had a female nor black president. One of these two will most likely become the next President of the United States of America. But no avowed atheists have been announced, although in an early debate, three Republican hopefuls admitted that they don't believe in evolution: Senator Sam Brownback of Kansas, Governor Mike Huckabee of Arkansas and Representative Tom Tancredo of Colorado. Frighteningly, from my perspective, there was potential for one of these politicians to lead the country.

## More Readings on God and the Afterlife

Compared to 2003, consumer spending in the U.S. on books increased 3.4% in 2004. However, during this same period, there was a 17.3% increase in religious books, which, accounted for most of the change[77].

Tippler's ***TPOI*** provided partial differential equations to prove the existence of the afterlife. George Hammond in 1997 "accidentally discovered scientific proof of God (*SPOG*)," and, as a by-product, also "confirmed the entire theology of Christian Science (*proof-of-god.freewebsitehosting.com*)." A simple equation: GOD = GUV. No advanced calculus. Also provided is a "God Test," with a warning: there is very little chance that you can comprehend the scientific proof of God if you can't answer at least half of them. There are all kinds.

Scientology is a particularly today topic. Just ask Tom Cruise, John Travolta and 8 million followers in 154 countries. Founded by the very controversial L. Ron Hubbard in 1950, you can purchase a used copy of ***Dianetics: The Modern Science of Mental Health***, for as low as $1.48 on Amazon.com. Of course, you can get free Bibles. Sociologist David Bromley of Virginia Commonwealth University says[377] that "Scientology is a 'quasi-religious therapy' that resembles Freudian 'depth psychology' while also drawing upon Buddhism, Hindus, and the ancient, heretical offshoot of Christianity known as Gnosticism." One controversy is that the therapy sessions could end up costing hundreds of thousands of dollars to reach a kind of Nirvana, called Clear. Belgium and Germany might put the Church of Scientology on trial for extortion and fraud. They could well then be labeled a criminal organization.

***God, a Biography***[202] by Jack Miles, a Pulitzer Prize national bestseller, cited as "A tour de force....of the character God," by The New York Times Book Review, is, well, a biography of God. At the end, one can't help wondering how valuable the experience was. Was there anything particularly reinforcing? Historically relevant, yes. Gracefully written, yes. Am I now convinced? No.

***Searching for God in America***[139] by Hugh Hewitt reports on his conversations with people like His Holiness the XIV and the Dalai Lama of Tibet, then extracts tidbits from events (*Mayflower Compact*), dignitaries (*Thomas Jefferson, John F. Kennedy, Muhammad Ali*) and authors (*Mark Twain, Isaac Asimov*), and ends with a number of three minute sermons and songs. Quite an achievement, actually, and, maybe, symptomatic of the very high belief rate of Americans. Does it add to the body of evidence that there is a God? No, but that is true with all other publications of this type.

Francis S. Collins, director of the National Human Genome Research Center, wrote ***The Language of God: A Scientist Presents Evidence for Belief***, and is noteworthy because he is one of the very few reputable bioscientists who believes in God. Perhaps his home schooling in the Shenandoah Valley of Virginia provided some basis for his views. He uses the term BioLogos instead of Theistic Evolution to explain why scientific discoveries about our universe do not conflict with the existence of God. He does believe in evolution, but is not convincing in his attempt to reconcile science with religion.

The ***Left Behind*** series by Jerry B. Jenkins and Tim LaHaye sells because people who believe in God many times adhere to a cataclysmic ending to this all. The Armageddon and the Apocalypse, whether in the book title, or as a theme, this eschatological finality from the ***Book of Daniel, The Revelations***, and their like, serve as symbols leading, ironically, to an afterlife, for this offers an escape from doom. I can almost identify with that. ***Publishers Weekly*** calls it "the most successful Christian-fiction series ever." Maybe a bit of redundancy, though, in adding fiction to Christian. But can science aid the critic and/or reinforce the wishes of the believer?

As the afterlife is so crucial to the logic of this chapter, I must include the works of Elizabeth Kubler-Ross (*KBR*), who claims to have studied 20,000 people who clinically died, but returned to life. She was one of triplets born in Switzerland, the two pound runt of the brood, who early on had to, she says, work extra hard to prove she was worthy of living. When she was a teenager, she voluntarily found her way to concentration camps at the end of World War II and decided that she wanted to work with Mother Theresa in India. She became, though, a psychiatrist in New York City, and went on to practice at the Manhattan State Hospital. Her seminal book was ***On Death and Dying***[177], but ***On Life After Death***[178] is typical of the type of publication that tries to reach for scientific credibility, and sells well. Three points from this book are memorable, to me. Dr. KBR reported:

- God, 7 million years ago, gave us free will and the ability for our soul to leave our body, certainly at death, but at other times, too. Interesting that this capability was provided at that relatively precise moment in the past when our earliest of ancestors split off from chimpanzees.
- She and her team spend their holidays (*Memorial, July 4$^{th}$, Labor) at hospitals, because this was the best chance to interview children who survived headlong collisions. What a life! Morbid, but dedicated.*
- A rather troubling admittance is presented on page 42, when she writes: "We have never published any of our research for many reasons."

I mention ***ODAD*** and ***OLAD*** because there is something sincere and almost plausible about her efforts. Yet, I feel she fails that key test of scientific credulity because I, for one, am not convinced.

Another book mentioned again is a fictional tale by Dan Brown, ***The Da Vinci Code*** (*TDVC*), because it fits into the theme of this section. Succinctly, ***TDVC***, which has sold more than 60 million copies since 2003, traces the Holy Grail and indicates that Mary Magdalene bore a child with Jesus, with this line continuing today. For eons, people have been searching for a cup. Well, the chalice that carries the blood of Jesus, it is portrayed, is that human line of descendants. What has Leonardo Da Vinci got to do with the plot? Well, his ***Vitruvian Man***, in combination with the ***Mona Lisa*** and ***The Last Supper***, give you the clues to the code, where the Knights Templar and Opus Dei serve as watch guards. How accurate is this novel? No less than most of the other publications indicated in this segment.

The fact of the matter, though, is whether scientists should even bother searching for God or the afterlife. Sir John Templeton has been paying to find an answer since 1972, feeling that the Nobel Prize overlooked spirituality. Templeton is an American born businessman and billionaire who was named ***by Time Magazin***e to their 100 most influential people in 2007 and who will reach the age of 92 in 2008.

The Templeton Foundation wants to know whether the universe is the product of design or accident. In 2000, Freeman Dyson, a churchgoing agnostic from Princeton who did not pray and did not consider God omnipotent, was awarded the $1 million Templeton Prize for Progress Toward Research or Discoveries about Spiritual Realities. This sum always just exceeds the Nobel Prize. Mother Teresa won in 1973 and Billy Graham in 1982. Dyson's ***The Sun, the Genome, and the Internet***[94] proposes using the sun for energy, genetic engineering to create more efficient plants and the internet as a way for the poor to raise themselves. There is a lot in common with these simple solutions. He has indicated that, as an agnostic, he does not know (*of God and the afterlife*) and doesn't know what is true. Strange that they gave him this prize, but understandable that he accepted. Dyson, one of the biggest thinkers of our generation, is no longer around, but it is symptomatic of the challenge that after more that almost two decades into the Templeton Prize, science has gotten nowhere towards clarifying this mystery. That, perhaps, is the motive of Templeton.

The 2005 Templeton Prize winner was Charles Townes, a Nobel laureate and co-inventor of the laser. He has been reported to say that the insight of such a device came to him as a revelation, a striking example of the interplay between science and religion. Scientists propose hypotheses from ideas without initial proof. Thus, like religion, science builds on a form of faith. Professor Townes played an inspirational role in my Chapter 4, and in his waning years, seems to again be focusing on space. So maybe everything is connected to each other and there are logical links among all the chapters in both books.

## The Golden Evolution

All things considered, then, should religions be disestablished? Thomas Jefferson and his Constitution makers, many of them highly religious, nevertheless drew up a wall between religion and government. Yet, Jefferson, although he equated ***The Bible*** to fables and mythology, was adamant that no atheist would ever serve in his Cabinet. Times have not changed much. Notwithstanding the seeming illogicality of these few sentences, the point is that there is a place for religion. It serves an important societal purpose. Religion can be, on balance, good. Why get rid of something that works, and reasonably well? Recognize the flaws and enhance the system. But this might not be possible, for, if you remove an underpinning, such as an afterlife, or miracles, the whole concept falls apart.

This chapter could not prove that there was no afterlife, nor, no God. Yet, I am inclining more and more towards a future world with no religion, as people can still be good without an enforcer and a society functional. The worth of this discussion is to stimulate and provoke, in some quarters, a golden revolution in spiritual thought so that the best of what religions can offer can be synthesized with the latest knowledge and societal standards, which itself is continuously evolving, to, in their own way, help mold our future society, which could well be godless.

Society mores are changing. Science and technology are creating ever new issues for a largely conservative and historically unwavering establishment, where the gospels or Koran or equivalent early writing has supposedly sacred beginnings. How to reconcile, adapt and strengthen will need to prevail over obsolete, unsupportable and illogical strictures.

Eighty three percent of the world population adheres to some religious or spiritual belief. So, how best to proceed?

Let me be brutally specific. I would say to an interdenominational group, you can start by:

- Taking a closer look at changing social patterns and making appropriate adjustments. At one time, women in the United States could not vote. Blacks until fairly recently had to drink from different public water fountains and seat at the back of the bus in the South. For all intents and purposes, most religions still follow this form of practice in their own obsolete ways. Pope Benedict will excommunicate any female from the Catholic Church who is ordained. Women's rights are just not allowed in many Muslim societies. The Episcopalians might have a clue. In 2006 they selected Bishop Katharine Jefferts Schori as the first female leader of the U.S. branch of the Anglican Church. They also in 2003 caused controversy by naming an openly gay bishop. One very "simple" change: give women equal leadership and religious rights. There should be more, but just one progressive step could well set the table for the rest.
- Appreciating that science and technology have been, and will continue to, change the world. Religions have tended to act like Luddites (*Spartacus.schoolnet.co.uk/PRluddites.htm*) or ostriches that hide their head in the sand when seeming danger appears (*which, by the way, happens to be a myth....but you get the point*). Take abortion, for example. Life, indeed, is sacred. But this is a simple matter of realistically agreeing to the point at which life truly begins. Stem cell research is being obstructed by people with strong religious convictions, and President George W. Bush is the poster man for this faction. All this because "life," somehow, is being jeopardized. There is also the fear of cloning. Wake up! Genetic engineering is happening and will go underground or to another country if governmental control occurs.
- Frankness is no way of approaching this matter, but, heck, appreciating the advent of science, accept the ***Bible***, ***Koran*** and other religious manuscripts as a perpetuation of superstitions and fables, and if a document is necessary to maintain some order, create one, and make it up to date and rational. The ***Bible*** is the best-selling book of all time…and yearly. A unified next generation guide will someday supplant this, and other religious relics.
- Stop crucifying people. Just in this publication alone:

- Nicolaus Copernicus (*1473-1543*): In 1514 he distributed a book called ***Little Commentary*** to only his close friends, setting out his theory of the universe with the Sun at the center, although he was wise enough to claim that these were merely mathematical theories. He died of old age because he generally kept quiet about the actual reality of heliocentrism, and when he finally did publish his ideas, he used Poland and was already very old.
- Giordano Bruno (*1548-1600*): A priest, who had the impertinence to suggest that there might be other Suns with other planets, was kept in a dungeon for eight years, tortured, and condemned by the Inquisition and, at the age of 51, executed.
- Galileo Galilei (*1564-1642*): Maybe the most famous of astronomers, who perfected the telescope and supported the Copernican Theory, he was found guilty by the Inquisition of heresy and condemned to lifelong imprisonment. In 1992, 350 years later, Pope John Paul II admitted that errors had been made by the Catholic Church.
- Charles Darwin (*1809-1882*): His theory of natural selection removed the need for a God, was condemned by the Catholic Church, but by 1859 when ***Origin of the Species*** was published, as there was no Inquisition, Darwin lived. The Church is either getting more mature, or losing power.
- Salman Rushdie (*1947-*): An Anglo-Indian novelist, he was condemned to death by the former Iranian spiritual leader Ayatollah Khomeini in 1989 after publishing ***Satanic Verses*** [269] which was his fourth novel, and won the 1988 Whitbread Award. The Prophet Muhammad was cast in a bad light and liberties were taken with the Koran. There was a $2 million reward for his death, and in 1998, Ayatollah Hassan Sanei raised it to $2.8 million. Rushdie remains alive, but goes in and out of hiding. What a life.

- Sam Harris (*still alive, too*): awarded the 2005 PEN Award for Nonfiction, challenges all religions about the irrationality of blind faith. The problem, he says, is religion, and, worse, moderation, poses dangers of its own. Is there an upcoming fatwa?
- Reach out and work with your constituency and enemy. The day before Pope Paul II died in April of 2005, then Cardinal Joseph Ratzinger, speaking in the village of Subiaco, just outside Rome, said that Europe now "excludes God from the public conscience."[86] He further indicated that this disdain for God has led us "to the edge of the abyss." This is no attitude to take when you want to embrace the people. Religious leaders need to think, act and react positively, not revert to the fire and brimstone mode of operation which might have worked in the past.
- Eliminate the sexual abuse problem involving priests and, mostly, young boys. Not only the Roman Catholic Church, but other religions, throughout the world, for centuries, have failed to resolve this morality issue.
- Strive towards a universal religion with one God. Good, the Irish Republican Army has taken that important first initial step towards reconciling the Protestant versus Catholic dilemma in Northern Ireland. The Cardinals should begin to groom a stunning, female, Chinese as a future Pope candidate. Combining all—one God, common dogma—a United Religions of the World, would be a worthy and magnificent challenge. **Better yet, leap over that step and agree on no god**.

Why, then, don't Pope Benedict, the Dalai Lama and the other prominent religious leaders meet to arrive at a universal solution? As a matter of fact, this Golden Revolution has begun, for something like this occurred at the end of August in the year 2000, when 2000 of the preeminent religious and spiritual leaders gathered at the United Nations for a Millennium World Peace Summit (*www.millenniumpeacesummit.co*m). This unprecedented forum pledged to take concrete actions for the achievement of world peace. An International Advisory Council of Religious Leaders (*IACRL*) was formed to function as a resource for the Secretary General of the UN to resolve international conflicts.

IACRL has leaned on the Group of Eight (*G8--U.S. Japan, Russia, Canada, Germany, France, Italy, and United Kingdom*) meetings, and taken on the elimination of poverty as a common goal. This is certainly a good start because the poorest countries with less than a $1000 Gross National Product/capita already pay 83 percent of their entire budget on world loans.[369] Will they consider the role of women, the issue of abortion and the afterlife? What about no god?

There are those who have called for an Islamic Reformation. Yes, women's emancipation and how science fits into the logic can certainly be woven into what makes sense from the now obsolete Koran. There was Martin Luther's Protestant Reformation in the 1500's, fracturing Christendom, which provides a message. The next great movement, though, should be a unification, not endless fractionation.

A great first step is for the two largest religions, Christianity and Islam, to determine that they are one and the same religion, for they have virtually identical beliefs:

- One God, miracles, seven deadly sins.
- That Jesus was born to Virgin Mary and rose to Heaven.
- That Abraham was the Father of their religion.
- Use the Jewish Old Testament and New Testament as sources of faith.
- Have a Hell, with a Satan, as the nether world to Heaven.
- Share the Creation, Adam and Eve, and Moses with his Ten Commandments.

The early attainment of this accommodation will no doubt be equated to a major miracle, for as negligible as the Sunni/Shiite differences might be, centuries of mistrust and history are what stand in the way of amity. But, if the Christians and Muslims can "somehow" find a way just to talk about integrating their religion, the lower order disparities of sectarian discord in both religions could then become a tertiary matter to be settled when the attitude of future generations changes. Hinduism and Buddhism can also readily be incorporated, for they tend to be inherently more accommodating, anyway.

The amalgamation of traditional beliefs will take many generations. The Supreme Court has ruled that Secular Humanism is a religion and a Court of Appeals has indicated that Atheism, too, is a religion. The Neo Atheists and their brethren might have difficulty being accepted into this partnership, but they could well serve as the catalysts, for the humanistic sect of these non-beliefs can serve as that rainbow bridge.

Is the Golden Evolution that ultimate step we must take, while surrendering the obsolete beliefs of the past, to reach out for the future by unifying science and new reason with the best of world cultures to attain security, quality of life and happiness forever? Religion is a necessary partner for this simplest of solutions.

The city of Rome began building in 753 B.C., took 250 years to become a Republic, and went on for a millennium. Daniel Dennett believes that religion will lose command in a quarter century. Is there a way, then, for us to bypass all the above in one monumental act?

Yes! The Golden Evolution, in my simple solution (*hold your breath, this is as crazy as making hydrogen free in Chapter 3 of* ***Book 1***), then, is the process by which there is general acceptance that Man created God when it was vital for our early ancestors to have an all-watching and morally satisfying divinity, but that an omnipresent protector is today obsolete. The only way for the Dennett revolution to happen is first for the sudden emergence of a global test of monumental proportions. Step One, to challenge our survival: a cataclysmic series of events, such as, perhaps, oil suddenly jumping to $200/barrel and tens of millions perishing through global heating one hot summer, with the prospects of Planet Earth converting to Planet Venus (*where the surface temperature is 900°F, see Chapter 5 in* ***Book 1***) to arise with such fury that all elements of Mankind compellingly unite and take coordinated action, which would be Step Two. Having overcome this global crisis (*let's be at least positive about the outcome*), Step Three would be that evolutionary transcendence towards a higher respect for the environment and a fading away of the supreme being concept.

As we today don't need a feared deity to serve as an enforcer, for earlier reported studies have shown that most of our citizens, religious or not, choose the righteous and ethical pathway in life, maybe we can shift our belief and have faith in ourselves, instead. Mind you, there really isn't any real requirement for worshipping as such, but, in the transition, as our current society appears to have a psychological need for some higher order symbol, perhaps Planet Earth can serve as that tangible object. Instead of depending on our environment to take care of us, though, while in the midst of overcoming Peak Oil and Greenhouse Effect, the Golden Evolution will be the process by which we switch roles and take on the necessary task for remediation and sustainability as a common goal for humanity. In time, and this may take many millennia, we will then expand our vision to our Galaxy as our domain. In anticipation, ***Book 3*** could well be called ***SIMPLE SOLUTIONS for the Whole Universe***.

# CHAPTER 6: THE BEST PLACE IN THE WORLD

Ah, but why worry about such doomsday nonsense. If you have religious inclinations, then you will most probably go to Paradise or Heaven at the end anyway. But then, you need to die to get there, and you will only make it if you meet all the requirements, whatever they may be, or be some kind of martyr. But what if there is no Heaven? What proof do you really have to put all your faith into something that might not actually exist?

Say, nevertheless, you truly believe in some afterlife. It would still be smart to also pick a site on Planet Earth where you can optimize your lifestyle while you are alive, just in case. Maybe, even be part of the Green Enertopia movement (*Chapter 2*) or the Blue Revolution (*Chapter 4*) from ***Book 1***. Clearly, where to get involved to make this difference is Hawaii, but let us do a quasi-systematic analysis to determine the closest thing to heaven on Earth.

## The Greatest Civilizations

Let us start from the beginning, when discovering fire was certainly pretty great. But that was just some earlier hominoid who observed a forest fire started by lightning providing warmth, scorching some animal, and, wow, that cooked flesh tasted better. There is evidence of human-like fossils as old as 1.8 million years ago in Indonesia, and in the Caucasus and China 1.6 million years ago, but these were Homo erectus (*Peking Man, around one million BC*) and ergaster.[23] We, Homo sapiens sapiens (*wise or knowing man*), are said to have originated in the African savanna—the Serengeti, or Kenya and Tanzania—about 200,000 years ago.

Around 70,000 years ago, when the world population was in the millions, the Toba supervolcano in Indonesia erupted, with an energy equivalent 3,000 times that of the 1980 Mt. St. Helens explosion, placing a considerable volcanic ash into the atmosphere, triggering an ice age, and reducing the human population to, perhaps, a thousand breeding pairs, most probably where temperatures were the warmest. This, or similar cataclysmic events, is probably a good a reason as any for our roots beginning in Africa, where the climate was favorable during that cold period.

Over time, migration led to human colonies in Eurasia and Oceania by 40,000 BC, then to the Americas around 10,000 years ago, just around the time when agriculture was developed in Iraq by the Sumerians, or in China, and when the world population was in the range of 5 million.

There are signs of a Chinese civilization as early as 12,000 BC., and farming can be traced back around 9,000 years. The earliest known dynasty was around 1700 BC. The Chinese are credited with having invented: gunpowder, wheelbarrow, compass, spaghetti, kites, iron casting, harnessing of animals, clock, modern boats, abacus, rudder, silk, anesthesia, printing press, and much more.

Soon after 1200 AD, Genghis Khan governed over 12 million square miles, almost twice the size of Russia, with a population of 100 million. In the early 1400's, Admiral Zheng He, who started as a palace eunuch in the Imperial court, but with family connections to Mecca, led seven naval expeditions to establish Chinese trade and presence, and may well have reached America before Columbus. On his initial 1492 voyage, Columbus had the Nina, Pinta and Santa Maria, the largest with a length of 59 feet (*18 meters*). In his 1405 expedition, Zheng had 62 treasure ships, with several more than ten times longer, up to 600 feet (*183 meters*) with 9 masts, plus 190 smaller support craft. Regarding the Orient, a case can be made that China spawned the culture of Korea and Japan, declined for a spell, but again looks promising into the future.

Likewise, India, which has been inhabited for hundreds of thousands of years, began to organize in the Indus Valley around 6,000 BC, with major trading as far back as 3,000 BC with Egypt, China and Arabia. Like China, India could well only now be maturing, again.

Ancient Egyptians ground grain by 11,000 BC, with the Pharaohs coming into power around 3150 BC, which was ended by the Roman Empire in 31 BC, more than three millennia later. Remember, if you go back an equivalent period from today, you are talking about 1000 BC.

The combination of Nile silt deposition for agriculture and papyrus served to bring eminence to the country. The Egyptians invented the first known writing system—hieroglyphics—paper, and the decimal system almost 5,000 years ago. They also built the first wine cellar (*3100 BC*), performed the first surgery (*2700 BC*), used the first alphabet (*1800 BC*), blew the first glass (*1500 BC*) and signed the first peace treaty (*1258 BC*). The Great Sphinx of Giza was built around 2600 BC, and remains today as the largest single-stone statue. The Great Pyramid of Giza, around 2580 BC, stood as the tallest structure until AD 1300, almost 4,000 years. But what happened to Egypt? I've been to Cairo, gazed at the pyramids and wondered how such a great past could lead to that grayish-brown present teeming with subsistence life.

The Fertile Crescent incorporates the Nile, Tigris, Euphrates and Jordan rivers, today corresponding to Egypt, Israel, West Bank, Gaza strip, Lebanon and parts of Jordan, Syria, Iraq, south-eastern Turkey and south-western Iran, now with a population of 120 million. The Sumerians came into prominence around 5000 BC, and in 4000 BC Mesopotamia gained eminence in what is now southern Iraq. The capital city of Babylon, with its Hanging Gardens, was particularly of consequence, where Hammurabi codified laws around 1800 BC. Today, Babylon, located 55 miles south of Baghdad, is dust and shrub, although one of Saddam Hussein's former grand palaces is built close to it. The origin of Judaism was also around 1800 BC, where the supposed Diaspora (*scattering from ancestral homeland*) around 100 AD dispersed the Jewish population, only to return as Israel in 1948. The Persian Empire, today Iran, around 700 BC, was the largest the world had seen, but fell to Alexander the Great in 330 BC. Then the Golden Age of Islam blossomed, to never recover from the Mongol invasion of 1258 AD. Certainly, you don't today want to live in this Cradle of Humanity today.

The early beginnings of Greece can be traced back more than 5000 years. Homer's period, when Greece was more a tribal society, flourished around 1400 BC during the time of the Trojan Wars; Socrates, Plato and Aristotle arrived a thousand years later; and the end came with the Romans in 146 BC. Remember, the USA has been in existence for only a little more than two centuries. But some scholars say that Ancient Greece really began in 776 BC with the first Olympics and ended with the death of Alexander the Great in 323 BC, a period of 453 years. From 800 BC to 400 BC, the population of Greece increased from less than a million to more than 10 million, and was the most advanced economy of the world. Greece is a tale of two cities: Athens and Sparta. Sparta won the war, but is today a city of around 20,000, compared to Athens, already 3000 years old, with a metro population approaching 4 million. Not unlike Egypt, what happened to Greece, and why did Sparta largely disappear? Aside from olive oil and the early culture, the legacy seems to be a blockbuster movie every decade or so. Athens can be stricken from the list of best places to live.

The Roman Republic was formed in Rome, Italy with the overthrow of the monarchy in 509 BC. The Roman Empire, a product of the 500 year-old Republic, became a superpower just before the birth of Christ. The Romans had already conquered Greece (*146 BC*) and Egypt (*31 BC*), and went on to control 2.3 million square miles—from Western Eurasia to northern Africa—by 106 AD, paltry by Genghis Khan standards. Gaius Julius Caesar Octavianus, more popularly known as Augustus, was the first Emperor. His mother was a niece of Julius Caesar. Earlier in the book, mention was made of Gaius Flavius Valerius Aerelius Constantinus, or Constantine the Great, who ruled from 324 to 337 AD, and because he was the first Christian emperor, re-worked the Bible through the Council of Nicaea and, also, moved the Roman capitol to Constantinople, which was formerly known as Byzantium and Nova Roma, and in 1930 was renamed Istanbul. The end came in 476 AD when Romulus Augustus was deposed and not replaced, while the Empire fell to an assortment of invaders.

Tuscany is too hot in the summer, Rome is too crowded, northern Italy is too French and southern Italy…well, there is more crime. Then, there is the Mafia in Sicily. Hey, I'm kidding! Italy has great wine, spectacular food, art, and opera and is actually a fine place to live, if you don't mind train strikes, the stagnant economy, their government and the attitude of the Vatican. As you can imagine, I'm building the foundation for the best place in world today, and it will not be Rome or Athens or Baghdad or Cairo.

Back in the New World, there were three noteworthy civilizations:

- o The Maya region (*today, Guatemala, Belize, western Honduras, El Salvador and southern Mexico*) was first inhabited around 10,000 BC, flourished in the 250 AD to 900 AD classical period with a population of 20 million, having developed written language, art and architecture, but, then, mysteriously declined. When the Western World came calling in the form of Spaniard Hernan Cortez in 1519, the Mayas were already on a downward spiral through droughts and dubious planning, with the population perhaps as low as 30,000. You can experience one version through Mel Gibson's ***Apocalypto*** *(although some have criticized the effort as distorted, including use of the wrong Maya dialect*). However, the last Maya Kingdom actually survived until around 1700. It is reported that there are today, perhaps, 10 million

Maya still living in this region. The Mayas were particularly advanced in mathematics and astronomy, with an early prophesy having to do with "God communication" on October 21, 2012, when our Sun and the center of the Milky Way align in such a manner that the northern steps of the pyramid at Chitzen Itza (*CI*) in the Yucatan Peninsula will be pointing exactly towards the Pleiades star cluster, or December 21, when the world will supposedly come to an end. Make your reservations now for what could be a SETI (*search for extraterrestrial intelligence*) experience in 2012, just avoid the local popsicle. I stayed at the Cancun Westin Hotel, climbed up the C.I. pyramid with a colored ice concoction in hand, but soon thereafter suffered from Montezuma's revenge, and later, saw on TV the hotel seriously damaged by a hurricane. Moctezuma (*the preferred spelling today*), of course, is an Aztec, and his civilization follows.

- The Inca Empire began as a tribe in the Cuzco area of Peru around the 12th Century, but only prospered beginning in 1438 for less than a century. At the height, the Empire also included Ecuador, Columbia and north Chile, with a total population of 6 million. Architecture was exemplified by the site on Machu Picchu. Surgery was practiced, coca leaves chewed for endurance, alcohol fermented and an incredible system of roads (*14,000 miles*) was built. Gold was mined and there was no crime, as such. They believed in reincarnation. The Inca army consisted of 40,000 warriors, so how did Spanish conquistador Francisco Pizarro (*who came before, and was a distant relative of Cortez*), with only 180 men and a cannon prevail? The coming of Spanish invaders introduced smallpox. Civil war was rampant. Pizarro cleverly used allies and the Christian religion to gain some control, and in 1533 executed the last sovereign, Atahualpa, bringing an end to the Inca Empire.
- The Aztec Empire began in what is now Mexico City in the 13th Century, and reached a peak population of 19 million just around the time Columbus discovered America, when Motecuzoma Xocoyotzin (*yet another spelling, better known as Montezuma*) was ruler. A monetary system was in use, song and poetry were in high regard, and cannibalism and human sacrifice were practiced. Also in 1519, Hernan Cortez, fresh from conquering the Mayas, added the Aztecs to his list. A smallpox outbreak that soon followed killed up to 50% of the local population. By 1581, the population dropped to 2 million, so black slaves were imported. This combination of Aztecs, blacks and Spanish now represents the Mexican race around 500 years later. In high school I belonged to a social club called the Aztecs. I'm pretty sure no one, certainly not me, knew much of the above.

While we might want to accuse those Europeans for so blatantly infringing on the rights of these indigenous people, the fact of the matter is that they were all already collapsing, some more than others, mostly from environmental factors. In any case, do you want to live in Guatemala, Peru or Mexico? Oprah and other celebrities have third mansions there, but also like Hawaii.

Thus, it appears that global climate change played a significant role in the rise and fall of civilizations.[85] In ***Collapse***, Jared Diamond comes to a conclusion that environmental problems were mostly responsible for the downfall of empires and societies. The worry, then, is the next big one, Planet Earth, as the developed nations, per capita, today utilize 32 times more resources than developing countries. ***Book 1, SIMPLE SOLUTIONS for Planet Earth***, treats this problem, or, at least provides some potentially outrageous solutions.

Finally, then, we have Modern Western Civilization, the only mandatory history course when I was in college. Last thing you want is a history lesson, but, in keeping with the above, Greek philosophy, Roman law and Christianity were pillars of Western Culture. Combined with Germanic, Slavic and Celtic customs, the transitions occurred during the Dark and Middle Ages, or medieval period. Then came the Renaissance in the $14^{th}$ to $16^{th}$ Century interlude, largely centered around Italy with Dante Alighieri, Leonardo Da Vinci and the like, although England, with Geoffrey Chaucer and William Shakespeare, Germany (*Albrecht Durer, who originally coined the term*), France (*after all, this is a French word, but the names are more associated with reigns, such as of Charles VIII or Henri II*), Netherlands (*Desiderius Erasmus, Hieronymus Bosch and Martin Luther*), Poland (*Nicholaus Copernicus*), and so on, all contributed. Colonialism also began around this period, first by Portugal and Spain, but Britain soon dominated with an empire about a quarter of the land surface where the Sun never set. The Enlightenment or Age of Reason occurred in the 1700's with the French Declaration of the Rights of Man and the Citizen and the American Bill of Rights, Immanuel Kant, Adam Smith, all linked with the Scientific Revolution inspired by Galileo Galilei and Isaac Newton, leading to the Industrial Revolution in the $18^{th}$ Century and continuing to today. The spark was Great Britain, with coal, low interest rates (*5%, compared to China at 30% during those days*), victory over France and Napoleon, and the Protestant work ethic. Finally, there were those three world wars: I, II and Cold.

The United States prevailed and became the supreme world power. Certainly, then, the choice to live is here, and immigrants are still coming, although we seem to be hassled by too many wanting in.

## The Best and Worst of the World

I have flown 2 million miles, just on United Airlines. Certainly, I've used many tens of other airlines, and journeyed many hundreds of thousand miles on them. I have made, perhaps, ten around the world trips. My wife and I have spent a month on Amtrak around the U.S., throughout Japan on the Shinkansen and Europe on trains. We have driven from Stockholm to Milan and three times across the USA. Then there were those cruises across the Pacific, from Alaska through the Panama Canal and into the Caribbean, plus the Mediterranean. Here are some of my worst, well, make that, challenging, trips, indubitably eliminating them from those sites making any best list of places to live.

### Bombay was Eye-opening

It was during the mid-70's when my wife Pearl and I left on an around the world trip: Tokyo, Bangkok, Bombay, Frankfurt, England, Washington, D.C., then finally back to Honolulu. I have only two memories.

First, we flew into Bangkok during the monsoon, and it was in a state of flood. This means that sewers overflowed, and the whole city was a smelly mess. At our first meal in the President Hotel, Pearl ordered a fruit salad, but a vegetable salad came. All the alarm bells rang. Avoid leafy salads in Bangkok, and certainly, oh my gosh, during these conditions. She ate it, anyway. Nothing happened.

Second, we went to Bombay, which still went by that name then. *(However, Bombay is a corrupted western version of Mumbai, so, in 1995, the change was made to Mumbai. The power structure also attempted to eliminate the term Bollywood—a type of movie form initiated in this city, where frantic dancing intersperses a love story. That failed, as Bollywood films are now even shown in the U.S. I used to wear Madras shirts in college. Ever try looking for Madras on the Indian map? It is now called Chennai.*) However, as we went through customs, the agent sent us to the back of the line because we had no visas. No one told us about that before the trip, but, sure, that was our fault.

At 2:30 in the morning, we were the final two in line. The temperature was in the 90's (*degrees Fahrenheit*). That agent—and, sorry, he looked like a crook—said he had to keep our passports, and we could enter the country, but we should hire someone to get them back before we checked out of the country. What choice did we have? This is scam city, and a more active form than in Cairo, yet to come.

There was a very large sign behind him warning anyone not to exchange money with these officials. So he proceeded to ask us how many rupees we wanted. Oh, great, now what? Do we ignore him and walk out, invoking his rage to purposely lose our passports, or get thrown in jail for exchanging money? We got a few rupees. No problem.

The taxi ride was uneventful. We checked into the Holiday Inn, and got a room with the noisiest air conditioner I have ever experienced. But it worked. We specifically picked this hotel because it was a Holiday Inn. Certainly, it would be sterile.

The next morning, we went down to breakfast in their coffee shop, which was swarming with flies. Yes, this was a Holiday Inn.

Pearl walked just outside the hotel area to the beach, and came running back, as a whole mob of children was chasing her to sell rocks. Not gemstone quality, but plain old rocks. What a cultural shock.

We took an arranged tour of the city. I can still remember the utter poverty. People living in cardboard boxes…mothers with deformed children begging…carts hauling dead people to special areas for vultures to pick on…this was a totally different world. Bombay was shock to our senses.

The tour guide was especially proud of a church basement where 8-10 year old children were sewing in semi-darkness, almost swollen with pride because at least they had shelter and food. The Hanging Gardens of Bombay approximated my hanging roof garden in Honolulu. The Gateway of India was swarming with a million people. People bumped into you at this tourist attraction because of crowd surges, but as far as I could determine, there were no pickpockets. Singapore has about 2,000 people/square mile…Bombay is almost ten times that density. 20 million people? I can go on, but a couple of days later we finally found ourselves back at the airport six hours before our flight, to retrieve our passports.

You can imagine our anxiety as we waited for 5 ½ hours with our baggage, waiting to check in. Through a major miracle, the youth we hired came running back…we barely were able to check through…just got on board, and the plane left India. That was our last trip to this country. Eliminate India, and, while you're at it, Thailand, from the best places to live.

**Moscow was an Experience**

The 7th World Hydrogen Energy Conference was held in Moscow in September of 1988. With my wife and several of my staff in the party, we flew first to London, then on to Moscow. David Block, director of Florida Solar Energy Center, and his wife Sharon, also attended, and joined us on our trip back. We stayed at the Hotel Rossia, then, the largest hotel in the world with 5,000 rooms. Picture a gigantic World War I military barracks and you get a sense of the accommodations.

From the first morning session to the final at the end, the conference room was packed with mostly Russians. I guess in those days anyone who received permission to join the meeting felt committed to be present at all times. In other worldwide technical conferences, many times the speakers were the only ones in attendance, and by the last gathering, most would have left town.

There was one incident where our group missed our subway stop and got lost. We walked up to the street level, and a very nice gentleman in a black leather jacket topped with a furry cap inquired if we needed help. We explained our plight and he so courteously guided us back down and, even, paid for our trip to the correct stop. I later learned that he worked for the KGB.

The one factor still sticking with me, though, is that all the Soviet delegates were very cordial and competent. The Seoul Olympics were being held at the same time, and one morning, a Russian scientists came up to us and painfully reported that they had beaten the American basketball team, eliminating us from the gold medal. It wasn't sarcasm. He truly felt terrible that they had won.

However, the food was dreadful (*the best vodka and caviar were exported*). We pretty much were forced to eat at the conference and hotel, featuring rubber chicken and cold oil slabs. There were no such things as restaurants then.

We had one final ghastly experience, but, nothing like what was to come in Cairo. There were no real lines at the airport. You had to fight to get to the window for changing money and the like.

We boarded Aeroflot, which took me back to those movies of World War II bombers. Well, we made it to East Berlin, and were able view a tad of this grayish town before checking through to West Berlin, almost like Dorothy stepping from the black and white of Kansas to the colored land of Oz. After a couple of days, we picked up two cars and drove through the corridor to the real West Germany. We were twice stopped by the East German police: first, for missing a turnoff, and a second time, for pausing at a rest stop, but where buses are supposed to park. Totally unnerved by then, at the gate to freedom, we passed on six passports, but the guard counted seven people, so there was a frantic search, only because I had dropped one on the floor of the van. We then found our way to Kiel, a picturesque harbor town. The rest of the trip was wonderful, but uneventful. Moscow is never on a list of best places to live, for good reason.

**My Adventures in Papua New Guinea**

I traveled to the Independent State of Papua New Guinea (*PNG*) in 1989, no doubt one of the three most stressful experiences of my life. Most of what follows comes from pure memory, although I do keep files of all my trips, and I did obtain a conference proceedings of why I went there. The reason why I went had to do with a professor friend from Michigan who convinced me that I should give a talk at his energy conference in PNG, where he had temporarily moved.

To bring you up to date, PNG, located in the southwest Pacific Ocean just north of Australia and south of the equator, has a current population of 5.5 million with 600 islands and the land area the size of California. Port Moresby, the capital, has about a third of a million people and Lae of something just below 100,000. It is a constitutional monarchy, meaning that they recognize the Queen of England as their head of state, with an elected parliamentary democracy, and they mostly deal with Australia. "For each village, a different culture," is an apt folk saying, as there are some 800 languages spoken. It is rich in natural mineral resources, and could well increase in importance because fossil fuel deposits are yet largely untapped. Interesting that Exxon Mobile and Chevron Texaco abandoned operations there, but I think I know why. Read on.

The U.S. State Department now has online security information for Americans traveling abroad. This was not available then. Visitors in 2006 were warned, don't go to PNG. Many incidents of assaults and robbery occur in Port Moresby and Lae, and individuals are especially at high risk. Golf courses, parks and beaches are to be avoided, as are taxis and buses. In May 2006, the Australian government was a bit more descriptive, underscoring that there are high levels of serious crime, especially in Lae.

It was worse in 1989. A rebellion was running rampant on Bougainville Island and there was a series of no confidence votes against the government.

This visit should have taught me a lesson of never going anywhere unless you know where you are going. But there were extenuating circumstances. There was some combination of Nejat Veziroglu and F. Welt involved with the planning for the gathering in Lae, PNG. My original response was, no, sorry, can't make it, but thanks for asking. But persistence sometimes pays, and at the last moment, as the travel reimbursement seemed unusually attractive, I made a late booking and found myself going through customs at Jackson International Airport in Port Moresby.

As I was picking up my suitcase, I noticed a sign saying, "Don't enter the country if you have not taken Malaria precautions!" My initial reaction was, whoa, go home. But I had to physically proceed through the process to get out, and the customs official asked me about my visa. Aha, I thought, become an arrogant American and let them kick you out. I had a good excuse, for I again did not bother about a visa. At least I could report to the conference sponsors the "I tried" part. I said, "I am an important speaker from the United States and you must let me through even though I don't have a visa." He said, "okay," and I could not think quickly enough to irritate him any further.

After the hour flight to Lae on Air Niugini, I was picked up at the airport by conference planners. Professor S. L. Hall, Head of the Mechanical Engineering Department at the University of Technology from Australia, was on the plane. She casually mentioned that the president of Papua New Guinea University of Technology in Lae was the brother in law of the current head of state, and there was a move to evict him by the opposition party. At the hotel, over drinks, we were told don't walk around in town, not even in the daytime. And don't think of doing that at night. There are marauding packs called Rascals, who are mostly cannibals from the jungle who can't find jobs in town and must rob and kill to stay alive. I thought they were exaggerating, but no one was smiling.

What really caught my attention, though, was when I mentioned that I had not bothered with malaria precautions and asked, "just how serious was it?" One of them dropped his drink and the others, wide-eyed, expressed alarm. First, Lae is a lot wetter than Port Moresby, and the problem is amplified here. Second, it was too late. Third, those trying to prevent malaria as a resident by taking medication can go blind. However, S.L. (*don't remember her first name*) gave me a bunch of pills and said, all things concerned, it might help. I asked one of them about the getting blind part and asked for some details. He said he decided not to take that chance, the blind chance. So, he had malaria.

I went back to my room and only then saw that can of insecticide and black splotches on the wall. I was so exhausted after a flight that took more than 30 hours that I quickly fell asleep.

We were picked up the next morning and taken to the conference, which was held in an open auditorium with a roof. As I was glancing at the program, a strange brown mosquito wafted unto the page. Before I could panic, it flew off somewhere. Just then, the moderator opened the program and mentioned that some of the out of country conferees might be concerned about malaria. He said not to worry, for the only mosquitoes to give you malaria suck you just around sunset. And don't worry about the male of the species. He was trying some humor. I later learned that there are various anopheles varieties capable of inflicting this disease, and they sort of look like those found in Hawaii.

I made one of those command decisions, and this time, to be smart and decisive about it. I remembered that someone in my family was sick with something more serious than a cold and went up to my friend the organizer, F. Welt, and said that I noticed my talk was to be at the banquet two days away. Unfortunately, there was a sickness in the family and I had to leave first thing tomorrow, so could I give my talk today. This was not an outright lie, but close. After some anguishing and discussions, we agreed on my presenting my message at the morning session the next day so I could catch a noon flight to Port Moresby and connect to a Quantas flight to Brisbane. He would be glad to make the adjustments for me. It was difficult for me to disagree with this kind of cooperation. So I was stuck at least a second night.

The foreign guests were invited to dinner at one of the professor's home after the end of the meetings that day. We dawdled around for a while and walked to his residence. He was not there. No one was there. After waiting for an hour, I noticed that dusk was approaching, and imagined that those malaria mosquitoes were readying themselves for their evening meal. Then the family returned with groceries. Waiting outside did not matter much because the home was open to the elements. At some point a siren sounded and the local staff began to exhibit a high sense of anxiety. Finally, a phone call came and we were "reassured" that the problem was that students advocating the fall of their university president had invaded the faculty club and had stolen all the liquor. In addition, there was a riot in town and those with hotel rooms there were told to remain overnight at this home. The campus was a barbed-wire enclosure, not unlike a jail.

Unexpectedly, at about 10 PM, a government official showed up in an open air jeep and said that he would take S.L. and me back to the hotel. They were more apprehensive about her, being female. I asked, what about those rioting protesters, and he said he thinks we're covered, as he had a case of beer in the back and if a group attacks us, we give them the beer. He was serious. But we made it back without incident.

The next morning, I gave my talk and was rushed to the airport. The plane was late. I was worried about the connecting flight, for if we left at noon, the 1:30 flight time seemed awfully close. The uneasy state of politics was such that this was to be the last plane out of New Guinea that day. I was told that on Fridays those who worked get paid, and become drunk and dangerous. Whatever happens, they said, don't get stranded at the airport.

Finally at 12:30 PM the plane came and immediately left with me. We landed at Jackson at 1:35 and Quantas was still there. I grabbed my luggage and began running to the plane...but was told I first had to go through customs. Well, it took a long time to clear, as first, they wondered about my visa. Finally, finally, I was allowed to board the flight. It turned out the airline was waiting just for me, and till today, I have joyful feelings about Quantas. Brisbane is, maybe, among the most boring cities in the world. Those three days there were about the best I spent anywhere in my life. This is part of the reason why Australia is way up there as among the best places to live. However, scratch PNG from the list.

**My Seoul Dinner with Two Kims and a Chun**

In 1990, wearing my vice-president for development hat in service to the Pacific International Center for High Technology Research, I went to Seoul, Korea to discuss cooperative ventures. I had frequently been to Korea, so the trip in itself was not supposed to be particularly memorable, but I earlier mentioned something about my dinner with a former president of the country, so here it is.

An intermediary arranged for me to meet with some "important" people from his country at the Hilton. The information was sketchy as to the purpose of the gathering or who was to attend. The Lotte, where I was staying, was no more than a couple of miles from the Hilton, so I attempted to catch a taxi at 6:30 for the 7PM dinner.

While traffic at 6:30PM can be a problem in Seoul, I had not in the past had difficulty. Well, it was raining, so that was a complication. The taxi stand had, perhaps, 25 people waiting, and after ten minutes, all of one cab showed up. I then walked to the street to try to hail one down. All the taxis were full. Nearly sopping wet, I came back to stand in line, which had grown. It was now 6:45PM.

I remembered that the hotel had a limousine service, so, at ten to seven, I arranged to be dropped off at the Hilton. The cost was manageable. The traffic was terrible, and if you have tried to navigate away from the Lotte, you might remember that you have to traverse through two full circles, to finally head in the right direction. At 7:35PM I finally arrived at the Hilton, and with some help from the staff, found the special room in which the dinner was to be held.….45 minutes late and somewhat bedraggled, being still wet.

All three individuals, who I had not previously met, were sitting over a drink waiting for me. They all knew each other very well. They were reasonably nice about my tardiness and introduced themselves. The first Kim was the current director of the Korean Intelligence Agency, the second Kim was a high level government official who was the first Minister of Science and Technology, and the Chun was none other than Doo Hwan, who was president of Korea from 1980 to 1988. The second Kim, Kee Hyong, mentioned that if he had known of my plight, he would have arranged something, as his wife was the brother of the person who owned the Lotte. While in an advanced state of shock, I somehow managed to survive the dinner.

Till today, I don't know if I, somehow, got shown into the wrong room, and these dignitaries were waiting for someone else. Certainly, they must have wondered why it was so important for all three at the same time to have dinner with me.

I never did see the KIA Kim, nor ex-President Chun, again, but in 1996 he was sentenced to death for the Gwangju massacre. Korean presidents have historically gone through this charade, for Chun was pardoned by President Kim Young-sam, just before Kim Dae-jung replaced him as president. Chun had two decades earlier sentenced Dai-jung to death.

Perhaps there was some good reason for that dinner, as I did get to become good friends with Kim Kee Hyong. He had obtained a PhD in materials science at Penn State University and at a very young age was summoned back to his country to become a Minister. He later became chairman of the board of the Korea Advanced Institute of Science and Technology, and was a key architect of technology development for his country. He came to Hawaii on several occasions and served on one of my advisory boards.

One of our later lunches was held at the Renaissance Hotel in Seoul, where, Kee, Kiryun Choi (*a professor from Ajou University who at one time signed most of the research contracts for his government*) and I came up with the Renaissance Project. You can go to Chapter 3 of ***Book 1*** for some details on this hydrogen competition. At this writing, Professor Choi is translating ***Book 1*** into Korean. Kee and I, until very recently, had dinner once or twice a year to discuss the future.

**My Day in Hangzhou**

In the Fall of 1997 I made a two day stop in Shanghai, China. I had arranged to give a talk to the engineering students at Zhejiang University in Hangzhou, generally ranked #3 to Tsinghua University and Beijing University, but the Paris Tech 2007 ranking placed it at #1 in China and #35 in the world. While the city was around 100 miles from Shanghai, in those days, there was no superhighway. Today of course there is one and plans are being readied for a magnetic levitation train to become operational for the 2010 Shanghai Expo. That trip will take only 27 minutes. But that's the future.

Thus, I woke up that fateful morning to catch a flight to Hangzhou. I got a call saying the area was fogged in, so wait in my room until further notice. Finally, I was picked up and boarded the plane, but it was till foggy. The flight nevertheless took off, and I never saw land until a short while later, a sudden bump announced our arrival at the Jianqiao Airport. I was initially impressed with the unbelievable radar system, but then decided they had just winged it. I was alive, so all was well.

Hangzhou is located in the Yangtze River Delta. The city is 2,200 years old and is famous for its natural scenery. While the population today is greater than 6 million, in 1276, already a million people lived there. Marco Polo then called it the finest and noblest in the world.

Like many universities in the Orient, the full range of study options is available, but engineering rules. I made the usual protocol visits, but by the mid-afternoon a concern surfaced that all airline flights could be cancelled until at least the next day. The only other option was a train, which did not worry me, but seemed to distress the administration. So, it was determined that I had to miss the sightseeing part of the trip, and go immediately to the airport. Well, all the flights were, indeed, cancelled, so my faculty guide said that we needed to catch a taxi to the Hangzhou East Railway Station.

He found out that there was only one more train left with any seats to Shanghai, but that the departure time was in about half an hour. The cab line was at least 100 yards long, so, he went up to the policeman monitoring that area and explained how important I was I think, in Chinese, anyway, and magically, we were whisked away. However, with the rain and flooding, the normal roads were at a standstill, so I was told that the driver would take the country alternative, where I learned that most of the roadway was essentially wide enough for one vehicle. It was now dark and the ride was harrowing. At one point, a large truck headed in our direction at full speed, and, till today, I don't know how we survived a head-on collision (*remember, the traffic death rate/vehicle in China is more than 20 times that of the U.S.*).

Well, we made it to the station, and you need to recall that Paris station where Humphrey Bogart waited for Ingrid Bergman in ***Casablanca***, as the German army was entering, but ten times worse. Again, there were long lines, which were outside in the rain. He somehow cut in line and came back crushed. No seats remained unless we paid a bribe. After some anxious minutes of determining what could be done (*I was leaving Shanghai early the next morning to Narita, so staying over was not an option*), it turned out the bribe was only a few cents, so back he went, I got a ticket and he rushed me to the train, which was just pulling out—five minutes early—when I jumped on, soaking wet. This escapade was the longest half hour of my life. The din, the mass of humanity, no signs in English…I now know why the university was apprehensive.

But the story continues, for two hours later, the train arrived in Shanghai for a long cab ride to my hotel, which was close to the airport, but outside of town. (*Since then, the Westin moved to a new location on the Bund.*) Unfortunately, the cab line was another mass of humanity, but I noticed that the subway was also located in the terminal. In those days there was nothing to the Westin, but the Hilton (*where I had stayed in a previous trip*) was only a couple of stops away, and it's always easy to get a taxi at a major hotel. As no one spoke English, I struggled to get a ticket, which was all of ten cents or so, got on and off, which was a challenge, because the signs were in Chinese. The exit to the outside was jam packed as the rain was really coming down. There was no sense in getting an umbrella as I was still wet. So out I went, heading in the general direction of the Hilton, and for no good reason, began waving my hand in hopes that a cab would stop…and one did. So I jumped in and gave him the Westin card. He nodded, but after half an hour, I began to get nervous, as the hotel was not that far away. The thought of being shanghaid in Shanghai came to mind. After another fifteen minutes of anxiety, he made it to the hotel, and I don't think I paid even $2, with tip.

**My Message from Purgatory, Also Known as Cairo**

This section consists of a series of e-mails I sent to colleagues as a stop on an around the world trip.

> *Dear Friends:*
>
> *The overall world trip itself has been fantastic, with the only unusual portion being our current stop:* ***Cairo****. The trip started in Tokyo on August 15, 2000, then, Frankfurt, Hannover (for the Expo), Marlburg, Edinburgh, Athens, Delos, Mykonos, Santorini, Rhodes, Kusadasi, Istanbul and* ***Cairo****. We hope to eventually get to Munich, Wash. D.C., Orlando, Chicago, Las Vegas, San Francisco and Honolulu (September 26, 2000).*
>
> *We are now more than halfway through our world odyssey, and, as we seem to be trapped in a kind of purgatory, I thought this would be good time to communicate with our friends, while summarizing the current technical essence of my trip for the University of Hawaii. Much of the following many of you will find boring, but, if you harbor any thoughts of someday seeing the pyramids in Egypt, you might at least want to refer to that portion of the message, for* ***Cairo*** *has been a distinct surprise for us.*

*Our first stop was Tokyo, where we met with Hiro Nakahara and Toshitsugu Sakou, ending the evening with Yoko and Toshi at an Italian restaurant in Ebesu. We left the next morning for Frankfurt, and, over a couple of days, first took in the Hannover Expo, and followed with a stop in Marlburg. No matter what you have read, Expo 2000 was very impressive, and featured most of the world, except for the USA. While Outer Mongolia and various countries at war had decent exhibits, for our nation, only companies had a presence. We had lunch at Horst Senger's home in Marlburg with Shigetoh Miyachi, and formed a Japan/European/U.S. "emeritus" advisory team on the photo-bio production of everything from hydrogen to global climate remediation. Professor Miyachi is the grand old man of biotechnology from the University of Tokyo and Professor Senger is his equivalent in Germany.*

*In Edinburgh, we were joined by Yayoi and Takeo Kondo, and met with Grant Burgess and Phil Wright to plan for a major international marine biotech gathering to be held at Heriot-Watt University in August of next year. We added a session on the biotechnology of next generation fisheries. Andrew Sprague earlier this year received his PhD from HWU, and obtained an offer from St. Andrews University to stimulate the commercialization of biotechnology. He had spent some time at HNEI in our Marine Bioresources Laboratory, and is leading the search for marine algae colors for the pearl project. As he is a world class surfer, he is torn between teaching Prince Andrew/picking up golf, or becoming a pearl entrepreneur in Hawaii.*

*As Professor Kondo is a specialist in marine recreation, we accompanied him on one of his official duties, and flew to Athens to board the Crown Odyssey for a cruise to Istanbul. To say that I had more than my fill of ruins is a mild understatement. Acropolis, Delphi, Santorini, Ephesus...we saw it all. Our biggest accomplishment is that Pearl and I walked from the Topkapi Museum in Istanbul, to the Grand Bazaar, on to the Spice Market...then back to the Intercontinental Hotel. At 95 degrees F, completely across a hilly city, that was a major achievement.*

*As using your computer to retrieve e-mail from your room on the ship cost $350/hour, and their internet room cost about $50/hour, we fortunately could find on each Greek Island internet cafes, which only charge about $4/hour, and some even had free coffee. You might consider getting a HOTMAIL address, which is the cheapest way to communicate on international travel.*

*PEARL AND I THEN FLEW TO* ***CAIRO****. This is where it gets bizarre. Getting a visa was trivial, but as in life itself, agonizing, if you don't know how to do it. First, you are not told that you needed one until you got there, and then, no one seemed to know how to get one. There were numerous lines for various things, and the one that gave the visa was the one that exchanged money, so we lucked out.*

*IF YOU PLAN ON GOING TO EGYPT, JOIN A PACKAGED TOUR. Don't just show up and expect to catch a taxi to your hotel. Well, this "government official" came up to us and said that she needed to escort us out of the airport. She even had a badge, and this was before you went through customs. It turns out this is a scam, and she diverted us to a tour desk, where we were badgered to sign up for inflated tours. We somehow were able to resist, and they gave up and charged us 50 Egyptian Pounds (3.5 pounds to the dollar) to take us to the Nile Hilton. We were kind of spooked, and did not then realize that they did us a favor, for if we caught a taxi off the street, who knows where we would be now, although I somewhere read that, because of the culture, Cairo is the safest Western metropolis. The air-conditioned van ride to the hotel was comfortable, the driver spoke English and he gave us a free tour of the city. Only in afterthought did I realize that the government passed us through this process because there were no other options for tours. If this is not making sense to you, read on.*

*The Nile Hilton is the worst Hilton I have ever experienced. Staff attitude was atrocious. The place was going to seed. We were given a room with an overpowering odor of tobacco, and was moved to one where the door safety latch was previously forced open, and just hung on one screw. There is no information guide in the room, and when I asked for a map at the Concierge Desk, was told to buy one at the book store. However, there was an internet café close by (hotels typically charge about 6 times more than these coffee shops), the Egyptian Museum was next door, and the Nile was across the street. Just walking around (outside) the hotel, though, is an adventure, as there are swarms of people just sitting on the curb or standing and doing nothing. Everything here ranges from brownish gray to grayish brown, even the Nile, and the entire city is like a ghetto for 20 million people.*

*That night, we decided to move. I had previously made a reservation at a Sheraton which was scheduled to open earlier this year. We somehow got their telephone number, and at 5AM called to see if they would honor something I had cancelled two months before. To my surprise, the person who answered said come on over, and even gave me a $95 rate, which compared well with the $165 Hilton room. We checked out the next morning and were asked by the uniformed person, who was picking us up. When we said that we needed to catch a taxi, he flinched, and showed body language like, you're kidding. He said he'd do what he could to arrange for a safe taxi. (By the way, you might recall that Bangkok had a serial taxi robber/murderer that lasted about a year. He mostly killed Europeans. It turns out he wasn't Thai, but was an Egyptian.) He waved a couple of cabs on and selected one where they settled on a 25 pound rate to take us to the Sheraton Royal Garden, which was surprising in two respects. First we were changing hotels, and he was good humored about it, and second, no one knew where this hotel was located, as it had just opened.*

*We caught our last taxi in Cairo, I hope. The temperature here ranges from 95 to 100 degrees, and no taxi is air conditioned. The vehicles themselves are used car rejects from Yugoslavia, or something close.*

*In Athens, Istanbul and Cairo, for a ten day period, we never saw any blue sky or even a cloud, for air pollution obscured the sky. The airport and traffic in Cairo are reminiscent of Manila and Bangkok 15 years ago. If a road had three lanes, there were two more, if the road was wide enough. No one paid any attention to the lines, and not much to traffic lights. Our taxi was bumped and the driver just gave the offender an evil eye and moved on. The thought of us stopping in the middle of this traffic with our baggage would have been nightmarish. There were people on street corners selling one cigarette and individual bandages. Interesting that we saw a number of older adults with what looked like their head completely covered like a mummy. Well, the taxi found our hotel, a true miracle, because even the hotel staff said no one can find it.*

*The Sheraton Royal Gardens is an oasis. It has been operating since March, but portions are not yet completed. The staff is incredible, so much so that I began to worry...and still do. They call us up twice a day to ask if there is anything else they can do.*

*Let me share, though, some concerns:*

*1. You've seen those movies where you show up at the Pearly Gates and they can't find your name. The person on the phone I talked to must have screwed up because the attendant at the desk hotel said it was full, and for us to wait in the nice lounge, where they served us a refreshing drink. After a short wait, they showed us to our room, which is beautiful. They must have opened up a new area, at least that's what Pearl suspects, because there is no one else on our floor. We walked around the large pool and an Egyptian song was blaring. Later, I learned that the music was Mexican.*

*2. We had dinner the first night at Trader Vic's, that international chain. You ask, why didn't we catch the dinner cruise on the Nile or the sound and light show at the Pyramids? Well, this Sheraton does not subscribe to any services for these kinds of things, so we needed to hire a private driver. We thus made arrangements to go to the Egyptian Museum, bazaar and Pyramids/Sphinx the next day. The Concierge found a driver with car for a cost about half of what that airport tour desk quoted. Anyway, at the hotel restaurant, where the food was good and service impeccable, there were a dozen people manning the tables, but we were the only customers. We stayed from 8PM to 10:30PM, and finally left when three more people finally showed up. It was weird. This is as large a Trader Vic's as any of the others in the world. The person running this restaurant came from Thailand, and he said that his father was manager of the Trader Vic's in Munich, at the hotel where the HyForum Conference, our next stop, was to be held. What a coincidence. All the restaurants here are being run by people from Bangkok—Inakaya and Senor Pico are the other to places to eat.*

*3. The next day, the front desk wished me happy birthday, and everyone knew our name. Strange. It was recommended that we not walk outside because all we'd see were street people. We could not catch a taxi. So we were effectively trapped. At about this time it occurred to me that the bump in traffic the previous day might have been more serious, and maybe, we have passed away, and this hotel was purgatory. Starwood is owned by God and this is just a stop to heaven, I hope. The Hilton here is purgatory for hell, surely. Interestingly enough, I had a Sheraton Year 2000 directory, and, of all the things, there were no Sheratons listed for Egypt, which made no sense because I earlier booked this one, and we saw at least three more obvious Sheratons in town on the way in from the airport. Maybe they were all recently disenfranchised, but kept the name. But like in the movies, they, apparently, allow you to make one more trip to Planet Earth, so we were picked up by our guide, who had an air-conditioned, purple Toyota RAV. One problem was that he did not speak English. The tour itself would take a whole page, so I'll skip it (except to say that the Egyptian Museum—you know, that King Tut home—was very dusty with a few rooms set aside where the guards allow you in only for another fee, which is blatantly illegal, just another scam), but to editorialize that if you are not into this kind of adventure, hate the heat and dust, and don't care much for death and the afterlife, go to Las Vegas. The Luxor is about the same size as the largest pyramid, and I think the new Sphinx on the Strip is on the order of the ancient one.*

*4. We were delivered back to good purgatory, and Pearl and I celebrated my Yakudoshi at Inakaya. The food was excellent and, again, the service was great. The toro (fatty blue-fin tuna) cost about 10% what it would have in Tokyo. However, again, we were the only ones eating in the table area. It seemed that there was a group of five at the teppan yaki grill way on the other end, but that could have been a hologram to make us feel more comfortable. The restaurant itself was huge, maybe the largest Japanese restaurant I have ever been in. The cook was from Bangkok, and he told us he learned everything at a Japanese restaurant in Texas. Oh yes, they brought us a chocolate cake with candle, and the staff sang happy birthday. The two Thai employees in addition sang a Japanese equivalent of happy birthday. But again, we were the only ones eating, and this hotel is supposedly "full." Except we never see anyone around. We have not seen a real tourist in this hotel.*

*5. We still had two days left, with nothing to do, so we decided to sleep in and fast for one day. We have been eating too well on this trip. Surely, we had gained several pounds from the cruise alone. About 1PM Pearl gave up because she got hungry. So much for our fast. But we ate in our room some stuff we had collected throughout the trip. For dinner we went to Senor Pico's. Twelve waiters were there to greet us, and we had one of the finest Mexican dinners we have ever had. The margarita (Professor Miyachi, you might want to consider passing through this purgatory) was perfect. There were seven in the Mariachi Band, dressed in traditional costume, and they entertained us through our entire meal. We were the only customers.*

*6. Today, we ate the fruit in our room for breakfast and went to the pool barbeque for lunch. People were swimming and sunning, our first real tourists, but again, we were the only ones who ate. The food was great, with free beer. Certainly, something is not quite right.*

*7. I have kept asking about the trip to the airport tomorrow, and the response is always that they are looking for the most cost-effective way for us to get there, and this has not yet been determined. The same people seem to work at the same stations, 24-hours a day. There is also this lighted room in a separate part of our floor—we remain the only ones, except for them—which overlooks the hotel area and pool, and there are people in white always there—sort of like a Ku Klux Klan revival meeting.*

*At 4AM this morning, they seemed to still be in conference. Maybe they are the ones planning our future.*

*Of course, there are explanations for all the above, and perhaps, there are some minor exaggerations here and there. But isn't this all very interesting? If you receive this e-mail and never hear from us again, you are the very first to receive a communication from the afterlife, or, at least, purgatory. Send someone to the Sheraton Royal Gardens in* ***Cairo*** *to check out the place. Maybe rescue us. We still have one more dinner tonight, and we are planning to fool them. Stay tuned.*

*Aloha.*

*Pearl and Pat*

## The Mystery Continues (8Sept2000)

*Hi Friends:*

*These are the latest developments. We learned that people in Egypt eat quite late, so we decided to go to all three restaurants beginning at 9PM. We first went to the Japanese restaurant, and had 15 people leave while we were there, and ended up alone after half an hour. We only had sashimi and a drink, and went on to the Mexican restaurant. We had a snack with a frozen margarita. Again, a very lively Mexican band, but no customers. At 11PM we finished up at Trader Vic's, and were the only ones there until two ladies showed up just before we left. Maybe there is hope, although I again went up to the front desk and asked (the same person who has continuously been there since we first checked in) on details regarding transportation tomorrow morning to the airport, and his response was that they were still working on it.*

*Aloha.*

*Pat*

## Escape from Cairo (9Sept2000)

*Hi All:*

*We woke up on the day of our flight and I immediately checked with the desk about transportation to the airport. They said they found a reliable person who would be by at 10AM for our 3PM flight. It would take about half an hour to the airport. I wondered why so early, but was nevertheless relieved.*

*Surely enough, at 10 or so he showed up. He could barely speak English, but was told in Egyptian our flight number. The bags were loaded into the back of his strange looking car, which was not air-conditioned. About ten minutes into the drive, he mumbled something about needing to fill gas. So, he went way out of his way into a strange neighborhood. Apparently, you fill his car through a hole below where our bags were, so they had to unload virtually all the baggage. I thought, oh no, they're going to steal our luggage. Well, after about ten minutes, they put everything back in and he drove to the airport.*

*He dropped us off, but the airport was closed. Closed!!! Apparently, for security reasons, they now and then stop any entry for a couple of hours because it gets too congested inside. After half an hour in the hot sun, they opened up one door, and the crowd funneled into the airport check-in area. There was no system and it was every person for himself. With all our luggage, it was a very painful process. After another 45 minutes, we made it to our Lufthansa check-in area, where they first had to scrutinize every bag in detail. This was after another half an hour wait in line. We got our tickets and proceeded into the actual airport, where there was a horrendously long line, as again, every article had to be hand-checked. At this point we had about an hour before our flight left.*

*Then we had to go through customs. That was another experience not worth even repeating. This took half an hour. We then walked to the gate area of our flight, where again, there was a long line, because everything again had to be hand-checked. We walked straight to our seats and the plane left in ten minutes, some customers still in that line, for the plane was only half full. You think airport security is a pain? Try Cairo!*

*We're alive and well. Munich is Heaven!*

*Aloha,*

*Pearl and Pat*

It is thus safe to say that we can eliminate Cairo as the best place to live.

**The Challenges and Promise of La Reunion Island**

I embarked on an $18,000 (*just expenses*) trip in October and November of 2005 to La Reunion Island, located in the Indian Ocean, then going on to Paris, Oslo, Bergen and London. The expense was high because there were some paid upgraded segments. This was certainly in the top 10 of worst and best trips, showing enormous promise for future interaction (*see The Free Hydrogen Age and the Blue Revolution in **Book 1***). Mauritius was a late add-on, and a pleasant one.

*Dear Friends:*

*By now you have probably received at least one of eleven chapters of my month long trip to the Indian Ocean and Europe. For some, it will only take you a second to delete this as SPAM. For others who actually might be interested in gaining some closure, this is a collection of the most memorable experiences and anecdotes, in chronological order:*

*a. After flying (actual air time) about 28 hours, I landed in La Reunion Island, east of Madagascar in the Indian Ocean. La Reunion, about the size of Oahu, at the same Latitude (but they are South and we are North—close to being our antipode), with about the same population and a balanced, but different, ethnic mix of Africains, French, Chinese and Indian, is a "welfare" department of France. There seem to be tolerable racial relations, although those walking the markets look only to be brown/black. I actually asked someone why I don't see too many Chinese, and the response was: they are in their shops. Perhaps true, but nevertheless, disconcerting. Unemployment might be as high as 50%, but the government payments are quite good (the unemployed take vacations to Mauritius), although crime is distressing, most probably because of an underlying drug problem. However, I don't think I saw a beggar or homeless person. The French government subsidizes gasoline and electricity prices to maintain equality with the nation. But, to cut future costs, there is heavy pressure for conversion to coal, a policy being questioned by the island president, Paul Verges, who is someone I could well look like if I lived to the age of 82.Verges wants renewable energy and ocean resources, thus the reason why I am here, for they are just where we were 30 years ago: dying sugar industry, potential geothermal resources and a wealth of renewable options. Their meetings typically started with breakfast at 7AM and ended after dinner at 11PM. Worse, 95% of all official discussions were in French. My PhD language was French, but I know more Japanese than French, and anyone who knows me, knows that I don't know any Japanese. Amazingly, though, among the 100 or so conferees over the two weeks, I never saw anyone doze off. Even more of a surprise, as fatigued and jet-lagged as I was during these psychologically arduous sessions, I must have been too tired to fall asleep during these interminable discussions, as I hardly knew what was being said. They were all genuinely interested and dedicated to do something about their energy problem, and the planning staff was like super-humans: spoke a variety of languages, were nice, helpful, progressive and well educated. My primary contact, Laurens Gautret, from France, had a PhD in astrophysics, and recently returned from Chile, where he had a project on search for extrasolar planets, an interest area of mine, to settle on this island (his wife is from Reunion). There are two other problems: mosquitoes and cockroaches. In Norway, if you see a leaf rolling on the ground, it is a leaf. In Reunion, it will probably be a roach, especially at night. Actually, I exaggerate, for there are probably more large cockroaches on my roof area on warm nights than in any equivalent space on that island. I did, though, have an encounter here with the largest flying cockroach I have ever seen. The mosquitoes, though, were the truly worrisome factor. Just this year, Chikumgunya appeared. 5,000 now have been infected, and the symptoms are like Dengue Fever, but with a lot more pain. Week One was like hell for me, as my glasses fell apart on the flight over, I contracted a cold, had an uneasy stomach, experienced marginal hotels, was subjected to Creole food (okay once a month, but not six meals in a row), and always, there was the worry about Chikumgunya. My body was very unhappy with me for subjecting it to this ordeal.*

*b. Week Two began at an especial nadir. We were asked to appear at 9AM for an "easy" hike up a mountain to visit a renewable energy site, stay overnight and hike back the next day. However, the directions were to douse yourself with mosquito repellent (Chikumgunya!!) and bring a change of clothing. I showed up in hush puppies and a Wal-Mart shopping bag with my clothes. They were passing out large—two liter—bottles of water, a yard long French roll and some cheese to the hikers. That was to be the food for the next two days. Save for me and one other, everyone else had professional backpacks and hiking boots. Someone had mentioned to me that there was a water shortage and there were no showers available at the site. As I looked so out of place, in one of my best ever exhibitions of extemporaneous brilliance—escape became a mandatory solution—I went up to my contact and indicated that my room reeked of tobacco smoke and I had a bad cold (both necessary exaggerations, although this hotel, or, at least, my room, was pretty bad), and instead of joining them, I would be moving hotels (there was a recently built Concorde I read in the travel guide that looked appealing). He hesitated, then said he would drive me up there and sign me in, for he was an experienced hiker (at some point in the potential challenging march, he had to assist that other person who, like me, was not prepared to undertake this expedition) and could easily catch up with the group. I weakly objected, but he fortunately was insistent, which was a good thing, because you essentially needed to speak French to make this transition into the Concorde.*

*c. My Week Two was like Purgatory (which is a huge step up from Hell). This new hotel had an exercise room, plasma TV screen, a view of the city/ocean, an excellent French restaurant and, because of the relative elevation and dry climiate, no prospects for Chikumgunya. When the group returned, they stayed at that dump, while I luxuriated in the Concorde. This is one of the reasons why Americans are just not appreciated around the world. It's an attitude thing. However, I endeared myself with the conferees by repeatedly mentioning that, I, too, had severe problems with President George Bush. It turned out that, better yet, I could now opt out of certain whole morning and afternoons of meetings because I was sort of inconveniently located for the pick-up bus (that hill was a challenge). Anyway, I would not understand most of the discussion, so it was a relief for all involved. Week Two was actually enjoyable, for my comfort level was fine and I think I actually said a few things at rare opportunities that someday will help the island.*

*d. To be serious, La Reunion has a shot at succeeding because, contrary to our beginnings, oil prices are now much higher, solar technologies are now largely proven (Hawaii was the international laboratory for renewables, which meant that everything that we tried essentially failed) and there is the fear of global climate warming. This is using some hindsight, but when we completed all those island energy self-sufficiency projects in the mid-seventies, the electricity part was deemed to be a given once the price of oil climbed higher (I think we will be right on this), but hydrogen was to be the key to the future, for if biomass (sugar cane) could be converted to bio-methanol, the production can be DOUBLED, if cost-effective hydrogen can be added in the process, and, the most promising aviation future had to be hydrogen jetliners. Unfortunately, because of the farm lobby, our Nation went ethanol, which will in time, be a mistake because, given fiber, it is much more economical to produce methanol, which, in addition to replacing gasoline, also can be readily utilized by fuel cells. It is a shame that the National Aerospace Plane (which was supposed to use hydrogen fuel), which we helped create through the Matsunaga Hydrogen Act, was eventually killed by the Department of Defense, so the future of air travel will remain a problem. A tiny island in the middle of the Pacific can affect the energy future of the nation and world. I now and then mentioned this potential for Reunion, and, later, in Mauritius. Someday, they will be energy independent and provide resources for Europe.*

*e. Well, for Week Three, go to next section on Mauritius...*

*f. Go on to following section on Norway...*

*h. Go on to London...*

*I'm now back home and this is also the 14th day since I left La Reunion, so I, apparently, escaped the curse of Chikumgunya. This is also my final trip anywhere. Almost for sure.*

*Aloha.*

*Pat*

But, that was in 2005. In 2006, the staff of President Verges volunteered to look closer at the Free Hydrogen Economy. Let's see, now. They are about the same size and population as Oahu. Tourism is important; the sudden calamity of Chikumgunya has left them in a pickle. They have a dying sugar industry and their mother country wants to convert them into a coal economy. They just might be at that critical stage to enter doomsday, which is almost a necessary requirement for human societies to transcend normality. If France can be convinced to pick a year, say, 2020, for good vision, when renewable hydrogen is suddenly made free, La Reunion might have as good a chance as any to tap her nation's deep pockets to get a jump on what might be the only solution for humanity, too. Stay tuned. La Reunion Island might just someday make my top place to live in my update of ***Simple Solutions, Book 2***.

## *e. The Paradise Known as Mauritius*

*Well, for Week Three, I was next scheduled to fly back to Paris to meet with UNESCO on the Blue Revolution, but riots had started, so, instead, by their request, I flew to Mauritius, a half an hour away, which is smaller than Reunion, but has 1.2 million people, just like Hawaii. It has a sugar industry on the edge of going bankrupt, a declining textile industry (because of China) and a smaller and smaller fishing fleet. However, there is low unemployment, religious/ethnic harmony (Lee Kuan Yew, evidently, some time ago, came here and copied the system for Singapore) and an inspired leadership, which has selected the Blue Revolution as their future. (A small team visited Hawaii a year later.)*

*I was housed for three days at a resort that was a combination of Mauna Lani Bay and Mauna Kea Beach Hotels. The dinner buffet was at least twice as large as anything I'd seen anywhere, with various stations for carvings, creole food (yes, same kind as Reunion...and Louisiana—but at least this one was temperature hot), pasta, etc. There was also a stage show at dinner time, very similar to those you see on a cruise. The one distracting factor one night was another large cockroach that seemed to enjoy running from the stage to my table and back, with the lead singer and me subtly and unsuccessfully trying to kill it.*

*The breakfast buffet was equally impressive, with free champagne every morning. I gave my talk on THE BLUE REVOLUTION to their government planning group of the Mauritius Research Council, headed by Arjoon Suddhoo, a PhD aerospace engineer and past chairman of the board of Air Mauritius (Air Madagascar is on the "don't fly" list.....Air Mauritius is doing quite well, unlike United Airlines and most American airlines, and is the only one, I think, to still pass out metal knives with their meals). Mauritius is a nation (same vote as the U.S. in the United Nation) and linked historically with Great Britain, meaning they all speak English. As Brisbane was an oasis, Mauritius reminded me of what Heaven might be.*

*The flight from Mauritius to Paris was, courtesy of Arjoon Suddhoo, in First Class, and wonderful. However, I soon noted that virtually every notable location we flew over started with an M: Mauritius, Madagascar, Mombasa, Mogadishu, Misratah, Mediterranean Sea (and several other seas, which, when you approach Italy, become Mer, for Sea), between Marseille and Monaco, at which point I began to get worried. I still had that M Curse in my mind. Clearly, this was a clue that the plane would be hijacked and flown to Munich, or, more probably, Moscow. However, as we approached Paris, it was, indeed, burning. There was ongoing civil unrest, so I immediately transferred planes at Charles De Gaulle for Oslo.*

I might mention that, while Mauritius is in the Indian Ocean, it is considered to be the most successful African nation in progressive business development. It is the only African country to have eradicated malaria. The government has been stable for forty years, and featured are free education and free health care. I was very impressed with their success at racial relations and they have taken on the challenge of the Blue Revolution.

### *f. Norway, the Next Best Place in the World*

*Week 3 in Oslo was enjoyable. Norway has for the past five years now been selected as the best place to live (until displaced by Switzerland this past year). Yes, it is far too cold, although, apparently, when I was there, 15 degrees F warmer than normally. It was still, though, too cold, and this was only November.*

*Prices are very high for everything, and their best restaurants charge ridiculous amounts for very pedestrian cuisine. I noted that their newscasters surely sounded like they were speaking English in reverse. Serious climate warming can only help this country, but, then, with sea level rise (as much as 250 feet can occur over a long period of time) both Oslo and Bergen would go underwater.*

*Why, then, is Norway so terrific? There is no homeless, nor insects, true peace of mind (you can actually walk the parks at night), and everything works. The bathrooms and airports (when you want to leave Bergen, there is no check-in desk-you must use those scary looking machines, but someone is there to help you) are well engineered, elevators arrive within 10 seconds (if not already there—in London, the average wait is more than a minute), cities and public lavatories that are really clean, with soft paper towels, and a transportation system that is frequent and dependable. The people are attractive and nice, with no obvious obesity problem.*

*Hydropower supplies their electricity, oil has been a godsend, plus, they have vast quantities of natural gas yet to tap. I gave several PowerPoint talks on THE BLUE REVOLUTION and NEXT GENERATION FISHERIES, for, many decades from now, when they run out of fossil fuel and have overfished their still OK stocks, the open ocean will need to be their future, something they have not needed to think about. I think I planted a seed for their future.*

*Then, on to Bergen, another fine city. In a special summit with Chile, Norway and the USA, we created the Bergen Declaration for Next Generation Fisheries. A century from now, some historian will discover this document and trace the relative abundance of seafood to this international agreement.*

*Bergen rained about 8 inches in a 24 hour period and then snowed 4 inches, but the one day we were free, the sky was sunny, the snowfall looked majestic and the various touristy sites educational, enjoyable and almost free. Yes, Norway deserves its high world ranking.*

### g. London

*Next, London was experiencing frigid conditions, but, with no wind and a lot of sun, walking around was a very tolerable experience. This was about the tenth time I had visited this sprawling city. I had the pleasure to have lunch with Don Lennard (who has since passed away), the OTEC guy from the U.K., at his stately club: dry sherry, followed by a bottle of Claret (British term for Bordeaux), with a kind of cream soup and hare—a large bunny, which tasted exactly like the Minke whale I had in Bergen, both of which had the odor and consistency of a tough piece of beef liver. So much for trying the food of the region. We connived on the future of OTEC, which appears now to be experiencing a measurable revival. I chatted with Professor Bill McGuire of University College of London, who gave the annual Science Museum lecture on monumental disasters, two chapters of my upcoming book. I saw THE PRODUCERS, to next month (remember, this is the continuation of my letter to colleagues) be released for the second time as a movie, with Lane/Broderick, and SATURDAY NIGHT FEVER, probably the best stage musical I have ever seen, mostly because the sound (there were 20 foot tall speakers—if you have a pacemaker, don't go) was incredible, and the cast, after the usual bows, kept singing and dancing, with the audience, for another half an hour, they said, because it was Saturday night, which it was that night.*

*In London, reading newspapers like the* **Financial Times**, *I noticed that gold, at nearly $500 / troy oz, is the highest it has been in 18 years (in 2008, the price rose to $900 / toz), and copper hit an all time high. In case you don't keep up with these things, almost always, these signs mean that inflation is coming. (Well, it never came, but wait till 2012!) The Japanese Nikkei hit a 4.5 year high and the South Korean stock market has never, ever, been any higher. Sell!!! On the other hand, I'm usually wrong on stock prices. Google, which was less than $100/share a little more than a year ago, is now at $400 (but soared past $700 in 2007, dropping some in 2008). Of course, I didn't buy. Twelve of the most respected fifteen international companies (Toyota at #3; British Petroleum, an oil company that has a progressive view on sustainable resources; and Siemens, also a company with good attitude are up there) are U.S. corporations, with Microsoft as #1. I guess we're doing fine as a Nation, even though no one likes us.*

This entry completes my travel report to the Indian Ocean and Europe. A few of the stops were ideally arranged for me to confirm decisions for this chapter. I took the trip, I guess, at least partly, for this purpose.

## Scotland and Ireland

Why am I reporting on these two countries? First, because they are among my favorites. Second, these two countries serve as the backdrop for a story I just had to share, which follows this section.

August is the finest month to visit Scotland. Make it the only good month. The Arts Festival, single malt scotches and the home of golf make for an idyllic combination. Let me, though, write Scotland off with two words—too cold—but, still provide an entertaining story featuring Professor Grant Burgess, favorite son of Edinburgh, who when this tale occurred a decade ago, was the biotechnology expert for Heriot-Watt University located in his home town.

When a small group of us first visited that campus, their vice provost, or something similar, welcomed us into his capacious conference room, and this being the late afternoon, wheeled out a cart of six single malt scotches. He proceeded to provide some background of each, from the lightest up to Lagavulan, a peaty 16-year old malt, which soon became my favorite. We came to talk marine biotechnology, but never got around to that subject.

Grant later took us to his office, and pointed out that his two neighbors were the Scotch Professor of Scotland and a biology faculty member who, while also a specialist in malting and brewing, had a membership in the Royal and Ancient Golf Club of St. Andrews. Dr. James Bryce had a single digit handicap and took us to his home course on occasion.

I've challenged Carnoustie, the home of the Open in 2007, and even toyed with the Old Course of St. Andrews, or, make it the other way around. Anyway, will come back to Scotland later, but one day, Grant Burgess, Mayumi and Tadashi Matsunaga and I golfed at the Royal Dublin Golf Course, in Ireland, which was on that other island to the West. Ireland is a favorite of many, and the town of Dublin has terrific character, with a good many bars and a lot of artworks consisting of painted cows. There's a reason for this, and I'll need to Google the reason. Anyway, the day I landed, I had transferred through Heathrow, and London had, for the first time in recorded history, hit 100 degrees Fahrenheit, with Dublin at 98°F. The major news item was a warning to place sun block on cow udders.

Of course, I thought about protecting myself, too, so I went to a department store but couldn't find any for humans. After much scurrying around, I finally was able to purchase a small tube of Johnson and Johnson for a ridiculously high price. It went on fine, although it seemed stain everything white, but just wouldn't come off, even with soap. I think I bought something for cows.

Well, back to the Royal Dublin, Grant and I each rented a golf set, while the Matsunaga's had brought theirs. We were going to buy golf balls, which were very, very expensive, but Tadashi said, we could use his, for he brought a lot of them. We teed off, but by the fifth hole, were down to one ball each. The rough grass just consumed our balls, and Tadashi had not brought that many, maybe only 35. Well, anyway, the more interesting story occurred at St. Andrews, where golf was invented. But I eliminate Ireland from contention because it also is normally too cold and you're never quite sure about some terroristic threat, although that is, really, in Northern Ireland, a part of the United Kingdom. Ireland is its own nation and deserves a top ten standing.

What has this got to do with Scotland and being the best place to live? Nothing much, but serves as a link to the next story.

## Revenge of the Green Buggies (circa 2000)

Leaving Edinburgh in Scotland, seven of us were led by Grant, bon vivant and champion karaoke singer, on about a one hour drive to St. Andrews, home of golf, which reeked of history. He arranged for us to stay at the dormitories of St. Andrews University.

We had back to back times at the New Course, which started play more than 100 years ago. The hallowed Old Course of Open fame initiated golf in 1574. We signed up and some of us rented pull carts. No riding here, except for the dreaded Green Buggy, a golf cart, and weapon of choice for the Course Marshalls, who maintain a vigorous regime of discipline at the club.

We were shown to the first hole by the Starter, a tough ex-military type with a large moustache, who clearly put up with no nonsense. He gave us a few derisory looks. There were four all–American jocks standing behind the tee off area, immaculately dressed, with real golf shoes and the latest golf technology. In fact, I recall two of them were actually wearing tweed plus four trousers with sky blue socks. They were anxious to tee off and get going but had the misfortune to have a 9:13 tee off time after our groups.

At 9:01 AM four of us went to tee off (*they move things along promptly here at St Andrews*), and a few obviously snide comments were heard. No problem. I was in the foursome with Tadashi Matsunaga and two of his colleagues from the Tokyo University of Agriculture and Technology, one of whom, Professor Miyata, went on to become President at this university, the institution where Grant spent his post-doc period under the mentorship of Professor Matsunaga, who himself, seems destined for that same honorable position, president of the university, that is.

In group two were Phil Wright (*from Australia, but a faculty member of HWU*), Visanu Meyoo (*from Mahanakorn University in Thailand*) and old pro, Grant Burgess. Actually, Grant was not quite ready, and, had last golfed sometime the previous year or so.

The story is taken up by Grant Burgess, then with Heriot-Watt University (*HWU*), but now with the University of Newcastle:

> *The Fife wind was howling cold, and, actually, the first group did not tee off at 9:01, for Tadashi, more used to the climes of Hawaii and the relaxed pace of Japanese courses, had come dressed in a T shirt, but urgently required his windproof St Andrews top he had purchased the day before. Unaccustomed to the police state regulations in force at the New Course, requiring that one must tee off within the 6 minute allocated time slot, Tadashi began to saunter back to the car park to retrieve his windproof top, a stroll of about ten, maybe fifteen, minutes. Recognising immediately the ensuing catastrophe, Jim Bryce, Royal and Ancient Club member with a two handicap, and my close colleague from HWU, who had come to see us off, flung him his own sweater and urged in almost panic to TEE OFF NOW! The wind lifted, the tension mounted, sweat trickled down Jim's temple, and his reputation was at stake. All eyes were on Professor Matsunaga, who now was reasonably warm and confidently strode to the tee box. The American Foursome was scrutinising his every wiggle with piercing blue eyes and voluminous quantities of derision.*
>
> *Tadashi swung and struck the ball well, it curved up beautifully and we all watched as it veered majestically straight into the metal grandstand with a loud "bong," a central strike on the metal scaffold pole, and ricocheted into the gorse. The grandstand was in place for next week's Open. The American's rolled their eyes skyward, the Starter began to frown, but I thought it was quite a good shot! The panic continued and Pat teed off next, fast and hurried, but unbelievably straight down the perilously narrow fairway. Professor Takahashi was not much of a golfer himself, actually. Dr. Wake was next, then Professor Miyata. "Quick quick," Jim implored, urging them on, the clock ticking...already three minutes late..."walk up the fairway and crack on." The green buggies had started to gather, like storm clouds. I should just clarify: St Andrews has "Course Marshals," whose job it is to "oversee play," and they do this with Stasi like efficiency. They chivvy and chase you at any delay, for slow play is a crime in St Andrews, on a par with murder. It is not to be tolerated and must be rooted out at all cost. The Green Buggies, dark, worryingly dark green, ferry the Marshal's all over the course watching, and, as you will see, striking down those who do not comply.*

*So, somewhat shakily, the first group was off, but the Americans again began to make loud and disparaging remarks, and another Marshal in his Green Buggy drove up to the tee off area and watched the proceedings solemnly. Three of us were left. No racial comments as such. It was just that Visanu, who had never golfed in his life, was wearing a World War II Eisenhower jacket (it was really cold, slightly drizzling, and this was August), jeans and army boots. Not regular St Andrews golf wear, while my own garb also left a lot to be desired. My Hawaiian Aloha shirt was bright orange rayon with real coconut buttons and a foot long blue flying fish swimming across the front. I must enquire of the Royal and Ancient Club byelaws whether such dress is allowed on the New Course. Flapping in the wind, as this shirt did, I had the feeling that it did not endear me to the gathering throng of Course Marshals. The next sequence of events to unfold left us all in shock. Bear in mind, that by now, tempers were frayed at the delay, plus the obvious insult of our ensemble, and, frighteningly, yet to come, golfmanship.*

*Visanu had no clubs of his own. Another major felony. But it was OK, I thought, he was sharing mine. My own golf bag was a 1930's antique orange canvas bag, which matched my Aloha shirt. It had seen better days and had holes and significant leather failure. But it was equipped with fully four clubs. A rusty five iron, a brass putter, a sand wedge and a club of indeterminate identity. All with the grips falling off in tatters. Well, as a beginner, I wasn't going to splash out on expensive clubs now, was I? My lack of any drivers did not worry me at that time, as I always teed off with my five iron, and was always happy to chip my way round a course in under 150 or so. At least I rarely lost my ball! The Starter, Marshals and American Jock Pack were aghast. We were by now four minutes late. High treason.*

*Visanu had trouble placing the golf ball on the tee, something he was doing, maybe, for the first time in his life. His major error was pushing the tee into the turf at a slight angle so that the ball rolled off two seconds after he had straightened up. This happened three times. He then realized, being an internationally recognized engineer, that the angle of the tee was of paramount importance, and gravity must be allowed to do its work. The summer howling winds so prevalent in these links courses did not help.*

*He finally laid his club calmly on the ground, and with two hands, succeeded to insert the Tee vertically and balanced a dirty ball perfectly on top. He took a practice swing and almost fell down, as his attempt was more reminiscent of American baseball.*

*At this point, the Starter, in utter apoplexy, leaped out from his Starter's Box and stormed across the tee off area, screaming: "You....OUT!"*

*Visanu, in stunned embarrassment, backed away. But you can appreciate the situation. Every golfer was supposed to have his own bag and Visanu and I were sharing a bag, very much against bout four or five byelaws. The Americans' equipment made the difference too intolerable, for mine was a decaying mess and the Marshals had, of course, noticed every detail.*

*"You've got nae clubs, and YOU (pointing to me) CANNAE PLAY GOLF !"*

*"Get off my course!"*

*Despite this, I knew that Scottish anger was quick to dissipate and we succeeded somehow in placating the Starter as his colour returned from purple to russet. Extremely reluctantly, he allowed us a second chance, I had convinced him that we could play on, and that Visanu was actually my caddy.*

*I gallantly teed off under immense pressure and was happy because I hit the ball, and it was quick. I knew the waiting Americans and the Starter would be pleased. Not my best shot, a 30 meter skiff into a vicious looking gorse bush (all gorse in St Andrews is vicious, it's a special breed). And it was freezing, but, after all, I grew up in Edinburgh, and this was to honor Pat. As my ball hit the gorse the Americans went ballistic. The Marshall crossed his arms, and appeared perturbed. Disregarding all this, I began walking up the fairway, followed by Visanu, carrying, very professionally, I might add, my bag, and I with the demeanour of Arnold Palmer, stalked off.......*

*We almost pulled it off.*

*The Marshals jumped unto their Green Buggies and followed, stalking us with field glasses. There were two. They travel in pairs you know, like policemen.*

*My second shot dribbled left, only a few meters, but with unbelievable fortitude and a hockey like chopping action with my five iron, I made it to the fringe of the first hole in eight shots.*

*At this point, the Green Buggy drove up to me, and the Marshall, showing considerable authority, said, "if you quit now, we will refund your green fees." I really had no choice. But for a Scottish professor to be kicked off St. Andrews! I'll never live this down. Visanu and I went back to the clubhouse to drown our sorrows, and discuss Tee physics. I also later visited Argos to remedy my lack of drivers, determined to do better! Funnily, things got worse later that day, as Pat continues.*

The four of us finished our delightful round in less than three hours. Well, there was little choice! We were sweating profusely, but had avoided the green buggies, and Tadashi had only lost fourteen balls. We were surprised to see Grant and Visanu already in the clubhouse. (*Not sure what happened to Phil. The ignominy of the whole thing must have distressed him.*) When they told us their story, we couldn't stop laughing through several beers. The unsmiling old Scotsman remarked at the next table in gruff Highland accent, "Highly Irregular!" Needless to say, he was not amused.

Then, it occurred to us that we should sign up tomorrow for the Old Course. The previous time I had played there, Jim Bryce signed up and joined us. There is another system there (*where the British Open is played*) called the daily ballot, whereby, if you registered by 4PM the day before, a lottery is held, and you can check back by 6PM to determine if your foursome lucked out. So, Grant and I went to the computer lady located in the clubhouse. I gave my name, showed my club golf card and placed my order for a foursome. You needed to have a minimum 24 handicap to play the Old Course (*36 for females*), and our foursome qualified, but more by counterfeit. A poor golfer shoots about a 24. As mentioned earlier, Grant can get around a course in about 150 strokes...in fact, his golf more closely resembles hockey. Of course he did not have a handicap card.

Grant then was asked by the nice lady the name of his "home" golf club. Grant, in perfect brogue, nevertheless stammered, ehm, "Blackhall" (*actually a 9 hole ladies course in Edinburgh, which would have set the silent alarm bells ringing—intruder...intruder*). The extremely experienced lady had senses worthy off the El Al check-in staff, and immediately spotted a flaw. Probing further, this now vice-marshal in green became stern and asked, glowering, "what is your handicap?" Grant couldn't think of what to say, although he had heard the word "handicap" used in reference to the sport of golf, we shall give him that. She remarked with heavy irony, "you don't golf, do you?" Then, ominously, she closed her clipboard with a crushing finality. Grant, thus, became the only native Scotsman to get kicked off both the New Course and Old Course of St. Andrews on the same day.

Be on the watch for The ***Return of the Dreaded Green Buggy***! A movie script is being discussed.

## Surveys on the Best Place in the World

What criteria do you use to pick the best place in the world? Let me first try happiness. Supposedly, psychologist Ed Diener of the University of Illinois has been studying this subject for decades. Positive psychology, a relatively new field, is kind of the opposite of traditional psychology, which mostly focuses on mental illness. Wellness and happiness lead to the good, pleasant and meaningful life. Happiness results in a stronger personal immune system, longer life, larger social rewards, and greater success. Chapter 3 on education refers to those studies and publications.

The University of Michigan's World Values Surveys has for two decades now tracked the happiest countries.[152] They simply asked, how happy are you. Never would you have guessed the top three. They are: Nigeria, Mexico and Venezuela. Why Nigeria? They've been through so much that with relative stability, their faith and family, they are really satisfied today, and happy. At a higher complexity level for subjective well being, the results were: Puerto Rico, Mexico and Denmark. The U.S. ranked #15. Something about Americans' focus on materialism made them less happy. Those in the former Soviet Republic dominate the bottom. They are not very happy. Let's see, now, would you like to live in Nigeria?

Notice that Mexico fares well. The impression of Mexico tends to be one of squalor, sin and illegal immigrants. But border towns such as Tijuana and Juarez cater to Americans, and are not representative of the country as a whole. Mexico, further, now has an educational process that makes sense. Only after stopping through Cabo San Lucas, Puerto Vallarta, Acapulco, Huatalco and Puerto Chiapas did I understand why their happiness quotient is so high.

Adrian White of the University of Leicester publishes a World Map of Happiness. His current top 10 are: Denmark, Switzerland, Austria, Iceland, Bahamas, Finland, Sweden, Bhutan, Brunei and Canada. The U.S. was #23 and Russian #167.[164]

You'll notice the usual list of cold temperature countries, but Bhutan? In 1972, His Majesty Jigme Singye Wangechuk, King of Bhutan, created Gross National Happiness as the goal for his country. They're not into ha ha happiness, but more, contentment, nurturing relationships and subsistence farming, with a GDP/capita of $1,400. The theory is that material and spiritual development must occur together. Yes, there are only 2.3 million subjects, and the country zoomed from nothing to 50 cable channels and American Idol virtually overnight in 2006. Thus you can almost predict some growing unhappiness in the near future. A 233 page paper is available on "Gross National Happiness and Development," from the first International conference on the subject, held in Bhutan. The third gathering occurred in Thailand in 2007.

Brunei, a mostly Muslim country, located next to Malaysia, is happy mostly because they have oil to sell with a benevolent dictator serving less than 400,000 people. The GDP/capita was $25,600 in 2005, and is much higher today.

For those Americans who missed it, the Pew Research Center released their happiness study in 2006. To summarize:[235]

- Money buys happiness (*a very happy tally of 50% was indicated with an annual family income over $150,000, but only 23% at less that $20,000*).
- Only 16% of Americans are not too happy (*or don't know*).
- Married people (*43%*) are happier than unmarrieds (*24%*).
- Those with children are about as happy as those without.
- Religious types (*43%*) are happier than the irreligious (*26%*).
- Republicans (*45%*) are happier than Democrats (*30%*).
- Whites (*36%*) and Hispanics (*34%*) are happier than Blacks (*28%*), but 12% of Whites are unhappy, while 23% of Blacks and Hispanics are unhappy.
- 27% of single parents with minor children are unhappy.
- Pet owners (*dog or cat, about the same*) are no happier than those with no pets.
- Sunbelt residents are happiest of all. (*Another reason why you might want to live where the temperatures remain salubrious and comfortable.*)

The National Opinion Research Center of the University of Chicago spent 18 years studying job satisfaction and general happiness.[290] Well, I might have been too critical about religion, for 67% of clergy were at the top in happiness. The average American worker showed a score of 33%. At the very bottom were gas station attendants.

The British New Economics Foundation published their Happy Planet Index in 2006, measuring people's wellbeing, and ranked the tiny South Pacific archipelago of Vanuatu at the top, followed by Columbia, Costa Rica, Dominica and Panama. #178 was Zimbabwe.[107] The U.S. ranked #150. The low rating was because Americans don't treat our planet well. People, the study concluded, are happy because they are satisfied with very little. Clearly, many of you wouldn't want to live where you only have a very little, save for those with the hermit complex.

There are other rankings that could sway you. In the 2007 Mercer Cost of Living list, for the past five years, Asuncion, Paraguay has been the least expensive city. Moscow is the highest and Tokyo is next. Oslo is #10, New York City is #14 and Honolulu is not in the top 50 (*this is surprisingly good*), while Singapore is. However, in the ***Economist*** Intelligence Unit's Worldwide Cost of Living Survey, Oslo is the most expensive, with Paris #2. Manila is the cheapest city. Want to live in the Philippines or Paraguay?

The Mercer best quality of life list ranks these cities: #1 Zurich, #2 Geneva, #3 Vancouver, #4 Vienna, #5 Auckland, #6 Dusseldorf, #7 Frankfurt, #8 Munich, #9 Bern and Sydney. Honolulu is #27 as the highest rated U.S. city, although San Francisco is #28. Oslo is #31 and Singapore #32. Baghdad received the worst score. More recently, though, Switzerland has been tarnished by an electoral campaign featuring three white sheep standing on the Swiss flag, as one of them kicks a single black sheep away. The matter of immigration has suddenly become an issue.

In Gross National Income, Switzerland is #1, Luxembourg #2, Japan #3, Norway #4 and the U.S. #5. If you divide Gross National Income by Gross National Product: #1 Argentina, #2 Uruguay, #3 Kiribati, #16 Japan, #35 U.S., #53 Switzerland, #107 Norway, #166 Libya. If nothing else, these rankings should confuse you.

Then, there are some bizarre surveys. The University of Chicago international study reported that 71% of Austrians were satisfied with their sex lives, ahead of Spain at 69%, Canada 66%, Belgium 65% and the U.S. 64%.[181] There were only 29 countries, with Japan at #29 and Taiwan #28. The bottom five were countries of the Orient. The study was funded by Pfizer, which sells Viagra.

The World Economic Forum, based in Europe, annually reports on the Global Gender Gap. The Scandinavian nations are the best, and European nations represent eight of the top ten, with the Philippines and New Zealand the only exceptions. The U.S. wallows in 32$^{nd}$ place, with Yemen at the bottom.[270]

However, the World Economic Forum also has a business competitiveness ranking. One hundred thirteen factors contribute to the process, and the USA is ranked #1. Venture capital availability and a large domestic market help. Seven of the top ten nations are from Europe, with Singapore (#7) and Japan (#9).

The most credible of all surveys is the United Nations Human Development Report, all 444 pages in 2006.[245] To gain a quick understanding of the scope of the effort, go to Human Development Index, ***Wikipedia***. The top ten in 2006 were #1 Norway, #2 Iceland, #3 Australia, #4 Ireland, #5 Sweden, #6 Canada, #7 Japan, #8 United States, #9 Switzerland and #10

Netherlands. European countries dominate. Singapore is #25, Paraguay #91, Vanuatu #119 and Bhutan #135. Niger at #177 was the lowest, but that is because Iraq and Afghanistan were not included. However, in 2007, Iceland was rated #1, with Norway #2, Australia #3 and U.S. #12.

Analyzing all the above surveys, incorporating my world travels and being influenced by Chapter 1 where I concluded that, darn it, the U.S is the best country, the best place on Planet Earth is the United States of America. Norway is great, but too cold. So are Iceland, Switzerland, Canada and, even Ireland. Singapore is appealing, but they take life too seriously. Australia deserves to be in the top three.

But the USA is a big country. Where is the best of the best? The latest ***Money Magazine*** top ten are: #1 Middleton, WI, #2 Hanover, NH, #3 Louisville, CO, #4 Lake Mary, FL, #5 Claremont CA, #6 Papillion, NE, #7, Milton, MA, #8 Chaska, MN, #9 Providence, PA and #10 Suwanee, GA. Chances are, if you're reading this, you've never been to most of these cities. So we can justifiably delete this ***Money*** list.

Statemaster.com has a livability index by state, incorporating 44 factors. The top three are: New Hampshire, Minnesota and Vermont. Hawaii is #26. Hawaii does poorly because it has the highest gas price and tax burden, plus second highest housing cost (*next to California*). Yet, Honolulu was rated #1 by Men's Health for the lowest incidence of insomnia and #2 by the Center for Digital Government in digital access. Of the eight communities in the country with the highest percentage of solar-water heated homes, eight are in Hawaii. These must count for something.

Sperling's healthiest cities has San Jose as #1 and Washington, D.C. as #2. I've lived in both locations, and agree that something good has happened to San Jose since I was a college student, but D.C as number two is startling. Maybe crime was not a factor. Hawaii is not listed in the top 50, but perhaps we did not take enough Centrum pills, which sponsored the study. But, the ***Environmental Almanac*** ranked Hawaii #1 on environmental quality. I didn't see San Jose or D.C. in the top 75. The EPA rated Texas as the worst in toxic discharge and Hawaii as best. The American Lung Association monitoring 700 U.S. counties, rated Honolulu air among the cleanest in the Nation.[114]

Let's face it, you want to live in a healthy location:

- Hawaii was ranked #2 to Minnesota by Northwestern National Life Insurance Company in their survey, incorporating 17 indicators, such as infant mortality, access to health care, smoking rates and violent crime.
- The Anne Casey Foundation looked at the 50 largest cities in the U.S. for well-being of its children, and Honolulu was ranked first. Hawaii also leads the nation in longevity, and is the only state with an average life expectancy topping 80.[218]
- Children born in Hawaii will have a life expectancy three years longer than the national average, with lower death rates from heart disease and cancer.[284]
- Hawaii is home to more centegenarians (*those 100 years or older*) per capita than any other state.

- o Honolulu has the smallest temperature range of any major U.S. city, with a low of 57 °F and high of 88 °F, an average of 76.6 °F (*the national average is a chilly 53.2 °F*)
- o ***Men's Fitness*** regularly indicates that Honolulu, for all the Spam (*canned mystery meat made by Hormel, said by some to contain more cholesterol per gram than anything else*) we consume (*leads the nation in pounds/capita*) is the fittest city. San Francisco or Seattle is normally #2.

Sperling's Best Places did list Honolulu in the top ten of least stressful cities (*Tacoma, Miami, New Orleans, Las Vegas and New York City were the most stressful*), and #5 to Charlottesville, Santa Fe, San Luis Obispo and Santa Barbara as the best place to live. There were 331 metropolitan areas profiled. The surprise is that Honolulu was recommended not only for your next vacation, but as a good place to live. Unemployment is low (*during the past decade Hawaii has been #1 or #2 in the Nation with the lowest unemployment rate*) and so is violent crime. However, Hawaii tops the nation in thefts. Ah, this is not good.

Cited by Sperling is a remarkable economy, although **Forbes** and ***Money*** regularly dump on the state as Death Valley for business. All three are correct, as the economy is improving while the labor unions do have an influence on legislation that pains the private sector. The 2005 Milken Institute survey showed that Hawaii was the most expensive state to do business. But do you want to do business in South or North Dakota (*the least expensive*)?

Also mentioned were the infectious people. No, this has very little to do with communicable diseases. There is an aloha spirit that tends to pervade the community. We do the right thing, being the #4 state on charitable giving and are among the lowest on DUI traffic fatality rate (*2.02 versus a national average of 4.74*). The people of Hawaii were voted best-looking, friendliest and most laid-back by ***Travel & Leisure***. Is this a hint of the best place?

## So Where are the Best Places in the World?

As I'm just about to send this to the publisher, I read that there was a brand new book, published in 2008, called ***The Geography of Bliss***.[342] Eric Weiner, a National Public Radio correspondent and known grump, travelled to the most happiest sites, and wrote a book of his experiences. He mentions that journalists travel to the worst places in the world to get the most sordid stories. So, he did just the opposite. In many ways, this is just what I did for this chapter. Some of the locations mentioned in this publication can be compared with his observations. Someday soon I'll do just that.

I have landed in Japan at least a hundred times, been to Seoul, Hong Kong and Bangkok perhaps on 20 occasions, Singapore at least ten times and various parts of China. Australia and New Zealand are favorite spots for travel. Europe I generally love. Switzerland and the Scandinavian countries deserve their high ranking. Tahiti is charming.

At one time I thought that Australia looked like the country of the future, with vast resources and a pioneering attitude. Then, Jared Diamond's ***Collapse*** reported that a lack of predictable rainfall makes this country already over-urbanized, for very little of the land is livable. Worse, the soils and surrounding marine coastal space are generally unproductive for a lack of nutrients. Scratch Australia from the final list, but it deserves at least a mention.

Buenos Aires has the tango and a European flair. With a Gross National Product per capita of $16,000, versus $9,000 for Brazil and $13,000 for Chile, Argentina seems poised to make a recovery from their economic free fall. But it will tumble again, so nothing in South American makes the A list.

While safety is a plus for those developed countries of the Orient, on the Continent, it decreases with warmer temperatures. Yet, America's two most dangerous cities, Detroit and St. Louis, are a lot more terrifying than anything in those areas. In any case, we are trying to determine the best place on Earth, so let me share some of my favorites.

My preferred international cities are Tokyo, Osaka-Kobe, Bangkok, Hong Kong, Seoul, Shanghai, Singapore, Perth, Paris and Oslo. But most of the world wants to come to the USA, so the top spots are littered with American cities and regions.

With these surveys and my travel experience, I then bravely ventured forth with a top ten list, then expanded it to twelve, and ended up with a sweet sixteen. It was getting too large, so I created an honorable mention category and went back to only a top ten. The best? Drum roll, please……

**The Honorable Mention Finalists**

## Andorra

A tiny (*population of 82,000 and 181 square miles*), mountainous (*starts at 2,854 feet and goes up*) and rich (*$38,800 GDP/capita, easily in the top ten*) country which belongs to the United Nations, I included Andorra because it has the highest life expectancy (*83.52 years in 2007*) in the world and draws 9 million tourists each year. It is located between France and Spain in the Eastern Pyrenees.

## United Arab Emirates

The United Arab Emirates was formed in 1971 after Britain left the Persian Gulf. There are seven states (*Bahrain and Qatar almost joined, but decided to go independent that same year*) and you know of only two, as described below. It's an Islamic country with hereditary leadership. The population is around 4.5 million, where in the 16-65 age group, there are 2.75 males to each female because 85% of the population are foreigners, mostly laborers. The GDP/capita is $42,275 and is ranked #3 by the ***CIA Factbook*** to Luxembourg and Equatorial Guinea (*no, you don't want to go there*), but #12 by the International Monetary Fund (*IMF*).

Abu Dhabi is the capital and one of the seven emirates of the United Arab Emirates. The city has a population of 2 million and is actually an island. It is said to be the richest city in the world. Each natural citizen is worth an average of $17 million. In 2008, this emirate announced a $15 billion clean energy and hydrogen program, a breakthrough, being the first major Arab commitment to solar energy. The first paved road came in 1961, but in 2011 will open the $200 million Guggenheim Museum, designed by Frank Gehry.

Dubai, the other known emirate, has no personal, corporate nor sales tax, and, surprisingly, less than 6% of its revenues comes from oil and natural gas. The twin World Trade Center towers had 110 floors. While the tallest current building (*in Taiwan*) has 101 floors, the Burj Dubai has shot past 158 floors and is expected to rise to 164, 170 or 200 stories by 2009 at a cost of around $4 billion, finally returning this honor to the Middle East. The Great Pyramid of Giza had the title for 4000 years. Samsung, from South Korea, which built the Petronas Twin Towers in Kuala Lumpur and Taipei 101, is handling the construction. To discourage competitors, Al Burj, on the Dubai Waterfront, has been proposed to be nearly 1000 feet taller.

It was a quarter century ago that I landed in Dubai when Pan Am had a world route. I did not see anything of consequence then, but, certainly, times have changed the landscape, and I look forward to returning to the United Arab Emirates by 2010 and staying at the Burg Dubai, while also venturing forth to Abu Dhabi.

## Iceland

As the 2007 UN Human Development Index rates Iceland as #1, you can't leave out this pioneering country. In 1944, it separated from Denmark and became a representative democracy. More than 30,000 of the 313,000 total population were born abroad, and there has been a recent surge of immigrants because of a labor shortage. While Icelandic is the spoken language, English is widely used.

It ranks next to Andorra with a life expectancy of 82 years. Their GDP/capita of $63,000 puts it at #4 (*U.S. is #9*) by the IMF. It is a welfare state with high taxes. There is no standing army, but they participated in the Afghan War. While by my standards it is cold, even if it is just south of the Arctic Circle, the weather is surprisingly temperate because of the Gulf Stream.

Bjork, that singer who wore what looked like a swan for her dress at the 2001 Oscar ceremony, comes from Iceland. The dress was auctioned off for charity, so it served a useful purpose.

Two centuries ago a quarter of its population died from a volcanic eruption, thusly providing for natural steam and geothermal energy. There is also abundant hydropower, so 70% of the energy used is renewable. Iceland has partnered with Shell Oil towards a hydrogen economy.

## Australia

Australia is a continent in itself, with an indigenous population that can be traced back almost 50,000 years. First settled by Europeans as a British penal colony in 1788, the Commonwealth was formed in 1901. It remains a constitutional democracy, with Elizabeth II as Queen of Australia.

Today, with a population of 21 million, it has a GDP/capita of around $42,000 (*better than the UK, Germany and France in purchasing power parity*) and is ranked #3 in the United Nations' Human Development Index of 2007, beaten only by Iceland and Norway. The U.S. was #12.

I've been through much of the country, and can say that there is a uniting spirit that transcends the disparate topography and diverse cities. One troublesome future has to do with Jared Diamond's hinting about a collapse because of the unpredictable rainfall. There remains, though, a continuing and ambitious immigration program should you wish to relocate there.

## Jewels of China

The capitol of China began forming during the first millennium BC, and was earlier called Zhongdu in 1153, Dadu under the Mongols, eventually to Peiping, then Peking, now Beijing. In periods from 1425 to 1825 it was the largest city in the world. Today, it is remains too crowded with horrific air pollution, but this is the power base for the country. Beginning with Peking Man (*who was not one, but many, and not Homo sapiens*) to tea (*yes, the Chinese were the first*) and the Great Wall, Forbidden City, Tiananmen Square, Beijing Opera, Peking duck to the 2008 Olympics, much can be experienced around this grand city.

Shanghai is the most populated in China, and eighth largest city in the world. However, while Mumbai is supposedly #1 with 13 million people, it is said that Shanghai might well have 20 million residents, depending on whom you count and who you ask. This world class municipality has long been China's international port and is emblematic of a progressive economy. The city more recently wallowed until provided with a mandate for market-economic redevelopment in 1992. The result has been spectacular. The skylines are extraordinary with fascinating architecture. I ordered a one person scallop soup at the Tokyo Westin, costing around $50. For this price at the Westin on the Bund, my wife and I got a full Asian fusion meal with wine. From a magnetic levitation train connecting their airport to downtown, with a link planned to Hangzhou, 106 miles away, to the coming 2010 World Expo, astonishing things are happening here.

Xian has a history longer than 3000 years, is one of the four ancient capitals and is the Eastern terminus of the Silk Road, connecting to the Roman Empire in the West. Today, with a population in excess of 8 million, it is said to have nearly 100,000 ethnic minorities. In 1974, the Mausoleum of the First Qin Emperor was accidentally re-discovered by farmers drilling a water well. Emperor Qin Shi Huangdi was buried with 8,099 life size clay figures of warriors and horses. It is reported that the effort began in 286 BC with 700,000 workers over 38 years. The Terra Cotta Warriors are now the prime tourist attraction of the region. Also try the Xian Dumpling Banquet, with 32 varieties, although another 120 different types can also be ordered.

Hong Kong, meaning fragrant harbor (*which it most definitely is not*), was a crown colony of the UK from 1842 until 1997, when China regained control upon the U.K. actually acquiescing to a former treaty. The transition has been satisfactory, with the economy still booming. Less than 16 miles away by train, Shenzhen was a fishing village of 25,000 when, in 1979, it was made a Special Economic Zone. In two decades, the population of the city and environs zoomed up to 18 million, surging past the entirety of the Hong Kong metropolis. What used to be the thrifty shopping attraction of Hong Kong has been transferred to this new city. But height restrictions have been removed from Kowloon, located across the harbor from Hong Kong Island, so look for spectacular buildings to sprout. This is the only Chinese location where English can generally be spoken and understood by a third of the people.

In 1670 Portugal leased Macao, but in the Beijing Treaty, China ceded to Portugal perpetual occupation. Through a series of political dealings, China officially regained jurisdiction in 1999. Both territories (*including Hong Kong*) are now Special Administration Regions, meaning that the central government will attempt to keep hands generally off the economic imperative of those locations. Beginning with the invasion of the Sands casino in 2004, mostly American investments of more than $25 billion have converted this almost dingy gambling destination into the world leader, surpassing even Las Vegas in revenues.

I know of colleagues who went to work in Hong Kong and Shanghai, and ended up living there. In both cases the wife was a mainland Chinese, so the transition was smooth. Not many will want to permanently relocate to China if you don't have important connections, but it is possible, and something to consider if you are on the adventurous side.

## Japan

Japan has 3,000 islands, the highest life expectancy (*81.25 years*) of a developed country, second biggest world economy and tenth ranking world population. Tokyo is the largest metropolitan area on the globe with 30 million people. The country is a constitutional monarchy with an emperor, plus an elected parliament.

My ancestors came from Japan. I've been everywhere (*well, not quite to all those islands*) in that country and, save for the regrettable fact that I don't speak nor read the language, I feel comfortable with the lifestyle there and safe in any city there. The food is fabulous, science and technology leading edge, culture everywhere prevalent with all those temples and such, Mount Fuji imposing (*especially when covered with snow*), Shinkansen (*bullet train*) efficient and, unlike Europe, there are almost no strikes. The Fall colors are magnificent and the Spring Sakura (*cherry blossom*) season dazzling. I regularly in April spend a hanami (*picnic*) with, perhaps, a sake, Kirin beer and Kentucky Fried Chicken lunch. I try to make the meal as hybrid as possible around local imbibibles. The Kyoto Protocol to combat global warming was drawn up there and Hokkaido is the site of the 2008 G8 summit, focusing on the global environment.

There are hurricanes (*called typhoons there*), earthquakes and tsunamis. Anyone who is not a native Japanese is referred to as a gaijin, or alien. Even though I look Japanese, I cannot be accepted into their society. I can imagine how much worse it must be for a Korean or any other nationality. Conversely, if you are obviously not Japanese, anyone in that country will go way out of his way to help you find your way, even though very few speak conversational English. Visit Japan, certainly, but move there? Probably not.

## European Union

The European Union (*EU*), in this section, excludes UK, Ireland and Norway, because these are featured separately. I almost felt compelled to add Switzerland, but, like the grand cities of Paris, Berlin, Munich, Madrid, Seville, Stockholm, Copenhagen, Brussels, Rome and dozens of other remarkable treasures, I've lumped them into one pot called the EU.

Formed in 1957, now with 27 members, it features a common market and currency (*euro, adopted by 13 nations, so far*), and remains a work in progress. With a population of nearly 500 million, the EU represents almost a third of the world gross national product and is the largest exporter. Unemployment is 7%. The people are more concerned about the environment than in the U.S., and member countries have taken significant steps towards energy sustainability, even though their natural prospects are not outstanding, in fact, poor.

My first exposure to the Continent was in my first around the world adventure, when one of the flights was from Bangkok to Frankfurt. Bangkok had just suffered a typical monsoon flood, the traffic was horrendous, living conditions somewhat squalid and air pollution was worse than Los Angeles at its worst. Germany was so clean, scrupulous and enjoyable. Much of Europe turned out to be the same. Of course, like anywhere in the world you need to use some good judgment about where not to go at night, but, the history, character and variety of Europe make it a favorite of many.

One of my dreams is to spend a year on a series of cruises and river boat experiences to optimally appear at the key festivals and assorted events throughout Europe. This way, you avoid those train strikes and intimidation on the Autobahn. My wife and I have several times Eurail Passed throughout the region and driven across the "continent" from North to South and East to West.

There is a problem: immigration. All countries are now reviewing their in-migration policies. There is a Muslim challenge that will only get worse, especially in France, Germany and the Netherlands. Spaniards believe that immigrants increase the crime rate. Portugal has tightened asylum rules. Denmark has taken steps to dissuade anyone from going there. Sweden is complaining that those policies are shunting refugees into their country. Thus, from all reports, the EU doesn't want you.

## United Kingdom / Ireland

The United Kingdom of Great Britain and Northern Ireland (*also known as Britain or UK*) is a parliamentary democracy and constitutional monarchy. Scotland (*5 million people*), Wales (*3 million*) and England (*50 million*) are constituent countries within the kingdom. A good case can be made that the UK in the 19$^{th}$ Century was greater than the US today, having stimulated the Industrial Revolution, expanding into a world-wide British Empire where the Sun never set.

The urban area of London, having been founded 2000 years ago by the Romans, alone has a larger population than Wales, Scotland and Northern Ireland combined. Buckingham Palace, Big Ben, Piccadilly Circus, Hyde Park, London Eye…the city has everything to offer. Cambridge and Oxford are in the top ten of best world universities. Stonehenge, St. Andrews (*where golf was invented in 1552*), Welsh rarebit (*no, not rabbit, but cheese on toast*), Richard Burton (*Welsh actor*), the Highlands, Dolly (*the cloned sheep, named after Dolly Parton*), Tattoo (*Scottish military music festival*), Fat Duck (*currently a London restaurant*), Stilton (*lighter than Gorgonzola, richer than Danish blue and somewhat goldish, it is a blue cheese*), claret (*a British name for the French Bordeaux wine*), Lagavulan (*my favorite single malt scotch*)…there is much to see and consume in the UK.

The Republic of Ireland (*officially declared in 1949*), with Dublin as the capitol, occupies five-sixths of this third largest European island, with Northern Ireland (*most populated city, Belfast*) still part of the United Kingdom. After three decades of Protestant-Catholic unrest with 3600 deaths, a cease fire came to the North in 2005. To make a complicated story simple, Northern Ireland is aligned with the UK because the majority are Protestants. In Ireland, 80% are Catholic. While the entire island has 6 million people, in the early 1800's, before the great famine, it was over 8 million. Known as the Emerald Island, it is, indeed, green.

Druids, St. Patrick, Gaelic games and music, Boyle's Law, Blarney Kilkenny Castles, Molly Malone (*fictitious*), Jamison Whiskey (*worth a tour*), Guinness (*although the beer was originated in London, with headquarters there, and, yes, they started the world records book*) stout, pubs, Trinity University, satirist Jonathan Swift, James Joyce and a host of Nobel literature laureates, Bono and U2, expanding high tech economy, cow statues…there is something distinctly Irish about the country.

In 2005, Ireland was ranked as the best place in the world to live by ***Economist*** magazine. Once a country of out-migration, it is now just the opposite. Opportunities are available, as immigrants from Romania, Nigeria and China are coming in larger numbers. This welcome mat is why the UK/Ireland is ranked high.

## Gems of Canada: Vancouver / Toronto / Montreal

While the Canadian outdoors are what are truly grand, their cities are neat. You can camp in the wilds, but you more probably will want to live in proximity to some metropolitan area. Vancouver has a Chinese tinge and Montreal a French overtone, no, make that, prominence. A memorable way to appreciate Toronto is to drive over the Windsor Bridge into Detroit.

Canada is the second largest country in area (*Russia is almost two times bigger*). It severed its federal dominion status from the United Kingdom in 1982 and became a parliamentary democracy. However, Queen Elizabeth II remains the head of state, so it is also a constitutional monarchy. Canada, while a close partner of the U.S., maintains full relations with Cuba and chose not to participate in the Iraq War.

The country ranked #6 in the UN Human Development Index, Foreign Policy Magazine Globalization Index and Yale/Columbia Environmental Sustainability Index. The Economist gave Canada a #8 rating in the Global Peace Index, the Wall Street Journal ranked it #10 in the Index of Economic Freedom, and IMD International listed it as #10 in World Competitiveness.

What's wrong with Canada? Perhaps a mediocre national medical plan, there is that French flap about secession and their women's Olympic curling team only won the bronze medal in Torino 2006 (*the men got gold*). By the way, the Winter Olympics are coming to Vancouver in 2010. You can't find too many bad things about the country, except, maybe it might be too cold for some of us.

Canada tends to have an easier immigration policy, so you might not need to jump over an electric fence to enter. Also, it has the highest per capita immigration rate in the world, with most now coming from Asia. Go to www.canadavisa.com and see if you qualify. If you are not in the U.S. and are looking for a better place to live, try Canada.

### Florida

Florida was named by Spaniard Ponce de Leon in 1513. He never found the fountain of youth, but did plant the flag that allowed Spain to cede this area to the U.S. in 1819 (*actually, Britain gained control in 1763, but lost jurisdiction back to Spain after the American Revolutionary War*) in exchange for America renouncing any claims on Texas. But that's another story. Florida gained statehood in 1860 with a population of 140,000, 44% being slaves. In a few years, it is expected to become the third most populated state, replacing New York. California is #1 and Texas is #2.

Disney World, Epcot Center, national parks, growth (*when I first visited Central Florida University twenty years ago, the University of Hawaii was twice the size of CFU; today, CFU has more than twice the number of students than the UH*), mild weather, easy nautical access and the good life. There are only a few earthquakes, but they do suffer from hurricanes. If global climate change becomes truly serious, and all the ice melts, the sea level will rise 250 feet and 99% of Florida will go under water. But, this will take a lot longer than your lifetime, so enjoy the Sunshine State while you can.

## The Top Ten

#### #10: Jewels of the American East: New York/Boston/D.C. /Chicago

Like the EU, these cities are such great places that I amalgamated them all into something called the Jewels of the East.

I don't love New York, but appreciate its economic and entertainment virtues. It remains the largest city in the USA, with the Statue of Liberty, Wall Street, New York Stock Exchange, Broadway and several tallest buildings of their time, including the Empire State Building (*102 floors, #1 from 1931 to 1973, currently #10, but the current tallest is Taipei 101 with only 101 floors*) and the World Trade Center twin towers (*in 1973 became the tallest, 110 floors*), which were demolished by terrorists on September 11, 2001.

I like Boston, the so called Cradle of American History. The Red Sox, high technology, finest universities, lobster, history…it has almost everything. The weather is generally bad.

I lived in Falls Church, Virginia, just outside of Washington, D.C. Across the street one way was Alexandria, and the other, Arlington. For three years I toiled in the U.S. Senate, but had a chance to enjoy the various concerts on the Mall, free museums, change of season (*D.C. is the most beautiful city on the globe a week in the Spring and a week in the Fall*) and easy access to the Eastern Jewels. If not for the safety factor and frequent crummy weather, D.C. itself could have been considered as a serious finalist.

The Town of Chicago in 1833 had a population of 350, but grew to 1 million in 1890, even after the Great Chicago Fire of 1871. By the time of the Great Depression in 1929, the population tripled to 3 million, which is, amazingly enough, about the same as today. But the metropolitan area is pushing 10 million. Like New York City, the crime rate has dropped. Chicago was the original skyscraper city, and has the Spire being readied for occupancy in 2010 with 150 floors. In 2007, Chicago was the only North American city to have had a champion in all five major sports, and is the official national entry to bid for the 2016 Summer Olympics. The Loop, Chicago-style hot dog (*no ketchup, please*), chop (*steak*) houses, Oprah, bone-chilling windy weather, Chicago has a distinctive style.

The frenetic pace of these metropolitan areas, and you can add Philadelphia, Baltimore, and half a dozen others—all almost equivalently exceptional—are not quite the lifestyle that makes for an enjoyable life. Sure, a few years to gain exposure and experience, but not a full life. Important locations, but not necessarily the best places to permanently live.

**#9: Pacific Northwest**

The Pacific Northwest, in this application, includes the whole region incorporating the States of Washington, Oregon and Idaho, with a focus on the former. Earliest habitation has been recorded as far back as 15,000 years ago. English Captain Francis Drake arrived in Oregon in 1579, followed by Juan de Fuca, Greek captain working for Spain in 1592. During the mid 1700's, Russia dispatched Danish explorer Vitus Bering to the area, leading to the coming of Russian settlers later in the century. Captain James Cook also made a stop during this period, and so did several Spanish expeditions. British mariner George Vancouver worked with the Spanish to map the territory around this period, while French explorer Jean Francois La Perouse also laid claim, but unfortunately became shipwrecked in Australia on his way home and officially missed this opportunity. But fresh from the 1804 Louisiana Purchase, President Thomas Jefferson sent Americans Meriwether Lewis and William Clark overland to the Pacific Northwest, strengthening the American claim to the Oregon Territory.

Washington has Microsoft, Starbucks, Amazon.com and the Grand Coulee Dam (*largest concrete structure in the U.S.*) Wineries are sprouting (*429*), the state produces 90% of the national raspberries and Mt. Rainier is majestic. Seattle is too rainy, although, granted, their average rainfall is actually half that of Hawaii. The operative parameter should be how gloomy a place feels, as Seattle's precipitation comes mostly as a mist, while Hilo is known to have the largest raindrops in the world.

Likewise, Oregon has Nike, more than 300 wineries (*Portland has more breweries than any city in the world*), no sales and minimal corporate taxes and much to do in the wilds. The state has always been that much more concerned about the environment and a touch more humanistic than most. Their general tolerance probably makes Portland a tad edgy, with more homeless than they need and an uncomfortable drug scene, though nothing close to Vancouver.

There are several derivations for the name Idaho, but probably the most accurate has to do with a lobbyist, George Willing, who suggested the term from the Shoshone language, meaning "gem of the mountains." He later said he made this all up. Yet, this is called the Gem State. Idaho produces one-third the potatoes, has a growing science and technology sector and, from Boise State University, the only undefeated football team in 2006 (*the University of Hawaii had the only unblemished regular season record in 2007*).

There was the 1700 Cascadia earthquake, and a fear that a really big one could be forming just off the coast of Oregon. Washington's Mount St. Helens erupted in 1980 killing 57 people. The glacier/snow topping Mt. Rainier has been featured on various Discovery-type channels as showing potential for collapsing and causing havoc to the area surrounding Seattle. However, the combination of the great outdoors, progressive lifestyle and job opportunities make this a most attractive area for living.

**#8: Mauritius**

The Republic of Mauritius is a Paradise in the Indian Ocean in the approximate location south of the equator as Hawaii is north. It's slightly larger than the Hawaiian Island of Oahu, with just about the exact same population as Hawaii. The ethnic mix is a mélange from India, Africa and Europe, with 30,000 Chinese. Great Britain gained control from the French after winning the Napoleonic Wars. Independence was gained in 1968, the year Mauritius became a member of the United Nations, and in 1992, it was announced to be a republic within the Commonwealth with a parliamentary democracy.

There is the sad plight of the 3 foot tall, 50 pound pigeon called the Raphus cucullatus, or Dodo, which became extinct just before 1700 due to man. However, this was a bad tasting and tough bird, so more probably, the animals brought by settlers were the real cause.

As reported earlier, Singapore observed the racial policies of this country in fashioning their own. The country rates well in the various indexes of economic freedom, press freedom, corruption perceptions and human development. Also previously mentioned was my effusive review of their resorts and lifestyle.

The country is moving into the future with progressive policies, and is slated to become a duty free island in a few years and have total wireless internet access soon. Unemployment is very low, the official language is English and the politics are stable.

I was particularly taken by their sincere interest in considering the Blue Revolution for their future economic well-being. In many ways, Mauritius is today undergoing a similar predicament as Hawaii faced forty years ago: dying sugar industry, increasing energy prices and declining fishing prospects. The deep, surrounding ocean could be their salvation.

Of particular importance to this section is that Mauritius is open to immigration. There are web sites advertising "How to Retire to Paradise for $19/day," with Mauritius as an option. Otherwise, officially, you need a good reason to move there, but the attitudes are positive and cost of living quite suitable.

Say you go there as a visitor and decide, heck, this is a great place to live. You can acquire for $500,000 a luxury home with all the amenities, which you can rent in your absence. In 2006, the Business Facilitation Act was enacted, permitting non-residents to obtain an initial three year permit, renewable for 10-year periods of permanent resident status.

**#7: Denver**

Indians are recorded to have inhabited this region from before 10,000 BC. Partly through the 1803 Louisiana Purchase and also from the Mexican Cession of 1848, Colorado was formed and became a state in 1876. The population then was in the range of 100,000. Today, the state is approaching 5 million, with the greater Denver/Boulder area at around 3 million.

The lowest point in the State of Colorado is higher than 1000 meters (*1010 meters or 3314 feet*), and there are more than 500 mountain peaks exceeding 4,000 meters (*13,123 feet*). Most of the population occupies the eastern side of the Rocky Mountains (*51 peaks higher than 14,000 feet*), where Denver is located.

There are sound reasons for living in Colorado, for there are the Rockies (*mountain range and World Series baseball team*), the National Renewable Energy Laboratory, museums, the outdoor lifestyle and a special high. Colorado ranks last for obesity (*Mississippi is #1, and the top eight are from the South*), which is good.[226]

Denver was selected to host the 1976 Winter Olympics, but the voters declined to provide financial support. So the games went to Innsbruck. While the weather is fickle, and generally too cold, and there is that prevalent brown cloud over the city, the views are still magnificent and the way of life sterling.

**#6: Singapore**

The first settlement in Singapore occurred around 200 AD, and largely remained a fishing village until the Portuguese came around 1600, then the Dutch. However, British adventurer Sir Thomas Stamford Raffles established a trading post in 1819, clashing with the Dutch, which nevertheless ultimately decided to instead focus on Indonesia. Occupied by the Japanese in World War II, the British regained authority in 1945. In 1963, Singapore and Malaya combined to form Malaysia, but Singapore split off in 1965 and joined the United Nations as a parliamentary republic with a representative democracy.

From a backwater trading post with high unemployment, lacking land and resources, the country has grown into a major financial and high technology power, thanks to Lee Kuan Yew and his "benevolent dictatorship." Singapore now has a population approaching 5 million and a Gross Domestic product/capita at $31,000. The unemployment rate in 2007 was 1.7%. Their K-12 students general rank #1 in comparative standardized tests. Racial harmony is good. Singapore Airlines and Changi Airport generally are also rated #1 or #2. They just spent $1.2 million on Terminal 3 because Bangkok in 2006 opened a new international airport at a cost of $4.7 billion, and China, Dubai and Kuala Lumpur have taken steps to unseat Singapore as the best in the Orient.

In my visits there, I felt a bit uncomfortable about their intense focus on profits and relationships which lacked warmth. Not flushing public toilets is a crime and gum chewing until recently was, too. Remember, they flogged American Michael Peter Fay, which was, actually, deserved. But there is a basic humanitarianism missing, but, evidently, being addressed.

Should you wish to move to Singapore, check out the following website: www.smcmc.com. There is an e-relocation corporate online program at: www.entersingapore.info/relocation/e-relocation.php.

**#5: Las Vegas**

The city of Las Vegas was established in 1905. By 1920, there were still only 2300 residents. Today, the metropolitan district has 1.7 million and is the fastest growing area in the nation. It has among the highest suicide, marriage and divorce rates in the country. The former is embodied in ***Leaving Las Vegas*** with Nicholas Cage and the latter two because industries are built around them.

Water could someday become a serious problem, and there are those nuclear facilities in the region. A serious blackout one hot summer could prove fatal and the city is on the terrorist list of priorities.

However, on the plus side, Las Vegas has become a global city with the very best restaurants and hotels. From Zagat's recent survey for an expensive meal: Tokyo *($70)*, Paris *($75)*, London (*$80*) and Las Vegas (*$113.78*). At one time food was gratis. Now, what is a $500 meal when you are losing $5k at craps anyway, and not enjoying it very much doing that? People from Hawaii stay at the California Hotel chain because food and lodging are still almost free there, so that they can lose their few thousands gambling the night and morning away, as they almost surely tend to do. In 2010 will come Boyd Gaming Corporation's Echelon Place Resorts to enhance those contributions. Shows now cost upwards from $100. They were also once almost free. And people keep coming and spending.

Las Vegas reminds me of religion. There is an illogical faith influencing the mind of the human. Many go there because they think they can win at gambling. All those luxurious casinos should provide a clear warning that someone is paying for them. But, like in religion, some have faith. For most, okay, so you lose a few hundred dollars. The excitement, enjoyment and cheaper food/rooms should be worth it.

Why then is this city rated #5? Las Vegas represents the city of the present and future. You can get anything there, for a price. It is the virtual sports capitol of the globe and a growing must stop for other entertainers and jet setters.

Yes, visit Sin City every so often and enjoy yourself. If you're sensible, the buffets show good value, exhilaration palpable and New Year's celebration grand. Plus, you must believe.

My brother and most of his family love it there, but I don't think he has bothered to place a quarter in a slot machine. That is an important key to comfortable survival. Many have moved there, especially from Hawaii. But the best place in the world? Nah.

**#4: Southern California**

Let's include everything from San Luis Obispo to San Diego in Southern California, anchored by Los Angeles. Which reminds me of an experience I had nearly half a century ago. John Laing (*Stanford classmate*) and I in his temperamental Pontiac, driving back to campus, when we heard an emergency radio report as we approached San Luis Obispo that several particularly dangerous inmates from the Atascadero State Hospital had just escaped. Atascadero is 13 miles north of San Luis Obispo and the hospital was located next to Highway 101. At just about the point where the hospital had to be, John's car died. A strange looking man approached us...(*wait for my, maybe, **Book 5***).

The region has 25 million people (*could be more, as this depends on what you count*), the second most active international airport (*LAX*) in the nation, busiest commercial port (*Port of Los Angeles*) in the U.S., 85% of adult film production in North American, surfing, skateboarding, freeways, professional sport teams and the latest restaurant trends.

I first lived in Southern California in 1958. The smog was terrible. It is still bad today, but, somehow, better. Hollywood, Santa Barbara, La Jolla, Disneyland, Getty Museum, you want it, you can get it. More specifically, I resided in Oxnard, located about 60 miles north of LA, when it was then a land of lima beans and lemons. Today, they are largely gone, but homes are now more expensive than in Honolulu. A bit further north through Santa Barbara and up to San Luis Obispo are fine wineries, Hearst Castle and Solvang, a Dutch town. This was the general locale, not Napa Valley, for ***Sideways***, that wine tasting film.

I've never lived in San Diego, but the weather, La Jolla, the zoo, access to Mexico, outstanding biological and medical research, golf courses and the Pacific Ocean argue for inclusion as a finalist. But those fires will return.

All in all, this would be a nice place to live if you find that ideal niche. I highly recommend this part of the world.

**#3: Norway**

Archaeological findings indicate people living in this region for 12,000 years. The Vikings of Norway explored the Americas way before Columbus. In 1349, the Black Death killed half the population. Norway peacefully separated from Sweden in 1905.

Norway has not joined the European Union and has no plans to do so. There is a kind of superiority complex exhibited by this country because of their fossil fuel resources, and independence remains, by a small margin, the prevailing sentiment. Yet, they comply with most of the requirements anyway, and would probably gain by converting to the Euro.

The Kingdom of Norway is a constitutional monarchy with a parliamentary system of government. Depending on the report, either Norway or the U.S. has the second highest GDP/capita in the world in terms of purchasing power parity. Luxembourg is #1. The cost of living in Norway is 30% higher than the U.S, another disadvantage of remaining non-EU. With a relatively small population of less than 5 million, Norway is well endowed with petroleum, natural gas, hydropower, minerals, forests and fisheries.

Why then with so high a cost of living and truly cold temperatures is Norway rated #3 as the best place to live? Easy:

- #1—Global Peace Index by the Economist.
- #2—in the 2007 Human Development Index (*life expectancy, literacy, standard of living, etc.*) by the United Nations, but #1 the previous six years.
- #1—Press Freedom Index by Reporters Without Borders.
- #1—State of World's Mothers by Save the Children.
- #2—Environmental Sustainability Index by Yale University/Columbia University.
- #3—Worldwide Quality of Life Index by the Economist.

About ten percent of Norwegians are immigrants from 200 countries, accounting for more than half of the country's population growth. There are various internet portals on how to immigrate to Norway.

Their foreign aid is cunning. They don't just give money away to needy nations. They have tended to invest in disadvantaged, but even developed, areas, in a manner which might utilize local brainpower to create joint efforts, thus linking that country to future investments and trade agreements.

With all the above, why isn't Norway #1 as the best place to live? Too cold, for sure, and their cost of living is quite high. Yet, opportunities abound and I can highly recommend trying Norway first because they seek immigrants (*not as much today as in the past with some welfare problems and Muslim unrest*), while the U.S. is not as accommodating.

### #2: San Francisco and the Bay Area

Next to Hawaii, I enjoy the area around San Francisco most. Having spent four years at Stanford University, several assignments at the Lawrence Livermore National Laboratory and Ames Research Center, and regular forays through the wine country of Napa, Sonoma and down south all the way to Santa Barbara, there is a lot of variety in this region. BART, culture, Chinatown, SoMa, cable cars, the Golden Gate Bridge, Union Square, Nob Hill, Silicon Valley, genome hotspots, outstanding colleges, all the professional sports you might want and generally acceptable weather, a case can be made for this area being #1.

There are earthquakes and the western side of the San Andreas Fault could fall into the sea someday. My most memorable trip ever with regard to natural disasters occurred in October 1989 when I participated in an engineering conference in New Orleans, but left town a bit early to avoid a hurricane heading towards Texas or Louisiana. I flew to San Francisco, then on to Tokyo for another meeting, where I felt an earthquake. I then needed to testify in Congress, so I stopped off in San Francisco and stayed at the AmFac Hotel at the airport. The next day I flew to Dulles. The first scene I saw on my room TV was the elevator shaft of the AmFac Hotel, which had caved in from the Loma Prieta earthquake that postponed the World Series. My room that previous night was next to the elevator.

But, in 2007, for the $18^{th}$ consecutive year, San Francisco was named by Conde Nast as the number one U.S. city. Even if home and rental prices are higher in San Francisco and vicinity than anywhere else (*Honolulu is only #9*) there are very good reasons for picking this area. I was that close to leaning in this direction, but, perhaps, for the second edition of ***Book 2***.

## #1...Hawaii

...HAWAII has more people (*approaching 1.3 million*) than 8 states and a larger land area than 7. Actually, counting the Exclusive Economic Zone (*the 200 nautical mile region surrounding our country*), we <u>are twice as large as Texas</u>.

This is the most isolated island chain in the world, but because of volcanoes as high as 13,796 feet (4,205 meters), the islands enjoy the full range of micro-climates and environments. While Mt. Waialeale on the island of Kauai is either second or first as the wettest spot (*about 460 inches/year*), just ten miles away are beaches that sometimes experience only 5 inches/year.

We have tended to be ahead of the curve on matters sociological. There have been a lot of ethnic political firsts:

- Chinese U.S. Senator, Hiram Fong.
- Japanese Congressman and U.S. Senator, Daniel Inouye.
- Female Japanese Congresswoman, Patsy Mink (*and second in Pat Saiki*)
- Hawaiian in Congress and Senate, Daniel Akaka

- Japanese, Hawaiian and Filipino state governors, George Ariyoshi, John Waihee and Ben Cayetano.
- Korean Mayor, Harry Kim.

Hawaii is the most multi-racial state, that is, percentage of citizens of combined races.

We have the only unified statewide educational system, partly explaining why state taxes are the highest in the Nation. Our diverse ethnic mix and interface location between East and West provide a model for universal peace.

Our agriculture industry is changing. At one time, sugar and pineapple were king. Today, freshwater sold from the reverse osmosis of deep sea water is our largest export commodity. However, unofficially, marijuana production is our leading agriculture crop, said to be worth in the range of $4 billion/year.[298]

How did Hawaii become Hawaii? It is not absolutely clear if "Hawaiians" first arrived in 200AD or 1000AD, but they came from the Marqueses and Society Islands, followed by Tahiti in 1300AD. Then, in sailed British explorer Captain James Cook in 1778, followed by assorted missionaries, mostly from the New England states. In 1810, King Kamehameha the Great united Hawaii.

The sugar industry started in 1835 in Koloa, Kauai, largely by the sons of these religious families, who were instrumental in having Hawaii annexed to the United States in 1898, to stabilize higher sugar prices and obtain other legal expediencies. Koloa is where my father resettled in 1903 after his father passed away.

Largely beginning in the mid-1800's, the industry brought in nearly 400,000 laborers from China, Japan, Puerto Rico, Korea and the Philippines, and supervisors from Portugal, Norway, Germany and Scotland. Considering that the total population of Hawaii was only 154,000 in 1900 and less than 500,000 in 1950, when much of this practice stopped, it is clear that the sociological mixing pot and resultant society today were due to sugar, which happened to be my first job in 1962. Statehood was attained three years earlier when Hawaii became the 50$^{th}$ and last state to enter the Union, and in 2009 will celebrate half a century of being an equal member of the U.S.

Hawaii has passed monumental land and water use legislation. We tried the gas cap, but a year later, our gasoline prices were still the highest in the Nation. So we gave up on that one. We kicked homeless people out of parks before the community could react, and, guess what? Solutions appeared. Churches, it turns out, do have purpose and value. Some offered a place to sleep at night (*for there is a lot of space not used at night*) with a start-off breakfast in the morning. Members sometimes interacted with the "guests" and part-time jobs resulted. Trusting relationship began to form, and some of the homeless problem was ameliorated, for a while. And Hawaii did not even have to resort to using public schools, which also aren't used at night, or the military, which offers another dimension of cooperation. This is still a work in progress, for parks are again beginning to be settled.

But all is not perfect, as, while we don't have malaria or chikumgunya mosquitoes, we do have large cockroaches. In fact, they are referred to as B-52s, because they fly and can frighten you. However, they are not as large as those from Ecuador (*try 6 inches long with a one foot wingspan*), which are also poisonous, nor Le Reunion Island, where I encountered a monster. Honolulu is #5 on the list of most roach-infested cities in the U.S., according to Vernard Lewis of the University of California at Berkeley.

More seriously, today, as I am continuing to write, ***The Honolulu Advertiser*** reported that Hawaii ranks (*in addition to those entries cited earlier*):

- #47 (*out of 50, edging out San Francisco, Oakland, New Orleans and Miami, from SustainLane.com*) as the worst place to live based on potential natural disasters. In case you want to be safe, Mesa (*Arizona*), Milwaukee (*Wisconsin*) and Cleveland (*Ohio*) are the top three.[310] Yes, we do have earthquakes, volcanic eruptions, tsunamis, hurricanes…name it, we probably are the most exciting place on Earth. Keep in mind, though, that at my advanced age, I have not yet felt a strong earthquake, seen a tsunami, or had to deal with a hurricane. And I've lived here most of my life.
- #3 by the United Health Foundation as the healthiest state in 2007, next to Vermont and Minnesota. We were #9 in 1990. Thus, terrific, and getting better.[165]
- #2 from the bottom (*this is really good*) with respect to the prevalence and severity of depression, next to South Dakota.[319] Yes, South Dakota. Utah was #51 and West Virginia #50. Mormon Church? Lack of alcohol? Coal? South Dakota is the least depressed state?
- #41 (*good*) by Mental Health America on suicides. Utah was #1 (*bad, very bad*). Heart disease and cancer kill more people, but suicide is next, so there must be something about Honolulu that makes it just of opposite of Las Vegas and Salt Lake City.
- #5 (*of medium sized metropolises, from the Bailey's Irish Cream and Sperling Best Places ranking*) for most "Chilled Out" city. For those who are not in the know, being chilled out is good, with no relationship to getting frozen. It relates to a neat place to hang out. The best cities are Phoenix (*Arizona, mega*), Portland (*Oregon, large*) and Colorado Springs (*Colorado, medium*). Honolulu was hurt by being rated the lowest for cool coffee houses. I guess the swarm of Starbucks doesn't count, for there must be one every few blocks.
- #4 (*with Essex County in Massachusetts and San Francisco and San Jose, California being even worse, from Forbes.com*) in the top 10 of most overpriced places to live in the U.S. The average price of a home in Honolulu is $625,000, with San Jose at $746,800, even higher than San Francisco at $720,400. When I was matriculating at Stanford, my freshman roommate, Jim Seger, came from San Jose, and he would have agreed with me that San Jose was then a hick town. What a difference half a century can make. Similarly, I spent my summers in Oxnard, 60 miles north of Los Angeles, in those days known as the lima bean capital of the world. Today, home prices are higher than Hawaii's.
- #4 (*with New Jersey, Maryland and Connecticut #1 to #3*) in millionaires per household in 2007.[121] We were #1 in 2005 and 2006. We'll be back if you move here.

The point, too, of course, is that Honolulu and Hawaii, as isolated and small as they are, always are included in national and world rankings. I can further add that Hawaii, at 52%, has the highest rate of people killed in alcohol-related traffic accidents. Utah is lowest at 24%. Do you want to live in Utah? Soon in Hawaii will come a mandatory DUI preventative device to reduce this partying downside.

Where will Hawaii be by the turn of century? Sea level rise could impact our famous beaches and resorts. But the sea itself will be alive with floating cities, tending next generation fisheries and marine biomass plantations, while helping to remediate global climate warming. The Blue Revolution could by then serve to prevent the formation of these giant storms, and, also, reduce the impact of the Greenhouse Effect.

We should someday be totally powered by sustainable energy (***Book 1*** of ***SIMPLE SOLUTIONS***). Solar energy, windpower, ocean energy and biofuels (*also from the sea*) will prevail. Perhaps a renewable hydrogen economy will be in place. No coal, no nuclear.

Our ethnic diversity already has made us the world melting pot. Today, 20% of our citizens are multi-racial. Crime will be in check and there will be peace on Earth, of course, partly due to Chapter 1. Some of you will be contemplating eternal life (*Chapter 2*) and education will become a rainbow experience (*Chapter 3*). We might have begun communicating with other worlds (*Chapter 4*) and there will be the Golden Evolution of religion (*Chapter 5*). The Hawaii 2050 Sustainability Task Force, which is reporting to the public as I write this sentence, will set the tone for a progressive Hawaii, and so will Fred Riggs' sustainability group through his web page at:

http://webdata.soc.hawaii.edu/fredr/SUSTAIN%20OUR%20WORLD.html#rigg

Early in 2008 there was a best place contest to pick Hawaii's top 25 sites to visit. Maui's Haleakala Crater at sunrise? Kauai's Waimea Canyon at sunset? The volcanoes, green sand beach and macadamia nut plantations of the Big Island? The Green Flash from my penthouse? That secret fishing ground off Molokai? The Manoa Valley rainbow? You can contact WAdams@HonoluluAdvertiser.com with the secret password, Na Wahi Heke, and gain access to the poll results.

You, too, can become a part of this future. Can you imagine a better place on Planet Earth? **This is not heaven, but is the closest thing to paradise**. If you can't afford it, certainly don't come, but if this is to be your last life, you might as well make it exciting, memorable, enjoyable and lengthy.

# SIMPLE SOLUTIONS: A SUMMARY

## ONE: Ending Crime and War Forever

- Crime: three strikes and you're dead.
- War: convert all nations to democracies, starting with the establishment of a World Peace Center, where diplomats can obtain a universal degree to promote peace, and find a way to give the United Nations enforcement powers on world solutions. In parallel, strive towards total world disarmament.
- The looming world economic cataclysm caused by Peak Oil and Global Heating can serve as the stimulus for the United States to work with the other G8 Nations to immediately (2009) shift military funds towards remediation of this dual hammer.

## TWO: Eternal Life

- Develop the necessary computer technology to store knowledge from a brain and perfect human cloning.
- Find the aging gene and disable it.

## THREE: Teaching Rainbows

- Incorporate Rigor, Respect, Relevance and Relationship as equals with Reading, Riting and Rithmetic to convert the one marshmallow students to become productive citizens, and further enhance the capabilities of the two marshmallow group. There will further be the bonuses of a lower crime rate and a more peaceful society.
- Anytime there is a budget surplus, local, statewide or nationally, give at least 50% of those funds towards education, preferably to deliver on the new R's.
- For the U.S. to maintain #1 status, continue to refine the greatness of our universities, from where will come the leaders, thinkers and producers to maintain our pre-eminence.

## FOUR: Seeking the SETI Light

- Provide $10 million/year for coherent optical techniques to confirm the presence of Earth-sized exoplanets.
- Establish a Chinese connection by seeding the prospects of a SETI program in China, and nourish it so that it becomes a threat to American egos.

- Re-start an official NASA SETI program at $100 million/year to coordinate the world effort. Alas, we might need to wait a while for that galvanizing spark, whatever form it might take.

## FIVE: The Golden Evolution

- Grow up and accept the notion of a Supreme Being as, while once necessary for the survival of our species, now obsolete.
- Acknowledge miracles as impossible.
- Recognize that there is no afterlife.
- As our society has a fatal flaw in anticipating and subverting future economic calamities, should something like the looming giant asteroid of Peak Oil and Global Warming become a monumental threat to our survival, first, overcome the unparalleled crisis, but more so, learn a lesson in societal maturity by transferring now archaic religious beliefs towards the sustainability of humanity itself.

## SIX: The Best Place in the World

- Dream about living in Hawaii.
- Come to Hawaii…if you can afford it!

# REFERENCES

1 *Time*, June 24 1996, p. 62.
2 *Parade Magazine*, March 23 2004, pp. 4-5.
3 *Time*, August 2 1999, p. 100.
4 *Honolulu Advertiser*, December 13 1998, p. G5.
5 *Honolulu Advertiser*, December 31 2002.
6 *Honolulu Advertiser*, November 17 2001, p. B3.
7 *Honolulu Advertiser*, January 5 2004, p. A3.
8 *Free Inquiry Magazine* 1991.
9 Carey Gilliam (Reuters), 'Dupont, Bp Link up for Biofuels Production', *Washington Post*, June 20, 2006.
10 Bob Abernethy, 'America's Evangelicals' [Accessed April 23, 2004.
11 ACLU, 'The Case against the Death Penalty' [Accessed July 25, 2007.
12 Abdullah Shihri and Ahmed Al-Haj, '7 Suspected Terrorists Escape from Saudi Prison and 19 Al-Qaida Suspects Acquitted in Yemen', *The Honolulu Advertiser*, July 9, 2006, p. A22.
13 Sheldon Alberts, 'Gore Defends Live Earth Concerts', National Post, [Accessed July 7, 2007.
14 Jodie Allen, 'Iraqi Vote Mirrors Desire for Democracy in Muslim World', ed. by Pew Research Center, 2005.
15 Jonathan Alter, 'Monkey See, Monkey Do', *Newsweek* 2005, p. 27.
16 J. P. Chaput Angelo Tremblay, et al, 'Study: Less Sleep Ups Obesity Rate', *International Journal of Obesity* (2006).
17 Thomas Aquinas, *On Law, Morality and Politics*. Second edn, Hackett Publishing Company, 1988.
18 et al Arthur Aron, *Journal of Neurophysiology* (2005).
19 Patrick Barry, 'The Great Dying', NASA, January 28, 2002.
20 National Education Association, 'Teacher Pay 1940-2000 Losing Ground, Losing Status' [Accessed September 16, 2007.
21 Eric Bailey, 'Pot Is Called Biggest Cash Crop', *Los Angeles Times*, December 18, 2006.
22 Ronald Bailey, 'The Rise of Stem Cell Research', *Reason Magazine*, January 19, 2007.
23 Nicholas Bakalar, 'Did Early Humans First Arise in Asia, Not Africa?', *National Geographic News*, December 27, 2005.
24 Frank Barnaby, *How to Build a Nuclear Bomb and Other Weapons of Mass Destruction,* Nation Books, 2004.
25 Antony Barnett, 'Vatican Told Bishops to Cover up Sexual Abuse' [Accessed August 17, 2003.

26 BBC, 'Animal Experiments' [Accessed August 17, 2004.
27 Deanna Bellandi, 'Boiled Nuts Help Protect against Illness', *FoxNews.com*, October 29, 2007.
28 Bryan Bender, 'Economists Say Cost of War Could Top $2 Trillion', Boston Globe, [Accessed January 8, 2006.
29 Richard Benedetto, 'Faith-Based Programs Flourishing, Bush Says', *USA Today*, March 10, 2006, p. 5A.
30 Eric Berger, 'Still More Evidence It's Ok to Be Overweight' [Accessed April 23, 2007.
31 Claire Bertschinger's, *Moving Mountains,* Doubleday, 2005.
32 Don Bierle, *Surprised by Faith,* Emerald Books, 1992.
33 Dana Blanton, 'More Believe in God Than Heaven' [Accessed June 18, 2004.
34 Deborah Blum, *Ghost Hunters: William James and the Search for Scientific Proof of Life after Death,* Penguin Press, 2006, p. 384.
35 Ronna Bolante, 'Our Schools: Has Anything Changed?' *Honolulu*, May 2006.
36 ———, 'Ready for the Real World?' *Honolulu*, May 2007, pp. 66-88.
37 Reporters Without Borders, 'Third Annual Worldwide Press Freedom Index', 2004.
38 Seth Borenstein, 'Virus Might Cause Obesity', *New York Post*, August 21, 2007.
39 Jeremy Bowen, 'Moses', ed. by BBC, 2002.
40 Peter Boylan, 'Hpd Unable to Solve 90% of Felonies in '04', *Honolulu Advertiser*, October 18, 2005.
41 Salynn Boyles, 'Fiber Not Protective for Colon Cancer' [Accessed December 13, 2005.
42 Pam Brooks, 'Bird Flu (Avian Flu)' [Accessed March 2, 2006.
43 Lester Brown, 'Wind Energy Demand Booming' [Accessed March 27, 2006.
44 Christi Brua, 'U.S. Highest in Gun Ownership' [Accessed September 12, 2007.
45 Nutrition Bulletin, 'Take It with a Grain of Salt', *Men's Health*, May 2006, p. 42.
46 Delan Butler, 'When Science and Theology Meet', *Nature,* 443 (2006), 10-11.
47 Dennis Camire, 'Early-Education Funding Sought', *Honolulu Advertiser*, January 24, 2008, p. B4.
48 International Agency for Research on Cancer, 'Working the Graveyard Shift Could Be Bad for Your Health', ed. by World Health Organization, United Nations, 2007.
49 Tony Cappasso, 'Go to Church, Live Longer', in *Click10.com*, 2001.
50 Robert Todd Carrol, *Shroud of Turin*. ed. by The Skeptics Dictionary, 2006.
51 Joseph Carroll, 'Public Divided over Money Spent on Space Shuttle Program' [Accessed June 30, 2006.
52 The United States Census, 'Education', ed. by U.S. Census Bureau, 2000.
53 Alex Usher and Amy Cervenan, 'Global Higher Education Rankings', ed. by Educational Policy Institute, 2005, p. 77.
54 Maria Cheng, 'Graveyard Shift Work Linked to Cancer', in *Foxnews.com*, 2007.
55 ———, 'Want to Live 14 Years Longer?' *Seattle Times*, January 8, 2008.
56 Cary Cherniss, 'Emotional Intelligence: What It Is and Why It Matters', ed. by The Consortium for Research on Emotional Intelligence in Organizations, 2000.

57 Robert Chessnoff, *The Arrogance of the French: Why They Can't Stand Us--and Why the Feeling Is Mutual,* Sentinal, 2005, p. 208.
58 Nick Childs, 'Israel, Iran Top 'Negative List'' [Accessed March 6, 2007.
59 'Chimp Genome May Explain Human Diseases', in *myDNA News*, 2005.
60 Bill Christensen, 'Map of World Happiness' [Accessed August 25, 2007.
61 Vatican City, 'Catholic Priests Getting Scarcer', *The Honolulu Advertiser*, May 1, 2006, p. A3.
62 Bureau of Justice Statistics Clearinghouse, 'Opium' 2007.
63 Bill Clinton, *Giving*Knopf, 2007, p. 256.
64 John Cloud, 'Failing Our Geniuses', *Time*, August 27, 2007, pp. 40-50.
65 CNN.com, 'Study Claims Ice, Not Water, Kept Jesus Afloat' [Accessed April 4, 2006.
66 Philip Morrison and Giuseppe Cocconi, 'Searching for Interstellar Communications', *Nature,* 184 (1959).
67 Edward Cody, 'Chinese Rush to Have Babies in Year of Pig', *Washington Post*, March 5, 2007.
68 Steve Connor, 'Sleeping Better Helps Women Live Longer', in *The Independent*, 2002).
69 Alan Cooperman, ''Lost Tomb of Jesus' Claim Called a Stunt' [Accessed February 28, 2007.
70 A. Copland, *The Existence of Other Worlds: Peopled with Living and Intelligent Beings,* J.G. and F. Rivington, 1834.
71 Beverly Creamer, 'Teachers' Day: 15 1/2 Hours', *Honolulu Advertiser*, March 4, 2007, p. A1.
72 Matt Crenson, 'America's Stature Is Shrinking--Literally', *Honolulu Advertiser*, July 16, 2007, p. A1.
73 Stuart Creque, 'Killing with Kindness--Capital Punishment by Nitrogen Asphyxiation' [Accessed September 11, 1995.
74 Office on Drugs and Crime, 'World Drug Report', ed. by United Nations, 2006.
75 Lisa Takeuchi Cullen, 'Opening the Box', *Time*, August 14, 2006, p. A12.
76 Elizabeth Culotta, 'Spanish Fossil Sheds New Light on the Oldest Great Apes', *Science,* 306 (2004), 1273-74.
77 Farr Curlin, *Journal of General Internal Medicine,* (2005).
78 Donald Rusk Currey, 'Donald Rusk Currey', in *Wikipedia*, 2008.
79 Cathy Lynn Grossman Dan Vergamo, 'Gospel of Judas Believed Found', *USA Today*, April 7, 2006.
80 Nancy Dann, 'Taking a Leap of Faith' [Accessed February 21, 2007.
81 Richard Dawkins, *The God Delusion* (Boston and New York: Houghton Mifflin Company, 2006), p. 406.
82 ———, *Unweaving the Rainbow,* Houghton Mifflin Books, 1998, p. 352.
83 Wil Roebroeks and Robin Dennell, 'Are We All Asians?' *Discover*, May 2006, pp. 12-13.
84 Daniel Dennett, *Breaking the Spell: Religion as a Natural Phenomenon,* Viking/ Allen Lane, 2006, p. 488.
85 Jared Diamond, *Collapse,* Penguin Books, 2006, p. 576.

86 Christopher Dickey, 'Near 'the Edge of the Abyss'', *Time*, August 15 2005, p. 29.
87 Richard Dieter, 'A Crisis of Confidence: Americans' Doubts About the Death Penalty', ed. by The Death Penalty Information Center, 2007.
88 discoverthenetworks.org, 'A Guide to the Political Left', 2006.
89 Ian McKeague and Nathan Paldor Doron Nof, 'Is There a Paleolimnological Explanation For "Walking on Water" In the Sea of Galilee?' *Journal of Paleolimnology,* 35 (2006), 417-39.
90 Michael Duffy, 'Weapons of War: Poison Gas' [Accessed May 5, 2002.
91 Gary Dufresne, 'Interview', in *StopSylviaBrowne.com*, 2007.
92 David Duncan, 'Finding the Fountain of Youth', *San Francisco Chronicle*, May 29, 2005.
93 Maggie Kalev and Matthew During, 'Glass of Wine Aids Memory', *Journal of Neuroscience* (2007).
94 Freeman Dyson, *The Sun, the Genome, and the Internet,* Oxford University Press, 1999.
95 ECPM, 'Why Do We Need to Abolish the Death Penalty?' [Accessed July 25, 2007.
96 Melissa Eddy, 'Pope Benedict Contends Evolution Isn't Provable', in *Associate Press*, 2007.
97 Editor, 'Safeguards Can Protect Whales During Sonar Use', *Honolulu Star Bulletin*, September 1, 2004.
98 Global Business Network - Europe, 'What Road Ahead?' ed. by Nautilus Institute for Security and Sustainable Development, 2001.
99 'Evolution's Big Bang', *Time* 1995, pp. 66-74.
100 Bryan Farwha, 'Was Psychic Sylvia Browne Right?' *Skeptic,* 12 (2006), 10,11.
101 Finfacts, 'Gold Market and Price 1800-2007' [Accessed July 20, 2007.
102 Al Firdaws, 'Al Qaeda Woos Recruits with N-Bomb Website', in *Daily Times (Pakistan)*, 2005).
103 Brian Flemming, 'Greg Epstein Does Not Equal Humanism', 2007.
104 Tom Flynn, 'Prospect Impact: The Jesus Project', *Free Inquiry,* 27 (2007), 14-15.
105 B. D. Fontenelle, *Plurality of Worlds,* Red Lyon, 1728.
106 Hypography Science Forums, 'The First Blue Rose' [Accessed April 4, 2005.
107 New Economics Foundation, 'Vanuatu Is World's Happiest Country' [Accessed July 17, 2006.
108 Bill Frogameni, 'Toledo Native Barbara Blaine Crusades against Sexual Abuse in the Catholic Church', *Toledo City Paper*, April 29, 2004.
109 Kenneth Fry, *Beyond War: The Human Potential for Peace,* Oxford University Press, 2007.
110 Frances Fukuyama, *The End of History and the Last Man,* Penguin Books, 1992.
111 United Nations Population Fund, 'State of the World Population [Accessed April 11, 2006.
112 George Gallop, 'Origin of Human Beings', *USA Today*, September 11, 2005.
113 Stephen Garber, 'Journal of British Interplanetary Society', 52, 3-12.
114 Stephanie Gaskell, 'Honolulu's Air Is among Cleanest in Nation', *Honolulu Star-Bulletin*, May 1, 2002, p. C6.

115 Sonya Geis, 'Rich Donors Help California Fund Stem Cell Research', *Washington Post*, December 19, 2006.
116 Norman Geisler, 'Miracles and Modern Scientific Thought', Truth Journal, [Accessed July 14, 2002.
117 Jr George Gallup, 'Religion in American: Will the Vitality of Churches Be the Surprise of the Next Century?', *The Public Perspective,* 6 (1995), 1-8.
118 William Perry George Shultz, Henry Kissinger and Sam Nunn, 'A World Free of Nuclear Weapons', *The Wall Street Journal*, January 4, 2007.
119 Wayt Gibbs, 'Obesity: An Overblown Epidemic?' *Scientific American*, May 23, 2005.
120 Ian Williams Goddard, 'New Findings May Support Soy-Dementia in Men', in *Goddard's Journal*, 2003).
121 David Thompson and Ray Graber, 'New Jersey Has Highest Percentage of Millionaire Residents', Phoenix Marketing International, 2008.
122 Robert Greene, *The 33 Strategies of War,* Viking, 2006, p. 474.
123 David Gregory, 'Legal Arguments against the Death Penalty' 2000.
124 Frank Greve, 'Experts: Global Drug Abuse Largely Contained' [Accessed July 5, 2007.
125 John Griffin, 'Immigration Debate Affects Hawaii, Too', *Honolulu Advertiser*, June 25, 2006, p. B1.
126 Cathy Lynn Grossman, 'View of God Can Predict Values, Politics' [Accessed September 12, 2006.
127 Mercury Communications Group, 'The United States Is the Best Country on the Face of the Earth' [Accessed August 9, 2007.
128 Jonathan Gruber, 'Religious Market Structure, Religious Participation and Outcomes: Is Religion Good for You?' in *NBER Working Paper 11377*, 2005.
129 Joakim Hagelin, 'Religion and Opinion About Reproductive Human Cloning', *Eubios Journal of Asian and International Bioethics,* 14 (2004), 214-16.
130 Richard Halloran, 'War Memorial Peaceful, Inflaming', *The Honolulu Advertiser*, May 21, 2006, p. B3.
131 Rick Hamada, 'How to Deter the Bad Guys', *Midweek*, May 28, 2003, p. 55.
132 Sam Harris, *The End of Faith: Religion, Terror, and the Future of Reason,* W. W. Norton and Company, 2004.
133 Michael Hart, 'Settlements in Space, and Interstellar Travel, from Habitable Zones About Main Sequence Stars," Icarus', Vol. 37, pp351-7.
134 Victor Stenger and Charles Hayes, 'Scrap Yard: Does God Exist?' *Honolulu*, May 2007, p. 34.
135 V. Dion Haynes, 'Schools Report Urges Drastic Change, Higher Salaries', *The Washington Post*, December 15, 2006.
136 Robert Hazen, *Genesis: The Scientific Quest for Life's Origins,* Joseph Henry Press, 2005, p. 339.
137 Nanci Hellmich, 'Processed Meat Bad for You?' in *USA Today*, 2007.
138 John Hennessy, 'All of Us Own a Part of This Challenge', *Stanford*, December 2006, p. 6.
139 Hugh Hewitt, *Searching for God in America,* Word Publishing, 1996.

140 Mark Hitchcock, *55 Questions to Life after Death,* Multnomah Publishers, 2005.
141 Christopher Hitchens, *God Is Not Great,* Twelve, 2007, p. 307.
142 Miranda Hitti, 'Alzheimer's Blood Test in the Works', in *BetterInformation. BetterHealth*, 2007.
143 ———, 'Sleep More to Fight Obesity', in *WebMD Medical News*, 2004.
144 R. Joseph Hoffmann, 'The Jesus Project', *Free Inquiry,* 27 (2007), 50-52.
145 April Holladay, WonderQuest [Accessed December 10, 2004.
146 Nicholas Horrock, 'The New Terror Fear--Biological Weapons', *U.S. News and World Report*, May 12, 1997, p. 36.
147 Fred Hoyle, *Intelligent Universe,* Holt, Rinehart and Winston, 1984.
148 Vision of Humanity, 'Peace and Sustainability' [Accessed August 10, 2007.
149 Kasie Hunt, '1 in 32 Americans in Jails, on Parole', in *abc News*, 2006.
150 Samuel Huntington, *The Clash of Civilizations and the Remaking of World Order,* Touchstone, 1996.
151 Jin Hyun-joo, 'Entrance Exam Dominates Nation Tomorrow', *International Herald Tribune*, November 16, 2004.
152 Ronald Inglehart, ed., *Human Beliefs and Values* (Buenos Aires: Siglo XXI Editores, 2004).
153 Transparency International, 'The 2005 Transparency International Corruption Perceptions Index' [Accessed July 28, 2006.
154 Center for the Study of Religious Issues, *The Bingo Report* (Freeport: CSRI, 2005).
155 Susan Jakes, 'Sitting Pretty', *Time*, April 2006, p. A7.
156 Anick Jesdanun, 'China's Online Population Soon to Surpass U.S.' *Hawaii Business Today*, January 19, 2008, p. C7.
157 Patrick Johnson, 'Obesity: Epidemic and Myth?' *Skeptical Inquirer*, September 2005.
158 Mother Jones, 'The Iraq Effect', *The Foundation for National Progress*, March 1, 2007.
159 James Joyner, 'Black President More Likely Than Mormon or Atheist' [Accessed February 20, 2007.
160 Patrick Di Justo, 'For That Drain-Cleaner Fresh Feeling', *Wired*, October 2007, p. 50.
161 Marcus Kabel, 'Wal-Mart Nudges Foreign Suppliers', Washingtonpost.com, [Accessed October 21, 2005.
162 Ben Kage, 'Cattle Raised for Beef Cause More Damage to Planet Than Emissions from Cars, Report Finds', in *NewsTarget.com*, 2006.
163 Michio Kaku, *Parallel Worlds* (New York: Anchor Books, 2005), p. 428.
164 Marina Kamenev, 'Rating Countries for the Happiness Factor', *Business Week* 2006.
165 et al Karen Davis, 'America's Health Rankings', ed. by United Health Foundation, Minneapolis, 2007, p. 133.
166 Brandon Keim, 'Scientists Find World's Oldest Animal', in *Wired Science*, 2007.
167 Laza Kekic, 'A Pause in Democracy's March' [Accessed August 13, 2007.

168 Stuart Kingsley, 'The Search for Extraterrestrial Intelligence in the Optical Spectrum: A Review', *SPIE Proceedings, The Search for Extraterrestrial Intelligence in the Optical Spectrum, OE/LASE '93,* 1867 (1993), 75-113.
169 Brian Kladko, 'Russia Jumps to Top, England Drops on Reading Test', in *Bloomberg.com*, 2007.
170 Bradley Klapper, 'Wto: China Overtakes U.S. In Exports', *USA Today*, April 13, 2007.
171 Michael Klesius, 'The Persistent Poppy', *National Geographic* 2007.
172 Sam Knight, 'Bird Flu Will Cost $800 Billion, Says World Bank' [Accessed November 7, 2005.
173 Alfie Kohn, *The Homework Myth,* De Capo Press, 2006, p. 243.
174 Ah-Ng Tony Kong, 'Combined Inhibitory Effects of Curcumin and Phenethyl Isothiocyanate on Growth of Human Pc-3 Prostate Xenografts in Immunodeficient Mice', *Cancer Research* (2006.
175 Linda Thaler and Robin Koval, *Power of Nice,* Currency Doubleday, 2007.
176 Kenneth Krause, 'Dangerous Ideas on the Loose', *Skeptical Inquirer,* 32 (2008), 54-55.
177 Elizabeth Kubler-Ross, *On Death and Dying,* Scribner, 1997 reprint.
178 ———, *On Life after Death*, Berkeley: Celestrial Arts, 1991.
179 Steven Kull, 'How Muslims and Americans View Each Other' [Accessed February 18, 2007.
180 Paul Kurtz, 'Creating Secular and Humanist Alternatives to Religion', *Free Inquiry,* 2006, 4-9.
181 Edward Laumann, 'Gender Equality Leads to Better Sex Lives among People 40 and Over' [Accessed April 19, 2006.
182 Andrew Lawler, 'Nasa Budget: Crisis Deepens as Scientists Fail to Rejigger Space Research', *Science,* 312 (2006), 824-5.
183 War Resisters League, 'Where Your Income Tax Money Really Goes' [Accessed August 10, 2007.
184 Donna Leinwand, '1 in 11 Prisoners There for Life', *The Honolulu Advertiser*, May 12, 2004, p. A3.
185 Michael Lemonick, 'A Shortcut for Planet Hunters', *Time*, November 26, 2007, p. 48.
186 C. S. Lewis, *Miracles,* Harmat (Dew) Publishing House, 1994, p. 216.
187 Life, '100 People Who Made the Millennium', Time, 2000.
188 'Life Beyond Earth ', *National Geographic*, January 2000, p. 31.
189 Andrew Kohut and Luis Lugo, 'Religion a Strength and Weakness for Both Parties', ed. by Pew Forum on Religion and Public Life (Washington, D.C., 2005), 45 pages.
190 Landis Lum, 'Dangers of Ingesting Msg Likely a Myth', *The Honolulu Advertiser*, May 11, 2006, p. E5.
191 Colum Lynch, 'U.S. Won't Seek Seat on New Human Rights Body', *Washington Post*, April 7, 2006.
192 Martin Mahner, 'Council of Europe Approves Resolution against Creationism', *Skeptical Inquirer,* 32 (2008), 9.

193 Cynthia Hills Mark Herold, et al, 'Casualties in Afghanistan and Iraq' [Accessed July 16, 2007.
194 Spark Matsunaga, *The Mars Project,* Hill and Wang, 1986.
195 Thomas Maugh, 'Superbug Kills More People in U.S. Than Aids, Study Finds', *Los Angeles Times*, October 17, 2007.
196 Patrick McSherry, 'Relative Monetary Costs of American Wars' [Accessed April 3, 2007.
197 Beeth Ann Meehan, 'Exodus by Numbers', *Discovery*, January 1993.
198 Matthew Melko, *The Nature of Civilizations* (Boston: Porter Sargent, 1969), pp. pp 16-17.
199 Robert Mellert, *The Futurist* (1999).
200 Merriam-Webster, *Collegiate Dictionary*. Eleventh edn (Springfield: Merriam-Webster Inc., 2004), p. 1623.
201 Barbara Mikkelson, 'Soap Dope', in *Snopes.com*, 2005.
202 Jack Miles, *God, a Biography,* Vintage Books, 1995.
203 E.A. Milne, *Modern Cosmology and the Christian Idea of God,* Oxford University Press, 1952, p. pg 153.
204 Kepler Mission, 'A Search for Habitable Planets' [Accessed July 18, 2007.
205 Robert Mitchell, 'General Education Task Force Issues Final Report' [Accessed February 7, 2007.
206 David Moore, 'Public Divided between Death Penalty and Life Imprisonment without Parole' [Accessed June 2, 2004.
207 Richard Morin, 'Do Americans Believe in God?' in *Online Extras*, ed. by On Politics, 2000.
208 ———, 'Yes, It Still Pays to Get a College Degree', *Honolulu Advertiser*, December 11, 2005, p. A31.
209 David Morrison, 'Seti', ed. by Patrick Takahashi, 2007.
210 Tim Leedom and Maria Murdy, *The Book Your Church Doesn't Want You to Read,* Cambridge House Press, 2007, p. 497.
211 Corey Murray, 'Summit: High School Is 'Obsolete'' [Accessed April 1, 2005.
212 David Lloyd and J.T. Wichramasinghe, N.C. Wickramasinghe, 'Evidence of Photoluminescence of Biomaterial in Space', pp 255-260, *Proceedings of SPIE* 4495 (2002).
213 Nationmaster.com, 'Crime Statistics', 2000.
214 Ruben Navarrette, ''No Child' Changes Would Not Help Pupils', *Honolulu Advertiser*, July 24, 2006, p. A8.
215 NBC11.com, 'Report: Murder Rate Rises for Transgender Women' [Accessed May 22, 2007.
216 Lauran Neergaard, 'Ama Pushes to Cut American's Salt Intake', in *The Associated Press*, 2007.
217 ———, 'Food Poisoning Can Be Long-Term Health Problem', in *panagraph.com.*
218 ———, 'Hawaii No. 1 State in Study on Longevity', *Honolulu Advertiser*, September 12, 2006, p. A1.
219 ———, 'Nih Uses Live Viruses for Bird Flu Vaccine' [Accessed December 17, 2005.

220 Stephen Post and Jill Neimark, *Why Good Things Happen to Good People,* Broadway Books, 2007.
221 BBC News, 'World Bank Warns of Bird Flu Cost' [Accessed November 3, 2005.
222 Asra Q. Nomani, 'India's New Untouchables', *Honolulu Advertiser*, November 11, 2007, p. B1.
223 NoteBook, 'Numbers', *Time*, July 10, 2006, p. 19.
224 NOVA, 'The Elegant Universe' [Accessed July 19, 2006.
225 Beth Noveck, 'Wiki-Government', *Democracy,* 1 (2008), 31-43.
226 Bill Novelli, 'Living Large', *AARP Bulletin*, November 2007, p. 29.
227 Kevin O'Keefe, *The Average American: The Extraordinary Search for the Nation's Most Ordinary Citizen,* Public Affairs, 2005.
228 Large Binocular Telescope Observatory, 'About the Lbt' [Accessed July 18, 2007.
229 Congressional Budget Office, 'Wars Could Cost $2.4 Trillion', *USA Today*, October 24, 2007.
230 Ted Olsen, 'Go Figure', *Christianity Today*, January 2008, p. 18.
231 International Labor Organization, 'U.S. Remains 1st in 2006 Labor Productivity' [Accessed September 2, 2007.
232 Richard Ostling, 'Catholics Face Crisis over Retired Nuns' [Accessed July 28, 2006.
233 T.h. Orsi P. Fleischer, M.D. Richardson and A.L. Anderson, 'Distribution of Free Gas in Marine Sediments: A Global Overview', *Geo Marine Letters,* 21 (2001), 103-22.
234 Tom Parfitt, 'Mathematician Explains Parting of Red Sea', *Scotland on Sunday*, February 22, 2004.
235 Cary Funk and Peyton Craighill Paul Taylor, 'Are We Happy Yet?' ed. by Pew Research Center, 2006.
236 The Fund for Peace, 'The Failed States Index 2007', *Foreign Policy*, July/August 2007.
237 Penni Crabtree, SignOnSanDiego.com, July 29, 2005.
238 Matthew Pennington, 'Afghan Opium Crop Jumped 59% This Year, Un Says', *The Honolulu Advertiser*, September 3, 2006, p. A14.
239 Perspectives, 'To Reduce Crime', ***Time***, October 10, 2005, p. 23.
240 Michael Martin Phil Zuckerman, editor, *Atheism: Contemporary Rates and Patterns, in the Cambridge Companion to Atheism* (Cambridge: Cambridge University Press, 2005).
241 School of Public Policy, 'World View of U.S. Role Goes from Bad to Worse', University of Maryland [Accessed July 18, 2007.
242 PollingReport.com, 'President Bush--Overall Job Rating', 2007.
243 Daniel Porter, 'No One Can Explain the Pictures on the Shroud of Turin', ed. by drporter@optonline.net, 2006.
244 Associated Press, 'Finland "Least" Corrupt Country in the World' [Accessed September 13, 2000.
245 Human Development Program, 'Human Development Report 2006', United Nations.

246 Matthew Provonsha, 'Religious Belief and Societal Health', *Skeptic,* 12 (2006), 26-28.
247 Ram Ramgopal, 'India Begins Bird Flu Cell' [Accessed February 19, 2006.
248 Ronald Reagan, 'Remarks at the Annual Convention of the National Association of Evangelicals', RonaldReagan.com [Accessed March 8,1983.
249 Paul Recer, 'Scientists Hope to Create a New Form of Single-Cell Life', *Honolulu Advertiser*, November 22, 2002, p. A5.
250 ReligiousTolerance.org, 'Religious Identification in the U.S.', February 24, 2004.
251 John Remsburg, *The Bible,* Truth Seeker Company, 1905).
252 Coalition for the Advancement of Medical Research, 'New Poll Shows More Than Two Thirds of Americans Support "Therapeutic Cloning" Research to Produce Stem Cells' [Accessed March 19, 2003.
253 Reuters, 'Bird Flu Pandemic Could Cost Insurers $53 Billion' [Accessed March 27, 2006.
254 Anne-marie Reynaud, 'Killer Coconuts', in *Hot Summer Guide*, 2002.
255 Glenn Reynolds, 'Bachelor Degrees in Engineering' [Accessed April 5, 2007.
256 Brad Cooper and Mike Rice, 'Banned Lighters Might Fly Again', *The Kansas City Star*, July 17, 2006.
257 Paul Ridker, 'Bloodstream Inflammation Can Kill', in *cbsnews.com*, 2002.
258 Matt Ridley, *Genome,* HarperCollins, 1999, p. 344.
259 Sogyal Rinpoche, *The Tibetan Book of Living and Dying,* Harper, 1993.
260 Malcolm Ritter, 'Lad Linked to Aging in Older Brains', in *MiamiHerald.com.*
261 Zhisheng An, Rixiang Zhu, Richard Pott and Kenneth Hoffman, 'Magnetostratigraphic Dating of Early Humans in China', *Earth Science Reviews,* 61 (2003), 191-361.
262 et al Robert Lanza, 'Embryonic and Extraembryonic Stem Cell Lines Derived from Single Mouse Blastomeres', *Nature,* 439 (2006), 216-19.
263 Bruce Robinson, 'Capital Punishment--the Death Penalty' [Accessed July 25, 2007.
264 Russell Robinson, 'No Child Falls Short of a Realistic Approach', *Honolulu Advertiser*, July 31, 2007.
265 Jon Ronson, 'How to Make a Dirty Bomb', in *Guardian Unlimited*, 2002.
266 Isadore Rosenfeld, 'It's Ok to Eat Eggs-Enjoy!' in *parade.com*, 2006).
267 David Rothman, 'The Fountain of Health', *Technology Review*, March 2006.
268 R. J. Rummel, 'Iraq: Was Bush Right?' *Honolulu*, March 2006, pp. 54-60.
269 Salman Rushdie, *Satanic Verses,* Picador, 1988.
270 Jeffrey D. Sachs, *The End of Poverty: Economic Possibilities for Our Time,* Penguin Press, 2005.
271 Robert Sawyer, *Calculating God,* Tor, 2000.
272 Randolph Schmid, 'Poor Sleep May Raise Risk of Diabetes', *Honolulu Advertiser*, January 2, 2008, p. A10.
273 Barbara Schneeman, 'Qualified Health Claims: Letter of Denial - Green Tea and Reduced Risk of Cardiovascular Disease', ed. by U.S. Food and Drug Administration, 2005.
274 Douglas Schoen, 'Poll Shows American Dream Unaffordable and Unreachable', United Business Media [Accessed July 5, 2006.

275 World Science, 'Intelligent Bacteria?' [Accessed September 15, 2005.
276 ———, 'Sites under Review for Telescope That Could Detect Alien Tv' [Accessed July 10, 2006.
277 Union of Concerned Scientists, 'Scientific Integrity' [Accessed July 26, 2007.
278 Paul Wink and Julia Scott, 'Does Religiousness Buffer against the Fear of Death and Dying in Late Adulthood? Findings from a Longitudinal Study.' *The Journals of Gerontology Series B: Psychological Sciences and Social Sciences,* 60 (2005), 207-14.
279 Martin Seligman, *Authentic Happiness,* Free Press, 2004.
280 ———, *Learned Optimism,* Pocket Books, 1990.
281 Catholic News Service, 'Austrian Cardinal Says Darwinism Should Be Studied as Science' [Accessed August 24, 2006.
282 Anup Shah, 'The Arms Trade Is Big Business' [Accessed June 20, 2007.
283 Gwen Shamblin, *The Weigh Down Diet,* Muze, 1997.
284 Treena Shapiro, 'Hawaii-Born Beat U.S. Life-Expectancy Average', *Honolulu Advertiser*, June 6, 2006, p. B3.
285 Nadim Shehadi, 'Iran's Regional Position Is Key to Its Strength' [Accessed August 23, 2006.
286 Ben Sherman, 'Falling Coconuts Kill More People Than Shark Attacks', in *UniSci*, 2002.
287 Mark Sherman, 'Crime Rate Still at Record Low', *The Honolulu Advertiser*, September 26, 2005, p. A3.
288 Vandana Shiva, 'The Violence of the Green Revolution: Ecological Degradation and Political Conflict in Punjab', *The Ecologist,* 21 (1991), 57-60.
289 Doreathea Singer(translator), *Giordano Bruno: His Life and Thought,* Henry Schuman, 1950.
290 Tom Smith, 'Job Satisfaction in America', ed. by National Opinion Research Center, 2007.
291 Frank Drake and Dava Sobel, *Is Anyone out There?,* Delacorte Press, 1992.
292 Peaceful Societies, 'Alternatives to Violence and War', 2007.
293 Center for Genetics and Society, 'Opinions About Reproductive Cloning' [Accessed May 15, 2003.
294 Kurt Soller, 'Making Sure Death Is Fair' [Accessed June 15, 2007.
295 Park Song-wu, '48% of Youth Would Support N. Korea in Case of U.S. Attack', *The Korea Times*, February 2, 2006.
296 Bob Egelko and Kevin Fagan Stacy Finz, 'State Postpones Morales Execution', *San Francisco Chronicle*, February 22, 2006.
297 Staff, 'Comparing U.S. Religious Beliefs with Other Christian Countries' [Accessed February 21, 2007.
298 Advertiser Staff, 'Forget Sugar--in Hawaii, Pot's King', *Honolulu Advertiser*, December 2006, p. C1.
299 Mayo Clinic Staff, 'Germs', in *MayoClinic.com*, 2006.
300 StateMaster.com, 'Where Stats Come Alive', 2006.
301 Bureau of Justice Statistics, 'Violent Crime Measures', ed. by White House, 2005.

302 Rob Stein, 'Dangers of Being Overweight Less Dire, Researchers Say', *Washington Post*, November 7, 2007.
303 James Stephan, 'State Prison Expenditures, 2001', ed. by U.S. Department of Justice, 2004.
304 Claudia Wallis and Sonja Steptoe, 'How to Fix No Child Left Behind', *Time*, June 4, 2007.
305 Arthur Max and Toby Sterling, 'Researchers: Choices Spawn Happiness', *USA Today*, August 25, 2006.
306 Melissa Stevens, 'Which Is Better-- Butter or Margarine?' in *Cleveland Institute Foundation Chat*, 2003.
307 Lee Strobel, *The Case for the Creator* (Grand Rapids: Zondervan, 2004).
308 Office of Dietary Supplements, 'Vitamin B12 Fact Sheet', ed. by National Institutes of Health.
309 Ron Suskind, *The One Percent Doctrine,* Simon and Schuster, 2006, p. 367.
310 SustainLane, 'The Web's Best Community Resource for Healthy and Sustainable Living' [Accessed July 19, 2006.
311 Robert Sutton, *The No Asshole Rule*, 2006.
312 Sean Corcoran, Lawrence Mishel and Sylvia Allegretto, *How Does Teacher Pay Compare?,* Economic Policy Institute, 2004.
313 Public Broadcasting System, 'The Cambrian Explosion', 2006.
314 Patrick Takahashi, 'Edited From' [Accessed August 2005.
315 ———, 'Hi Dante', ed. by Mayor Dante Carpenter (Hilo, 1974).
316 Eric Talmadge, 'Extreme Monk Achieved Sainthood in 1,000-Day Run', *Honolulu Advertiser*, June 10, 2007, p. A21.
317 Robert Tanner, 'Death Penalty Works: Studies', *Chicago Sun-Times*, June 11, 2007.
318 Grances Grandy Taylor, 'Taking on the Catholic Church', Hartford Courant, [Accessed July 24, 2006.
319 James Thalman, 'Utah Leads the Nation in Rates of Depression', *Deseret Morning News*, November 29, 2007.
320 W.W.R. Sipe and Patrick Wall Thomas Doyle, *Sex, Priests, and Secret Codes,* Volt Press, 2006, p. 388.
321 Craig Timberg, 'U.N. Lowers Estimate of Global Aids Cases', *Washington Post*, November 20, 2007.
322 Time, 'Global Health', *Time* 2005.
323 Alexander Timoshik, 'Britain Used Indian Troops Like Guinea Pigs to Test Mustard Gas', *Pravda*, September 7, 2007.
324 Fuel Cell Today, 'London Mayor Comments on Fuel Cell Bus Vision' [Accessed February 28, 2006.
325 USA Today, 'Teachers Spurn Talented Rivals', *USA Today*, March 21, 2006, p. 12A.
326 Religious Tolerance, 'Human Stem Cells', August 29, 2007.
327 Robert T. Rood and James S. Trefil, *Are We Alone? The Possibility of Extraterrestrial Civilizations,* Charles Scribner and Sons, 1981.

328 Liz Sly (Chicago Tribune), 'Iraq Supports Iran on Nuclear Energy', *The Honolulu Advertiser*, May 27, 2006, p. A5.
329 Peg Tyre, 'The Trouble with Boys', *Newsweek*, January 30, 2006, pp. 44-52.
330 Guardian Unlimited, 'Keats Claimed Physics Destroyed Beauty' [Accessed November 22, 2005.
331 Steve Unwin, 'Fringes', in *Space Interferometry Mission Newsletter*, 2006.
332 Randolph Vance, 'How to Make an Atomic Bomb', in *totse.com.*
333 Andrew Walker, 'Richest 2% Own Half the Wealth', *BBC News*, December 5, 2006.
334 Claudia Wallis, 'The Myth About Homework', *Time*, August 29, 2006.
335 Roy Walmslely, 'World Prison Population List', ed. by Home Office U.K., 2003, p. 6.
336 Roy Walmsley, 'World Prison Population List', ed. by Home Office United Kingdom, 2003.
337 Jennifer Warren, 'Mental Ills Common in Prison, Jail', *Los Angeles Times*, September 7, 2006.
338 Matthew Warshaw, 'Polling Iranian Public Opinion', ed. by Terror Free Tomorrow, 2007.
339 Teresa Watanabe, 'Islam Fatally Flawed, Says Voice from Corona Via Al Jazeera', *Los Angeles Times*, March 13, 2006, p. Dl.
340 La Vita Weaver, *Fit for God,* Doubleday, 2004.
341 National Crime Victims' Rights Week, 'Cost of Crime and Victimization' [Accessed April 10-16, 2005.
342 Eric Weiner, *The Geography of Bliss,* Twelve, 2008.
343 Elizabeth Weise, 'Scientists Create a Virus That Reproduces' [Accessed November 13, 2003.
344 Jeffrey Weiss, 'Sight Unseen: Are We Wired to Serve God?' *Dallas Morning News*, August 7, 2006.
345 Rick Weiss, 'California Firm Breaks New Ground on Human Embryo Cloning', *Washington Post.*
346 Michael West, *The Immortal Cell,* Doubleday, 2003, p. 244.
347 John-Henry Westen, 'Why Embryonic Stem Cell Research?' [Accessed May 9, 2006.
348 Elizabeth White, '2.2 Million Now in Prison Population', *Honolulu Star-Bulletin*, May 22, 2006, p. A8.
349 Josh White, 'Hidden Costs Drive Wars' Tab to $1.5 Trillion, Study Says', *The Washington Post,* 2007.
350 Matthew White, 'Source List and Detailed Death Tolls for the Twentieth Century Hemoclysm' [Accessed February 12, 2005.
351 Wikipedia, 'Biological Warfare' [Accessed April 17, 2006.
352 ———, 'Diamond' 2006
353 ———, 'Jesus' 2006.
354 ———, 'Terrestrial Planet Finder' [Accessed July 18, 2007.
355 Daniel Williams, 'Italy Grants Asylum to Afghan Convert', *Honolulu Advertiser*, March 30, 2006, p. A10.

356 Maria Rose Williams, 'Grads Revel in Bumper Crop in Jobs', *The Honolulu Advertiser*, May 22, 2006, p. C3.
357 Gavin Peebles and Peter Wilson, *Economic Growth and Development in Singapore: Past and Future,* Edward Elgar, 2002, p. 328.
358 Margie Wilson, 'Bird Flu Explodes in Indonesia', forbes.com [Accessed May 31, 2006.
359 Stacey Wilson, 'Fatigue at the Wheel: Root of Serious Traffic Accidents', in *Buzzle.com*, 2006.
360 Stephen Wilson, 'Russia Awarded 2014 Winter Olympic Games' [Accessed July 5, 2007.
361 Edward Larson and Larry Witham, 'Scientists and Religion in America', *Scientific American*, September 1999, pp. 88-93.
362 Marcus Wohlsen, 'Test Created for Wine Headache Chemicals', in *Associated Press*, 2007.
363 John Donohue and Justin Wolfers, 'Uses and Abuses of Empirical Evidence in the Death Penalty Debate', *Stanford Law Review* (2006).
364 Lewis Wolpert, *Six Impossible Things before Breakfast: The Evolutionary Origins of Belief,* WW Norton, 2007, p. 243.
365 Bob Woodward, *State of Denial,* Simon and Schuster, 2006, p. 560.
366 Adrian Wooldridge, 'The Class of 2006', *Economist*, (2007).
367 New Commission on the Skills of the American Workforce, 'Tough Choices or Tough Times', ed. by National Center on Education and the Economy, 2006, p. 170.
368 Pocket World, 'Highest Obesity', *Economist*, August 22, 2007.
369 Worldwatch, '"Forgive and Forget" Will Not Fix Third World Debt', April 26, 2001.
370 Pippa Wysong, 'Microbial Life in the Oceans More Diverse Than Previously Believed', in *Access Excellence*, 2006.
371 Cardinal Ottaviani and John XXIII, 'From the Supreme and Holy Congregation of the Holy Office', The Vatican, 1962, p. 39.
372 'Love and Brain Scan'
373 Yahoo, 'How Many Stars Are There in the Sky?' [Accessed July 19, 2006.
374 Katie Young, 'A High School Relationships Class', *MidWeek*, November 16, 2005, p. 60.
375 Chester Yung, 'Expert Urges Mainland to Start Cloning', *The Standard*, March 7, 2007.
376 Bill Powell and Adam Zagorin, 'The Sopranos State', *Time*, July 23, 2007, pp. 45-48.
377 William Zellner, *Alternative Religious Groups in the United States,* Syracuse University Press.
378 Yuwei Zhang, 'Reducing Environmental Risks Could Save 13 Million Lives Globally', United Nations [Accessed June 13, 2007.
379 Carl Zimmer, 'Did DNA Come from Viruses?' *Science,* 312 (2006), 870-2.
380 Robert Zimmerman, 'Seeking Other Earths', *Astronomy*, August 2004, pp. 43-47.
381 Greg Zoroya, 'Veteran Stress Cases up Sharply', *USA Today*, November 14, 2007.

382 Michael Martin and Phil Zuckerman, ed., *The Cambridge Companion to Atheism / Atheism: Contemporary Rates and Patterns* (Cambridge: Cambridge Press, 2005).

383 Phil Zuckerman, 'Is Faith Good for Us?' *Free Inquiry, 26 (2006), 35-38.*

# EPILOGUE: RAINBOW VISIONS for Planet Earth and Humanity

The Appendix from ***Book 1*** has been upgraded to an epilogue, with some adjustments, for this section is much more than a mere addendum. The concept of Rainbow Visions represents the concluding fusion drawing together the full contents of ***SIMPLE SOLUTIONS Book 1 and Book 2***, providing the final stimulus to inspire the reader into making that crucial difference for Planet Earth and Humanity.

While much of what is presented here transpired in Hawaii, and, more specifically, largely at the University of Hawaii, this is a guide for anyone from any State and any Nation on how to make a positive difference. While the examples are taken from the world of academia, the strategies should conveniently extend into the real world, for the intelligence and dedication quotient elsewhere surely cannot be as high as what I had to face.

I've always been strongly influenced by colors. I still marvel at the beauty of a rainbow. In Nuuanu where I live and Manoa where I ponder over simple solutions, I see a rainbow almost every day. The full spectrum represents the importance of a balanced life, advantage of broad skills and an open attitude. The consequence is Rainbow Vision.

Surveying my life, I've found that my greatest accomplishments came as a necessary reaction to failures. Mistakes, bad fortune, call it what you want, are, in reality, a beneficial, and maybe almost necessary, stimulus for success. There is something about embarrassment, physical ailment or hopelessness that forces you to try harder, think out of the box, maintain perseverance and strive for triumph. In a way, then, this book is for those who have something yet to prove. Some of you might have been a loser most of your life, or, perhaps, unlucky.

The first example might sound too much like bragging, and while it has something to do with underdog status and not giving up, more so is the notion of compassion, for if you need to be driven, it is more important to focus on your surroundings and those around you, than you, yourself.

The most noted public school in Hawaii is McKinley. But that is because it is one of the oldest. The nationally respected private school is Punahou, from where came Barack Obama, Michelle Wie (*early golf fame*) and Steve Case (*AOL founder*). Punahou regularly provides a number of students each year to Stanford University and the Ivies. I'm sure there must be some, but I don't know of one person from McKinley, before or after me, who went to Stanford as a freshman.

Well, a couple of my close friends played on the high school tennis team, and, as they were desperately looking for any able body, I was coaxed into joining them some time in my junior year. Only my left wrist was broken, so I could still use my right hand. Picking this sport up for the first time, I think I must have played something like 398 out of 400 days, and when the season started as a senior, I was third singles, which meant I was the 5th best player on the team. (*I might also add, no one used sunscreen in those days, so I am now feeling the effects.*)

I'm going on pure memory here, but McKinley normally did not win any tennis matches against Punahou. They gave scholarships, and almost all of their players had been playing since birth. Well, one remarkable day, I proceeded to lose 6-0 and was behind 5-0, when something happened, and I eventually won the match. That was the pinnacle of my tennis career, and you would think giving the full effort was the point, and to some degree it should be, but I also a couple of weeks later slaughtered someone from another private school, Mid-Pacific, 6-0, 6-0, and this was, actually, the more important lesson. My opponent was so distraught and embarrassed—a factor here being that people were watching—that I learned never to again humiliate anyone at any time. These lessons come from experience and provide something called maturity, but more significantly, with my now more responsible attitude, the 0-6, 0-5 comeback was of secondary importance.

There is a second example, and I again use a sporting case, first, to maintain some consistency, and second, because I'm not a good athlete. I am a really mediocre golfer. I drive the ball far, but in all directions. My handicap has wavered around 18 all my life. Well, a couple of years ago, I tripped, at the Ala Wai Golf Course—supposedly the busiest in the nation—and separated my shoulder. I could not play for at least six weeks.

I then went to a driving range and could hit a ball, but only with some pain. But I played the following week anyway, and shot a 76, the best in my life. A week later, a 78, the first consecutive 70's scores ever. Then, I began to crush the dimpled spheroid harder with each passing week and my scores rose into the 90's. Was there a lesson to be learned? Sure, don't swing too hard. Did I change my game? No.

Well, about a year later, I happened to join Kenji Sumida's golf safari to Las Vegas and environs, playing 7 days in a row, on some days through 36 holes, in temperatures hovering close to, if not beyond, 100 °F. I did about average, for me. It was physically a strain, and the whole experience was agonizing, but, in an odd way, enjoyable. I'm scheduled to undergo the same torture in a couple of months.

Well, the first time I returned home and played, I had a 74, the best in my life, again. Mind you, I'm accomplishing all this at an advanced age. Ken Watanabe, one of my current heroes (*similar to LESSON #2 below, Ken generally beats me and is in his mid-80's*), and who was also there when I had that original 76, signed the card, which I mounted. It proudly sits in my campus office. The point, I guess, is that you need to suffer through hardship and pain to improve your game. Have I finally learned my lesson? Maybe it was the frequency of play, or, more likely, the lesson to practice a lot. But nope, I am again in the 90's.

Will I change anything this time? Perhaps some combination of swinging less vociferously, compounded by more practice, might work. But one final point to all this athletic overachievement and why I am not yet on the Champions Tour. The camaraderie and exercise are what are important, not the scores themselves. In undertaking your mission for society, enjoy it. And, it is indeed true that the journey should be more satisfying than the conclusion. Life is more important than death.

So on to more important matters. For the rest of your life, you can mostly continue doing almost nothing, do something the right way, or make everything worse. While the first option is better than the third, you can't get to the second if you do zilch. While adversity helps, the best way, I've found, mostly depends on two things: good attitude and a personal goal. For me, it was a sincere desire to help others and work with them for a more progressive humanity.

Part of life, of course, is that we all have ups and downs. Some things will go wrong no matter how successful you are. On any given day, the worst baseball team can beat the best, Chaminade can embarrass Virginia in college basketball and your toilet bowl could overflow.

So, if you have an IQ, started at a low socio-economic level, and have any kind of physical, ethnic or cultural defect, this book is just for you. Should you be so lucky as to start with more, than you already have an advantage. It will merely be a matter of absorbing the essence of the message and lessons to succeed in your quest by thinking simply with good conscience.

Some might be intimidated by the arena in which I operated, for how many will grow up to be a full professor in engineering, plus a research director of a sustainable resource institute? There is something chosen to being entrusted to do good things for humanity, although I think it was more actual effort and some luck. I regularly receive a wide variety of communications from those in the nuclear industry, academics from China, mining engineers from Australia, specialists from dot.com companies and those from the military-industrial complex, all wanting to work in solar energy. Yes, life is unfair, and, there are already too many who are just plain dissatisfied...but it could be worse. Remember, the most awful of conditions can bring out the best opportunities.

## Start with the Right Attitude

A more specific subtitle for this book could have been: the Art of Research Entrepreneurship. But, how many of you would care, and, anyway, that is far too limiting, for the whole point of this book and final guide is to aid in preparing the foundation to help you make this a better world. If all of this succeeded for me in competitive surroundings with brilliant people and a stultifying bureaucracy, success should be more easily attained in a "lesser" ecosystem manned by a bunch of losers, with your personally meaningful crusade where your goal can be more magnificent. After all, energy or ocean resources are about as prosaic as you can get. If it so happens that you are among those losers, this could be the last chance to justify your reason for being.

The first stage of decision-making is to determine whether you truly wish to take a monumental step and dedicate yourself to accomplish an epic goal. I suspect that, perhaps, only 10% of anyone reading this has the ambition and drive to even consider this option. Parents are busy taking care of their family and making ends meet. Nothing wrong with being an ordinary citizen, for you will live 13 years longer and are four times less likely to commit suicide compared to the typical celebrity.[227] But, suppose this is your one and only life. Just surviving seems, somehow, empty. Go ahead, try something!

For most you, if this is your first time, select a small, even almost trivial target, such as becoming the mother hen for compact fluorescent lamps, by, first, replacing all your incandescent bulbs with the latest conservation technology, but, more so, convincing those around you to do the same. It would help for you to encourage with some background information, so start by going to GOOGLE and type in "compact fluorescent lamps, Wikipedia." Or, another simple difference you can make is for you to follow-up with your child's teacher about the "one marshmallow child," and what the class is doing to convert that student into a two marshmallow child. Who knows where this will lead.

For those who did the small stuff, and want more, and for the few who truly want to make a big difference, keep in mind that you will not be able to do it alone. Your ability to orchestrate can leverage your base. As underscored in the chapter on education, first, almost forget what you learned in school. An important key to success will be to cultivate the right people working together in common purpose. But why would anyone listen to you? What is it that can set you up to take on any leadership role? In the salesmanship of teaming, there is something about good attitude that always works. Conversely, the wrong approach can royally screw up anything. There are books on these subjects, but let me provide just a few examples to get you going:

1. To attain success, work hard at it, but don't do anything illegal or shoot yourself in the foot (*the latter, from An Wang, founder of Wang Laboratories, a board member of an organization I helped start*).

2. On the very few things you can control, do the best job possible: be on time, say thank you, smile a lot, show enthusiasm, etc.

3. Regularly and carefully take risks, but remember to protect your feet *(see above)* and learn from your mistakes, because if you try anything different, you will no doubt fail now and then, if not regularly.

4. Always make that extra effort and take that extra step or two or three. If you think you are right, be persistent without being a pest.

5. Think, as, for example, something lawyers learn: never ask a question if there is any chance that you won't like the answer or be limited by that response. Also, be free about asking for assistance, for almost everyone really does want to be helpful.

6. Sincerely give credit when due, and take as little as possible. Also, too, personal relationships are more important than the attainment of any goals. Many times they conflict with each other. The choice to take should be obvious: stick with people.

7. For any reasonable task, you need a group of individuals from different organizations, and it's more effective if the whole village worked together. The 2004 Olympic basketball results showed how much teamwork matters. America had the stars, but we lost. Sport teams learn this lesson, but, unfortunately, and unconsciously, schools teach us to look out mostly for #1...me...you...ourselves. It will take a monumental shift in attitude for you to eliminate this flaw by leaning towards us.

8. It makes sense to trust others to do what you could have if you had more time, for you will never have enough to do everything well yourself. Then, too, most people around you actually can do certain things better than you.

9. Use good judgment by becoming invaluable to those around you and consider every interaction as an opportunity to build friendships. However, learn how to say no without alienation.

10. Use uncommon sense: understand, but do not be stymied, by life's contradictions: never lie, but you don't need to necessarily publicize certain truths; even without sufficient information (*which is at least 90% of the time*), make a decision, except for 5% of the time when no decision is the right one; never give up, but, sometimes, you must; and, while integrity is really important, you can't allow people who don't deserve it to run all over you, so, find a way. Most never get to appreciate the value of using common sense, which is a synonym for uncommon sense.

11. Neutralize the negatives, with only one example being: avoid insulting or embarrassing anyone, for these are the ones who will come back to bite you.

12. Enjoy life! Success comes with good health, both physical and mental, not only for you, but for your family and those around you.

Ah, a good dozen attitude pointers you can weave into your mission. These are not the LESSONS, which will come next, but the controlling attitudes for success.

## Rainbow Vision Lessons

To gain rainbow vision, combine the foundational roots of the above with the following lessons:

1. LESSON #1: determine what you want to accomplish where you have a natural advantage, and develop a sensible strategy. You won't be able to, with distinction, compete in traditional fields. If you're in Kansas, and water is running out, you must figuratively learn how to tame a tornado to produce water. In Hawaii, we are in the middle of the largest ocean, are endowed with a range of natural energy sources and rest at the interface of East and West. Clearly, an international sustainable resource project puts you at a distinct advantage. It is best to start with something you can accomplish...perhaps small, like inviting a promising new political campaigner to your

home to meet a few friends. They never say no. Then, who knows, she might win the election, with your assistance. You now have done some good and formed a base for something bigger in the future.

2. LESSON #2: invariably, other people will have better ideas than you. Be influenced by those around you. Your mentors change over time, and now, at a relatively advanced age, have learned to better appreciate my elders. Take Edward Jurkens, for example. You haven't read about him. He still picks me up for golf, we walk carrying our bags when we can, and has a beer, after which he drops me off, going home for two triple martinis, while completing both daily crossword puzzles. He is 90. Ken Watanabe, earlier mentioned, this past week, twice shot better than his age. He is 86. Fred Riggs, professor emeritus of political science, single-handedly developed a web page (*http://webdata.soc.hawaii.edu/fredr/SUSTAIN%20OUR%20WORLD.html#rigg)* on SIMPLE SOLUTIONS. He is also 90. Alas, he just passed away. They give me hope, and advice. Anyway, you must learn to listen and question, nicely, while always appreciating life. It is all in how you can synthesize the pieces and people to fit the situation and mandate. It will take a few mistakes, with small victories, gaining maturity and confidence, to recognize the value of doing the right thing in the right way most of the time. Fortunately for you, you can now start from here knowing all this, for you mostly don't know what common sense is until someone tells you what it is.

3. LESSON #3: optimize your social skills. Take politics, for example. The worst place to convince an elected official is in his office. You especially won't be able to change the mind of a legislator in a public hearing. Most of the effective selling, call it, even, lobbying, you will do needs to occur in a social setting. Consider golf, surfing, wine and karaoke to break the ice. Find your forte and apply it. Research awards are not only won by pure scientific brilliance, an academic corollary to LESSON 3. You need to first get that grant.

4. LESSON #4: work/volunteer for someone in Congress, the National Science Foundation, your State Legislature or an environmental group of your interest. A couple of years looking from the inside out, or, even, outside in, will give you a broader perspective, special connections and a competitive edge. Using politics again, LESSON 4B: go out of your way to help get someone elected. If that person loses, keep quiet and try again. A senator, any politician, will never turn down a sincere request for help, for the effort and effectiveness might suffer if there is no compelling need for them or their staff to want to really help you. There will be a hundred times more need than ability to deliver. Yours will be important enough only if they think you deserve it. It's amazing how important you can be if you have done something for them, even waving signs for the candidate.

5. LESSON #5: tolerate the small stuff, but ultimately, focus on something monumental. Why waste your time and that of others, for it only takes a little more effort to attain a higher goal than something too easy or simple. On the other hand, how can you be effective if you haven't had some experience? #5 is on the surface not consistent with

#1, but only you can resolve these apparent contradictions in life. Hint: start small and build.

6. LESSON #6: make your own luck. Bob Gibson, when he pitched, had incredible luck. Batters kept missing his ball. People still can't believe how lucky Rod Carew was, for while other infielders were almost always only inches away when the ball passed them, somehow he made the play. While you accept any good fortune, many times you need to make your own luck through uncommon effort and good people relations. Gibson and Carew made their luck through talent and practice.

7. LESSON #7: everyone has unique skills and friends. You must find something distinctive, with future utility, where you have a clear advantage. If you eventually undertake that monumental mission, find that niche or element ideal for you and your environment.

Thus, the **Seven Lessons of Rainbow Vision**. Combined with good attitude (*yes, be nice to people, please*), the combination should work every time.

As one of my personal case studies, take the field of hydrogen. The details are provided in Chapter 3 of ***Book 1***, but appreciate that Hawaii is in the middle of the Pacific and runs mostly on oil. We have a wide variety of natural energy resources, but there was something about hydrogen that made long term sense, especially as 40% of the energy used here went towards aviation, and this gas was ideal as a future jet fuel. Why not, then, make Hawaii a leader in this field, as no one was yet doing anything of any importance. Choosing the U.S. Senate as the launching pad for action, using all the lessons above, Hawaii eventually became the U.S. National Center for Hydrogen Research. This is only a very preliminary first step, but others, hopefully, will continue the effort.

Case two: Hawaii is surrounded by salt water, so what about tapping the riches of the seas? Again, we would have no competition if we could have our congressional representatives place funds to help build credibility. We had to take this step because the University of Hawaii had no national respect in ocean resource technology. In the Senate, I helped write the ocean thermal energy conversion bill. Also, I shepherded the Hard Minerals Act for strategic seabed minerals, so why not establish a center on these subjects in Hawaii? Finally, marine biotechnology: Hawaii as the biological equivalent of Silicon Valley would be as high tech as they come, and no university at that time had any engineering capability in this field. My PhD involved using a tunable laser to stimulate the DNA/RNA of E. coli. Thus came the Department of Interior Marine Minerals Technology Center and National Science Foundation Marine Bioproducts Engineering Center. I did not play superman to gain these leading research units, I hired the people to do it, and helped them. It is relatively easy to find unique themes in whatever makes sense from your experiences.

Combining all this ocean stuff, we could then have a Blue Revolution (*Chapter 4 of **Book 1***), the marine equivalent of the terrestrial Green Revolution, where the only product was better grains. The Blue Revolution had the promise of providing next generation seafood, sustainable energy, new habitats, and natural materials, while enhancing the environment, plus, perhaps preventing hurricanes and remediating global climate warming.

Now, there is a danger in floating a mega project, no matter how terrific it sounds, for funding and staff people are inherently afraid of ten year, $10 million/year initiatives that could lead to a billion dollar requirement. You need to start reasonably, and build up to the worthwhile adventures. Thus, while you must conceive of the total program, begin by suggesting an element of the system. This is a way to reconcile LESSONS ONE and FIVE.

Initial thoughts were imagined in the 1970's, and matured in the 1980's, for basic research at the Hawaii Natural Energy Institute of the University of Hawaii and technology transfer at the Pacific International Center for High Technology Research on hydrogen and ocean resources. A third of a century later, we are yet, only a third of the way there. But the seeds have been planted. That was the best I could do. But there will be others.

What if none of the above had turned out positive? Suppose nothing useful happened. That's okay, too, because I would have felt good trying to do well, and, in addition, improved my health, as indicated in the following books:

- ***Why Good Things Happen to Good People***,[220] reports that, by being good, mortality is delayed, depression is reduced and well-being and good fortune are increased. Thus, the act of giving results in better health, enhanced happiness and longer life.
- ***The Power of Nice***,[175] shows that nice people can be very successful, as well as healthier and happier, same as the other book.

Oh, yes, there is also the ***No Asshole Rule***,[311] which rather effectively informs you that assholes—also known as jerks, hotshots who alienate and dickheads—not only don't get hired nor promoted, but are the first to be fired. It should be clear which one you should be, I hope.

These lessons for Rainbow Vision, however, are mere personal strategies. You still need to get out there and do something, and the next sections should provide some confidence, as it sometimes takes only a spark to galvanize monumental deeds.

## How One Person Made a Difference: The End of Poverty

The simple solution is for each person to try to make a positive difference. It is as simple as that. Can one individual, for example, do anything about poverty?

In 2005, *The Lancet* reported on a study showing that $5.1 billion could save 6 million kids.[163] That sum is 6% of the expenditures for tobacco products. The average smoker does a pack a day. If these individuals can smoke only one less cigarette a day, and a way is found to effectively apply that savings, poof, we solve that poverty problem, and, maybe start the process of saving your life (*if you smoke or are in poverty*), too. How simple can it get?